THE COMPANION GUIDE TO

FLORENCE

THE COMPANION GUIDES

GENERAL EDITOR: VINCENT CRONIN

*It is the aim of the Guides to provide a Companion,
in the person of the author, who knows intimately
the places and people of whom he writes, and is able
to communicate this knowledge and affection to his readers.
It is hoped that the text and pictures will aid them
in their preparations and in their travels, and will
help them to remember on their return.*

LONDON · OUTER LONDON · EAST ANGLIA · NORTHUMBRIA
THE WEST HIGHLANDS OF SCOTLAND
ROME · VENICE · NEW YORK
PARIS · THE LOIRE · NORMANDY · THE SOUTH OF FRANCE
MADRID AND CENTRAL SPAIN · IRELAND
MAINLAND GREECE · THE GREEK ISLANDS
JUGOSLAVIA · TURKEY

In preparation
OXFORD AND CAMBRIDGE · THE SOVIET UNION

Contents

❧

Illustrations

❧

Preface

❧

'We are in a city with a good eye and a wicked tongue.'
Don Vincenzo Borghini to Bernardo Buontalenti, 1577

Of the great cities of the world, Florence is – always was – small. Never a metropolis and with a shorter history than most great cities, Florence nevertheless led the rest of the world in art, science and political idealism from the Middle Ages to modern times. No one has ever been able to decide if it was a miraculous coincidence or simply in the nature of the surrounding countryside that Dante, Giotto, Brunelleschi, Leonardo, Michelangelo, Galileo and so many other giants were all Florentines. The importance of their achievements and the great quantity of the visible remains which they have left behind make Florence as a city to visit at once immensely attractive and intimidating. There is so much to see, so much to understand, and time is never generous enough. In planning this volume, the most practical scheme seemed to be to use each neighbourhood as the pretext for a chapter with a theme devoted to a particular aspect of Florentine life and character. Each chapter starts out with a map keyed to a summary of the chief monuments to be found there. This information is intended for handy reference on the spot, and items particularly worth seeing are marked with a star. The text of the chapter, however, is meant for one's leisure either before or after the trip –or even during it, perhaps while resting one's feet in a loggia or under an umbrella pine overlooking the city.

This Companion Guide owes a very great deal to my own companions in Florence. Their gusto and generosity are part of the city's magic. I owe much to an almost daily companion: the Kunsthistorisches Institut and its former director, Dr Ulrich Middeldorf. Then there are the other friends and colleagues who have contributed stories and obscure information, or who have patiently read and benevolently criticized the text. Then there are the craftsmen, scholars and dedicated Florentines who also allowed me to take up their time. Among all these I must single out Signor

Baglioni of the Biblioteca Nazionale, Umberto Baldini, Paola Barocchi, Vittorio Batistini, Bruno Bearzi, Luciano Berti, Piero Bertolucci, my father Henry Borsook, Giulia Brunetti, Anna Maria Ciaranfi, Marco Chiarini, Leone Cei, Mario and Pier Paolo Feri, Riccardo Gizdulich, James Holderbaum, Irene Hueck, Karla Langedijk, Mario Mattei, Margaret Meiss, Kirsten Aschengreen Piacenti, Alberto Riccoboni of the Touring Club Italiano, Howard Saalman, Edward Sanchez, Enzo Settesoldi of the Opera del Duomo, Klara Steinweg, Peter Tigler, Leonetto Tintori, Frank Toker and Milton Waldman.

Soon after the original edition of this book appeared, the catastrophic flood of November 1966 struck Florence. As a result, many palaces, churches, entire museums, together with their contents, were engulfed by the Arno. Since then, the dogged courage of the Florentines, aided by help of all kinds from an admiring world, has done much to repair the damage. The original locations of many objects have changed; elsewhere hitherto buried murals and parts of older buildings have emerged; a few galleries have closed altogether. In this revised edition, note has been taken accordingly. Nevertheless, the work of repair continues and almost every week more changes occur. Therefore, the reader is bound to come across certain, I hope minor, discrepancies between what he sees and what he reads. Other changes in the text are due to new or more exact information which has come from the wealth of scholarly publications accumulated during the last six years. Some of the Florentines described in the text have since died or moved away, but like other colourful figures of the past I have preferred to leave them in their old homes where they still belong as shared memories.

The section on practical information at the end of the book has been thoroughly revised by my knowledgeable friend, Miss Sarah Fox-Pitt. My greatest debt is to Piero Bertolucci, devoted Tuscan and untiring critic, who has re-edited the text.

The text, of course, is based largely on the studies and essays of generations of scholars and other enthusiastic visitors to the city. Since footnotes acknowledging all the sources would be out of place in a volume such as this, a bibliography, listed according to chapters, is to be found at the end of the book for those caring to follow up special points on their own.

Florence is not just a collection of venerable objects and earnest ideas. It is full of its own peculiar humour which by turns is raucous and neatly elegant. The men, the objects, the ideas, cannot be torn from one another or from their unique setting. The flavour of

Florence is to be had not only in books and galleries but in the piazzas, markets and alleyways – at public meetings and along the near-by country roads. For me the perfect day in Florence includes a church, a stroll through a market, a chat with a craftsman in his workshop, a visit to a museum, a browse in a second-hand bookshop, a picnic lunch in the Boboli or up at the Fortezza di Belvedere, winding up (weather permitting), with a view over the city from one of the hillsides. If not 'everything' is squeezed into the visit, often 'less' turns out to be more. After all, the most perceptive visitor Florence has ever had, Hippolyte Taine, only saw the city for eight days!

Florence, September 1971

Note: Further additions and corrections made in September 1977. The hours and prices of admission to museums and galleries are subject to frequent changes.

Chapter 1

Introduction: The 'New Athens on the Arno'

✵

'. . . a city complete in itself, having its own arts and edifices, lively and not too crowded, a capital and not too large, beautiful and gay – such is the first idea of Florence . . . the ancient city of the fifteenth century still exists and constitutes the body of the city; but it is not mouldy as at Siena, consigned to one corner as at Pisa, befouled as in Rome, enveloped in medieval cobwebs . . . The Florentine, as formerly the Athenian under the Caesars, remained a critic and a wit, proud of his good taste, his sonnets, his academies, of the language which gave law to Italy and of his undisputed judgements in matters of literature and the fine arts . . . mind is an integrant force with them; they may be corrupted but not destroyed; they may be converted to dilettanti and sophists but not into mutes and fools.'

Taine, 'Voyage en Italie', 1866

Italians will tell you that Florentines are arrogant, sharp-tongued, miserly and great complainers. The Florentines themselves will agree to this. Dante's words for them were: 'That ungrateful, malicious lot . . . miserly, jealous, and proud' (*quello 'ngrato popolo maligno . . . gent' avara, invidiosa, e superba* – Inferno, xv. 61, 68). They do not particularly like to travel and they prefer their own city to what they see when they do travel. For this reason some modern critics, glad to be waspish, call them provincial. The Florentines have had this great pride for seven hundred years. Since the thirteenth century, they have been convinced that their city was unlike any other – save Rome or Athens, perhaps. Even during the worst moments in her history their civic pride was unbroken. Chiaro Davanzati, shortly after the humiliating Florentine defeat at the hands of a much smaller Sienese army at Montaperti in 1260, could still refer to his city as 'sweet and gay . . . the font of valour and seemliness'. Dante (1265–1321), after seventeen years as a public servant in Florence, was forced into exile, where he spent the last nineteen years of his life. Nevertheless, though embittered, petulant and sour, sure of Purgatory or worse for nearly everybody, he remained to the last an enthusiastic Florentine. It is characteristic of Florence that her statesmen were often poets (Leonardo Bruni, Lorenzo the Magnificent), and her poets statesmen or even musicians (Dante,

13

Petrarch, Salutati). There is even a poetic explanation for the city's name – 'Firenze', or the medieval 'Fiorenza': Varchi, a sixteenth-century historian (calling upon Dante for support), held that it was because she was built on a flowery meadow. From this same legendary meadow comes the Iris, or *giglio*, the emblem of the Florentine flag.

The great age of Athens was about a hundred years; for Florence it was two and a half centuries. In that long span of time no scheme of mind or hand was too large nor any detail so slight that both could not be refined into marvellously reasoned harmonies. One thinks of the scheme of Dante's *Divine Comedy* into which are woven the private jokes which make the heroes and villains so alive and piquant; or Brunelleschi's design for the interior of the Pazzi Chapel, an essay on the aesthetic possibilities of the circle and the sqaure which includes mouldings and narrow friezes of the noblest refinement. At first sight Florentine sculpture, Florentine buildings, appear so clear that they seem simple; they are compact, there is no over-statement – theirs is an inner life. The eye never tires of looking and the mind never seems to exhaust the ideas they evoke. The same may be said of Florentine slang. To make a debt is 'to hammer in a nail' (*piantar un chiodo*) – because of the ensuing difficulty of extracting it. Of credulous dupes there is the phrase 'in the good old days when goats wore clogs' (*quando le capre andavano in zoccoli*). Someone who is not repaid for his efforts is 'like the donkey who carries wine and drinks water' (*far come l' asino che porta il vino e beve l'acqua*). Florence, as distinguished from Siena or Venice, for example, was a city of philosophy. Even her artists were thinkers, her architects and painters were mathematicians, and all were touched with poetry. In everything she put her hand to during that wonderful two and a half centuries Florence set the world a new standard.

The great period began with a spurt of tremendous projects, all planned on a vast scale. The town hall, the Cathedral, the church of S Croce, the mural cycles of Cimabue at Assisi and of Giotto at Padua, and the *Divine Comedy* were conceived and for the most part completed in the four decades between 1280 and 1320. During the following one hundred years the Florentines continued to realize schemes bold in scale and often encyclopedic in theme: the Campanile with its multi-coloured marbles and its reliefs designed by Giotto, the didactic murals lining the big Dominican chapter-room at S Maria Novella (popularly known as the Spanish Chapel), and Brunelleschi's cupola for the Cathedral, which was the greatest engineering feat since Antiquity. From then on into the early sixteenth century, one bold experiment in the arts and sciences succeeded another. Individual achievement won new respect; craftsmen were now called artists. If the schemes for architecture and painting were smaller in scale than those realized in the previous century, the theories and plan for even vaster projects were worked out on paper. Leonardo had a plan for diverting the Arno from its bed and Michelangelo imagined how a mountain could be turned into a piece of sculpture. Rivers or mountains were no longer obstacles which could resist the will of the Florentine mind.

Material things no less than ideas are treated with seriousness and respect in Florence. Recently, after the street-car tracks were ripped out of the Borgo S Frediano (which is in a poor quarter), instead of putting down an asphalt surface as is done in most cities of the world, the street was repaved by teams of skilled masons who laid out the stones of perfectly cut porphyry into fine fan patterns. There is hardly an object so precious or so humble that Florentines cannot or will not repair it. Any old umbrellas, broken clocks, cracked crockery, pots and pans that need relining, old leather goods, are made elegantly useful again. So well do they know the old crafts that they can make almost perfect imitations of old jewellery, enamels and inlays. Florentine craftsmen are the world's best fakers when they want to be. The workshops around S Spirito, the Carmine and the neighbourhood around the Via de' Fossi supply the English with beautifully carved Baroque furniture and the Florentines with Chippendale and Hepplewhite.

The Florentines have always been aware of their great achievements even though the rest of Europe forgot them between 1600 and 1850. As soon as Florence succeeded in establishing her supremacy over Pisa as the leading city in Tuscany during the twelfth and thirteenth centuries, she began to have biographers. In other cities writers of civic histories were hired by the republic or the court, in whose interest and for whose greater glory they were paid to slant their writings. Florence was exceptional. From Villani in the fourteenth century to Varchi in the sixteenth, Florentine historiography was the work of native citizens and humanists who wrote in praise of the city out of a personal urge and patriotic feeling. Villani tells us that he set to work on the history of Florence after a visit to Rome in the jubilee year of 1300. There he was struck by the similarities between Rome and his native city. He saw Florence in the ascendancy – on her way, he says, 'to accomplishing great things'. Florence, which he called 'daughter and stuff of Rome', deserved a chronicle of her beginnings and of her recent affairs.

Villani loved statistics. He gave the following picture of the city during the first half of the fourteenth century. The population was estimated at 90,000 (about one-fourth of the present count), not counting clerics and about 1,500 foreigners. When a child was born a bean was dropped in an urn in the Baptistery (a black bean for a boy, white for a girl). By this means the annual birth-rate was calculated at about 6,000, with more boys. There were between eight and ten thousand children who could read and about a thousand more in six different schools learning mathematics. Four more schools were devoted to teaching 500 children grammar and logic. There were in the city and its suburbs 110 churches, abbeys, monasteries and convents. Among these were 30 hospitals with a thousand beds. The city's chief source of wealth, the wool-finishing industry, had 200 workshops employing 30,000 people. There were 80 'benches' (we would say banks) of exchange, 600 notaries, 60 physicians and surgeons, 146 bakers, and more hosiers, shoemakers, stonemasons, and carpenters than one could count. Such was the city's prosperity that there was hardly a 'burgher or lord' who had not a property with fine buildings. The amount of money spent on these, Villani said, was 'sinful', but they were 'a magnificent sight to see'.

Of these palaces and villas only the shells remain, although we know that they were richly furnished with paintings and hangings. But much survives of the private family chapels in the great new churches built between 1250 and 1320 (S Maria Novella and S Croce) which were covered with painted cycles taken from sacred history and set with monumental altar-pieces. Painting rather than sculpture was the great pictorial medium in Florence then. And the greatest master of the craft was Giotto. He was in such demand all over Italy that much of his time was spent outside the city – at Padua, Rome, Naples and Milan. In Florence he maintained a large crew of helpers and apprentices which probably included Taddeo Gaddi, Bernardo Daddi and Maso di Banco. They spread his style all over Tuscany. The modern notion of an artist had not yet arisen, but Giotto was recognized even by his contemporaries as one of the great men of his time. At the end of his life Florence entrusted him with the overseership (*capomaestro*) of the Cathedral works. Giotto was so sympathetic to the human situation that his paintings have a drama which endowed actions with a gravity never seen before. He recognized the critical moment in a narrative and fixed it in the whole composition of figures and setting with direct simplicity. Previously, narratives were diagrammatic and certain conventional masks were used to convey feeling. Giotto was the first teacher in the great tradition

16

of Florentine painting. A century and more later, Masaccio, Ghirlandaio and Michelangelo studied him.

Petrarch (1304–74) in literature belonged to the same movement as Giotto in painting. He dedicated himself to teaching his country-men that the great Romans were not musty figures of a dead past, but what Mommsen called 'living models for the present and harbingers for the future'. Although Petrarch was discontented with the conditions prevailing in his lifetime, nevertheless he was convinced that it was possible 'to come again in the former pure radiance'. He felt that he belonged to a new time and it is to him that we owe the concept of the 'Dark Ages' for the period from the fall of the Roman Empire to his own time. Petrarch was a champion of Italian unity five hundred years before it came to be. He believed that the best practical way to accomplish this ideal was to kindle in his fellow Italians an awareness of their Latin inheritance. Florence claimed Petrarch as her own despite the fact that he was born in Arezzo of exiled Florentine parents. He spent very little time in Florence but he maintained a warm friendship with Boccaccio (1313–75), who instigated the offer to Petrarch of a professorship at the University of Florence, which he declined.

Boccaccio was the leader of the circle in Florence who took to heart the ideas and the ideals of the absent Petrarch. They made Florence the first modern city in the world. By the end of the fourteenth century, Florentine statesmen and pamphleteers (we call them humanists now) such as Coluccio Salutati and Leonardo Bruni had translated Petrarch's vision of the moral greatness of ancient Rome into a new civic ideal for their own time and city. They were scholars and also men of action and they disapproved of a scholar's withdrawing from civic obligations.

Not long afterwards they were put to the test, which they met in heroic spirit. In the early years of the fifteenth century Florentine republican rule was threatened by Visconti tyranny, which had already seized the surrounding Tuscan cities. Florence had been ruled for almost one hundred and fifty years neither by a tyrant nor by a powerful family but by representatives of the commercial and professional guilds. There had been a few lapses – such as the attempted tyranny of the Duke of Athens in 1342–3 and the brief *coup d'état* of the rioting wool-workers known as the Ciompi Revolt in 1378. But by and large Florence had remained a stable republic. In the spring of 1402 she stood alone against the advancing Milanese troops of the Visconti. The city was saved by a stroke of luck: Gian Galeazzo Visconti died just as he was about to move on Florence.

And with his death Visconti power in Tuscany waned for a time. It was a stroke of luck but the Florentines persuaded themselves that they had won a great victory. It was felt as a great moment. Florentine virtue was revealed herioc in adversity. This inspired in the city an awareness of greatness, verve and vitality which found its supreme expression in the *Laudatio*, Leonardo Bruni's wonderful speech in honour of Florence which we shall quote from later.

The Visconti threat was renewed during the following three decades and the republican spirit of Florence again rose to meet it. 'Liberty is more useful than anything else, there is nothing that must not be risked for its salvation . . .' So spoke Rinaldo de' Gianfigliazzi after the defeat at Zagonara in 1424. Galileo Galilei (an ancestor of the astronomer) wrote at that time: 'The greatness of the Roman mind showed itself more in misfortune than in good fortune. The wood of the tree is an image of hope: wounded, it bursts into leaf and is covered again.' And Francesco Machiavelli (one of Niccolò Machiavelli's forefathers) spoke out: 'The enjoyment of freedom makes cities and citizens great: this is well known.'

These were the years of great experiences and many great men. Florence became the fountainhead of new political, intellectual and artistic ideas which have lived ever since. The whole of Italy, and to a degree the lands beyond the Alps, turned to 'the new Athens on the Arno' (Hans Baron). These same years were the heroic period of Florentine art. Brunelleschi's engineering genius invented the scheme for constructing the Cathedral's great cupola. The principles of perspective composition were being worked out by him, by Ghiberti, and Leon Battista Alberti. The first monumental bronzes were cast for Orsanmichele; a new scale and dignity were given to the human condition by Donatello's statuary and Masaccio's murals and altarpieces.

In both art and political thinking the ideals were the same and similar terms were used. In Goro Dati's accounts of central Italian politics there are paraphrases for concepts such as 'balance of power' and 'equilibrium'. Bruni in the *Laudatio* discusses the Florentine constitution as if it were a work of art, declaring that he wished: to bring out 'the inner order, neatness, and workmanlike construction' of the Florentine institution . . . 'For just as harpstrings are attuned to each other so that, when they are plucked, a single harmony arises from all the different tones . . . just as this farsighted city has so adapted all her parts to each other that from there results a harmony of the total structure of the republic . . . Nothing in this state is ill-proportioned, nothing improper, nothing incongruous, nothing left vague; everything occupies its proper place, which is not only clearly defined but also in the right relation to all the others.' All this, he thought, was a natural development of the harmony and geometry of the Florentine landscape.

Unhappily, the days of the heroic Florentine republic were brief. Since 1382, the Commune had gradually given way to the rule of 'Signori' – lords of commerce rather than of aristocracy, such as the Albizzi, Capponi, Medici and Strozzi. Eventually one of these – the Medici in 1434 – assumed total responsibility for the city's affairs. Florence then fell (the last of the great central Italian city-states to do so) under the rule of one man. However, Cosimo de' Medici was truly the benevolent tyrant. He was shrewd enough not to use the manners of one. He remained in title a citizen exercising his authority through already existing institutions which were, to be sure, carefully 'packed' with his supporters. Through sheer force of character, masterful management, and a healthy respect for public opinion, he succeeded in consolidating Medici control of the city with the backing of the masses. He carefully avoided flaunting his great wealth before the public in personal ostentation or in social climbing – virtues forgotten by his descendants in the sixteenth century. Cosimo chose local wine for his table and husbands for his daughters from Florentine merchant families. He was a student of classical literature and of theology, an experienced tender of vineyards and olive groves, an *aficionado* of architecture, and a bibliophile. His humour was famous. When, a few hours before his death, Cosimo's wife came to see him she asked why he kept his eyes shut. 'To train them!' (*per avvezzargli*) was the terse reply.

Cosimo's munificence was unique in scale. Yet his own palace on the Via Larga (now Via Cavour) was not more imposing than those built by other Florentine families such as the Rucellai or the Pitti. The style of the buildings Cosimo commissioned reflects his personal taste. The interiors designed by Brunelleschi and Michelozzo are spacious and clear, with a noble restraint which at times verges on Spartan bareness and economy of colour. In them there is no overt self-glorification; it is a perfect style for a ruler who seeks to discourage envy and abjures vainglory.

It is known that Cosimo's feeling for Donatello was a warm, personal one (whatever the crusty Donatello's may have been for him). He saw to it that Donatello was well looked after in his old age and he gave him a red coat. Red coats were worn by the city's highest officials. Cosimo himself wore one, but after a few times Donatello laid his aside, feeling that for him the garment was too dandified. Cosimo also supported Niccolò Niccoli in his translation of the Greek and Latin classics and he was the mainstay of Vespasiano da Bisticci's book business, if one may so speak of a shop devoted to the copying and illumination of old texts for the libraries of great bankers, princes and popes.

Cosimo's grandson, Lorenzo the Magnificent (himself a fine poet), continued Cosimo's interest in learning and the arts. As tutors for his children he hired Poliziano and Luigi Pulci. Pico della Mirandola was one of his companions. Lorenzo was famous as an arbiter of taste. The Pistoiese asked him to tell them which was the better of two models by Verrocchio and Piero del Pollaiuolo prepared for the Forteguerri monument. And he was proud to recommend Filippino Lippi to a Roman cardinal and Giuliano da Maiano to the Duke of Calabria. Like Cosimo, Lorenzo loved architecture although he commissioned very little of it. He liked to study the plans of some of the most beautiful buildings of the time – such as those for the Ducal Palace at Urbino and Alberti's church of S Sebastiano at Mantua. But he was less willing to lend his copy of Alberti's treatise to the Duke of Ferrara because he read so often in it himself. Lorenzo even submitted a design of his own for the façade of Florence Cathedral. It was he who erected the monuments there to the memory of Giotto and another to Filippo Lippi in the Cathedral in Spoleto. For these he had Poliziano compose the inscriptions. As a patron and collector, Lorenzo's taste was not so much for great buildings or large paintings. None of the known commissions was of a big, public nature. He especially prized small objects: bronzes, goblets, vases, medals and gems, many of which are today exhibited in the Museo degli Argenti of the Pitti. These show his appreciation of noble lines, rich materials and refined proportions.

Other Florentine families undertook the subvention of large public building projects. The Rucellai paid Alberti to complete the façade of S Maria Novella and eventually Castello Quaratesi provided funds for the church and cloister of San Salvatore al Monte. Such enterprises in the past had been sponsored by the major guilds; now they were the work of the great merchants. By 1470 such was the splendour of the city that a miniature in an edition of S Augustine's *City of God* shows the 'City' in the guise of Florence.

Not long afterwards the Florentines suffered an acute case of guilty conscience. Lorenzo the Magnificent was hardly in his grave two years when his son Piero lost the family's dominion of the city. Savonarola preached sedition and convinced the masses that Florence was a pit of sinfulness. Piero stood passively by, unable to cope with either the dissident faction or with the angry prophet of S Marco – until at last he was forced to flee for his life in the autumn of 1494. Savonarola was not a Florentine either by birth or temper. He was a fanatic. Yet, in a remarkable lapse, the Florentines took him seriously. Before the crowds that packed the Cathedral, Savonarola compared the city to the world just before the Flood. When, in the last of these sermons, he declared to his thunderstruck audience that the doors of the Ark were now shut, his listeners wailed in despair. Savonarola warned the Florentines of Divine punishment; he scolded them for looking to Aristotle, Plato, Virgil and Petrarch instead of to the Saints and Apostles for the guidance of human affairs.

The Heaven-sent punishment foretold by Savonarola materialized in the form of a brief French occupation. Charles VIII, leading the largest standing army Europe had ever seen, entered Florence in November 1494. On his way down the peninsula to conquer the kingdom of Naples, he exacted from the Florentines a forced loan and the cession of their coastal fortresses. Clever bargaining saved the city from sack. After the departure of the French, the city put itself into the hands of Savonarola, who restored the republic along Venetian lines. In spite of his earlier condemnation of civic pride, Savonarola in his way also fell under the spell of Florentine idealism. He spoke as if he now believed that the Florentines were a chosen people who could set the world an example by acknowledging Christ as their only ruler and Savonarola as their prime minister. In little more than three years the experiment was wrecked by Savonarola's virulent attacks against an unreformed clergy and the revolt of Pisa. Under papal orders, a fickle populace burned him at the stake in the public square.

The next regime, which included Soderini and Niccolò Machiavelli, succeeded in keeping the republic free of the Medici and of papal and foreign interference. It was this government which commissioned Michelangelo and Leonardo to do murals for the main council-chamber of the town hall.

Machiavelli was the last Florentine statesman who, in the tradition of Salutati, Bruni, Cosimo il Vecchio and the magnificent Lorenzo, fused learning with living and practical politics. In Autumn 1512 after the defeat of the republican forces at Prato, Machiavelli fell from office and retired to his farm near San Casciano. A few months later he wrote a friend how he spent his time following his fall from office. During the day he worked with his woodmen and played cards in the tavern with his neighbours, the local farmers, but in the evening, turning homewards, he tells us: 'On the doorstep I shed my everyday clothes covered with mud and dirt, and I put on regal, curial garments; thus appropriately dressed I enter once more the venerable halls of the ancients where, affectionarely received by them, I feed on that food which is for me alone and for which I was born . . .'

Machiavelli's food was the art of governing. *The Prince* and the *Discourses* were written between 1513 and 1519 during his enforced retirement at S Casciano. It was in this work that he gave the famous advice on how a prince could maintain a strong position: '. . . make everything in the state new . . . new institutions with new names, with new authority, new men, making the poor rich as David did when he became king . . . to build beside this a new city, destroying all that is old, shifting the inhabitants from one place to another, in short, leaving nothing as it was before . . .'

With the fall of the republic Medici authority was re-established in Florence and shortly afterwards Giovanni de' Medici became Pope Leo X. With the detachment of a scientist, which he was, Machiavelli looked back on the history of Florentine politics, keenly appreciating the artistry of Cosimo il Vecchio's shrewd calculations and the refined diplomacy of Lorenzo the Magnificent. Full of hope, he dedicated *The Prince* to Lorenzo's grandson, the young Duke of Urbino, who sadly disappointed him.

From 1513 onwards the Medici steered a tricky course amid the expansionist ambitions of the great lords cf Europe: the Pope and the kings of Spain, France, and Austria. Duke Cosimo I assumed the role, if not the title, of absolute monarch of the city in 1537, setting the pattern of Medici rule for the next two centuries. Never again was there the wonderful fusion of art and intellect with civic ideals.

The last Medici, the widowed Electress Palatine Anna Maria Luisa, died in 1743. She left all the Medici collections to the state of Tuscany with the proviso that none of them should ever leave Florence and 'that it should be for the benefit of the public of all nations'. It is these collections which today fill a large part of the great Florentine galleries: the Uffizi, Pitti and Bargello. She also left the Laurentian Library, Michelangelo's Medici Chapel, and the splendid villas of Castello, Petraia, Poggio a Caiano and Cafaggiolo. But eighteenth-century travellers remained unimpressed. In the age of neo-classicism, Rome and Naples were the great attractions. Few came to Florence for its own sake. The only thing that Goethe noticed about Florence as he passed quickly through the city was the efficiency and grandiose aspect of its roads and bridges. Stendhal's sympathy for Florence was more deeply engaged. On descending from the Futa Pass in January 1817 and beholding the city for the first time on the plain below, he exclaimed: 'There is the noble city, the queen of the Middle Ages. It is inside these walls that civilization began again!' But even for him Florence was only a noble cemetery. His first visit was to pay homage to the men of ideas: to the cenotaphs of S Croce commemorating Michelangelo, Alfieri and Galileo. 'Florence,' he said, 'is nothing but a museum . . .' After a poor performance of *The Barber of Seville* he was provoked to say: 'In general Florence's reputation has been usurped. I like Bologna a hundred time more, for its pictures; and beyond this, Bologna has character and spirit. In Florence there are beautiful liveries and long phrases.'

It was through a pedantic Englishman and a Swiss historian that in the nineteenth century the full import of the Florentine achievement was recognized. Perhaps it was something to do with the affinities between the English and Swiss liberal traditions and that of the old king-hating Florentine republic at a moment when Italy was struggling for her unity and independence. John Ruskin and Jacob Burckhardt rediscovered and proclaimed the ancient greatness of Florence. Ruskin made Florence seem quaint rather than vigorous, but he scolded his public into taking seriously not only Michelangelo and Leonardo but the very stones of the city – the rough masonry and the anonymous tombstones. '. . . My general directions to all young people going to Florence or Rome would be very short: know your first volume of Vasari and your first two books of Livy; look about you, and don't talk, nor listen to talking.' Ruskin's public apparently liked the tone of the cross-patch, arrogant pendant; on his advice, generations of English-speaking travellers made Florence the goal of their pilgrimage.

Ruskin saw in the great period of Florentine art models for the aesthetic and moral education of his countrymen. He was not interested in modern Florence at all and saw no connection between its participation in the *Risorgimento* (the movement for the unification of Italy) and the ancient political ideals of the city. As a counterbalance to Ruskin there were the Brownings, Leigh Hunt, and Margaret Fuller.

Burckhardt's *Civilization of the Renaissance in Italy* was published in Basle in 1860 – the year before Italian unification. Its title and table of contents set forth Burckhardt's broad vision and his poetic insight. From the history of Italian city-states from the thirteenth to the mid-sixteenth centuries he drew a grand design in which Florence stands as the paragon – the steadfast opponent of tyrannies papal and monarchial; the home of the free spirit and the inquiring mind. 'Renaissance' and 'Risorgimento' have much in common besides their names; both were heroic, both were humane.

Hippolyte Taine was the first nineteenty-century critic to see that the old Florentine spirit was still alive. Although a political conservative as far as France was concerned, he sympathized with both the Renaissance and the Risorgimento. Taine's visit to Florence occurred in the spring of 1864; the city was already a part of the kingdom of Italy and she was shortly to become for six years its capital. Taine wrote:

Two traits distinguish their revolution from ours. In the first place the Italians are neither levellers nor socialists. The noble is on a familiar footing with the peasant, he converses with the people in a friendly manner; the latter, far from being hostile to their nobility, are rather proud of it . . . the system of cultivation is the same as under the Medicis, which was much advanced for those times, but far behind for these (this is now changing: the teams of white oxen are fast disappearing). The proprietor comes in October to superintend his harvest and then departs . . . he loves economy and, formerly, sold his own wine (actually many families still sell their own wine, often from their palaces and villas – the Ricasoli, Antinori, Gondi, Frescobaldi, and Serristori). For this purpose every palace had an opening through which customers passed their empty bottles and received them full on paying the money . . . The master 'lives and lets live'. There is no pulling and hauling, the meshes of the social web are relaxed and they do not break. Hence the ability of the country to govern itself since 1859 . . . it is a great feature in the organization of government or of a nation not to feel your feet resting on communistic instincts and theories . . . They are too imaginative, too poetic, and besides that, are endowed with too much good sense; they are too conscious of social necessities, too remote from our logical abstractions . . .

Florentines of the working classes to this day are proud of their city's ancient history. The photographer's assistant at the Uffizi is called 'Guelfo'. The name 'Dante' is, of course, very common. Under Mussolini, a girl was named 'Repubblica'. The city officials refused to register the name and she remained officially nameless until the fall of Fascism. A baker gave his children Persian and English names ('Nadir' and 'Donald') from the characters in novels he was reading because he was ashamed of Italy under Mussolini and wouldn't give his children Italian names. Florentines are still stubborn idealists.

Chapter 2

Piazza della Signoria: 'Firenze bizzarra'[1]

SUMMARY OF THE CHIEF MONUMENTS

1. Palazzo Vecchio or Palazzo della Signoria

Exterior – Very likely, the original facade was on the north side of the building (the actual left flank). There the organization of windows and doors is symmetrical. Nucleus of the building 1299–1314; additions on Via della Ninna flank 1342–3; the Salone dei Cinquecento and adjacent rooms 1495–1511; rest of building 1549–55, 1588–92. Upper sections reworked in the 16th c. Below crenellated gallery, coats of arms of the Commune, city wards and public offices (all repainted): Commune (their first insignia half red, half white; then white lily on red field; after Guelph defeat of Ghibellines in 1251 – red lily on white field); Parte Guelfa (gold keys on blue field, keys indicative of their loyalty to the Church; after alliance with Charles of Anjou against Manfred, King of Naples in 1265, they adopted insignia of red eagle with gold crown holding in talons a green dragon); House of Anjou (gold lilies on blue field adopted when Charles of Anjou became lord of Florence for ten years); Popolo (red cross on white field adopted in 1292 during Giano della Bella's reform of the Commune); the wards: Oltrarno (the Bridge), S Piero Scheraggio (the *Carròccio*, or chariot), Borgo Santi Apostoli (the Ram for the butchers' quarter), S Pancrazio (a lion's paw), Porta del Duomo (the insignia – 'Opa' – meaning 'Opera'), S Piero (keys); the districts: S Spirito and Oltrarno (white dove on blue field), S Giovanni (gold octagonal temple on blue field). Over the main portal between two lions (1528), Christ's monogram and the inscription, which is a replacement of the original since lost.

Interior – Because the Palazzo Vecchio is still the city hall of Florence some of the rooms are often closed to the public. Hours: 09.00–19.00 weekdays; 09.00–12.00 Sundays and holidays; admission fee 250 lire except Sunday, which is free, closed Saturdays.

[1]Bizarre Florence.

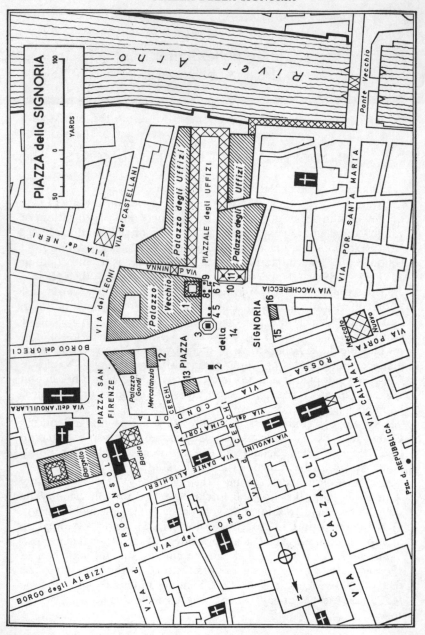

PIAZZA della SIGNORIA

100

50   0   YARDS

The Cortile – rebuilt by Michelozzo, *ca.* 1444. In 1565 Vasari had the columns stuccoed and gilded as part of the festive decor to welcome Joan of Austria, the bride of Cosimo I's eldest son, Francesco. At the same time the lunettes were painted with views of towns under Austrian rule. These murals are all the work of Vasari's pupils – Marco da Faenza, Giovanni Lombardi, Cesare Baglioni and S. Vini. At the same time, Verrocchio's *Fountain* (1476) of the *putto* holding the spouting fish was brought down from the old Medici villa at Careggi. The present bronze *putto* is a copy of the original now exhibited in a room upstairs. The marble shaft is part of the original fountain, but the porphyry basin by Francesco del Tadda dates from *ca.* 1555. The marble group of *Samson and the Philistine* in a niche on the eastern side of the cortile by Pierino da Vinci was probably based on a model by Michelangelo.

After the cortile, a double flight of stairs by Vasari (1560–3) leads to the *Sala del Maggior Consiglio* (also called the Salone dei Cinquecento). This room more than any other in the palace registers the course of Florentine civic life after the expulsion of Piero de' Medici in 1494. When Savonarola assumed the direction of the city's affairs, he reformed the republic along Venetian lines, instituting a Grand Council consisting of 500 members. A hall was built to accommodate them by Simone del Pollaiuolo ('il Cronaca'), assisted by Francesco di Domenico and Antonio da Sangallo. Work began in July 1495 and the hall was ready for the council in February 1496. An inscription stated that the government was divinely inspired and that whoever attempted to ruin it would come to a bad end. At the same time, the Consiglio ordered the trustees of the Medici estate to give them Donatello's bronze *David* (now in the Bargello) to be set on top of a column in the cortile downstairs.

During Savonarola's administration the walls of the room were bare. Between 1503 and 1504, under Soderini, the grandiose pictorial decoration of the room was begun. Two great battle pieces to go on either side of the eastern wall facing the entrances to the room were commissioned from Leonardo da Vinci and Michelangelo. These were the *Battle of Anghiari* and the *Battle of Cascina*. Neither was ever completed. Michelangelo was called to Rome and Leonardo's interest was distracted by an irrigation scheme (*see* chapter 6). The cartoons of these murals were widely copied and engraved.

With the return of the Medici in 1512, the great hall's function became obsolete. The woodwork was dismantled and turned over to the Opera del Duomo. Leonardo's unfinished mural was boarded up and the room was shared by a barracks and a tax office. Between

27

1527 and 1530, during the brief revival of the Republic, the hall once more served its original purpose. But the room's appearance seems to have remained unaltered until Cosimo I moved in from the Palazzo Medici in 1540. The hall then became the Duke's audience chamber. Baccio Bandinelli built the podium at the northern end of the room to serve as a background for Cosimo. In the niches Bandinelli set statues of *Cosimo I, Giovanni delle Bande Nere, Leo X* (finished by Vincenzo de' Rossi), and *Duke Alessandro.* The statue of *Charles V kneeling before Clement VII* and the *Francesco I* (both by Giovanni Caccini) were added in 1594. While Bandinelli worked at the northern end, Ammannati devised a great wall fountain for the opposite end in which Florence was allegorically shown as the counterpart of Parnassus (*see* chapter 9). This project was never finished and the statues were dispersed. Some are in the Bargello and others are in the Boboli Gardens. What stopped the project was a consequence of Michelangelo's death in 1564. The sculptor's nephew was induced to present the Grand Duke with a figure originally meant for the tomb of Pope Julius II. This is the *Victory** (carved in the late 1520s) now in the central niche. At this point Cosimo commissioned Giambologna to carve the *Fiorenza* to go at the opposite end of the room, but this statue too has been moved to the Bargello.

In 1563 the ceiling was raised and a pictorial scheme was devised for it by Vasari and Don Vincenzo Borghini. There are 39 painted compartments illustrating the provinces of Tuscany and events from Florentine history. The work was carried out by Vasari, Naldini, Stradano, Zucchi, Santi di Tito, Michele Tosini, Prospero Fontana and others. Between 1567 and 1571 Vasari painted the murals on the west and east walls illustrating famous Florentine victories. The 17th c. tapestries illustrating the life of the city's patron saint, John the Baptist, were woven in the Grand Ducal tapestry factory. The compositions are based on Andrea del Sarto's murals in the Scalzo. The crudely conceived marbles illustrating the *Labours of Hercules* are the work of Vincenzo de' Rossi (*ca.* 1566) but were not installed here until about 1592.

Cosimo's personal apartments were on the first floor. We are told that his wooden bed was gilded and was hung with golden damask curtains. At the head of the bed was a *Madonna* by Pontormo. A room next door was lined with embossed leather and at each corner was a marble statue: a *Bacchus* by Baccio Bandinelli, another *Bacchus* by Sansovino, a *David* by Michelangelo, and an ancient Roman *putto.* The Duke's wife, mother and children occupied apartments on the floors above. Also housed in the palace were the gem-cutters, weavers, pages, and the barber.

At the south-western end of the Salone dei Cinquecento a door leads to the **Studiolo of Francesco I***. Vasari built it for Francesco I along the lines of the famous study in the old Medici palace and Borghini suggested the subjects for its decorations. The pictures are a treasury of later Mannerist art. Looking down on the scheme from the lunettes are Bronzino's portraits of Francesco's parents: *Cosimo I* and *Eleonora of Toledo*. The scheme consists of two rows of pictures (the upper row are painted on slate, the lower ones on the wooden backs of the cupboard doors), with small bronzes at the corners of the room. Starting at the middle of the entrance wall (proceeding from left to right and from top to bottom) are: a *Gold Mine* by Jacopo Zucchi, *Deucalion and Pyrrha* by A. del Minga; *Opi*, a bronze by Ammannati, *Atalanta's Race* by S. Marsili; *Amphitryte*, a bronze by Stoldo Lorenzi, *Perseus and Andromeda* by Vasari; *Alexander gives Campaspe to Apelles* by F. Morandini called 'il Poppi'; *Passage Through the Red Sea* by Santi di Tito, *Neptune and the 'Teti'* by Carlo Portelli; *Whale Fishers* by Naldini, *Sacrifice of Lavinia* by M. Cavalori; *Fetonte's Sisters turned to Poppies* by Santi di Tito, *Circe bewitching Ulysses's Companions* by G. Stradano; *Wool-workers* by M. Cavalori, *Dreams* by Naldini; *Pearl Fishers* and *Feast of Cleopatra* by Alessandro Allori; *Venus*, a bronze by Vincenzo Danti, *Venus takes back her Girdle from Juno and gives it to Paris* by F. Coscia; *Juno*, a bronze by G. Bandini, *Aeneas's Arrival in Italy* by G. M. Butteri; *Diamond Mine* and *Fall of Icarus* by Maso da Sanfriano; *Zephyr*, a bronze by Elia Candido; *Apollo*, a bronze by Giambolonga, *Daniel at Balthasar's Feast* by G. Fedini; *Baths of Pozzuoli* and *Medea and Jason* by G. Macchietti; *Invention of Gunpowder* by Jacopo Coppi called 'il Meglio', *Hercules slaying the Dragon* by L. dello Sciorina; *Glass Making* by G. M. Butteri, *Hercules and Iole* by Santi di Tito; *Goldsmith's Atelier* by A. Fei called 'il Barbiere', *Looting of a City* by Niccolò Betti; *Alchemist's Laboratory* by G. Stradano, *Medicinal Distillery* by Domenico Buti; *Bronze Foundry* by F. Morandini called 'il Poppi', the *Family of Darius before Alexander* by J. Coppi; *Vulcan*, a bronze by Vincenzo de' Rossi, *Vulcan at his Forge* by V. Casini; *Pluto*, a bronze by D. Poggini, *Danaë* by B. Traballesi.

A small staircase from the Studiolo leads to the **Tesoretto** (ask custodian to show the way) with murals and stuccos representing the arts and sciences by L. Ricciarelli and G. Boscoli.

Opposite the entrance to the Studiolo is the **Hall of Leo X** rebuilt and decorated under Vasari's direction between 1556 and 1562. This and the adjoining rooms are lined with murals alluding to Medici history. A staircase from the Hall of Leo X leads to the second floor. On the right, at the top of the stairs, is the *Quartiere degli Elementi* – an apartment consisting of five rooms and two terraces built by Battista del Tasso (*ca*. 1550–6). The rooms are furnished with precious cabinets, tapestries of the hunt, and antique busts. Giambologna's bronze *Diavolino* is exhibited in the *Loggia of Saturn*. This terrace was originally painted by Bachiacca (1552–3). Splendid view.

Returning through the apartment and crossing the gallery overlooking the Salone dei Cinquecento, one reaches the *Apartment of Eleonora of Toledo*. The chapel was painted by Bronzino (1540–5). The ceilings of the other rooms were carved by Bernardo del Tasso and painted with subjects of famous women of legend and ancient history.

In the corridor leading from Eleonora's apartment are hung some of the pictures left to the city by Charles Loeser (more works from this collection are installed in the mezzanine). Also here is the 14th c. mural of the *Expulsion of the Duke of Athens on St Anne's Day* (*ca* 1343) which was originally painted in the debtors 'prison known as the Stinche. The stairs farther on, on the left, lead down to the *Sala dei Duecento* (usually closed), begun *ca* 1444, and hung with tapestries designed by Bronzino, Salviati and Pontormo, and upstairs to the tower of the Palazzo Vecchio. Inside the tower is a small room known as *l'Alberghettino* here Cosimo il Vecchio and Savonarola were held prisoner. At the end of the corridor is the *Sala dei Gigli* rebuilt by Benedetto da Maiano (1476–80), who was also responsible for the carved and gilded ceiling. The murals by Domenico and Davide Ghirlandaio (1481–5) represent at the centre: *S Zenobius Enthroned, flanked by SS Lawrence and Stephen*. In the fictive arcades on either side are six republican protagonists of ancient Roman history: *Brutus, Camillus, Cicero, Decius, Mucius Scaevola* and *Scipio*. Opposite is a marble doorway with the figure of the *Baptist* carved by Giuliano da Maiano (1476–81). Dante and Petrarch are set into the intarsiaed doors by Giuliano da Maiano, and 'il Francione'. In this room the members of the Pazzi Conspiracy took brief refuge in 1478 after the murder of Giuliano de' Medici in the Cathedral.

Off the Sala dei Gigli, through the doors on the wall with Ghirlandaio's murals, are two rooms. On the left is a small room in which are exhibited Verrocchio's *bronze putto** of 1476 (formerly in the cortile fountain), Santi di Tito's *Portrait of Machiavelli*, a polychromed terracotta bust of *Machiavelli* by an unknown master, and the relief of *S George and the Dragon* (*ca* 1270–80) from the Porta S Giorgio. The second door on this side of the Sala dei Gigli leads to the *Guardaroba*, or *Sala delle Mappe Geografiche*, surrounded by cupboards carved by D. Nigetti and painted with 53 maps of Tuscan territories begun by Egnazio Danti (1563) and completed by Stefano Buonsignori (1576). The scheme was begun under Cosimo I and derives from a Venetian decoration in the Doge's palace.

Returning to the Sala dei Gigli, the doors inlaid with Dante and Petrarch lead to the **Sala dell' Udienza** (closed for restoration), built by Benedetto da Maiano. The carved ceiling is the work of his brother Giuliano, aided by 'il Francione' and the Tasso brothers. Above the portal is the figure of *Justice* by Giuliano and Benedetto da Maiano (1476–8). The murals designed by Francesco Salviati (*ca* 1550–60) illustrate the history of Camillus.

Beside this room is the **Cappella dei Priori** built in 1511. The murals, commissioned by Lorenzo di Piero de' Medici, are by Ridolfo Ghirlandaio (1514). The altarpiece of the *Holy Family* is by Ridolfo's assistant, Mariano da Pescia.

Downstairs, adjacent to the Sala dei Duecento, is the **Mezzanino** where most of the pictures, sculpture and furniture from the Loeser Collection are installed. These include Bronzino's *Portrait of Laura Battiferri* (the poetess and wife of Ammannati), a *Madonna* by Pietro Lorenzetti, a marble angel by Tino di Camaino, and Giambologn'a *Hercules and the Hydra*.

2. Equestrian Monument to Duke Cosimo I de' Medici by Giambologna, 1587–99. The horse was finished in 1594, the Duke's portrait in 1595, and the reliefs in 1598.

3. Neptune Fountain designed by Bartolomeo Ammannati, 1565–75, bronzes executed by Ammannati, Giambologna and possibly others.

4. The Marzocco,* or heraldic lion of Florence, copy of original by Donatello now in the Bargello, 1418–20. The base dates from the 15th c. The statue (made for the papal apartments at S Maria Novella) was brought to the Piazza in the last century to replace a 14th c. image of the Marzocco.

5. Judith and Holofernes* by Donatello, 1456–60.

6. David, copy made in 1873 of the original by Michelangelo now in the Academy.

31

7. Hercules and Cacus by Baccio Bandinelli, 1533–4.

8. Male herm by Vincenzo de' Rossi, *ca* 1535.

9. Female herm, by Baccio Bandinelli *ca* 1535; the pair of herms served originally as posts securing the chain across the main entrance to the palace. The identity of the pair is uncertain; Philemon and Baucis have been proposed.

10. The Loggia dei Lanzi – built by Simone Talenti and the Opera del Duomo, 1376–82. Reliefs on attic: nine coats of arms of the Commune and the Parte Guelfa by Jacopo di Piero Guidi and Niccolò di Piero Lamberti and painted by Jacopo di Cione and Vanni di Bono, 1381, 1331. Reliefs of Virtues designed by Agnolo Gaddi (executed by Jacopo di Piero Guidi, 1383–6) on flank facing palace: *Hope, Charity,* and *Faith* – the *Charity* carved in the round but not installed until 1395; its tabernacle is modern. Recently it has been discovered that the head of *Faith* is a work of Donatello (possibly taken from his statue of *Dovizia* which once stood in the Mercato Vecchio). No one knows exactly when the substitution of the heads occurred. Virtues on front of Loggia: *Strength* and *Temperance* by Giovanni di Francesco Fetti and Jacopo di Piero Guidi, 1386; *Justice* and *Prudence* by Giovanni d'Ambrogio, 1383–6. Originally all Virtues painted by Lorenzo di Bicci, niches lined in blue mosaic edged with golden stars.

11. Statuary inside the loggia – first row: *Perseus** by Benvenuto Cellini, 1553, with a base containing statuettes of *Jove, Minerva, Mercury, Danae and infant Perseus* (recently replaced by copies) and a relief of *Perseus liberating Andromeda* (all these are now in the Bargello); two lions flanking staircase – that on the right is ancient, that on the left is a copy by Flaminio Vacca; *Rape of a Sabine* by Giambologna, 1583. Second row: the *Rape of Polixena* by Pio Fedi, 1866; *Ajax or Menelaus supporting the Body of Patroclus,* perhaps a Roman copy of a 4th c. B.C. Greek original; *Hercules fighting the Centaur Nessus* by Giambologna, 1599. Third row: six statues of ancient Roman matrons purchased by Ferdinando I de' Medici when in Rome as Cardinal but probably not brought to Florence until 1789.

12. Palazzo or Tribunale della Mercatanzia (No. 10) – finished in 1359, restored in 1905; the old commercial court established in 1308. During the 14th c. also functioned as a public post-office. Now seat of local bureau of agriculture.

The Lily of the Commune of Florence, from a fifteenth-century doorway in the Zecca (the old Mint), now part of the Uffizi

The Palazzo Vecchio, the town hall of Florence, with the hill of Arcetri
in the distance

13. Palazzo Uguccioni – facade by Zanobi Folfi called 'l'Ammogliato', 1550–9; remodelling of medieval building in the Roman Renaissance style. The structures on either side occupy sites on which the palaces of the Rinuccini and Guidacci once stood. Bust of Francesco I by G. Bandini.

At No. 5 on the *piazza*, a floor has recently been taken over by the city to install a gallery of modern Italian art donated by the Genoese collector, Della Ragione, which includes works by De Pisis, Marini and Manzu.

14. Tablet marking site of the stake at which Fra Girolamo Savonarola and two of his followers were burned and hanged by order of Pope Alexander VI on May 23, 1498.

15. Palazzo delle Assicurazioni Generali di Venezia – built in 1871, occupies site once filled by the so-called Loggia dei Pisani and the church of S Cecilia.

16. Caffè Rivoire, the pleasantest spot from which to view the Piazza in good weather.

'FIRENZE BIZZARRA'

THE PIAZZA. The heart of Florence consists of three great piazzas: the Piazza del Duomo, the modern Piazza della Repubblica, and the Piazza della Signoria. The Piazza del Duomo is the oldest, but the vigour of Florentine idealism was in its secular life and the Piazza della Signoria was its centre. The free spirit of the Commune has its echo in the breadth and irregularity of its Piazza. Each building has something of stubborn self-sufficiency. Not a façade resembles its neighbour (which moved a Lucchese to mutter knowingly: '*Firenze bizzarra*'). In Siena the palaces facing the town hall bend as if in curtsy and their façades are swept into a conforming pattern around the fan-shaped piazza. In Florence each facade is sharp and clear – oblivious of any master plan. Yet the marvel is that there is no cowering confusion, no medieval huddling together. The harmony lies in the material – undressed stone of gold or golden-grey; and in the character – solid, severe, economical – but *bold*.

Building stone is so abundant in Tuscany that it was used for houses whether humble or noble. Before the simple, forthright masonry of the Piazza della Signoria one feels that the distance between peasant house and palace is, after all, not so great. The very streets of Florence served as quarries. The chief source of the golden-brown *pietra forte* or *macigno*, which was used in the Palazzo Vecchio, the Mercanzia, the Palazzo Strozzi, and the Palazzo Uguccioni, lay in the area between Piazza S Felìcita and the Porta Romana. All one had to do to build a house in Florence, remarked a sixteenth-century wit, was to dig into the site and pile up the stones. During the fourteenth and early fifteenth centuries, buildings and towers were lined with stone inside and out. But in the Renaissance economic as well as aesthetic considerations worked a change. The dearness of quarrying, cutting and transport favoured the use of plastered rubble. Stone began to be restricted to ornamental rustication, to articulating columns and cornices, or to the frames of doors and windows.

The Piazza della Signoria and the town hall were not planned together. The first ground was cleared before the Palazzo Vecchio was even projected. This was the cursed land of the degli Uberti family, whose property was confiscated in 1268 and deliberately left in ruins as a public reminder of Ghibelline perfidy and defeat. In order to build the Palazzo Vecchio, property was purchased from other Florentine families. Subsequently, the degli Uberti land was turned into a paved piazza so that any hope that the exiled family might have had of rebuilding there was eliminated for ever. The space to the south of the Palazzo was occupied by the church of S Pier Scheraggio, which was left intact until it was absorbed into the fabric of the Uffizi in the sixteenth century. This accounts for the curious angle at which the town hall was built and why it proved impossible to accord it either an axial or a centralized position in the Piazza. Villani foresaw this difficulty, which arose only because of the building committee's reluctance to use any of the degli Uberti ground – a sentiment with which he had no sympathy: '. . . The palace should have been given a square rectangular shape and should not have been carried so close to S Pier Scheraggio.' Throughout the fourteenth century efforts were made to enlarge the Piazza in front. But for many decades whatever space was cleared served only as an unsightly building yard while the Palazzo Vecchio and the Loggia dei Lanzi were being raised.

The widening and paving of the Piazza was left to the Opera del Duomo – the largest construction company in the city. Although it was permanently attached to the Cathedral fabric, the Opera was often hired out for other public enterprises. Its administrators were lay representatives of the great guilds and many of these officials also held public office. It was easy to shift jobs and materials between

Cathedral and Commune. And thus it came about that the Palazzo Vecchio was completed early at the expense of delays in the construction of the Cathedral, which had been begun almost at the same time. By 1330 the Piazza, however, was still defaced by ripped-up house foundations and piles of broken masonry. A contemporary document declared that the Piazza should at last be regularly paved with tiles (or bricks) and paving stones because it 'must look more seemly and as regular as every other square and street in the city'.

To have the Piazza 'seemly and regular' still nagged Duke Cosimo I de' Medici two hundred years later. It was characteristic of the age of absolutism that Cosimo tried to impose some sort of comprehensive scheme on the Piazza. Vasari informs us that Cosimo consulted Michelangelo on this problem. One might have expected Michelangelo, as an old Florentine and a militant republican, to have vigorously opposed doing anything to the Piazza or touching any of its monuments. But the artist got the better of him and he proposed that the motif of the Loggia dei Lanzi be continued all around the Piazza. It was too costly and Cosimo never seriously considered it. Instead, he let sculpture accomplish the task. The existing startuay and the works subsequently commissioned by Cosimo and his heirs were marshalled into military order in front of the palace which had by then become the ducal residence. A *Marzocco*, Michelangelo's *David*, and Bandinelli's *Hercules* were already there. The rest of the statuary, the Neptune fountain and the monument to Cosimo I, were aligned along an axis which cuts across the Piazza. The public was confronted with a parade of civic symbols and political propaganda. The equestrian monument to Duke Cosimo I is the last in line and stands in the middle of the Piazza. It aimed to copy the Marcus Aurelius monument in Rome, which had but a few decades earlier been transferred from the Lateran to the centre of Rome's public square – the Capitoline Hill. An explicit comparison was drawn between *Roma Caput Mundi* and Florence Capital of all Tuscany. Such were Medici pretensions in the late sixteenth century.

Today the Piazza functions in summer as a parking lot and on S John's Day (June 24th) as a soccer field in which the teams of competing districts of the city play in costume for the benefit of visiting hordes of *forestieri* (foreigners). But during the autumn and winter Florence belongs to its citizens and the Piazza returns to the life of the Commune. On Fridays the cars in the parking area are drowned in throngs of farmers and *fattori* who gather here, spilling into the near-by streets, to trade and gossip about wine, oil and grain; to bargain for livestock and to make contracts with a gruff nod or a laying on of hands. Cosimo on his bronze horse is caught in the hubbub of voices from the Arno valley, the Mugello and the Chianti. Steam rises in the crisp cold air from heavy bargaining. The Mercatanzia, the old commercial tribunal where every bankruptcy and every maritime question was deliberated, is now the official agricultural centre (Consorzio Agrario), but the real affairs are conducted in the open-air stock exchange in front of it. There the sun is warmer and rendezvous are easier to arrange at the feet of Cosimo I and Neptune, or before the *trattoria* called the Cavallino or in front of the Palazzo Uguccioni.

The Florentine beast of burden also has his day on the Piazza; on the last day of the year the Commune offers free oats to all the city's horses, donkeys and asses which are brought here.

During the election season, politics are shouted from the *ringhiera* (or platform) in front of the Palazzo Vecchio or from the Loggia dei Lanzi. Not even pouring rain can keep a crowd from packing the Piazza when a really vociferous *urlatore* (a shouter) or a Communist is promised them. Before the speeches the crowd is roused to the proper heroic spirit by deafening martial music or political 'hymns'. Much the same is done in Rome for the crowds who on Easter Sunday wait in front of St Peter's for the Pope's address delivered from a balcony. A political rally in the Piazza della Signoria is a kind of entertainment. The event is announced as a great *festa* with gaily coloured broadsides plastering the walls of the city. Besides the singing and shouting, these gatherings are usually well-staged affairs. The Communists, who are the most experienced, are masters of the art. They organize troops of youngsters from the neighbouring towns (S Casciano, Tavernelle, Impruneta) to burst into the Piazza at appropriate moments so as to punctuate the speaker's arguments with their enthusiasm, their waving banners and slogans.

THE PALAZZO VECCHIO. From the Via dei Leoni, the Palazzo Vecchio thrusts its cliff of golden-brown rock into the Piazza. For miles down the Arno valley one can see its crenellated battlements (the *ballatoio*) and its beacon tower, with their counterpart, the Cathedral's great cupola. The Palazzo Vecchio is at once a fortress of municipal liberty and a monument to the victorious Guelphs, who finally crushed the Ghibelline or Imperial party at Benevento in 1266. Although the Florentine part in the battle was minor, her strength in Tuscany was established by having backed the winning side, and a relatively stable government followed. The city was ruled by seven priors from the major guilds, and before the building of the Palazzo dei Priori (as the Palazzo Vecchio was at first called), they met either in a fortified tower or in the church of S Pier Scheraggio. Before long, however, a place of permanence and security was required. Plans for the new palace were already under way in 1284. But the cornerstone was not laid until 1299, five years after the new Cathedral was begun. The name of Arnolfo di Cambio, the Cathedral's architect, has since Vasari been traditionally associated with the Palazzo Vecchio, but no document substantiates the connection.Once under way, the Palazzo dei Priori rose with a speed remarkable for those times. Whether because of Arnolfo's death or because of the building of the town hall, work on the Cathedral stopped in 1302. Such interruptions never afflicted the Palazzo Vecchio, which by 1301 was far enough advanced to permit the priors to move in. By 1314 the building was finished except for the tower, which was to be built on to that of the demolished Foraboschi palace. In 1322 the great bell known as the Lion was cast. The Florentines boasted that it was the world's largest. But it was not of Florentine make; the best bronze-founder of the time was a Sienese – Lando di Pietro – and it was he who was given the job. He was paid an honorarium of 300 gold pieces – triple the annual salary Giotto received when he was *capomaestro* of the Opera del Duomo. The bell was removed in 1530 from the tower and smashed in the square as a symbolic execution of the republic.

The lion is the heraldic symbol of the city, like Venice's lion of St Mark. Since the thirteenth century living lions were kept at the Commune's expense – a custom which persisted into the eighteenth century. At first their cage was situated opposite the Baptistery in the Piazza del Duomo where the Bigallo now stands. Citizens paid to see the lions and they interpreted the behaviour of the wild beasts as omens. In 1319 the lions were brought to the Piazza dei Priori, where the Loggia dei Lanzi is now. A permanent pen was made for them in a big courtyard behind the new palazzo. Duke Cosimo I (ruled 1537–74), however, found the stench too much for him and had them moved out. The stone lions in the present inner courtyard and the Via dei Leoni behind it commemorate their stay there.

The fortress-like nature of the Palazzo dei Priori soon changed. With the decision in 1323 to build the *ringhiera* ('a noble and fitting *arengheriam*', says the document) communal life was carried out of doors. The *ringhiera* was a raised stone platform from which the communal officials addressed or 'harangued' the populace. Literally a *ringhiera* is a 'haranguing-place'. In its present state the *ringhiera* is a reduction of the original one, which was largely demolished in

1812 at the order of French troops.

In 1342–3, the Palazzo became a fortress again for a short time during the attempted tyranny of Gaultiero di Brienne, the Duke of Athens. He walled up the steps of the *ringhiera* and reinforced the palace's already formidable defences by adding a keep around the entrance door and extending the flank along the Via della Ninna. A picture of the palace in this state exists in a detached mural of the period now exhibited in the Palazzo Vecchio. The Duke of Athens was in such a hurry that he took away beams and masonry from the Ponte Vecchio, then under construction.

Throughout the Trecento the town hall was known as the Palazzo del Popolo. But during the next century this name was used less and less. Gradually, the government by representatives from the major craftsmen's guilds was replaced by government by the leading lords of commerce, or Signori, as they were known. Thus came into being the 'Palazzo dei Signori' or 'della Signoria'. When Duke Cosimo I moved over from the Medici palace on the Via Larga in 1540, it became a 'Palazzo Ducale'. And when, in 1565, Cosimo moved out into the new ducal residence prepared for him in the Palazzo Pitti, the old town hall became the Palazzo Vecchio (Old Palace). Cosimo's move was the result of his son Francesco's marriage to Joan of Austria, Emperor Ferdinand's daughter. The bride was melancholy and homesick. To give her a cheerful welcome into her new home, the walls of the grim cortile just inside the entrance were painted with views of towns under Austrian rule, the grey columns were hidden behind gilt stucco, and as the joyful centre-piece of it all, Verrocchio's *putto* with a dolphin was moved down from the old Medici villa at Careggi.

During the next three centuries the Palazzo Vecchio became less and less the centre of the city's public life. Sometimes it was used as a courtly residence, sometimes as an office building, as a meeting-place for learned academics, or simply as a stage-setting for ceremonies of official pomp. For a time the city magistrates were even forced to move over to the relative obscurity of the old Palazzo della Parte Guelfa. The public had no part in the Palazzo Vecchio. Only once a year, on the day after St John's Day, were the citizenry, as a sop, allowed free entry; the palace was thrown open for dancing, feasting and general *baldoria* (loud merry-making). But with the rising of 1848 and the later unification of Italy this changed. The Florentines again took the government into their own hands. The granducal coats of arms were knocked down and much of the palace's displaced décor was reinstalled. One of the leaders in this was Gino Capponi, another member of the same family, who three and a half centuries earlier, had produced the brave and cocky Piero. This was the Capponi who had the courage to stand up to Charles VIII, King of France. When Charles uttered some threat against the city, Capponi replied. 'If you blow your trumpets, we shall ring our bells,' meaning that the populace would fall on the French troops. In 1528 Niccolò Capponi, in the spirit of Savonarola, composed the inscription set over the town-hall entrance proclaiming Christ the elected king of Florence: IESVS. CHRISTVS. REX. FLORENTINI. POPVLI. S. P. DECRETO. ELECTVS. It was republicanism as well as piety which inspired the line, for who would dare to pretend to be Christ's successor as the lord of Florence! But in 1851 the grand duke had it replaced with the present REX REGUM ET DOMINUS DOMINATIUM.

Its centuries-old tradition is no hobble to the city government of Florence. It is still actuated by the ancient spirit. Employees feel passionately about the city, and their personal initiative, sometimes from a low echelon, carries forward to speak for the whole city. For example, few remember the significance of the two little white dresses (*due vestitini bianchi*) which every June are sent to Anghiari in commemoration of the Florentine victory over the Visconti in 1440 (the subject of Leonardo's great battle-piece). The dresses commemorate the two boys dressed in white sent by the Milanese to ask for a truce. In exchange for the white dresses, Florence receives from Anghiari a candle which has been blessed. A Florentine lawyer remarked bitterly that this was typical of what happened to the city under mayor La Pira: 'We send them dresses and all we get in return is a candle!' Another example: it is customary to have wreaths mounted on the houses of Florentine heroes. A minor official, an accountant, discovered that no annual wreath was being sent to the birthplace of Francesco Ferrucci (the last defender in 1530 of the doomed Florentine republic). He took it upon himself to see that as long as he was a municipal employee the wreath should each year reach Ferrucci's birthplace at Via S Spirito No. 32. Again, it is an annual event for the city to send Florentine oil to Ravenna in September to light votive lamps at Dante's tomb. The custom dates back, so the mayor's office says, to the '*notte dei tempi*'. The oil had been sent by train without any ceremony. Whether due to La Pira or to competition from the city of Turin (which also sends a gift of oil at the same time of year), oil from Florence has since 1949 been sent 'with pomp' on the Sunday closest to September 14th, the day Dante died.

THE LOGGIA DEI LANZI. The graceful Loggia dei Lanzi was built by the Commune alongside the grim town hall. It showed that by 1376 the Florentine state felt so secure that it could now afford leisurely grandeur. Its wide open arches and easy access, even its choice of material (smooth *pietra serena* instead of rusticated *pietra forte*), all speak for the changed mood of the city. The *ringhiera* upon which public acts had been proclaimed was exposed to sun, wind and rain, and the speakers must have appeared dwarfed by the fortress-like wall behind them. A need was felt for a larger, more impressive and more protected space for public ceremonies. The Commune of S Gimignano already had such a loggia by 1338. In Florence the matter had been discussed since 1356 but little was done until 1374, after a particularly rainy season when all the public ceremonies scheduled for the *ringhiera* had to be given up. The Commune acquired the property for the Loggia and began demolition of the houses. The workmen of the Opera del Duomo were again called away from the Cathedral's construction. Indeed, the arches, the vaults and the shape and scale of the enormous piers (two of which required the labour of thirty-five masons) resemble those in the Cathedral's nave. By November 1382 the Loggia was finished. Here the Bishop of Ravenna was officially welcomed in 1384 and the Queen of England in 1961. On such occasions tapestries line the Loggia's walls and the city herald sings out verses honouring the illustrious visitor. (The same herald also used to have the task of doing the labels for the effigies of rebels and criminals which were painted on the walls of the Bargello.)

Later, the Loggia became important for more everyday events. Fifty years after its completion, Leon Battista Alberti, who was a great figure in Florence, wrote: '. . . One of the greatest ornaments either of a square, or of a Crossway, is a handsome Portico, under which the old Men may spend the Heat of the Day, or be mutually serviceable to each other; besides that the Presence of the Fathers may deter and restrain the Youth, who are sporting and diverting themselves in the other part of the Place, from the Mischievousness and Folly natural to their Age.' The Loggia is shown thus in Ghirlandaio's mural of 1485 in S Trinita.

The Loggia dei Lanzi got its name from Duke Cosimo I's Swiss lancers (*Landsknechte*) who were housed in barracks in the near-by Via Lambertesca. Its other name, 'Loggia dell' Orcagna', comes from Vasari and not from any document. The only connection with Orcagna was the painting of one of the reliefs done by his brother, Jacopo di Cione.

Towards the end of the sixteenth century, after the roof of the Loggia was joined to the Uffizi, the Grand Duke had Bernardo Buontalenti turn the top of the Loggia into a roof garden, or 'Giardino Pensile'. Fruit trees, spices, peas and flowers grew there. There was even a pergola and a fountain with a small bronze of the Court's favourite dwarf, Morgante (now in the Bargello), cast after a design by Giambologna. Sometimes orchestras played there for the amusement of the Court and the public.

During the course of centuries, the Loggia became an open-air sculpture gallery. Donatello's *Judith and Holofernes* was the first statue moved there, in 1506. In 1554 Cellini's *Perseus* was set up beside it as a sort of pendant. Both were bronze and both described the decapitation of a vanquished enemy. As civic symbols, however, the comparison would have been ironic. Donatello's group had come to the Piazza from the Palazzo Medici when Florence expelled the family in 1495 and an inscription on its base proclaimed the city's liberation from their rule: EXEMPLUM. SAL[UTIS]. PUB[LICAE]. CIVES. POS[UERE]. MCCCCXCV. The *Perseus*, on the other hand, commissioned by Duke Cosimo I, celebrated the absolute power of the Medici, who since 1513 had regained their hold on the city. It has been suggested that the *Perseus liberating Andromeda* on the relief at the base is symbolic of Florence; Cosimo did bring a stable government to the city, but it was a tyranny. Perseus holds up Medusa's head towards the Piazza; according to the legend, Perseus used the head to turn his enemies to stone. Was Cellini's bronze intended, then, as Cosimo's challenge to the Florentines?

Cellini's *Perseus* marks another development in the concept of free-standing statuary in the Piazza. Not since Donatello's *Judith* had figures been composed with more than one view in mind. For example, Michelangelo's *David* and Bandinelli's *Hercules* have but one main view – an unconscious survival from the time when monumental statuary was set inside an architectural framework. Eventually Donatello's *Judith* was moved from the arch of the Loggia on the Via Vaccereccia side in order to make room for Giambologna's *Rape of a Sabine*. This marble group, finished in 1583, is thought to have been carved as a virtuoso's reply to Cellini's *Perseus*. Giambologna sought to prove that it was possible, even in the more difficult material of marble, to realize a monumental composition with several figures all in violent action with many views in spiral. It was Vincenzo Borghini, a critic and inventor of allegorical schemes for the Medici court, who suggested the subject after the sculptor had considered continuing the Andromeda theme.

Although it was one of the largest blocks of marble ever brought to Florence, so far there is no clear evidence that this group (unlike most of the statuary in the Piazza) had any veiled political meaning. It was a purely formal performance. This loosening of the relationship between subject and formal composition, with the emphasis on the latter, is characteristic of Florentine art after 1530, which thus associates itself with the style known as Mannerism.

THE STATUARY IN FRONT OF THE PALAZZO VECCHIO. Here statuary acquired a new significance as an expression of changing civic ideals. Elsewhere in Florence, monumental statuary was incorporated into a frame of architecture – as in the Cathedral bell-tower or the outer walls of Orsanmichelle In the Piazza della Signoria, all the statuary is free-standing. The range of scale is very revealing of the time and of those who made and commissioned the statues. Donatello's *Marzocco* and the *Judith* are both life size, but beginning with Michelangelo's *David*, the scale becomes superhuman. Perhaps Michelangelo and his contemporaries remembered Livy's mention of colossal statues of Hercules which once stood on the Capitoline Hill. The *David* looms so large that it almost overpowers the Palazzo behind it. Save for its axial arrangement, the statuary, formally, is entirely unrelated to the adjacent architecture – thus acquiring a life of its own.

THE MARZOCCO. The *Marzocco* was the first civic image to enter the Piazza. Since 1350 smaller versions of the heraldic lion had been set up in the public squares of towns conquered by Florence. The *Marzocco* was the sign of Florentine jurisdiction, and part of the customary treatment of prisoners was to force them to kiss its backside. Probably the name *Marzocco* was a corruption of the diminutive of Mars – *Martocus* – whose ruined image long stood at one end of the Ponte Vecchio. Donatello's monumental lion, carved between 1418 and 1420, though a civic symbol was not made for the piazza but for the papal apartment which had been built at communal expense within the convent of Santa Maria Novella. Originally, he wore a gilded crown inscribed with a patriotic verse composed by Franco Sacchetti some fifty years earlier:

Corona porto per la patria degna,
a ciò che libertà ciascun mantegna

(The crown I wear for the deserving homeland, so that liberty is maintained by everyone.)

Elsewhere in Italy the lion as a popular image symbolized Justice. Donatello's *Marzocco* was conceived as a defender of liberty. Its heroic size and the almost human character that Donatello gave it were new then. Donatello's lion was brought to the *ringhiera ca* 1812 but was replaced by a copy in 1885. The original is now in the Bargello.

THE JUDITH AND HOLOFERNES. The history of Donatello's *Judith and Holofernes* is that of a displaced monument. It was cast for the Medici some time between 1456 and 1460 after Donatello's return from Padua. In 1495 the Commune acquired it as part of the spoils of the exiled Medici and set it up as a symbol of tyranny crushed. Originally, the group was a fountain which spouted water from the four corners of the pillow. It was, in fact, the most monumental piece of fountain statuary of the Quattrocento. Even when it still belonged to the Medici, the statue already had the character of a public monument. It had an inscription stating that Piero the Gouty had the statue made as a symbol of Florentine liberty (*see* chapter 8, p. 228). *Judith and Holofernes* also stood for another theme: they were symbolic of pride vanquished by humility, or incontinence crushed by chastity. The bacchanalian scenes on the base, as well as the water which spouted from Holofernes' wineskin-cushion, continue this secondary theme.

Donatalleo cast the bronze in several pieces, which by that time was unusual. Judith's head, raised forearm, and Holofernes's legs were cast separately; her gown was cast from a wax model based upon actual cloth draped over a nude or nearly nude figure, and traces of the material, clearly visible across Judith's forehead, are reproduced in the metal.

Between 1495 and 1504 *Judith* stood on the *ringhiera* not far from the *Marzocco*. But before long the Commune became dissatisfied with her: '[it] does not befit us whose insignia are the cross and the lily, nor is it good to have a woman kill a man.' Furthermore, it was said that ever since *Judith* had been adopted as a personification of civic virtue, matters for the Florentines had been going from bad to worse. On the arrival of Michelangelo's *David*, the *Judith* was banished from the *ringhiera*. After various migrations she at last in 1919 regained her former place.

THE DAVID. Michelangelo's *David* was commissioned in September 1501 by the Opera del Duomo, twelve days after the republic's constitution was revised and the sculptor's admirer, Piero Soderini, was installed as its leader (*gonfaloniere*). The piece of marble was not Michelangelo's choice. He was given an old block quarried years before on which an abortive beginning had already been made by Agostino di Duccio. The very defects of the block were a challenge to Michelangelo. His conquest of such technical difficulties contributed to the popular enthusiasm which greeted the finished work early in 1504. A commission of thirty of the city's leading artists (including Leonardo da Vinci, Botticelli, Filippino Lippi, Perugino, Lorenzo di Credi, Andrea Sansovino, and Andrea della Robbia) was then convened to decide where the colossal *David* was to stand. A minority suggested the steps of the Cathedral. Botticelli and Leonardo were for putting it in the Loggia dei Lanzi. The final decision was to mount it in front of the Palazzo Vecchio, where it remained until 1873 when the original, which was moved to the Academy, was replaced by the present copy.

The character of David was a favourite with the Commune. In 1416 the priors acquired from the Opera del Duomo a marble *David* by Donatello for their audience hall. And in 1495 the bronze *David* (now in the Bargello) which Donatello cast for the Medici was brought to the central courtyard of the Palazzo Vecchio. As a civic symbol, David was particularly apt for Soderini's government, which defended Florentine liberty and independence from the Goliath of papal ambition, Medici plots and foreign intervention.

Unlike Donatello's statues of David, Michelangelo's suppresses the narrative aspects of the subject: there is no trace of Goliath's corpse and the timing of the action is deliberately left unclear. It is David's character which is the dominating element; his is a heroic conception of human will – vigorous, troubled, brave and free. Perhaps for this reason Michelangelo did not give David ideal physical proportions, as Donatello had done in the bronze; the head and the limbs are too large for the body, thus discouraging admiration of physical beauty as an end in itself.

During and after this commission Michelangelo was given the city's highest honours. In 1503 the Opera del Duomo decided to build him a house and studio in the S Croce quarter (at the corner of Borgo Pinti and Via delle Colonne) and, through Soderini, the Signoria commissioned him to do a great mural representing the Battle of Cascina, which, however, was never completed.

THE HERCULES. The *David* was a great success and the Signoria bid Michelangelo execute a companion piece: a *Hercules*. Both Hercules and David were republican symbols of Fortitude; David personified valorous defence against foreign attack. Hercules conquest of domestic enemies. Dante had compared David's victory over Goliath to Hercules's over Antaeus (*Monarchia*, Book II, chap. 9). In 1427 Rinaldo degli Albizzi had compared Florence to a 'new Hercules' who would overcome evil tyrants. There was also a tradition that Florence was built on swampy land dried out by the legendary hero, and from 1308 until the end of Savonarola's regime Hercules's image was the city's official seal. Even Michelangelo's *David* bears a likeness to medieval and ancient figures of the god.

The Hercules project had bad luck. The commission was set in 1508. Seven years later Michelangelo had done nothing on it because of other commissions and difficulties with the quarries. In 1513 Florence had fallen again under the Medici yoke (the yoke, or '*giogo*', was indeed one of the Medici's favourite emblems) and in 1515 the Medici Pope Leo X took the commission away from Michelangelo and gave it to Baccio Bandinelli. This was not the end of it. The struggle between Florence and the Medici popes Leo X and Clement VII went on for a quarter of a century. In 1525 when Clement VII gave Bandinelli the marble block originally intended for Michelangelo, the Signoria, on its side, told Michelangelo it was the general wish of Florence that he execute the statue. He agreed and offered to make a present of it to the Signoria if the Pope would release him from his current obligations. The Pope, of course, refused.

Tolnay believes that the Medici deliberately kept Michelangelo from doing the *Hercules* partly in order to monopolize his genius and partly because they feared he would give a republican twist to the work which would stress Florentine sovereignty. The Medici did not dare do away with the project altogether because public demand for it was too great. Although Bandinelli had had the block since 1525, the affair dragged on until 1530. After the fall of the Florentine republic, Clement VII ordered Bandinelli to finish his muscle-bound brute. It was at last unveiled in 1534. There was bad feeling in Florence about it. Michelangelo was reserved for popes, Bandinelli's 'sack of poatoes' was good enough for the Piazza of Florence.

Nevertheless, Hercules continued to be an emblem of Florentine rule during the reign of Duke Cosimo I. An early portrait of him as the eighteen-year-old victor of Montemurlo shows him with a medal in his cap of Hercules crushing Antaeus. During the first months of his reign a medal was struck with Cosimo's portrait on the obverse and the same Herculean subject on the back.

THE NEPTUNE FOUNTAIN. The Herculean pretensions of Florence's ruler are even reflected in the *Neptune*, an allegorical portrait of Duke Cosimo which is the centrepiece of the fountain to the left of the Palazzo Vecchio. In 1550 the project was given to Bandinelli, who wished to replace the *Marzocco* with a 'great giant' and he swore to surpass Montorsoli's Neptune fountain which was then being made for the city of Messina. But he died before the design got off the drawing-board. The marble for the *Neptune* had already been quarried, and on Bandinelli's death it was the ambition of every sculptor in Florence to have a chance to show off his talent with one of the largest blocks ever brought from Carrara. The competition narrowed down to the four best entrants: Cellini, Ammannati, Vincenzo Danti and the young Giambologna, whose model received the highest praise. Ammannati, however, was the winner – probably because he was Vasari's protégé and because of his greater experience with fountains and colossal statuary. The foundations of the fountain were built in 1565. Meanwile the *Neptune*, soon nicknamed '*Biancone*' (big white fellow), was finished. Even Ammannati, at the end of his life, admitted that the *Biancone* was a failure. The peculiar proportions of the block constrained him to give Neptune narrow shoulders and to keep his arms close to the body. The job was not made any easier by Bandinelli's beginning on it. In 1565 a temporary construction of stucco and *papier-mâché* surrounded the *Biancone* for the occasion of the Duke's welcome to his new daughter-in-law, Joan of Austria. The fountain's bronze nymphs and satyrs, designed by Ammannati, Giambologna and possibly others, were not finished until 1575. The completed ensemble is in the character of Florentine fountains in that they are for the display of sculpture rather than of water. This was due as much to the scant water-supply as to the general interest in sculpture. The bronze nymphs and tritons are images of sheer enjoyment of physical existence; they spread their limbs, force out their muscles, kick up their legs and fall backwards towards the water.

The Neptune fountain originally had seventy jets. Possibly it was with the new fountain in mind that Cosimo in 1567 increased the city's water-supply. His choice of Neptune for a civic monument was more than an obvious allegory on water; it was intended to glorify his schemes to make Florence a great naval power. Since 1547 Cosimo had been building a fleet of galleys. A year later, in the hope of using Cosimo as an ally against France and the Pope, Emperor Charles V of Spain encouraged the Duke by giving him the harbour of Portoferraio on the island of Elba, which was developed into the strongest naval base in the Mediterranean. A medal was then struck by Poggini (based upon an emblem devised by Lodovico Domenichi) which showed Cosimo's portrait on the obverse with the figure of Neptune reclining before Portoferraio on the back. The fountain symbolically alludes to Cosimo's debts to his imperial ally. On the bases of the two bronze nymphs, eagles or falcons (the emblems respectively of Charles V and Cosimo's father, Giovanni delle Bande Nere) flank a he-goat's head (Cosimo's symbol because he was born in the sign of Capricorn). These birds probably once held metal crowns in their beaks – which may have referred to Charles's help in strengthening Cosimo's position and the latter's eventual claim to the title of Grand Duke of Tuscany in 1569. Cosimo was fond of astrological symbolism. The *Neptune* stands on a sea chariot, its, spokes are covered with astrological signs which, if deciphered would undoubtedly reveal even more of Cosimo's maritime ambitions. The Duke was especially proud that his horoscope, in which Capricorn was in the ascendant, was the same as that claimed by Augustus and by Charles V. Under Capricorn Cosimo's destiny had been cast; for in its sign in August 1537, which also happened to be St Stephen's Day, he (like Caesar) defeated his rebellious enemies at Montemurlo, thereby establishing his absolute rule. Capricorn, the he-goat with the fish's tail, had a special significance for Cosimo as a naval commander. Shortly before the *Biancone*'s completion, Cosimo founded in 1561 the naval knighthood, the Order of St Stephen, of which he was Grand Master, with headquarters in Pisa whose harbour he had recently re-opened. A contemporary admirer of the fountain, and a witness of the Medicean allegories woven around it, wrote that under Capricorn the sea becomes tranquil and safe, and under the Duke's sign the city flourished in peace.

The Florentines never took the fountain's allegories seriously. Only a few years after its completion a metal fence was put up to protect it from the animals who came to drink there. An inscription just behind the fountain, on the façade of the Palazzo Vecchio, warns that those who dared to do their laundry there or to throw ink or filth into the waters would be heavily fined.

THE MONUMENT TO COSIMO I. None of the earlier Medici had erected public monuments to themselves or their ancestors. Cosimo I had changed this. His son, Ferdinando, had hardly succeeded to the title in 1587 when he hired Giambologna to design a monument to Cosimo's memory. At fifty-eight, Giambologna had his chance at last to create a colossus for the Piazza. The Grand Duke built him a special studio equipped with a foundry and all the auxiliary furnace equipment. In 1591 the horse was cast in one piece by the Grand Duke's artillery founder and three years later the statue was unveiled.

Until then, the three great equestrian monuments of Italy were the *Marcus Aurelius* in Rome, Donatello's *Gattamelata* in Padua, and Verrocchio's *Colleoni* in Venice. All three subjects had been great military commanders and their statues dominate piazzas. In them horse and rider move together, there is an inner bond of sympathy between them. In the Cosimo monument, the rider in the aggressive pose of a conqueror sits rigidly indifferent to the horse beneath him, which is somehow held in check. The whole pose of man and horse conforms to the canons of late sixteenth-century horsemanship as set forth by the Spanish Court and described in Ferraro's *Cavallo frenato*, which was published in Venice four years before Giambologna received the commission.

The statue's base has three reliefs representing the chief events in Cosimo's career: his designation by the Senate in 1537 as Duke of Florence, his conquest of Siena in 1555, and the reception from the hands of Pope Pius V of the crown and sceptre for his new title of Grand Duke of Tuscany in 1569. The last was a compromise, because since the conquest of Siena Cosimo had schemed unsuccessfully for the title of king. Cosimo had found Florence a weak, small town dependant upon foreign powers, without troops, and with a ruined economy. He left her as the capital of all Tuscany (with the exception of the republic of Lucca), which he had consolidated into a state with a well-ordered administration and thriving commerce. He had also kept her free of both papal and imperial domination. The material prosperity of Florence was enhanced, but the great artistic and intellectual schemes were being created in those years in Rome and Venice. In Florence the quality of art and mind lacked the vigour and daring comprehensiveness of her great fourteenth and fifteenth centuries. The schemes of Cosimo and his heirs, no doubt well meant, succeeded only in being big and pretentious. These later Medici, unlike their illustrious forebears, were only fastidious amateurs in the arts. And – also unlike their ancestors – they loved rich complexes of a personal rather than a civic nature.

THE NEIGHBOURHOOD AROUND THE PIAZZA. Around the Piazza run the narrow streets which specialize in many of the same trades which were practised there five hundred years ago. The Via Condotta (which is the old Via de' Librai) is still a street of stationers and

The Cathedral cupola by Brunelleschi, seen from the Via dei Servi. The cupola's exterior was incomplete at Brunelleschi's death in 1446. The lantern, based on his design, was begun by Michelozzo between 1446 and 1452

Head of Niccolò da Tolentino, the victorious captain of a troop of
mercenaries, from his cenotaph mural in the Cathedral by Andrea del
Castagno, 1456

notaries. Just round the corner, near the Badia, the prince of Florentine booksellers during the Quattrocento, Vespasiano da Bisticci, had his shop which was known as that of a *cartolaio*, or stationer, which employed scores of copyists and illuminators. The shop itself was a favourite meeting-place for men of letters for three generations: Niccoli, Leonardo Bruni, Poggio Bracciolini, Ficino and Poliziano came to chat there. Today, if instead of a copy of an ancient manuscript one wishes to have tissue paper of any colour, boxes or paper cut to special measure, the order will still be filled by the stationers on the Via Condotta, at Mori's or at Scatolini's farther along on the Via dell' Anguillara.

Behind the Palazzo Vecchio, along the Via dei Leoni or in the Piazza S Firenze, instead of the seraglio of lions are shops specializing in caged birds – everything from canaries and all varieties of pigeons to ravens, robins, parrots and nightingales. And opposite the law courts, on the ground floor of the Palazzo Gondi, the family still sells its excellent wine.

The main street leading from the Piazza della Signoria to the Piazza del Duomo, the Via Calzaiuoli (the Way of the Hosiers), still specializes in footwear. There are so many shoe-shops concentrated here and scattered through the rest of the city that one marvels that there are enough feet to keep them all in business. It may be the cobbled Florentine streets and the amount of walking one has to do.

Between 1842 and 1870 the old commercial centre of Florence (the area to the north-west of the Piazza della Signoria including the Piazza della Repubblica) was largely demolished and rebuilt. The old city walls were torn down along the Mercato Vecchio and many old guild houses, towers, and palaces. The last war brought the destruction of the Via Por S Maria – the old street of the bankers and silk merchants issuing from the Ponte Vecchio – but in modern buildings now, banks and goldsmiths still crowd the street. The silks, however, have moved up around the Mercato Nuovo, clustering along the Via Porta Rossa. Above the Via Condotta, along the Via dei Tavolini (The Way of the Little Tables), the Via de' Cerchi and the Via del Corso are a bazaar of temptations. The light filters into the narrow streets lined with tall houses and the wares glow preciously. Fruits, nuts, mushrooms and cheeses from all over Italy are cradled in leaves of chestnut, fern or grape. There is the aroma of coffee which stands about in great sacks waiting to be roasted to suit one's pleasure. On the Via dei Tavolini, at Silvi's, are stacked hundreds of different kinds of galloon, fancy borders, and tassels which are destined for the bell-pulls of great palaces and convents or the replacement of worn-out borders on old tapestries and sofas. The same firm printed the kerchiefs of the Garibaldini. At the end of the street near the Via Calzaiuoli is one of the best ice-cream shops in the city. It is called with Florentine sauciness '*Perchè no?*' (Why not?) There are no tables here, only standing-room.

To the south of the Piazza one comes again to large spaces, a comprehensive scheme and a long unbroken view; the Piazzale degli Uffizi with its arcades framing the Arno at its farther end. Between five and seven in the morning it is the wholesale flower-market of Florence. Here, or in the Loggia dei Lanzi, are benches where one can rest one's feet, collect oneself, write a letter or meet a friend.

Chapter 3

Piazza del Duomo:
'Più bello che si può'[1]

☙

SUMMARY OF THE CHIEF MONUMENTS

1. Baptistery of St. John – Romanesque structure of uncertain date (perhaps built between 1059 and 1150).

Exterior: (*a*) **bronze doors**** cast from wax models prepared in 1330 by Andrea Pisano with scenes from the Life of the Baptist and the Four Theological and Four Cardinal Virtues; portal surrounds by Vittorio Ghiberti (1453–61), perhaps based on his father Lorenzo's designs; above, the *Decollation of the Baptist* – bronze group by Vincenzo Danti, 1570–1.

(*b*) **bronze doors**** designed and cast by Lorenzo Ghiberti between 1403 and 1424 illustrating the Life of Christ with the Four Evangelists and Four Church Fathers; above, the *Baptist between a Pharisee and a Levite* by Giovan Francesco Rustici probably assisted by Leonardo da Vinci, 1506–11.

(*c*) **gilded bronze doors**** (known as the East or 'Paradise Doors') with scenes from the Old Testament made by Lorenzo Ghiberti who worked on them from 1426 to 1452; on either side of the doors, porphyry columns from Majorca given to Florence by the Pisans in 1117 in thanks for services rendered against marauders based in the Balearic islands; above, the *Baptism of Christ* – marble group by Andrea Sansovino, 1502–5, finished in 1564 by Vincenzo Danti. (The angel is by I. Spinazzi, 1792).

Interior: inlaid pavements – signs of the Zodiac, early 13th c.; others from the 12th (cubes and zig-zag patterns), 13th and 14th c. (*d*) chancel mosaics – *Virgin and Child Enthroned* surrounded by prophets and saints, *ca* 1225–80; the red wheel supported by caryatids and Corinthian capitals is probably a late 13th c. addition – all much restored. Traces of Venetian craftsmanship in the ornamental bands around the entrance arch and in some of the saints and prophets. (*e*) **Vault mosaics**** illustrating the *Last Judgment*

[1]As beautiful as possible.

51

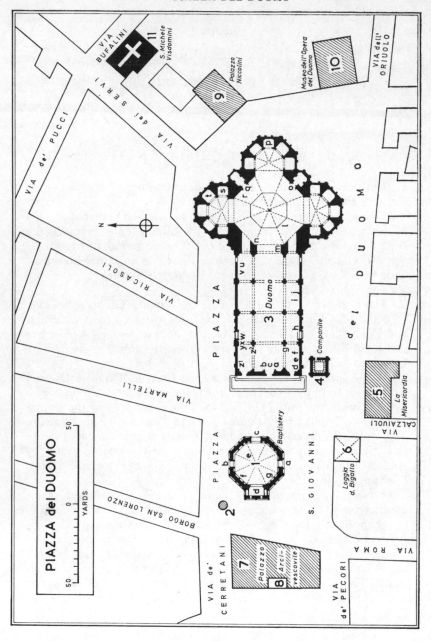

with cycles of scenes from the Creation, Joseph and his Brothers and John the Baptist, between *ca* 1270 and *ca* 1300 by some Florentines, an unnamed Venetian, and others. The mosaics have undergone restoration campaigns since the 14th c. (*f*) **Tomb of Baldassare Coscia*** (elected to the papacy in 1410 as John XXIII and deposed in 1415 by the council of Constance, d. 1419). Tomb paid for by Cosimo de' Medici. It was through this pope that the Medici became bankers to the curia. Monument designed by Donatello but, except for the bronze effigy, executed by his pupil Michelozzo between 1424–7). It has recently been suggested that the relief of the Virgin and the curtains were added at a later date. (*g*) **Magdalen*** by Donatello (*ca* 1455) now in Cathedral Museum.

2. **The Column of S Zenobius** – erected in 1384 on the site of an elm tree which legend says broke into leaf on a cold January day in A.D. 433 as the Saint's remains were moved from S Lorenzo to S Reparata. As the first Bishop of Florence, Zenobius is one of the city's patron saints.

3. **The Duomo or Cathedral,** known as **Santa Maria del Fiore.** Begun on a plan conceived by Arnolfo di Cambio between 1294 and 1302 and later continued with variants by Francesco Talenti (1352–64), Giovanni di Lapo Ghini (1364–7), Filippo Brunelleschi (1425–46), and others. The exterior of Brunelleschi's cupola was not completed before his death in 1446. The lantern, based on his design, was begun by Michelozzo between 1446 and 1452. It was not finished until 1467 after successive *capomaestri* including A. Manetti, B. Rossellino and T. Succhielli had worked on it. Verrocchio designed and cast the original gilt sphere (replaced by a somewhat larger version in the 17th c.) between 1468 and 1471. The gallery at the cupola's base which Michelangelo derisively called the 'cricket cage' was begun by Baccio d'Agnolo in 1508 but was never finished. The neo-Gothic façade designed by Emilio De Fabris and Augustino Conti was erected between 1875 and 1887.

Some fine sculpture and mosaic work is concentrated around the two main portals of the Duomo's flanks. A last whiff of Florentine Gothic clusters around the Porta dei Canonici at the south-eastern end. The *Madonna and Child* is variously attributed either to Lorenzo di Giovanni d'Ambrogio or to Niccolò di Piero Lamberti, 1396; the two angels (1401–3) are attributed to Lamberti. That on the right clearly shows the influence of Ghiberti.

On the opposite side, on the northern flank is the **Porta della Mandorla*.** Its decoration shows the first stirrings of the early

Renaissance side by side with the older, late Gothic masters. The earliest work on the archivolt (1391–7) includes work by Lorenzo di Filippo, Giovanni d'Ambrogio, Jacopo di Pietro Guidi and Piero di Giovanni Tedesco. The celebrated *Hercules* is by an artist of the younger generation – either Jacopo della Quercia (who worked in Giovanni d'Ambrogio's shop) or Nanni di Banco. This little carving already displays a thorough understanding of the heroic figure of classical antiquity. The two prophets on the pinnacles (1407–8) are variously attributed to Nanni di Bartolo (called 'il Rosso') or to the young Donatello. The large gable relief of the *Assumption of the Virgin* (1414–21) by Nanni di Banco is already a fully developed Renaissance work in which classical gravity and breadth merge with a graceful movement of line and supple surfaces. The *Annunciation* mosaic in the lunette is by Domenico and Davide Ghirlandaio (1491).

Interior: Between 1841 and 1843 the appearance of the interior was radically altered when a drastic restoration obliterated many of the murals and dismantled groups of sculpture. Since 1966, the remains of several earlier churches on the site have been excavated. This area, beneath the level of the present pavement, may be visited; entrance near the first pier on the right – 200 Lire. Among the interesting objects to be seen here are a 5th-century mosaic pavement, remains of Romanesque murals and tomb monuments, Brunelleschi's grave, and sections of architecture. Returning to the present Duomo (*a*) mosaic *Coronation of the Virgin ca* 1300 attributed to Gaddo Gaddi; (*b*) remains of the dismembered tomb of Bishop Antonio Orso (d. 1321) by Tino di Camaino, 1323; below, right, panel painting of *St Catherine of Alexandria* by an assistant of Bernardo Daddi, *ca* 1340; (*c*) clock face with four heads painted by Paolo Uccello in 1443; (*d*) bust of Brunelleschi by his pupil and adopted son, Andrea Cavalcanti (called 'il Buggiano') in 1447; (*e*) *Isaiah* attributed to Nanni di Banco (1408), originally made for a buttress on the northern tribune; (*f*) bust of Giotto by Benedetto da Maiano (1490) with inscription by Poliziano; (*g*) holy water font, copy of original (*ca* 1380) in the Museo dell' Opera del Duomo; behind it, mounted on the pillar – a panel painting of *S Antonio, Bishop of Florence* by Francesco Morandini (called 'il Poppi'), 1589, with a predella illustrating the *Founding of the Brotherhood of the 'Buonuomini di S Martino'* by Antonio Marini, *ca* 1850; (*h*) *St Blaise Enthroned* by Rossello di Jacopo Franchi (1408); (*i, j*) muralled cenotaphs by Bicci di Lorenzo of the learned Fra Luigi de' Marsili (d. 1394), 1439, and of Cardinal Piero Corsini (d. 1405), *ca* 1422;

(*k*) Brunelleschi's cupola with murals based on a scheme devised by Vincenzo Borghini involving the Last Judgment and allegorical subjects carried out by Giorgio Vasari and Federico Zuccari (1572–9). In the seven round windows, stained glass based on designs prepared by the following (reading from left to right starting with the east window): Donatello – *Coronation of the Virgin*, Ghiberti – *Ascension*, Ghiberti – *Agony in the Garden*, Ghiberti – *Presentation in the Temple*, Uccello – *Nativity*, Castagno –· *Pietà*, Uccello – *Resurrection*; (*l*) octagonal marble choir enclosure (1547–72) planned and partly executed by Baccio Bandinelli, finished by Giovanni Bandini called 'dell' Opera' (present structure reduced in 1842); Baccio himself signed the reliefs on the east and south-east faces in 1555; large wooden *Crucifix* by Benedetto da Maiano, *ca* 1490; (*m*) statue of *St Matthew* by Vincenzo de' Rossi; (*n*) statue of *St James the Great* by Jacopo Sansovino, 1511–18; (*o*) **Sagrestia Vecchia** (or 'dei Canonici' on the south side of the choir), lunette over the entrance: glazed terracotta relief of the *Ascension* by Luca della Robbia, 1446–51; over it was originally Donatello's choir-loft now re-assembled (after its dismemberment in 1688) in the Museo dell' Opera; inside, panel paintings by Mariotto di Nardo, *ca* 1404, and a lavabo by Buggiano after Brunelleschi's design, 1442–5, based on the design of the lavabo made in 1440 by the same sculptor for the Sagrestia Nuova; (*p*) **bronze shrine*** (below the altar) by Lorenzo Ghiberti (1432–42) containing the relics of St Zenobius. To see this properly, tip the sacristan generously or, if he is not about, sneak inconspicuously through the gate by unlatching it; on top of the altar are two kneeling angels by Luca della Robbia, picture of *Last Supper*, behind altar is by Giovanni Balducci; (*q*) **Sagrestia Nuova*** (or 'delle Messe' on the north side of the choir) bronze doors by Michelozzo and Luca della Robbia, 1446–69; lunette with glazed terracotta relief of the *Resurrection* by Luca della Robbia, 1442–5. Above this was installed Luca's choir-loft, now in the Museo dell'Opera. Inside: lined with cupboards and crowned by garland-bearing *putti* all made under the supervision of Giuliano da Maiano, 1463–8; intarsiae based on designs by Maso Finiguerra and Alesso Baldovinetti; gabled mable frame with *putto* head is by Mino da Fiesole – the lavabo designed by Buggiano; (*r*) brass plate in floor marking site of earliest meridian sun dial or 'gnomon', originally installed by Paolo dal Pozzo Toscanelli in 1468; (*s*) the **Pietà*** begun by Michelangelo *ca* 1550 and finished posthumously by Tiberio Calcagni; (*t*) altarpiece of the *Madonna and Saints* by a follower of Giotto painted on front and back, originally from the main altar of St Zenobius in the crypt;

(*u*) painting of *Dante holding a volume of the Divine Comedy* which sheds light on the city of Florence by Domenico di Michelino after a design by Baldovinetti, 1465; (*v*) *SS Cosmas and Damian* painted by Bicci di Lorenzo, 1429; (*w*) muralled cenotaph of the mercenary hero *John Hawkwood** by Paolo Ucecllò (1436); (*x*) muralled cenotaph of another military hero, *Niccolò da Tolentino** by Andrea del Castagno 1456 – both equestrian monuments restored in 1524 by Lorenzo di Credi, who was probably responsible for the ornamental borders; (*y*) bust of the organist Antonio Squarcialupi from the shop of Bendetto da Maiano, *ca* 1490; (z^1) statue of *Joshua* (the so-called 'Poggio Bracciolini') begun by Bernardo Ciuffagni and finished by Nanni di Bartolo ('il Rosso') between 1415 and 1421 – the figure was probably intended for the campanile; (z^2) *St Zenobius*, flanked by SS Crescentius and Eugenius, with Cruelty and Pride underfoot and Charity and Humility at his side, painted by Giovanni del Biondo, 1375–80.

4. Campanile, or Bell-tower* – built between1 334 and 1359 during the terms when the office of overseer or *capomaestro* of the cathedral works was held by Giotto (1334–7), Andrea Pisano (1337–42) and Francesco Talenti (1352–9). Copies of the hexagonal reliefs (originals now in the Museo dell'Opera) illustrating Genesis, the Seven Planets, the Seven Virtues (by Andrea Pisano based partly on designs prepared by Giotto), the Seven Sacraments (by Alberto Arnoldi, *ca* 1351–64), the Seven Liberal Arts (Grammar, Philosophy, Music, Arithmetic and Astrology, by Luca della Robbia – 1437–9, and the Professions and Sciences by Andrea Pisano). Together these reliefs originally served as a compliment to the iconography of the sculpture on the Duomo façade which is devoted to Mary as co-redeemer. On the campanile, man's gradual progress from original sin towards a state worthy of divine grace was shown via manual labour, the liberal arts, and the sacraments – all guided by astral influences and the cardinal and theological virtues.

5. Headquarters of the Brotherhood of Mercy *('L'Arcicon fraternita della Misericordia)* founded in the 13th c. Building acquired in 1576. Originally, the facade had muralled scenes by Bernardino Poccetti. The picture to the left of the entrance is by Pietro Annigoni. Inside: marble *St Sebastian* and *Madonna and Child*, both by Benedetto da Maiano, *ca* 1495–7; and other sculpture in the style of Antonio Rossellino and Giovanni della Robbia. In the adjacent oratory, altarpiece by Andrea della Robbia, *ca* 1480–90, originally made for the Badia Fiesolana and brought here in 1812. In rooms above, paintings by Sodoma, Santi di Tito, etc., and an archive with records from the parishes of the city going back to the 14th c.

6. Loggia of the Bigallo – built between 1352 and 1358, probably by Alberto Arnoldi (also known as Alberto di Arnoldo), who was responsible for the lunette on the façade and the statuary inside the loggia. Nardo di Cione's murals (1363–64) from the alter wall have, since the flood, been transfered to the south side of the oratory. Façade originally had murals with *Scenes from the life of St Peter Martyr* (the founder of the *Compagnia Maggiore di S Maria del Bigallo* organized originally to combat heresy) by Ambrogio di Baldese (*ca* 1392) and Rossello di Jacopo Franchi, now detached and re-installed in the Fortezza di Belvedere. Inside: detached, much deteriorated mural of the *Madonna della Misericordia* by a follower of Daddi which includes one of the earliest views of the city, 1352; other scenes showing acts of mercy performed by the society, late 14th c. Hours 14.00–19.00 weekdays; closed Sundays.

7. Palazzo Arcivescovile, the archbishop's residence – originally a medieval, loggiaed structure remodelled by Dosio (1573–84) and then reduced and rebuilt in 1895 in order to enlarge the Piazza. Vestiges of the old courtyard inside.

8. San Salvatore al Vescovo (Piazza dell' Olio, beside No. 6) – relic of a Romanesque church, black and white inlaid facade, *ca* 1221, when the original church of the 7th c. appears to have been rebuilt. In 1441 the pope declared it the bishop's chapel. Interior entirely redone in 1727 by B. Ciurini.

9. At No. 29 – red, the site of Donatello's workshop.

10. Museo dell' Opera del Duomo (No. 9) Museum hours: Summer – 09.30–13.00, 15.00–18.00 weekdays; Winter – 09.30–16.00; 10.00–13.00 Sundays and holidays; admission fee 300 lire – occupied by the administrators of the Cathedral fabric since the beginning of the 15th c. Originally, marble and other building materials were stored here. Michelangelo carved the colossal *David* (now in Accademia) in the courtyard. Since the last century the museum has housed displaced fragments of architecture and sculpture from early schemes subsequently dismantled, as well as *statuary** by Arnolfo di Cambio, Andrea Pisano, Donatello, Nanni di Banco and others which were originally installed in the Campanile and the Cathedral façade. A large part of the Cathedral's furnishings is now housed here: the *choir-lofts** (or *cantorie*) by Luca della Robbia and Donatello, the great silver altar frontal on which generations of Florentine craftsmen laboured (including Michelozzo, Verrocchio and Antonio del Pollaiuolo), embroideries, old panel paintings, Brunelleschi's death-mask, and a collection of wooden models for the cupola and the façade. Also: Archives of the Opera del Duomo.

11. Church of San Michele Visdomini – 'Visdomini' originally the name of an office in the episcopal administration which involved the management of church lands. The office, first held by a cleric, was given later to laymen. This administrative office called *'Vice domino'* was hereditary and subsequently became a family name. The original church of S Michele built in the 11th c. was demolished in 1368 to make way for the tribunes of the new Cathedral. Soon afterwards it was rebuilt on its present site by Giovanni di Lapo Ghini. The façade is by Bartolomeo Ammannati, *ca* 1577–90. Inside, in the second chapel on the right, is an altarpiece of the *Holy Family and Saints** painted for Francesco Pucci by Jacopo Pontormo in 1518 – a milestone of the Mannerist style.

'PIÙ BELLO CHE SI PUÒ'

'. . . one must not undertake public projects (*cose del Comune*) if the idea does not correspond to a heart made great through the soul of its many citizens joined together by a single will.'
—*from a document of 1294, the year when the Duomo was begun*

THE PIAZZA. As one strolls up the Via Calzaiuoli from the Piazza della Signoria a world of sober browns gives way to a view sparkling with white, rose and green-black marbles – the embroidery of the city's and the archbishop's main churches. Whereas the Piazza della Signoria is a wide open space, the Piazza del Duomo is not really a piazza at all; it is a setting for the Baptistery. Cathedral and belltower mounted jewel-fashion in its centre. 'A fine theatre', it was called in the eighteenth century. It is, in fact, still the stage for the two semi-profane pageants which have taken place here each year for more than five centuries – the '*Scoppio del Carro*' (a cart laden with fireworks) at Easter, of which more will be said later, and the ceremonies on June 24th honouring the city's patron saint, John the Baptist. To celebrate the Baptist's birthday there is a procession, fireworks, lotteries for dowerless girls and for (a modern addition) children's summer camps. In the old days, the entire piazza was covered at communal expense with blue canopies starred in gold to protect from the summer sun the crowds who came to see the processions, the horse-race and display of treasure. Tributes of painted wax mounted on great wooden and *papier-mâché* structures were carried to the Baptistery by the city's wards, the commercial and professional guilds, and by subject Tuscan towns such as Montecatini, Pistoia and Pisa. Today, it is only in the Umbrian hinterland, at Gubbio, that one can see a relic of this kind of festivity; the *Festa dei Ceri*, celebrated on May 15th, when brigades of the citizenry toil up a hillside shouldering the tremendous load of 'candle-towers' some fifteen feet high.

In the name of the Baptist, contracts were notarized and territories conquered. The Saint adorned the communal banner as well as the gold florin (first minted in 1252). This metal *fiorino*, or flower of Florence, was the earliest coinage in Europe to be accepted as stable international currency. Yet no one calls the piazza by its official name of San Giovanni. It is Piazza del Duomo. The very name Duomo (which comes from *Domus Dei* – ecclesiastical Latin for cathedral) has a large, deep, booming sound; its fabric engulfs most of the Piazza. The entire city takes shelter under the shadow of Brunelleschi's great cupola. Fifteen miles down the valley, in Pistoia, a street was named after the spot where the cupola first came into view (Via dell' Apparenza). So large is the Cathedral that there is no angle in the Piazza from which one can see all of it at once. To do so, one must climb to the top of a tower (the Campanile or the Palazzo Vecchio) or a near-by-hilltop (the Fortezza di Belvedere or Piazzale Michelangelo).

At the end of the thirteenth century, soaring communal pride launched the building of the Palazzo Vecchio and the new Duomo at the same time. More so even than the town hall, the Baptistery and the Duomo were the chief oranment of Florentine civic pride. Pisa had a Piazza dei Miracoli and Siena a gigantic cathedral; the Florentines were spurred to surpass them all. Nothing was too good, too rich, too costly or too large for their schemes. The phrase 'as beautiful as possible' (*più bello che si può*) was from then on a by-word in contracts for buildings, pictures, objects of all kinds. The phrase is not unique to Florentine terms of commission. But in Florence a procession of great talents came forward in the next three centuries to realize the city's unbounded ambitions – '*più bello che si può*'.

To obtain the best possible results, the secular administrators of the Baptistery and Cathedral Works often resorted to public competitions. Ghiberti's bronze doors, Brunelleschi's '*Cupolone*',

Uccello's muralled monument to John Hawkswood, even the ugly nineteenth-century Cathedral façade were all the results of such contests.

The Piazza and its buildings were occasions for adventures in science and technology. Ghiberti's Baptistery doors and Brunelleschi's cupola were unprecedented technical as well as great artistic achievements. The Florentines of the great age were never satisfied with being only superb craftsmen. They had an insatiable curiosity; they inquired, measured, experimented in their works, even on a great scale, to see into the heart of scientific as well as emotional and intellectual phenomena.

Standing in the main doorway of the Cathedral, Brunelleschi with paints, panel and a mirror rationalized a scheme of linear perspective composition with the view of the Baptistery as his subject. This octagonal building with its regular facets and its clear geometrical inlays was ideal for the experiment. But, realist that he was, Brunelleschi recognized that no system could capture a changing sky, a fleeting cloud. For these he relied on the reflection given by the mirror fitted to his painted panel. A few years afterwards, Brunelleschi's elegant linear system was formulated in more practical terms by Leon Battista Alberti, architect, theorist, courtier, and friend of the greatest artists of his time. The impact of Brunelleschi's discoveries, experienced directly or relayed through Alberti, found an immediate response in Masaccio and Donatello, who changed the course of European painting and sculpture.

The exploration of space – visual, pictorial, celestial and geographical – was a particular Florentine interest from Dante to Galileo. Already Dante in the *Divine Comedy* gave such a minute physical description of the universe that even the measurements of Hell were calculated from it. The heavens were explored by Brunelleschi's friend, Paolo dal Pozzo Toscanelli (1397–1482). He devised inside the Duomo the first meridian, or gnomon, for measuring the exact position of the sun during the summer solstice. The gnomon also served as a kind of regulator capable of registering the least sign of instability in the cupola's structure. A bronze plate pierced by a hole was set in the cupola's lantern through which the sun's rays fell some 277 feet to a measure laid into the Cathedral floor. From Toscanelli's astronomical calculations new maps were made, which guided another Florentine, Amerigo Vespucci, and Columbus to the New World.

From about 1300 onwards, the Piazza was a frame for these and many other great events in rapid succession. Yet up to almost the end of the thirteenth century the Piazza hardly existed. The area surrounding the Baptistery was a thoroughly medieval clutter. A graveyard lay to the south bounded by the tower houses of feudal lords. On the site of what is now the Bigallo stood the "Watcher of the Dead' – the *Guardamorto*, as the tower of the Adimari was called. To the east were the churches of S Reparata and S Michele Visdomini, and the house of the Cathedral canons. On the north flank of S Reparata once stood the porticoed Hospital of S John the Evangelist built about 1040. Running along the north side of the Baptistery was one of the city walls. The city's first cathedral for several centuries stood outside it. S Lorenzo was consecrated as bishop's church or cathedral in the fourth century by S Ambrose, Bishop of Milan, who had fled from his own diocese to take refuge in Florence. Only five centuries later it was decided to transfer the bishop's seat to the former parish church of S Reparata. It was believed that on Reparata's feast-day a great victory had been won over an invading Gothic army and so the first cathedrals of Pisa and Lucca had also been named after her. The predecessor of the present S Giovanni was the old S Reparata's Baptistery.

The development of the Piazza really began when the Margrave of Tuscany moved his headquarters to Florence in 1057. Until then, the Margrave ruled in the name of the Hohenstaufen Emperors from his seat at Lucca. He came only occasionally to Florence to attend tribunal hearings in front of his palace (on the site of the Palazzo Arcivescovile). In the Margrave's absence the only stable authority in the city was the bishop, who also ruled over secular matters. But this changed with the establishment of the margravate in Florence. There were radical ecclesiastical reforms and the bishop's powers were narrowed down. Lay officials now assumed the initiative, with the intention of constructing an organized complex of splendid buildings. The Baptistery was rebuilt, but the first sign of the great changes to come was in 1289 when what open space there was was paved with brick. In 1294 the cornerstone of the new cathedral was laid and the graveyard and the sarcophagi clinging to the Baptistery were cleared away. The Hospital of St John the Evangelist was demolished and the Baptistery and the Cathedral were left standing in a clear space facing each other almost on axis. To express the visual relationship between the two buildings, Arnolfo di Cambio, the new cathedral architect, applied black and white stripes to the corners of the Baptistery and to the pier buttresses of the Duomo façade (the first part of the new building to go up). Then for thirty years the work went very slowly. No one

61

knows quite why; there were wars and the masons were recruited as demolition squads (and when they were not at war they were probably building the Palazzo Vecchio, the city walls, and some of the Arno bridges). At last in 1334 the Campanile was begun under Giotto who in that year was appointed *capomaestro* of Santa Maria del Fiore. In 1339 streets were lowered so that the view of the splendid buildings from the south would not appear to sink as one approached them, and it was decided to make the main artery connecting the cathedral square with town hall more seemly. What is now the Via Calzaiuoli was widened and its buildings were given windows, arches and masonry that matched. The same was decreed for the houses on the Via Fondamenta behind the Cathedral's eastern end. An ordinance of 1363 decreed that unseemly façades and irregularly projecting porticoes on the Piazza were to be demolished or rebuilt. These ordinances were the first attempts in Florence at city planning.

The hard-headed Florentines would not have even their Piazza del Duomo dominated by ecclesiastical affairs. The splendid churches were its centrepiece; charitable societies, the Misericordia and the Bigallo, had their place there, but most of the houses on the Piazza were places of business. Even the bishop's own palace in the four-teenth century had its loggia walled up to accommodate thirty-seven small shops, and the façade above was more secular than sacred; on it was a mural of the *Seven Liberal Arts* – an echo of a theme on the Campanile's reliefs. In 1350 the Bishop, Angelo degli Acciaioli, added a *Crucifixion* to the scheme with, be it said, a portrait of himself alongside it.

THE BAPTISTERY. To the Florentine of the fourteenth and fifteenth centuries, the Baptistery was the supreme witness of the city's noble Roman origins. Throughout the Renaissance it was solemnly be-lieved that S Giovanni was a reconverted temple of Mars built to celebrate the Roman victory over the older Etruscan city of Fiesole. A favourite theme of inter-communal rivalry in Tuscany was the claim as to which city was the oldest. Siena had the last word by rigging evidence that she had been founded by no lesser personage than the son of Remus, one of the founders of Rome. The origin of Florence, as nearly as anyone so far has been able to tell, goes back only to 59 B.C., when a Roman colony settled there. Beneath the Baptistery is an ancient pavement of black and white mosaics – not part of a Roman bath, as was thought until recently, but probably of a bakery. During the Empire, Florence had a capitol, a forum, theatres, baths and an aqueduct. But these were all located in other parts of the city. By 1300 none of these buildings remained. A few columns from the old capitol were incorporated into the fabric of the Baptistery and some of its capitals were used in S Miniato. The subterranean chambers of the amphitheatre in the S Croce neighbourhood were absorbed into the foundations of the Peruzzi palace and on occasion these were rented out as prisons to the Commune.

Actually, the Baptistery is a Romanesque remodelling (*ca* 1059–1128) of an earlier structure built during the sixth or seventh century. Its prototypes in shape and function were royal chapels such as S Vitale in Ravenna and Charlemagne's in Aachen – Byzantine and Carolingian (but not Roman!) buildings. The important fact is that the Florentines believed in the Baptistery's Roman pedigree. Even Brunelleschi and Alberti, who knew actual Roman buildings well, accepted the Baptistery as the sole survivor of a great past. What lay behind this fond self-deception was a reverence for the imagined moral ideal of ancient Rome which bolstered contemporary Florentine civic pride.

The character peculiar to subsequent Florentine architecture, especially of the classic Renaissance type introduced by Brunelleschi and Alberti, was already set forth in the Baptistery. The clear articulations, the logical patterns of the decorative inlays which echo the actual structural members, the refined carving of friezes and cornices – even the black and white colour scheme, as well as individual motives (the flat grooved pilasters and the little lantern crowning the roof) – all these were taken over and elaborated upon by generations of Florentine architects up to and including Michelangelo himself.

But this declaration of a clear native style did not carry over to the Baptistery's early pictorial decorations. The immense mosaic lining the vaults perfectly expressed Florentine pretensions at the end of the thirteenth century. By then, the city could afford to be extravagant and in the manner of parvenus its citizens meant to outdo both Venetians and Romans. But neither the mosaic medium nor the monumental historical scheme into which it was worked were native to Florence. The Calimala (the guild of big business – not only of the importers of foreign wool, but also of jewels, silk, brocade and other precious stuffs from the Levant) which underwrote the Baptistery's expenses, was thinking of the gilded domes of St Mark's and the Biblical cycles which covered the nave arcades of the Early Christian basilicae then being restored in Rome and widely copied all over central Italy. Venetian workmen probably came to start the Florentine crew on the job of executing what was really a basilican scheme wound awkwardly around an octagonal vault. Nevertheless, the Baptistéry mosaic is the harbinger of what soon became a Florentine speciality: mural painting on a grand scale and of an expressive power which has never been surpassed.

THE BRONZE DOORS OF THE BAPTISTERY. After the vault, the Calimala turned to the decoration of the three entrances. Doors of bronze were what they wanted. Like the mosaics, these too were a borrowed idea – this time from the Pisans, whose twelfth-century bronze doors for their cathedral were renowned. Pisan craftsmen had made another set for the cathedral of Monreale in Sicily. During the first half of the fourteenth century, the workshops of Nicola Pisano and his son Giovanni turned out the best sculptors in Italy. Having decided to have them made *più belle che si può*, the Calimala in 1329 sent off a delegate to study the examples in Pisa and then had him proceed to Venice to find the bronze artisans, since just then the Venetians had the reputation of being the best masters of the craft. Early in 1330 Andrea Pisano came to Florence and in less than three months prepared the wax models for casting by Venetian bell-founders. But the casting and chasing of the reliefs and the job of setting them into their metal framework consumed almost eight more years of work.

Andrea Pisano's reliefs have been compared to manuscript illuminations. Gothic quatrefoils surround the scenes, and some of the figures (*Salomè before Herodias*) were indeed based upon painted models – Giotto's recently completed murals in the Peruzzi Chapel of S Croce. Soon after the doors were finished Andrea collaborated with Giotto in making the reliefs for the Campanile and in 1337 succeeded him as *capomaestro* of the cathedral works.

The first bronze doors, like the mosaics inside, though designed and executed by 'foreigners', are the beginning of another great tradition in Florentine craftsmanship. By the beginning of the next century, the Florentines became the great technicians and designers of bronze sculpture. Ghiberti, Donatello, Verrocchio, Pollaiuolo, Cellini and Giambologna were invited to supply monuments and *objets d'art* to courts and communes all over Italy. In 1339 Andrea Pisano's doors were installed in the east portal facing the new Duomo and plans were made for another set. At this point a wave of disasters overook the city (bankruptcies, pestilence, famine, political upheaval) and it was sixty years before the next doors were taken in hand.

Intarsia cupboards in the Old Sacristy of the Cathedral, made under the supervision of Giuliano da Maiano, 1463–8, with intarsiae based on designs by Maso Finiguerra and Alesso Baldovinetti

Self-portrait of Lorenzo Ghiberti from the bronze Paradise Doors of the Baptistery, designed and cast by him between 1425 and 1452

THE COMPETITION FOR THE SECOND DOORS. In the winter of 1400–1 the Calimala, still the Baptistery's financial guardian, announced the competition for the second pair of doors. It was a heroic moment: these were the years when Florence stood alone against the Milanese armies who had conquered all the other Tuscan communes. Apparently, the commission of bronze doors during such an emergency was not thought an extravagant outlay of public funds. Later in 1423, the Calimala decided to have them gilded stating that: 'The honour and fame of the guild count more than the expense and therefore the doors shall be gilded.' Andrea Pisano's doors were to be moved in order to make way for the new ones, but his scheme of quatrefoiled scenes was to be followed. The theme of the contest for the trial piece was the Sacrifice of Isaac; richness, technical virtuosity and high drama were desired. There were seven participants but the contest narrowed down to entries submitted by the two youngest competitors: Brunelleschi, who was about twenty-three, and Ghiberti, just twenty. This was probably their first public collision and out of it emerged what is now recognized as the Renaissance style.

Both artists were trained as goldsmiths. Both were students of ancient art. Both developed the principles of perspective composition and were writers and theorists as well. At first, their activity as goldsmiths meant that they were involved not with monuments but with small objects of precise workmanship and refined detail.

Although Brunelleschi had already made some figures for a silver altar in Pistoia, his real interest lay in the practical applications of his craft. For a time he made and repaired clocks, and these early experiences lay behind his later 'invention' which made the construction of the Cathedral's great cupola possible. Ghiberti, on the other hand, specialized in pictorial design and in developing the craft as a sculptor's medium. He was evidently also a skilled painter, and to enter the Calimala's competition he left a job in Pesaro where he was then busy doing a mural.

A comparison of the two competition reliefs, now in the Bargello, makes it plain why Ghiberti's was the winner. Brunelleschi's is more dramatic, but Ghiberti's is more beautiful to the touch and to the eye. His work perfectly satisfied the contemporary craving for splendour and elegance. Elsewhere in Europe it took the form of a final burst of Gothic flamboyance. In Ghiberti, grace and richness were laced with realistic details and recollections of antiquity. Technically also Ghiberti's sample was superior to Brunelleschi's. He used less bronze and cast the relief in a single piece.

In 1403, when the commission was formally awarded to Ghiberti, he was not yet a master in his own right, let alone an associate of the professional guild: he was only a precocious member of his step-father's shop. But the award of the project to him literally put Florence on the map as the sculptural centre of Italy. In order to make these doors and another set for the Baptistery, the Ghiberti shop expanded into the city's largest bronze foundry and Ghiberti showed that he had also the talent of an administrator. The shop employed hordes of craftsmen, and some of the city's greatest artists passed through it: Donatello, Uccello, Michelozzo, Gozzoli and Antonio Pollaiuolo.

THE 'PARADISE DOORS'. Ghiberti's first doors, which cost some 22,000 florins, were finally installed in 1424. Immediately another set for the Baptistery was ordered from him. These were the most splendid of all and on them the Ghiberti company laboured for twenty-seven years. 'I conducted this work with the greatest diligence and with the greatest love,' wrote Ghiberti. Sixteen years were taken up only with the chasing and finishing. These doors were greatly admired by sixteenth-century sculptors – by Cellini and Ammannati. Legend has it that Michelangelo himself gave them the name by which they are still popularly known: 'The Gates of Paradise'. The actual source of the name was probably more prosaic. The 'Paradiso' was simply the name for the courtyard which once existed between the Baptistery and Santa Reparata (as the Cathedral was known before the present structure was built) – and Ghiberti's second doors gave on this area.

In this scheme Ghiberti abandoned the pattern set by Andrea Pisano. Instead of the medieval system of quatrefoils he told the stories in ten large rectangular scenes which are like pictures painted in bronze. The comparison of the Paradise Doors to painted pictures is a clue to Ghiberti's entire artistic outlook. His *Commentaries* tell us of his admiration for painting (especially Sienese painting) of the previous century. His reliefs demonstrate his study of Duccio's narrative scenes and of the Lorenzettis' perspective composition. Even the panoramic views and the multitude of episodes are very Sienese. The Trecento was a painter's century for Florence and in many respects Ghiberti still belonged to it, even though his chosen medium was bronze.

BRUNELLESCHI AND THE CATHEDRAL CUPOLA. Brunelleschi, on the other hand, belonged almost entirely to the Renaissance. It is only in his early minor activity as a sculptor that there is any trace of the Gothic in him. Brunelleschi was not only a great artist and a lucid theorist, he was a brilliant inventor of engineering techniques, and in their boldness was a poet's fantasy. The year after Ghiberti won the competition for the Baptistery doors, the Opera del Duomo took Brunelleschi on as a kind of engineering consultant. Ghiberti, who had a finger in every pie, was already one of the consultants and for the next twenty years Brunelleschi had to cope with his old rival's conservatism as well as his pretensions as an engineer. Since at least 1367 the Florentines had intended to vault the Cathedral's crossing with a great dome. The question was how to build it. Since the construction of the Pantheon, no one had succeeded in building a dome of such dimensions. Practical experience was utterly lacking and confidence in these structures was badly shaken when the cupola of Hagia Sophia in Constantinople partly collapsed in 1346[1]. In 1400 the frightened Florentines hastily reinforced the Baptistery's vault when it showed signs of weakness. Apart from the formidable structural problem, there was the prospect of the enormous cost of a wooden scaffolding for the job which, according to conventional practice, had to be built from the ground up. The Opera's architects and consultants continued their bickerings until August 1418, when they finally threw the project open to a public competition. Two years later they chose Brunelleschi's scheme because of its technical superiority. But its execution was long delayed by lingering doubts and further demands for models and tests and by the stipulation that Ghiberti serve as a collaborator. The diameter of the space to be spanned was 140 feet. Brunelleschi proposed to do it without buttresses via a system of flying centerings and with a scaffolding based in the drum. The vault, which was to be octagonal like the Baptistery's, was to have a double wall made of bricks laid in a spiral fashion reinforced by a system of stone chains. Kitchens were eventually installed between the cupola's double walls, so that the labourers would lose no time in fetching their meals.

In order to overcome the fears of the sceptical officials, Brunelleschi built a large scale-model on the banks of the Arno and played a ruse on the Opera in order to rid himself of the nagging presence of Ghiberti, who always thought he knew better. Feigning illness, Brunelleschi left Ghiberti to direct the cupola's construction alone.

[1]Italians had been hired in 1317 to build supplementary buttresses for Hagia Sophia's dome, and after the collapse of 1346 Italian experts were again called in to rebuild one of the great supporting arches, together with part of the vault.

Left to himself, Ghiberti soon came to a standstill and thereafter he was gradually relieved of his authority in the cupola project. In 1423 Brunelleschi was officially recognized as 'inventor and chief director of the main cupola', but it was only in the last year of his life that he finally became the Cathedral's official architect.

It took fourteen years for the cupola to be raised. Entire quarries were reserved exclusively for it. *Macigno* came from Trassinare (near Settignano) and white Carrara marble was shipped from Pisa by ox-cart after Brunelleschi's patent for a special transport boat did not live up to expectation. During this period Brunelleschi had other important jobs besides the cupola: the Ospedale degli Innocenti, the Palazzo di Parte Guelfa, and the rebuilding of S Lorenzo. Meanwhile Ghiberti proceeded with the Paradise Doors, designed most of the Cathedral's stained glass windows, and filled orders from visiting popes for precious vestments.

In 1434, two years before the cupola's completion, Leon Battista Alberti came to Florence in the entourage of Pope Eugenius IV. Brunelleschi's dome was a sensation. Alberti wrote of it: 'A structure so great, rising above the skies, large enough to shelter all the people of Tuscany in its shadow, built without the help of any centering or of much woodwork, of a craftsmanship [which] perhaps not even the ancients knew or understood.' When Cosimo de' Medici sent Brunelleschi to Rome, he boasted to the Pope that his architect's talent was so great that his spirit alone was enough to change the world. The story goes that when the Pope met the cantankerous little Florentine he muttered, 'And this is the man who would turn the earth?' To which Brunelleschi, recalling Archimedes, spluttered, 'If your Holiness will give me a place to set up a crank you will see what I can do.'

Brunelleschi died in 1446. He was buried beneath his great invention with an epitaph comparing him to Daedalus. Brunelleschi's heirs are still to be found in Italy, if not particularly in Florence. The tradition of blending architecture and engineering as a single profession is still an Italian speciality. One thinks of Pier Luigi Nervi's use of flying concrete spans and a project for raising the ancient monuments of Abu Simbel in the valley of the Nile.

THE DUOMO. During the Middle Ages, the Cathedral was commonly regarded as a symbol of the eternal Jerusalem. By the end of the thirteenth century, in the eyes of the Florentines, the old cathedral of S Reparata no longer corresponded to such an image nor could it accommodate the growing population. Judging from the sermons of a popular Dominican preacher, Fra Giordano da Rivalto, it was consciously felt at the time that the city as much as the Cathedral was a reflection of a sacred model. In 1294 the new Duomo was renamed *Santa Maria del Fiore* – Holy Mary of the Flower – uniting the names of the Queen of Heaven and the Flower symbol of Florence in the place of Reparata, the obscure Syrian martyr.

The project for the new Duomo was the climax of a series of grandiose schemes: S Maria Novella, S Croce, and the new town hall. What was required was a church large enough to hold 30,000 people. As a measure of the range of opinion consulted, on a single occasion when a revision was proposed in 1366–8, 480 people gave judgment. There were hundreds of workmen for the construction. A century after its beginning the new Duomo (except for the cupola) was finished. The old S Reparata would have fitted into its nave.

How was such an enormous project financed? Communal subsidies paid for most of it. Fines, taxes and private donations in exchange for indulgences helped a little. The year the cornerstone was laid – 1294 – a special property tax was levied which raised $8\frac{1}{2}\%$ of the total cost. For town dwellers this amounted to a tax of only .4%, but those who lived on the land paid about 1%. Fines for raucous behaviour were also turned over to the Cathedral fabric as well as gifts from penitent usurers. At first the Calimala was deputized as the administrator of these public funds on behalf of the Opera del Duomo. After 1331 the Arte della Lana (the Wool Guild) assumed this responsibility.

Another source of income were the Casentino forests – part of the booty acquired by the Commune from the victory won over the Ghibellines at Campaldino in 1289. Casentino timber supplied the shipyards of Pisa, Genoa and Leghorn and the builders of many new palaces and churches. Until the eighteenth century this single property supplied the Cathedral fabric with a steady income. The Grand Duke then bought the lands from the Opera, since when the value of this invested capital has dwindled with the forests themselves. The hills of the Casentino are now bare and the annual income which the Opera gets from the Grand Duke's money amounts to a pittance of some 10,000 lire (about £6). Until 1800 every last will and testatement filed in Florence bore a tax of two *soldi* which was turned over to the Opera. Today the Cathedral fabric receives a little from the properties left it by pious Florentines and from the admission fees collected from visitors to the cupola, the campanile and the museum. The state makes an annual contribution to the Duomo as a national monument of 1,200,000 lire (about £700) for its maintenance – hardly enough to keep it in floor wax. For extraordinary repairs such as the recent restoration of the crumbling exterior (when about three-fifths of the entire marble revestment had to be replaced) the state made a special grant; four years were required to accomplish the task.

When the Florentines decided to build S Maria del Fiore they aimed to outdo every other church in Christendom in size and splendour. To obtain the very best talents for the architecture and sculpture, the Commune and the Opera del Duomo in 1296 once more sent for outsiders, and as was later also to be the case of the Baptistery doors, they turned once again to the Pisan–Sienese school. Arnolfo di Cambio was an architect-sculptor trained in the shop of Nicola Pisano. When he came to Florence to plan and supervise the construction of the new Cathedral he arrived fresh from commissions executed for the papal court in Rome, Viterbo and Orvieto. The stripes he ordered for the Baptistery's corners were the hallmark of his Pisan-Sienese heritage. Stripes dissipate the forcefulness of architectural membering and, until then, had been abjured by the Florentines even though the rest of Tuscany was partial to them. Another feature which Arnolfo imported from the Pisan–Sienese school was the role of sculpture in the design of the façade. Arnolfo did not live to see the façade completed; he died some time between 1301 and 1311; but his scheme was followed probably up to the middle of the century. Roughly a third of the façade was completed in the 14th century, but in 1587, at the instigation of Buontalenti, this was completely dismantled. Fragments of the sculpture which Arnolfo partly planned and executed (the great enthroned *Madonna*, part of a *Nativity* group and the figures of *Pope Boniafce VIII* and *SS Reparata* and *Zenobius*) are preserved in the Museo dell' Opera behind the Cathedral. Another fragment, a *Dormition of the Virgin*, is now in the collection of the Bode Museum, East Berlin.

But the fourteenth century in Florence was, as we have said, a painters' century. There were Giotto, Daddi, Taddeo Gaddi, Orcagna and his brothers. Even the new kind of architecture introduced by Arnofo developed in the trecento into what was really painters' architecture. '*Blumige Bellezza*' is Hetzer's gay phrase for it. Painters were advisers and designers on the committees of the Cathedral works. And when a competition for a revision of the Duomo's plan was held in 1366–7, the model submitted by the group dominated by painters (Taddeo, Gaddi Orcagna, Andrea Bonaiuti and Niccolò di Tommaso) won over that submitted by masons and architects. It was not until the next century that great sculpture and great architecture joined painting to become in Florence a supreme trinity of the arts.

With the sole exception of Orcagna's reliefs for the Orsanmichele tabernacle (*see* chapter 7), the fourteenth century was not a great period for native carvers because medieval Florentine architecture simply left very little room for sculpture. The Baptistery, S Miniato, the Badia Fiesolana, all relied entirely upon black and white re-vestments, the patterns of which look like intellectual games – a play with geometrical motives and architectonic forms which repeat the actual structural articulations. There were no niches, recessed lunettes, archivolts, loggias or pinnacles for sculpture to fit into. This is what distinguishes the Florentine Romanesque from the Lombard and Gothic architecture of the North, which was able, however, to penetrate the native styles of Pisa, Lucca and Siena; and it was in these cities that sculpture in Tuscany first developed.

While Arnolfo di Cambio and Andrea Pisano were introducing sculpture to Florentine buildings, Tino di Camaino, also from the Pisano shop, was invited to carve large groups for both the Baptistery and Cathedral. He carved a *Baptism of Christ* (now in a fragmentary state in the Museo dell' Opera) and also several figures (possibly three theological virtues) to go over another door. Between 1321 and 1323 Tino created the magnificent tomb for the Bishop Antonio Orso, part of which is still to be seen just inside the Cathedral's main entrance.

During the fourteenth century monumental sculpture gradually assumed a more important role in Florentine architecture. On the Campanile, the rows of hexagonal reliefs on the first storey (begun during Giotto's and Andrea Pisano's terms as *capomaestri*) were succeeded by rows of hollow niches lined in pink marble which eventually received the stone prophets by Nanni di Bartolo and Donatello (since moved to the Museo dell' Opera). A similar development occurred at Orsanmichele a few blocks to the south. Donatello, Nanni di Banco and Ghiberti all made their début in these buildings as masters of monumental statuary. Eventually Florentine architecture was to become a mere frame for sculpture.

A similar development occurred in the later history of the Duomo façade. During the fifteenth and sixteenth centuries designing for it became a kind of artists' sport. In 1489, Lorenzo the Magnificent sponsored a competition for a new façade because Arnolfo's (which had remained in a half-finished state) seemed so old-fashioned. The city's leading artists participated – among them Antonio Pollaiuolo, Verrocchio, Filippino Lippi and the da Maiano brothers. Even

Lorenzo himself contributed a design. But nothing came of it all. In 1515 when Lorenzo's son, Pope Leo X, made his triumphal return to the city, a pasteboard façade was made by Andrea del Sarto and Jacopo Sansovino. In 1587 the remains of the old Gothic façade were torn down to make room for an up-to-date scheme for which Buontalenti, Giambologna and Cigoli had prepared models. Again an entry was submitted by a Medici – this time by Don Giovanni. As far as we know, sculpture dominated all these schemes. But even these proposals did not get further than the drawing-board. In the end, after all the attempts to contrive a modern front for the Cathedral, the plan actually executed in the last century was in the neo-Gothic style.

It is interesting to reflect when pondering on the contrast between church and commune in the two piazzas that it is only in the Piazza della Signoria that free-standing statuary has a place. The numerous great statues in the Cathedral square were all absorbed into the Duomo's structure (both inside and out).

INSIDE THE DUOMO. Today the Duomo's sombre interior has the empty look and echoing sound of the abandoned hull of a great ship. Its magnificent decorations, the choir-lofts by Luca della Robbia and Donatello, the painted altarpieces, silver reliquaries, holy water fonts and embroidered hangings have been removed to the Museo dell' Opera. Gone too are most of the private tabernacles, votive images and cenotaphs left by illustrious Florentines. But the solemn grandeur of the Duomo's vast interior still breathes the air of great happenings. On the occasion of the Congo massacre of thirteen Italian U.N. aviators at Kindu, the old grave majesty came forth again. Three thousand soldiers and civilians walked slowly through the main portal escorting the great wreath. It was of blue-black laurel, magnificently austere, trimmed with only a few small silver spheres and a fluttering memorial scroll. For several days it stood in solitary splendour at the head of the nave, illuminated by a single slender candle.

In the fourteenth and fifteenth centuries Dante readings were held inside the Duomo during Lent. Boccaccio and the humanist Filelfo were among the readers. A memory of this custom remains in the north aisle in Domenico di Michelino's painting of the Poet declaiming in front of the city. It was commissioned by the Opera on the occasion of the bicentennial of Dante's birth (1465). Later, Lenten observances in the Duomo were more melodramatic; flocks of intimidated Florentines shivered at Savonarola's thundering sermons.

Outside the door of the New Sacristy, where Lorenzo the Magnificent took refuge from the assassins of the Pazzi Conspiracy (1478), is a plaque commemorating the final session of the Oecumenical Council held there in 1439 when the Greek Orthodox and Roman Catholic Churches formally declared their union on the eve of Constantinople's fall to the Turk. A platform was raised from the papal apartments at S Maria Novella all the way to the Cathedral's choir, so that Eugenius IV could pass to and from the council conveniently and in state above the heads of the crowd. Recollections of the exotic delegates – the bearded priests, the Greek philosophers and the gorgeous Emperor John Paleologus (the penultimate Byzantine emperor) – are to be found in Ghiberti's Paradise doors (the *Meeting of Solomon and Sheba*) and in Benozzo Gozzoli's *Adoration of the Magi* in the near-by Palazzo Medici.

The Pazzi, their crimes long since ignored if not forgotten, still occupy a place in the Duomo's ceremonial. Legend has it that Pazzino de' Pazzi brought back flints taken from the Holy Sepulchre on his return from a crusade. Early on Easter morning a Cathedral canon collects these relics from the church of SS Apostoli where the Pazzi deposited them. The flints are used to touch off a rocket shaped into a dove, which flies down a wire connecting the high altar to a festive cart full of fireworks standing outside in the Piazza. If the dove reaches the cart, sets off the fireworks, and returns to the high altar it is cheered as an omen for a good harvest. Originally, the *Scoppio del Carro* (the explosion of the cart) took place at Midnight Mass on Holy Saturday, but for the benefit of the many tourists visiting the city at this time of year it is now done at noon on Easter Sunday. The cart, which is popularly known as *il Brindellone* (because of all its wagging pennants) and which the Pazzi built during the seventeenth century, is stored in a house all its own on the Via Il Prato No. 48.

CENOTAPHS. Cenotaphs were intended for Dante, Petrarch and Boccaccio inside the Duomo, but only Dante's was ever carried out. Instead, the earliest surviving memorials honour men of lesser stature, one of them a foreigner. Only at the end of the fifteenth century, at the behest of Lorenzo the Magnificent, were the roundels made which commemorate Arnolfo di Cambio, Giotto and Brunelleschi. The two murals in the south aisle imitating stone catafalques painted by Bicci di Lorenzo honouring Cardinal Corsini (1422) and the learned Luigi de' Marsili. The Hawkwood memorial to an English man-at-arms painted by Paolo Uccello in 1436 imitates bronze statuary – because, according to Plutarch, Fabius Maximus (Hawkwood's model) had such a monument on the Roman capitol. Uccello's mural coincided with the revival in Florence of monumental bronze statuary in the ancient style. Not long afterwards his friend Donatello, with the Hawkwood in mind, designed the *Gattamelata* to go in front of the Santo at Padua. Even the Latin inscription (*Ioannes Acutus eques Britannicus dux aetatis suae cautissimus et rei militaris peritissimus habitus est*), which came from a eulogy to a Roman Republican hero (Q. Fabius Maximus), was repeated in Donatello's monument. Thrifty as ever, the Florentines had already settled for a painted substitute for real sculpture. Venetians and Milanese engaged Florentines – Pollaiuolo, Verrocchio and Leonardo – to devise bronze equestrian monuments; but republican Florence abjured the man on horseback. Her citizens might be willing to go so far as to honour a foreign mercenary with a painted imitation, but not even that for a native son. The equestrian monument carried associations of the deified emperor, the autocrat, of brute force triumphant – notions which were anathema to the proud republic. Such a monument made its first appearance only at the end of the sixteenth century when a Duke, not its citizens, ruled the city.

LUCA DELLA ROBBIA AND DONATELLO. The two choir-lofts carved by Luca della Robbia and Donatello represent still another innovation. Previously such lofts had consisted of simple wooden platforms with room enough to screen the organ and occasional singers and musicians. Already at the end of the fourteenth century when the massive crossing piers were completed, plans were laid for lofts of stone. Luca della Robbia's balcony was carried out between 1431 and 1438. Donatello began his in 1433 and finished it a year after Luca's. The size and shape of both were determined by Brunelleschi. In all other respects the two works disclose the different currents developing in the sculpture of the Florentine Renaissance.

Luca's balustrade, to be understood, needs to be seen in relation to its original site over the entrance to the New Sacristy (or Sagrestia delle Messe). At the end of lauds the 150th Psalm was sung – the words are inscribed around the balustrade and the reliefs illustrate them. Their exhortation had especial force and moment for the theme of the Resurrection, which Luca glorified in a glazed terracotta relief (1442–5) in the lunette below. For an architect, Luca della Robbia was the ideal sculptor. In his work are action, repose and a wealth of mood and loving detail, and also clarity, stability and symmetry. The central relief and those on either end reinforce the architectural divisions of the balustrade. His figures always observe the frame. The grooved pilasters are a Brunelleschian motive, and we know that Luca and Brunelleschi worked together in the Pazzi Chapel, where Luca contributed many of the roundels.

Donatello had a freer hand. He was a more turbulent, independent character. He was given no psalm or text for which he had to devise a pictorial equivalent, as Luca did. His are no disciplined singers or musicians, but a carefree, rowdy lot of winged street urchins, the personification of noise. Everything moves; even the column shafts sparkle with mosaics so that their function as frames and supports is reduced to a minimum. Action is the life of this frameless composition. The column shafts are only a screen to enhance the sense of speed and to give the boys depth to scramble about in. Donatello was never an architect's sculptor. He and Brunelleschi made the rounds of antiquities in Rome together; Donatello made the mould for a bronze winch which Brunelleschi designed for carrying up material to the crew at work on the cupola; but when Donatello was called upon to contribute sculpture for Brunelleschi's Old Sacristy in S Lorenzo, the result was anything but harmonious; he simply ignored the nature of his architectural surroundings.

The impact of ancient art on both sculptors was very different. On Luca it imposed a noble serenity on his otherwise realistic children. The stable, columnar dignity of his composition has, like Masaccio's and Piero della Francesca's designs, something of the calm reserve and ampleness of Roman republican relief sculpture. The high finish of Luca's reliefs is in the same spirit.

Donatello had spent the year immediately preceding the Cantoria commission in Rome, but with the exception of the ornament little influence of ancient sculpture is felt in his reliefs. Donatello was never overawed by the examples of others – be they contemporary or ancient – and he hardly ever resorted to direct borrowing. No pagan bacchanal has the abandon of Donatello's gang of street boys. We do not know whether the rough finish was deliberate or the result of shortness of time. One can find parallels only in late Imperial reliefs.

The *operai* waited nine years in vain for Donatello to do the bronze doors for both the north and south sacristies. In the end only the door of the New Sacristy was carried out. Luca della Robbia took the work in hand (1464–9) after Michelozzo had made a start on the frame. It is a curious mixture of old and new. From Donatello's doors in the Old Sacristy of S Lorenzo comes the general lay-out, but the heads protruding from the quatrefoils and the swinging draperies of the elegant figures have an old-fashioned Gothic flavour which one also sees in Ghiberti's doors.

THE NEW SACRISTY. The interior of the Sagrestia Nuova is one of the few Renaissance rooms in Florence in which a painter, a sculptor-architect, a goldsmith, and a crew of carpenters blended their efforts into a harmonious scheme. The decoration of the originally Gothic interior began with the marble gabled lavabo which Brunelleschi designed and had his adopted son, Buggiano, carry out. The lavabo brought the gaiety of children at play; saucy *putti* squirt water into the basin, their life size playmates (in wood) carry garlands around the top of the high cupboards. Others, in flat intarsia, bear pots of flowers and hop about the shrubbery. Wood is the unifying medium of the scheme. The great pilastered cupboards transform the medieval interior into a Renaissance studio. The intarsiae represent latticed cupboards and drawers left casually open, disclosing books, pen quills, empty candlesticks, an odd chalice or two and a bishop's mitre. There are laurel wreaths with curling ribbons, whorled medallions, garlands, balustrades, philosopher-like images of saints and prophets and a few scenes at either end of the room. For enthusiastic students of perspective, intarsia was an ideal vehicle for audacious fore-shortenings and long prospects – not only in Florence, but also in Pisa, Modena and Urbino. The decoration of church sacristies was rapidly becoming less piously didactic. The object was to please the eye and rest the spirit.

Giuliano da Maiano, who was a practising architect and sculptor, took charge of the project in 1463. He had his brother-in-law, Maso Finiguerra (a goldsmith and engraver), prepare drawings for the intarsiae. Alesso Baldovinetti, the painter, was invited to make a design for the Nativity scene and to tint the finished inlays.

THE CUPOLA DECOR. During the second half of the fifteenth century, the austerity of the early Renaissance was cast aside. Richness both in materials and design was sought after. Lorenzo the Magnificent encouraged the revival of mosaic painting. Baldovinetti and Ghirlandaio were appointed to keep the already existing medieval mosaics in good repair and to make new ones. Lorenzo even proposed to line Brunelleschi's cupola with a vast mosaic. He was thinking of the Baptistery's vault and the splendid domes of Venice. He probably knew that Brunelleschi himself had hinted at the possibility of such decoration, for he had lined the model for his cupola with gilt foil. Nothing came of this scheme. Instead, a century later, Vasari and Zuccari frescoed a pompous allegory boiling with clouds, draperies and personifications, religious and profane, which have no relation whatever to the style of the site save vastness of scale. The murals cost between 16 and 17,000 *scudi*. But there were some at the unveiling who felt that they had not got their money's worth. The murals belittled the cupola; 'without the painting', Lapini said, 'it seemed higher and greater.'

MICHELANGELO. Of the many great Florentines who left their mark on the Duomo, Michelangelo is among the few who left no work here made espccially for it. The Arte della Lana (or Wool Guild), who were then the financial guardians of the Opera, commissioned him in 1508 to carry out twelve apostles to be set into the great piers around the crossing and the tribunes. The master agreed to produce one figure a year and the Opera rented him a house for the purpose (this was probably the same house the Opera gave to Michelangelo some years earlier when he was commissioned to carve the *David*). The great blocks began to arrive regularly from Carrara but Michelangelo never got beyond the roughing out of a St Matthew (now in the Academy). Rome intervened. Pope Julius II commanded Michelangelo to paint the Sistine ceiling and prepare a monumental cenotaph for him. In the end the apostles were carried out by lesser men: Jacopo and Andrea Sansovino, Benedetto da Rovezzano, Bandinelli and others.

The Duomo's single Michelangelo, the *Pietà*, near the New Sacristy came to the Cathedral only in 1721 on the initiative of Grand Duke Cosimo III. Michelangelo began it around 1550, intending it for his own grave which was to be in S Maria Maggiore in Rome. The head of Nicodemus is a self-portrait. Before long he grew dissatisfied with the work, which was being carved from a faulty block. A servant kept pestering him to finish it, Vasari says. Then a piece from the Madonna's elbow broke off. Finally Michelangelo smashed it, letting the servant keep the pieces. After the master's death a pupil, Calcagni, tried to recompose the pieces according to the preparatory models and he finished the front of Mary Magdalen. Between about 1570 and 1721 the *Pietà* was virtually homeless. From a Roman vineyard it was brought to Florence and consigned to the murky crypt of S Lorenzo; from there it was finally brought to the Cathedral's high altar, where it remained until 1933. Even in its unfinished and mutilated state the group marvellously unites intense personal sorrow with a grand statement of the subject's eternal significance. This may explain why Michelangelo deliberately gave what is really a Deposition group the feeling of a *Pietà* and the form traditional to images of the Trinity.

CARITAS. Birth, death and charity all have their place around the Duomo. Births were registered in the Baptistery in front of the Cathedral. All wills were taxed and filed by the Opera del Duomo which stands behind it. The great public hospital founded in 1286 by Folco Portinari (the father of Dante's Beatrice) is in the street just behind the Opera.

S Maria Nuova, as the hospital is called, began with twelve beds. It now has hundreds and the complex of buildings has absorbed the old Camaldolese monastery of S Maria degli Angeli, as well as the church of S Egidio. Today it is administered by the University and its many clinics and dispensaries are open to everyone – natives and foreigners. The hospital's main source of income for several centuries was from properties left by grateful Florentines. Filippino Lippi left most of his possessions to it. Leonardo da Vinci left it drawings and a large part of the cartoon he prepared for the *Battle of Anghiari*.

The fact that in 1330, $12\frac{1}{2}\%$ of the populace lived on charity is an indication of the scale on which institutions of that time operated. Today the most beloved charity in the city is the *Misericordia*, which occupies the corner house opposite the Cathedral bell-tower. Since the thirteenth century it has done for Florence what the Red Cross does for American and English cities. There is an important difference: citizens from all levels of society devote to it at least one hour a week *for life*. There are over six thousand active members. Every day about three hundred are on duty. The minimum age for admission as a novice ('*Stracciafoglio*') is fifteen. To cloak their charity in anonymity members wear black hoods when on duty. The main activity now is a free ambulance service. For centuries the Misericordia also buried the dead, even in pestilence and war. They visit the sick and operate a free dispensary for all members, active and inactive (about 15,000) and their families. The doctors and nurses donate their time. On January 20th, the feast day of the patron, St Sebastian, tons of bread and pasta are distributed to the needy.

The Misericordia was begun in the thirteenth century by the porters who, at times, were called upon to bring the sick to hospitals. In order to raise funds for the confraternity they began by paying small fines when they were caught cursing. Eventually they absorbed an older religious society founded for the suppression of heresy. Today there are 452 chapters of the Misericordia all over Tuscany with more than 250,000 members. No institution can rival the Misericordia in the affection and sense of moral duty which binds it to the community. In Florence the administrative council of seventy-two members is evenly divided between noblemen, burghers (called 'artisti' for professional men, and 'grembiuli' – literally 'aprons' – for non-professionals) and prelates. Even the administrative head of the Misericordia is unpaid. At present he is Commendatore Crema, who happens to be the Prefecture's chief financial officer. At six in the morning he is at his desk above the Loggia of the Bigallo. At the beginning of normal office hours he rushes to his office at the Prefecture in the Palazzo Medici-Riccardi two blocks away. But at odd moments during the day he slips out again to the Misericordia. The confraternity operates on a slender budget of slightly more than £340,000 a year (595 million lire). It is still financed entirely from private support. Public appeals are never made. Everything comes from donations, membership fees (3,000 lire initiation fee, 1,000 lire annual subscription) and the income from property in the Val d'Arno acquired in legacies.

The doors of the Misericordia are open until eleven at night and anyone is welcome to walk in and inspect the marble *St Sebastian* and the marble *Madonna* by Benedetto da Maiano and the tabernacle by Andrea della Robbia.

Almost as old as the Misericordia is *la Compagnia di S Maria del Bigallo*. The name 'Bigallo', or 'near the cock', comes from a village above Bagno a Ripoli where the society since 1245 had run a hospital. During the thirteenth century the company's chief activity was the suppression of heresy, but gradually it became a charitable institution. Once a year the Commune allowed its officials to select prisoners for release. In 1352 the city gave it the property opposite the Baptistery, where the Bigallo's house and loggia were subsequently built by Alberto Arnoldi. The Bigallo's fame came from its care of foundlings and orphans, which it began around 1425 at the instigation of the Archbishop of Florence, Sant' Antonino.

The Bigallo was never as prosperous as the Misericordia; its services simply did not touch so many members of the community. To keep itself going, the society has merged several times with the Misericordia. Recently it has been set on its own again. Today the Bigallo's aid to the young is limited to helping two hundred needy cases with small donations and to preventing the exploitation of children for begging. A child found begging on the streets is taken by the police and a Bigallo official to a home for abandoned children. A heavy fine is exacted when the parent arrives. The Bigallo's main service now, however, is devoted to the aged – to running a small old folk's home.

In 1402 Bruni remarked at the conclusion of his *Laudatio* that the Florentines although desirous of glory were 'above all well-mannered and gracious.' These words were written when Ghiberti's doors were still to be cast and Brunelleschi's cupola was yet to be raised. Ambition never went wild in Florence, and through all sparkles the humour which even the names of the great Duomo bells reflect: *Grossa*, *Beona*, *Completa*, *Chierica*, and *Squilla* (the big one, the winebibber, the finished one, the priestling, and the shrill angelus bell or 'shrieker').

1758

Perspective drawing by Paolo Uccello

Vertical view of Baldassare Coscia (the deposed Pope John XXIII) from the tomb in the Baptistery (1424-7). Donatello designed the monument and cast the bronze effigy

Chapter 4

The Bargello – Santa Croce Neighbourhood: Justice, Dyeing and Franciscans

❧

SUMMARY OF THE CHIEF MONUMENTS

1. The Badia – founded in A.D. 978 by Willa, the mother of Ugo, Margrave of Tuscany. It was the richest monastery of medieval Florence. Rebuilt in the Cistercian Gothic style in 1285. Campanile, 1310–30. Radical reconstruction of church in 1627 following a plan by Matteo Segaloni. Originally, the church's façade was in the west. Entrance portal on Via Proconsolo by Benedetto da Rovezzano (1495). *Madonna and Child* in glazed terracotta over the door by Benedetto Buglione (early 16th c.). Portico leading from Via Dante Alighieri to entrance of church by Benedetto da Rovezzano (*ca* 1500). The loggia opposite by a follower of Michelozzo.

Interior (best light in the morning) – a Greek Cross plan. Carved Baroque ceiling designed by Segaloni.

1. *Apparition of the Virgin to St Bernard** by Filippino Lippi (*ca* 1486), includes portrait of donor – Piero del Pugliese.
2. Tomb of Giannozzo Pandolfini by the Rossellino shop (after 1456), design based on tomb of Orlando de' Medici in SS Annunziata.
3. An altar frontal including a relief of the *Madonna and blessing Child with SS Leonard and Lawrence* by Mino da Fiesole (1464–9).
4. Tomb of Bernardo Giugni by Mino da Fiesole (*ca* 1466) with Justice and Faith accompanying the effigy.
5. Altarpiece of the *Pentecost* by Mirabello Cavalori.
6. Tomb of Ugo, Margrave of Tuscany (d. 1001) – son of the Badia's foundress – by Mino da Fiesole (1469–81). A watered down version of Desiderio's Marsuppini tomb in S Croce. The dado with the racing angels is the best part. Overhead: Vasari's *Assumption of the Virgin* (1566).
7. *Giochi-Bastari Chapel* (ask sacristan to open it; tip) – remains of a fresco cycle by a follower of Nardo di Cione (*ca* 1350)

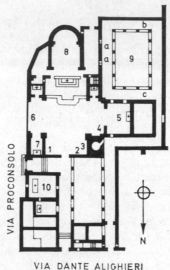

VIA DANTE ALIGHIERI

BADIA FIORENTINA

showing five scenes of *Christ's Passion*. Detached from the wall in 1958.

8. *Apse* – murals by G. D. Ferretti (1734); choir stalls by Francesco and Marco del Tasso (1501). On the right is a door leading to the sacristy and to the Chiostro degli Aranci.

9. *Chiostro degli Aranci* – a double-storeyed cloister with superimposed loggias probably designed by Bernardo Rossellino, 1435–40. (*a*) Fragments of Romanesque cloister on ground floor and on storey above. Until recently there were murals illustrating the *Life of St Benedict* painted by a Portuguese contemporary of Fra Angelico's (Giovanni di Consalvo) between 1436 and 1439. These beautiful murals together with their sinopia underdrawings have been detached and are for the time being in storage at the Soprintendenza alle Gallerie. Remaining *in situ* is the finished mural of *St Benedict chastising himself* by the young Bronzino (1526–8). (*b*) The detached surface layer of Bronzino's mural. (*c*) The *secondo strappo* – or second layer of colour which soaked down from the surface.

10. *Pandolfini Chapel* – dedicated to St Stephen; by Benedetto da

82

Rovezzano (1503–11) – a variation on Brunelleschi's Old Sacristy of S Lorenzo. Altarpiece by Bilivert. Recently a small tabernacle fresco of the *Transfiguration* by Taddeo Gaddi was uncovered in a room adjacent to the courtyard.

2. The Bargello (now Museo Nazionale, where the masterpieces of Florentine sculpture and arts and crafts are exhibited; hours: 9.00–14.00 weekdays; 09.00–13.00 Sundays and holidays; closed Mondays; admission fee 150 lire). Originally built as the city's first town hall, or Palazzo del Popolo; begun in 1255. Also served as a prison. From 1261 on it became the residence of the podestà and was thus known as the Palazzo del Podestà. Structural changes and additions between 1332 and 1367. Great hall on first floor built with wooden roof in 1254, later vaulted by one of the Cathedral architects, Neri di Fioravanti (1332–46), who was also responsible for the stairway in the courtyard (finished by 1367). In 1574, the palace became the residence of the chief of police known as the *bargello*.

In Loggia of Courtyard: on the wall beside the staircase – the arms of the governors and officials who resided here. Arcades of loggia on ground floor built in 1280–90; loggia above, 1316–20. Inside the loggia on ground floor are Giambologna's *Ocean* from the Boboli Gardens, and figures from Ammannati's fountain designed for the villa at Pratolino.

In the room off the north-eastern corner of the courtyard are medieval sculpture from the Badia and the Porta Romana including works by Paolo di Giovanni, Tino di Camaino, Alberto Arnoldi and others.

Crossing the courtyard to the hall facing the Via Proconsolo are works by Michelangelo and his contemporaries: Michelangelo's *Drunken Bacchus** (1497) made for Jacopo Galli's garden of antiquities, the tondo of *Mary with the Infant Christ and St John** (*ca* 1503) made for Bartolomeo Pitti, the unfinished *David* (1530) for Baccio Valori, and the bust of *Brutus** (*ca* 1540) for Cardinal Ridolfi. Nearby are gathered a series of terracotta sketches (or *bozzetti*) based on Michelangelo's works by Tribolo, Giambologna and others. Continuing around towards the right are Cellini's small bronze figures and the relief of *Perseus rescuing Andromeda* from the base of the Perseus statue in the Loggia dei Lanzi. Then there are two examples of virtuoso marble statuary involving several figures caught in violent action all worked into a spiral movement – Eganzio Danti's *Honour crushing Deceit* and Giambologna's *Virtue crushing-Vice* (also called *Florence conquering Pisa*). Looking at these allegories from the wall is Cellini's bronze bust of a glowering *Cosimo I de' Medici.*

Returning to the courtyard and going up the staircase: in the arcades above, works by Giambologna: the bronze animals were originally made for a grotto in the Medici villa at Castello; the *Mercury** (*ca* 1564) was once part of a fountain in the Villa Medici at Rome – a replica was sent as a present to Emperor Ferdinand of Austria when Francesco de' Medici married his daughter Giovanna. *On the first floor* are examples of ivory-carving, goldsmith work, and glazed pottery from the great Bargello collections. In the long room on the north side, the Carrand collection is exhibited which includes a charming altarpiece of the *Nativity* painted in the early 15th century by an unknown Bohemian master. Beside this room is the *Chapel* dedicated to St Mary Magdalen painted by a follower of Giotto (*ca* 1330–40). During 1970–1 these murals were repaired and freed from much of the repainting applied during the last century. *Scenes from the Lives of Mary Magdalen and the Baptist, Inferno, and Paradise.*

In the *Great Hall* to the right of the stairs, works by Donatello – the *St George** from Orsanmichele (*ca* 1417,) the *Marzocco** from the papal apartment at S Maria Novella (1420), the *David** from the Palazzo Medici (*ca* 1430–2), the *Amor Atys** or bronze faun (*ca* 1440,) the *bronze bust of a young man** with a Platonic emblem for the soul (*ca* 1440). Here also are the *competition reliefs** prepared in 1402 by Ghiberti and Brunelleschi for the Baptistery doors on the theme of the *Sacrifice of Isaac.*

On the second floor, in Room III: Verrocchio's *David** (*ca* 1475) and his terracotta *Resurrection* (*ca* 1478) made for the Villa Medici at Careggi and Antonio Pollaiuolo's small bronze of *Hercules and Antæus** (*ca* 1475–80); Antonio Rossellino's portraits of *Francesco Sassetti, Matteo Palmieri,* and two Madonnas; Benedetto da Maiano's *Pietro Mellini* (1474) and Desiderio de Settignano's *Madonna Panciatichi** and Francesco Laurana's *Portrait of Battista Sforza** (*ca* 1472).

In many of these rooms are splendid examples of sculpture, maiolica and decorative arts of the 16th and 17th c. In the *Sala del Camino* is Bernini's luminous marble bust of *Costanza Bonarelli** (*ca* 1636).

3. Reconstructed houses built on the site of property which tradition associates with the family of Dante Alighieri.

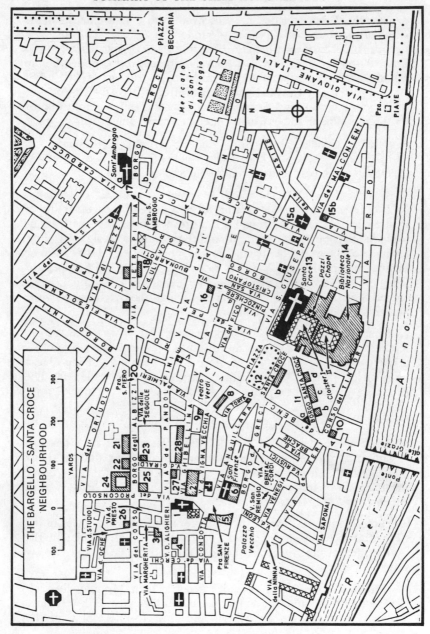

THE BARGELLO – SANTA CROCE
NEIGHBOURHOOD

4. Church of San Martino del Vescovo – the parish church of the Alighieri and Donati families; founded in 986, rebuilt in 1479. Became the seat of the *Compagna dei Buonuomini* instituted in 1444 by S Antonino for the relief of the *poveri vergognosi* (the poor who are ashamed to beg). Inside: muralled lunettes illustrating the deeds of St Martin perhaps by Davide Ghirlandaio (after 1479). Also: a *Madonna with Infant Christ and St John* by Niccolò Soggi, a follower of Perugino's. The church is usually open mornings only.

5. Palazzo Gondi – built for Guiliano Gondi by Giuliano da Sangallo after 1490. Southern façade facing Palazzo Vecchio added in 19th c. when part of the original palace was demolished to widen the street. Fountain in courtyard, 1604.

6. The Tribunal or former **Oratory of San Firenze** – occupies site of Roman temple of Isis. Present structure begun *ca* 1668 with funds provided by Giuliano Serragli and based on a design by Pier Francesco Silvani. The façade is the chief example of 18th c. architecture in the city. The left side was executed by Ferdinando Ruggieri in 1715. Between 1772 and 1775 Zanobi Filippo del Rosso copied it for the right-hand section and united the two façades by the palace-like elevation of the convent.

7. Piazza Peruzzi – the Piazza occupies one side of what was the old Roman amphitheatre, the medieval houses preserve the curve of its original shape (note its swing from the northern side of the Piazza on towards the Via Bentaccordi and the Via Torta on the left). The Peruzzi arms (the little pears) appear on many of the houses here. The family directed a great bank during the 14th c. In 1310 they received as their guest here King Robert of Naples.

8. San Simone – founded in 1192. Rebuilt in 1630 by Gherardo Silvani at the behest of the Galilei family. Inside, first altar on right: *St Peter Enthroned* painted in 1307 by the S Cecilia Master. Above the first altar on left, mural by a follower of Niccolò di Pietro Gerini: the *Birth of St Nicholas*.

9. Palazzo Salviati – one of the best-preserved 14th c. palaces in the city with projecting stone consoles which were later forbidden by the Commune because they obstructed light and traffic in the narrow streets.

10. Museo Horne (No. 6, Via de' Benci). Open Monday through Wednesday, 9.00–13.00; admission fee 300 lire. The 15th c. palace formerly belonged to the Alberti and then to the Corsi family.

Building sometimes attributed to Giuliano da Sangallo, but the most recent studies claim it as the work of Cronaca (Simone del Pollaiuolo). Its courtyard is a brilliant example of how a cramped, irregular space could be articulated into a structure of easy grandeur. The palace and most of its contents left to the city by Herbert Percy Horne (1864–1916). Among the items in this rich collection are a mural by Franciabigio of the *Noli me tangere* (1510) detached from a weaver's house formerly in Via Porta Rossa. Also: a terracotta tondo of the *Virgin, Child and Angels* attributed to Luca della Robbia; an octagonal panel of the 15th c. painted with the *Last Judgment* on the front and a *putto playing a bagpipe* on the back with the arms of the Albizzi and Soderini families.

On the first floor (according to the pre-flood installation) **Room I:** in a glass case, four Sienese panel paintings including (Nos. 18–19) a diptych, very probably by Simone Martini, and (Nos. 16–17) *SS Ursula and Apollonia* by a close follower of Sassetta; (No. 39) *SS Benedict, Catherine of Alexandria and Margherita** by Pietro Lorenzetti; (Nos. 44–5) panels by Bernardo Daddi; in a small glass case (No. 64) a *Man of Sorrows* by Filippo Lippi. **Room II:** (No. 26) *St Stephen*, often attributed to Giotto; (No. 27) cassone panel of *Esther leaving Babylon* by the young Filippino Lippi based on a design by Botticelli; (No. 45) a splendid 14th c. beaker of white maiolica with birds and griffons in blue and purple from Orvieto or Siena. **Room III:** (No. 4) early 14th c. altarpiece from the Badia a Settimo; (No 34) *Madonna and Child* by Taddeo Gaddi (active *ca* 1330–66); (No. 44) a *Miracle of St Julian* from the predella of the S Maria Maggiore altarpiece by Masolino and Masaccio.

On the second floor, **Room IV:** (No. 4) *Madonna and Child* by Pacino di Bonaguida; (No. 5) very fine, though badly damaged Sienese (?) *Crucifixion* painted late in the 14th c.; (No. 6) *Pietà*, Byzantine, 13th–14th c. **Room VI:** (No. 13) *Crucifixion* painted in the manner of Lorenzo Monaco; (No. 19) altarpiece of the first half of the 14th c. by the Master of the Horne Triptych; (No. 25) wood block print of *St Jerome* by Ugo da Carpi after Parmigianino's design.

11. Borgo Santa Croce; (*a*) *Tower and Loggia of the Alberti* – the original structure was destroyed by a Ghibelline mob in 1260. The present portico dates from *ca* 1400, now a *caffé* – one of the city's oldest. (*b*) No. 6 – *Palazzo Corsini* (now Istituto Araldico), early 16th c., courtyard in style of Giuliano da Sangallo. (*c*) No. 8 – *Casa Morrocchi.* which once belonged to Giorgio Vasari, who painted murals on the first floor with portraits of his contemporaries. (*d*) No. 10 – *Palazzo Rasponi,* late 15th c., style of Cronaca.

12. Piazza Santa Croce – (*a*) *Palazzo Serristori* (formerly Cocchi), Piazza S Croce No. 1: attributed to Baccio d'Agnolo. (*b*) *Palazzo dell' Antella* (formerly Cerchi), Piazza S Croce Nos. 21–2; built in 1619 by Giulio Parigi. Murals on facade painted in twenty days by twelve painters under the direction of Giovanni da San Giovanni. Bust of Cosimo II and commemorative plaque of February 10th,

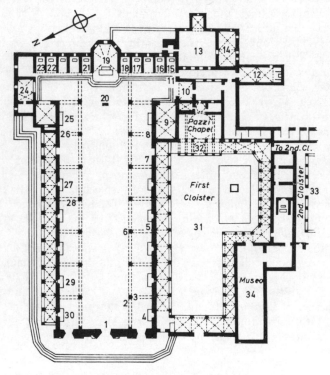

PIAZZA S. CROCE

BASILICA of S. CROCE

1565, which marked the centre line for the football games which were played in the Piazza. Dante Monument (1865) by E. Pazzi now on steps of S Croce.

13. Church and Convent of Santa Croce. First church built between 1228–52. Present structure begun in 1294–5; transept finished *ca* 1300; nave finished *ca* 1385; façade remained in rough state until 1863, when it was revested in polychromed marble based on a neo-Gothic design already prepared in the 17th c.; sculpture by Emilio Zocchi, Giovanni Duprè and Tito Sarrocchi.

Interior: the most richly adorned church of the city. Its original appearance altered between 1560 and 1584 by Vasari, who, on the Grand Duke's instructions, demolished the enclosure for the monks' choir together with the Gothic rood screen which spanned the nave. Then he added the symmetrical arrangement of gabled altars in the aisles. The subjects of these altarpieces illustrate the Passion and the events after Christ's death. The series begins in the right aisle at the eastern end and proceeds westwards and then goes back again down the left aisle. Walls and pavement heavily restored in the 19th c. Originally, the floor was crowded with tomb slabs.

1. Stained glass roundel, *Deposition*, designed by Giovanni dal Ponte, *ca* 1420. The other windows in the right aisle all date from the first half of the 15th c. All are heavily restored.
2. Holy water font, 1418.
3. *Madonna* by Antonio Rossellino (1478), made for the grave of Francesco Nori killed in the Pazzi Conspiracy.
4. *Tomb of Michelangelo,* designed by Vasari (1564) and with sculpture by Valerio Cioli, Giovanni Bandini and Battista Lorenzi – one of the initial projects of the Florentine Academy. To the right: *Crucifixion* by Santi di Tito (1569); to the left: the *Way to Calvary* by Vasari (1572).
5. Tomb of Vittorio Alfieri, poet and patriot, by Canova (1810).
6. *Pulpit by Benedetto da Maiano* (*ca* 1474–5), commissioned by Pietro Mellini, whose portrait by the same sculptor is in the Bargello. Note traces of gilding and polychromy in the scenes from the life of St Francis. Below: Faith, Hope, Love, Fortitude and Justice. The inlaid floor below was made at the same time.
7. *Annunciation** by Donatello (*ca* 1435) from the Cavalcanti Chapel. Most of the gilding dates from a late 19th c. restoration.
8. *Tomb of Leonardo Bruni**, humanist, historian and Florentine chancellor (1369–1444), by Bernardo Rossellino (1446–7). The Latin epitaph composed by Bruni's successor as state

chancellor, Carlo Marsuppini, translated reads: 'After Leonardo departed from life, history is in mourning and eloquence is dumb, and it is said that the Muses, Greek and Latin alike, cannot restrain their tears.'

9. *Castellani Chapel* – built after 1383, painted by followers of Agnolo Gaddi with scenes from the lives of SS Nicholas, Anthony Abbot, John the Evangelist and John the Baptist. Painted cross by Niccolò di Pietro Gerini (1380). Graves of Luisa Stolberg, Countess of Albany, Alfieri's great friend.

10. *Baroncelli Chapel* * – carved tomb at entrance (1327) and Annunciation group probably by Giovanni di Balduccio da Pisa. Murals probably painted in the early 1330s by Taddeo Gaddi – *Scenes from the Life of the Virgin*. Altarpiece: *Coronation of the Virgin* signed with Giotto's name but painted by his workshop. In the bay on the right: *Assumption of the Virgin* by Mainardi after a design by Domenico Ghirlandaio (1495). Marble *Virgin and Child* by Vincenzo Danti (*ca* 1570).

11. Portal frame by Michelozzo (1445), beside it a mural of *Christ among the Doctors* by Taddeo Gaddi (*ca* 1335).

12. *The Noviziata* or Novices' Chapel – built at the behest of Cosimo de' Medici *ca* 1445 by Michelozzo. Glazed terracotta altarpiece, *Virgin and Child with Six Saints*, by the shop of Andrea della Robbia (1490–1500), commissioned by the Company of Castel S Giovanni. Galileo was buried here in 1642.

13. *Sacristy* – built *ca* 1340 with funds provided by the Peruzzi family. Murals on south wall: *Way to Calvary* by a follower of Spinello Aretino (*ca* 1400); *Crucifixion* attributed to Taddeo Gaddi (*ca* 1340–55); *Resurrection* by Niccolò di Pietro Gerini (*ca* 1400); *Ascension* by a Gerini follower (*ca* 1400). Inlaid sacristy cupboards and benches by Giovanni di Michele (*ca* 1440), Giuliano da Maiano and the Tasso family. The great wooden '*Bancone*' in the centre of the room, used for laying out clerical vestments, is by Giovanni di Michele (*ca* 1440) commissioned by Tommaso Spinelli. The intarsias were recently discovered beneath layers of darkened varnish. Terracotta bust of Christ by Giovanni della Robbia. Wall font by Pagno Portigiani (second half of 15th c.).

Rinuccini Chapel * (at east side of the sacristy) – wrought-iron gate (1371); murals with *Scenes from the Lives of the Virgin and St Mary Magdalen* – the two uppermost tiers on either side by Giovanni da Milano (*ca* 1366), remaining scenes below by an unknown painter referred to as the Rinuccini Master. Altarpiece by Giovanni del Biondo (1379).

14. Room with terra-verde mural of *Christ and the Samaritan Woman* (*ca* 1450) in a niche over what was once a well. This room exhibits detached mural fragments from the Bardi Chapel which were painted by Gaetano Bianchi when he restored the chapel in the last century. Exhibition of photographs of the Bardi and Peruzzi Chapel murals before and after their recent cleaning.

15. *Velluti Chapel* – built *ca* 1300, murals with *Scenes from the Legend of St Michael the Archangel* by a follower of Cimabue.

16. *Riccardi Chapel* – rebuilt *ca* 1620 by Gherardo Silvani. Vault mural by Giovanni da S Giovanni.

17. *Peruzzi Chapel* * – murals by Giotto and his shop (*ca* 1326–30) of *Scenes from the Lives of St John the Evangelist and St John the Baptist*. These murals were painted almost entirely in tempera (in contrast to the Bardi murals next door, which were painted largely in true fresco).

18. *Bardi Chapel* * – murals by Giotto and his shop (*ca* 1315–20) of *Scenes from the Life of St Francis*. The gaps in the lower scenes caused by tombs which were once immured here. Altarpiece of *St Francis* by a Florentine painter *ca* 1250–60, known as the Maestro di S Francesco Bardi – one of the most beautiful and best preserved panel paintings of the 13th c.

19. *Chancel* – built and muralled at the behest of the Alberti family. Murals and stained glass windows by Agnolo Gaddi (*ca* 1390) of the *Legend of the Finding of the True Cross*. On the right wall, reading from top to bottom: St Michael presents Seth with a branch from the Tree of Knowledge; which is then planted on Adam's tomb; the wood from the tree, used later as a bridge, is recognized by the Queen of Sheba as the wood which will be used to crucify Christ – whereupon King Solomon has the wood buried; the Cross is recovered at the behest of St Helena. On the left wall: St Helena carries the Cross in triumph to Jerusalem; which is later taken by Chosroes, King of the Persians; the Persians idolatrously worship the wood; Heraclius the Byzantine Emperor, dreams of a victory against Chosroes fought in the sign of the Cross; Chosroes is decapitated and Heraclius, shedding his imperial garments, carries the Cross in triumph back to Jerusalem. Altarpiece: a composite of several dismembered altarpieces – the *Madonna and Saints* by Niccolò di Pietro Gerini (*ca* 1400), *Four Church Fathers* by Giovanni del Biondo (1363), predella and pinnacles by others

including Mariotto di Nardo. Painted *Triumphal Cross* hanging overhead by the Master of the Fogg Pietà (*ca* 1340). Choir stalls by Manno dei Cori (*ca* 1430).

20. Commemorative inlay to the Alberti family who were the patrons of the main chapel as well as of the old monks' choir.

21. *Tosinghi* Chapel – mural over entrance all that remains of a larger scheme dedicated to the Virgin: *Assumption* by the Master of the Fogg Pietà; altarpiece by Giovanni del Biondo (1372) with a predella by Neri di Bicci (*ca* 1440–50).

22. *Pulci-Beraldi Chapel* – murals of the *Martyrdom of SS Lawrence and Stephen* by Bernardo Daddi (*ca* 1330). Glazed terracotta altarpiece of the *Virgin and Child Enthroned* by Giovanni della Robbia (1520–30).

23. *Bardi di Vernio Chapel* – on the right wall: *Scenes from the Life of St Sylvester* by Maso di Banco 1335–38 heavily restored; left wall: carved tomb niche with mural of one of the Bardi rising from his grave to meet his Maker painted by Maso di Banco. The *Deposition* inside the grave niche beside it is the work of Taddeo Gaddi. Altarpiece of *S Giovanni Gualberto* by Giovanni del Biondo not originally painted for this chapel.

To the left, *Niccolini Chapel* built in a proto-Baroque style by G. A. Dosio (1579–85). Ask sacristan to open gate. Cupola frescoes by Volterrano, figures around tomb by Francavilla, pictures of the *Assumption* and *Coronation of the Virgin* by Alessandro Allori.

24. *Bardi Chapel* – contains Donatello's polychromed wooden *Crucifix* (*ca* 1412) which Brunelleschi is said to have disdainfully compared to a *contadino* (peasant).

25. Tomb of the bookseller and biographer, Vespasiano da Bisticci (1421–98).

26. *Tomb of Carlo Marsuppini**, humanist and Florentine chancellor (d. 1453), by Desiderio da Settignano (finished before 1464); one of the masterpieces of 15th c. Florentine sculpture. The epitaph in translation reads: 'Stay and see the marbles which enshrine a great sage, one for whose mind there was not world enough. Carlo, the great glory of his age, knew all that nature, the heavens, and human conduct have to tell. O Roman and Greek muses, now unloose your hair. Alas, the fame and splendour of your choir is dead.'

27. *Pietà* by Bronzino (*ca* 1560).

28. Grave of Lorenzo Ghiberti and his son, Vittorio.

29. Remains of a fresco cycle including the *Crucifixion* by Niccolò di Pietro Gerini (*ca* 1395).
30. Tomb of Galileo (1737, body transferred from the Noviziato).
31. *Convent and Museum of S Croce* (Piazza S Croce No. 16) – Hours: 09.00–12.00; 15.00–17.00 weekdays; 10.00–12.00 Sundays; admission fee 200 lire. This applies to the Pazzi Chapel, the cloisters, and the Museo dell' Opera di S Croce.
32. *Pazzi Chapel** – built as the chapter-room and as a family burial chapel. Begun by Brunelleschi between 1429 and 1430 but finished after his death. Giuliano da Maiano was involved in its completion. The porch has a vaulted ceiling adorned with glazed terracotta rosettes by Luca della Robbia and a frieze of cherubim by Desiderio da Settignano. Wooden doors by Giuliano da Maiano (1472). Inside: terracotta roundels of the Twelve Apostles by Luca della Robbia; the Four Evangelists in the pendentives are by another master. The dome over the altar painted with astrological signs. Stained glass window of *St Andrew* a copy of the original by Baldovinetti now in the museum.
33. *The Second Cloister* – the most beautiful in Florence, built by an unknown follower of Brunelleschi (*ca* 1452), variously attributed to Bernardo Rossellino or Giuliano da Maiano. Commissioned by Tommaso di Lionardo Spinelli.
34. *Museo dell' Opera di S Croce**. Most of the panel paintings belonging here are still being repaired as a result of the 1966 flood which here reached the height of 7 metres. The gravest casualty was Cimabue's great triumphal Cross reduced to a fragmentary state. The former refectory contains Taddeo Gaddi's mural of the *Last Supper* (*ca* 1340) – the earliest of the long series of Florentine *Cenacoli*. The mural includes an allegorical vision of the Crucifixion based on S Bonaventura's *Lignum Vitae* and scenes from the lives of SS Mary Magdalen, Benedict, Francis and Louis of Toulouse. On the walls are disposed – over the entrance: fragment of a *Deposition* painted by Taddeo Gaddi from the northern aisle of the church. To the right, as one enters: Cimabue's great *Triumphal Cross**; mural fragments by a pupil of Giovanni del Biondo from the porch along the southern flank of the church (*ca* 1375); fragments of Andrea Orcagna's *Triumph of Death* (*ca* 1360), other fragments on opposite wall, originally in the south aisle of the church and badly damaged by the construction of Vasari's altar tabernacles. To the left as one enters: Maso di Banco's muralled lunette of

the *Coronation of the Virgin*; Donatello's **St Louis of Toulouse***
(1423) originally made for the Parte Guelfa's niche in Orsanmichele (*see also* chapter 7, page 172) but moved to S Croce in
1463 where for several hundred years it was installed on the
façade in a niche over the main entrance.

In the second room (the small or winter refectory): *St Francis
distributing Bread on the Night before his Death* by Giovanni da
San Giovanni; fragments of 14th and 15th c. stained glass
including (upper left) the roundel of *St Andrew* by Alesso
Baldovinetti originally in the Pazzi Chapel.

In the third room (the former Cerchi Chapel): glazed terracotta altarpiece by Andrea della Robbia of the *Stigmatization of
St Francis* and *Tobias and the Angel*; on the northern wall:
fragments of mid-13th c. murals found in the earlier church
beneath the nave floor.

In the corridor on the right: an early 15th c. mural fragment
with the effigy of a dead cardinal.

In the fourth room: detached sketches for architecture and
wild-haired saints discovered beneath the white-wash in the
Pazzi chapel.

In the fifth room: fragments from the *Tomb of Gastone della
Torre**, patriarch of Aquilea, by Tino di Camaino (*ca* 1321);
a relief of *St Martin and the Beggar* (*ca* 1338) from Tino's
workshop for a part of the rood screen which once spanned
the nave.

In the sixth room: detached spandrels with *Angels* by Matteo
Rosselli.

14. The National Library (Biblioteca Nazionale; open Mondays
through Fridays 09.00–19.00; Saturdays 09.00–12.00. Hours during
summer may vary) – one of the world's great libraries for incunabu-
lae and illuminated manuscripts. Here too are collections of letters
by Poliziano, Machiavelli, Michelangelo and Tasso. There is an
architectural diary by Ghiberti's grandson and 300 volumes of
Galileo's papers. The nucleus of the Nazionale's collection is the
old Grand Ducal library (the Palatina) and the manuscripts and
codices assembled by Cosimo III's librarian, Antonio Magliabechi
(1633–1714). He was a learned, crabbed hunchback, so feared for his
bitter sarcasm that even the court dominated by the Inquisition left
him alone to tend the Medici library. 'Here,' he would say, standing
before the old Medici-Riccardi palace, 'letters were born again'; and
then, pointing to the Jesuit college across the street, 'there they
returned to the grave.'

15. (*a*) **San Giuseppe** – by Baccio d'Agnolo (1519); the façade 18th c.; originally the site of a miracle-working tabernacle known as the Madonna del Giglio. (*b*) *Tabernacle* with Virgin and Child, SS Peter and John the Baptist; a careful copy of the late 14th c. original since detached and exhibited in the Forte di Belvedere Museum. The original is possibly by Niccolò di Pietro Gerini and the tabernacle was first built in 1280 by the dyers' Company of S Onofrio.

16. Casa Buonarroti* (Hours: weekdays 09.00–14.00; Sundays 09.00–13.00; closed Tuesdays; admission fee 500 lire), Via Ghibellina No. 70 – built by Michelangelo's nephew Leonardo, on the site of two earlier houses belonging to the family. A public museum since 1858. Contains some of Michelangelo's earliest works; working models, and collection of his letters, and drawings. The ground floor rooms are arranged around a courtyard. Starting on the left, are two works attributed to Michelangelo – *Venus with two putti* (thought to belong to his first Roman period *ca* 1496) and an unfinished *Slave* for the tomb of Pope Julius II; room with Roman antiquities; other rooms contain: a fine mid-15th c. predella of the *Miracles of St Nicholas* by Giovanni di Francesco and several portraits of Michelangelo – some of which are contemporary (e.g. Bugiardini's of the *Artist in a Turban*).

On the first floor: two of Michelangelo's earliest works – the **Battle of the Centaurs*** (*ca* 1492) and the *Madonna of the Stairs* (*ca* 1490–2); in rooms nearby are wax and terracotta bozzetti attributed to Michelangelo; the polychromed wooden *Crucifix* recently discovered in the convent of Santo Spirito and accepted as the master's youthful work by many experts. In a room with facsimiles of Michelangelo's architectural drawings, is an original wooden model for the façade of San Lorenzo by Baccio d'Agnolo. '*La Galleria*' – a room lined with paintings glorifying Michelangelo's life and achievements painted between 1615–22 by Passignano, Jacopo da Empoli, Bilivert and others; the large *Madonna with Saints* was painted earlier by Ascanio Condivi based on a cartoon by Michelangelo. Many 16th c. painted copies after lost originals by the master (e.g. *Leda and the Swan* and *Noli me tangere*) are still in restoration because of flood damage.

17. (*a*) **Sant' Ambrogio** – probably founded in the 5th c. and thus one of the three oldest churches of Florence. Rebuilt late in the 13th c. and again in 1716 by Giambattista Foggini. The façade rebuilt in 1888. Buried here are Mino da Fiesole, Verrocchio, Cronaca, Francesco Granacci, and members of the del Tasso family. Much of the following awaits re-installation due to flood damage.

Interior: single-aisled church with wood-truss roof and raised choir. Four late Quattrocento tabernacles on either side of the nave containing earlier mural fragments and some pictures painted expressly to fit inside them. Right side: first altar – fragment of a late 14th c. *Annunciation* mural; second altar – *Virgin and Child Enthroned with SS Bartholomew and John the Baptist* by a follower of Nardo di Cione (*ca* 1370); third altar – *Deposition* by a follower of Niccolò di Petro Gerini (*ca* 1400). Left side: second altar – *Visitation* by Andrea Boscoli (1597); to the right – wooden tabernacle with *S Sebastian* by Leonardo del Tasso (1500) with *Annunciation* painted in monochrome – one of Filippino Lippi's last works; third altar – *Virgin in Glory with SS Francis and Ambrose* by Cosimo Rosselli (1498); fourth altar – *Tobias and the Angel with SS Anthony and Nicholas* and the *Annunciation* above by Raffaellino dei Carli.

Choir: on left – *Tabernacle of the Holy Sacrament** (containing a miraculous chalice) carved in 1481–3 by Mino da Fiesole. Earlier, Alesso Baldovinetti had painted a frame for the tabernacle (1470–3). This now hangs just outside the chapel near the steps; the opening in its centre was filled and a *Madonna and Child* was painted there by Giovanni Graffione. In 1485, Cosimo Rosselli painted the mural which shows a crowd gathered to adore the chalice in Piazza S Ambrogio. Chapel also contains two Andrea della Robbia candelabra in the form of angels (1513). On the right wall of the choir *Madonna and Child* by Giovanni di Bartolomeo Cristiani (*ca* 1380). Also: small marble tabernacle attributed to Buggiano (*ca* 1450).

(*b*) On the south-east corner of the piazza, glazed terracotta statue of *S Ambrogio* attributed to Giovanni della Robbia.

(*c*) Chapel of S Michele della Pace, headquarters of the *Compagnia del SS Sacramento*, built in 1414.

18. The Loggia del Pesce – reconstruction of Vasari's loggia for the fishmongers (1567), originally built for the Piazza del Pesce at the foot of the Ponte Vecchio, later moved to the Mercato Vecchio. Now it is the site of a 'flea market'.

19. Via Pietrapiana (formerly degli Scarpentieri). At No. 7 Mino da Fiesole worked; drawn studies made by him on the wall of his rooms have recently been removed and are now in storage with the Superintendancy of Galleries. At No. 32 the Palazzo Elaguine, a handsome late 16th or early 17th c. structure.

20. Arch of San Piero Maggiore – part of the portico and all that remains of the church. Portico built for Luca degli Albizzi in 1638 by Matteo Nigetti. It was the custom that every new archbishop came here to celebrate symbolically his union with the Church of Florence by giving a ring to the Abbess of S Piero. After feasting here and spending the night as the guest of the convent, the archbishop moved into his own palace the next day.

21. Palazzo Altoviti or dei Visacci (Borgo degli Albizzi No. 88) – built on the site of the house belonging to Cosimo il Vecchio's old rival, Rinaldo degli Albizzi. Façade adorned in the middle of the 16th c. at the behest of Baccio Valori with fifteen herms of famous Florentines (including Ficino, Amerigo Vespucci, Alberti, Guicciardini, Dante, Petrarch, Boccaccio). These are the *Visacci* or 'ugly faces'.

22. Palazzo Ramirez-Montalvo (Borgo degli Albizzi No. 26) – built by Cosimo I for his chamberlain who came from Spain as a young page. Begun in 1568. Façade attributed to Ammannati; graffito work attributed to Poccetti. Ramirez-Montalvo's grand-daughter founded the convent of La Quiete near Careggi.

23. Tabernacle on south-east corner of Via de' Giraldi – *Madonna and Child with SS Anthony, Peter and two Angels* by Bicci di Lorenzo (*ca* 1420).

24. Palazzo Nonfinito (Via Proconsolo No. 12) – built between 1593 and 1612. At first a plan by Buontalenti was followed by Nigetti. Later, Vincenzo Scamozzi took over the project which was carried on by Caccini, and later again taken up by Nigetti. The courtyard was planned by Cigoli and the stairway by Santi di Tito. The Museo Nazionale di Antropologia ed Etnologia now occupies the first two floors.

25. Palazzo Pazzi-Quaratesi (Via Proconsolo No. 10) – one of the finest 15th c. palaces in the city, recently restored. Architect unknown, recently attributed to Giuliano da Sangallo. It was built for Jacopo de' Pazzi between *ca* 1475–8. After the Pazzi Conspiracy in 1478, the palace was confiscated. It was used as a storage house for the Monte di Pietà (public pawn office) and later as the residence of the Medici, Cibò, Strozzi and Quaratesi families.

26. Palazzo Salviati (Via del Corso No. 6) – built on the site of the old Portinari houses (the family of Dante's Beatrice) for the Salviati family on a design by Bramante Lazzeri. The cortile is in the style of Baccio d'Agnolo. Cosimo I spent his boyhood here. Today it is the Banca Toscana. Inside: ceiling murals of the *Odyssey* by A. Allori, 1580.

27. Former Church of **San Procolo** – already in existence in 1036. Reoriented and rebuilt in the 17th c.

28. Palazzo Borghese (Via Ghibellina No. 110) – the finest neo-classical palace in Florence. Built in 1821 by Baccani for Prince Camillo Borghese on the site of a former Salviati palace.

JUSTICE, DYEING AND FRANCISCANS

No other Florentine quarter was until 1966 more densely populated than that bound by the Bargello, S Croce and S Ambrogio. In no other neighbourhood are the traces of the succeeding ages of Florentine history so visible. The streets and buildings forming the Piazza Peruzzi and the Via Torta still follow the lines of the ancient Roman amphitheatre. The criminal courts which for centuries were housed in the Bargello have only moved down the street (in the sixteenth century to Piazza dei Giudici; and in the last century to S Firenze). The lawyers' offices still cluster near by in the Via de' Rustici and the Via dell' Anguillara. The stationers, who supplied the lawyers, the bibliophiles, and the learned monks of the Badia, are still concentrated in the area where they were in the fifteenth and sixteenth centuries. Only the street names have changed: the Via dei Librai is now part of the Via Condotta, and the Via dei Cartolai has been absorbed by the Via Proconsolo.

It was these stationers who employed the scribes and illuminators for the books ordered by the great collectors – the Medici, Pope Nicolas V, Federigo da Montefeltro and Matthias Corvinus, King of Hungary. Even after the invention of printing it was some time before the technique was made much of in Florence. In the years between 1471 and 1474 when there were at least a dozen printers in Venice there were only two in Florence. Vespasiano da Bisticci, whose shop was in the Via dei Librai, tells us that one of his clients would have been ashamed to have a printed book in his collection. It was only the sudden rage for devotional literature that created the demand for cheap books at the end of the century.

Other street names retrace the route taken by condemned criminals from the Bargello to the gallows at the Porta di Giustizia (now Piazza Piave). Down the Via Proconsolo the grim procession turned up the Via de' Neri – named after the pious company of black-robed lay-brothers who comforted the prisoners on their last walk through Florence. After the Borgo S Croce they passed through the Via de' Malcontenti (the Street of the Malcontents), which ended at the gallows. The street is still a sad one, for many of the houses on it are squalid hostels for the aged. Curiously, when it came to commemorating Beccaria, the man responsible for ending capital punishment in Italy, the piazza chosen to honour him was not the site of the old public gallows but the next piazza up the Viale.

THE BARGELLO. From the outside, the Bargello is a grim fortress: the doors and windows are small and few, there is hardly any decoration. Its real façade is hidden within and faces the loggiaed courtyard which often served as a place of execution. Here are the beautifully proportioned gallery, the elegant outdoor staircase, the walls studded with the *stemmae* of its resident governors and the emblems of the city's wards. Many of these are splendid reliefs with fierce helmets, furling plumes and taloned paws. Fifty years before the beginning of the Palazzo Vecchio, the Florentines decided to build the Bargello *ca* 1250 to house the city's chief magistrate, or podestà. Law required the podestà always to be a foreigner: he had to come from a place at least fifty miles distant. The rules today for the modern garrisons of carabinieri are much the same; south Italians are sent to the Trentino, and northerners are dispatched to the south. The podestà's term was for only one year. Having a foreigner unfamiliar with municipal politics as the highest judicial official, the Commune hoped to have a fair judge in a city torn by factional strife and family feuds. Even so, the Florentines were often dissatisfied with their podestà. Workers stormed the building in 1292 and afterwards there were the legal reforms which were the closest thing to a constitution Florence ever got: Giano della Bella's *Ordinances of Justice*. After the expulsion of the Duke of Athens in 1343, the building was sacked, the prisoners released, a huge bonfire was made of all the accumulated documents and a citizens' committee took over most of the podestà's authority. The one surviving relic in the building of the Duke of Athens's regime are his arms on the keystone of the vaults in the Great Hall.

Often criminals were punished not only by explusion or execution. They were further disgraced by having their images painted on the walls of the Bargello's tower or those of its inner courtyard. All these have long since been cancelled out, but one such defamatory mural (the *Duke of Athens being chased from Florence under the vengeful eye of St Anne*) is still to be seen in the Palazzo Vecchio. Botticelli treated the members of the Pazzi Conspiracy to a similar pictorial fate on the walls behind the Palazzo Vecchio. When one of the plotters, Bernardo Baroncelli, was hanged from a window of the Bargello, Leonardo da Vinci made a drawing (now in Bayonne) of the pitiful corpse in its once exotic dress. It was really the dress that interested him and he carefully jotted down its details beside the drawing: 'Tawny cap; black satin vest; Black sleeveless coat lined; a turquoise blue jacket lined with fox; and the collar of the jacket appliqued with black and red velvet; Bernardo di Bandino Baroncigli; Black hose.'

Verses sometimes accompanied the defamatory murals. Here is one which was inscribed beneath a traitor in 1389 who was painted hung in chains and surrounded by devils:

> *Superbo, avaro, traditor, bugiardo,*
> *Lussurioso, ingrato e pien d'inganni,*
> *Son Bonaccorso di Lapo Giovanni.*

(Proud, greedy, traitor, liar, lustful, ungrateful, full of deceits, I am Bonaccorso di Lapo Giovanni)

Not all the Bargello's prisoners were given public execution. Bernardo Antinori was strangled in his cell in 1578, others were burnt, some hanged, many were decapitated. For the record, the deaths of political prisoners were explained away by formulas such as 'for affairs of state', or 'for speaking ill of the Republic', or even 'for unknown reasons'. But often men of influence eluded justice. They could flee the city and eventually annul their sentences by payment of a fine. Of the five members of the Medici sentenced to death between 1343 and 1360 not one was actually executed. In the middle of the Trecento, Matteo Villani complained: 'The powerful citizens who commit the greatest wrongs are never punished, while the small and weak are hanged, broken in pieces and decapitated for every petty misdemeanour.'

Here are some early statutes of the podestà. Once a year the residents of Rubiana in Val d'Ema were obliged to supply figs for the podestà's general council consisting of 390 men. Some regulations for town dwellers were very rigid and one does not know how strictly they were observed. If an armed servant was found on the streets without his master after curfew he risked losing a hand. No one was allowed on the streets after dark without a lantern. Lovers were forbidden to make dawn serenades under pain of a fine or forfeiture of the lute, viol, or other offending instrument.

THE DYERS OF SANTA CROCE. S Croce was always a workers' quarter. During the fourteenth and fifteenth centuries it was populated with carders, combers and dyers of wool. The Corso dei Tintori and the river front were packed with them. Even the basements of palaces belonging to the rich cloth merchants of the quarter were often built to accommodate the dyers' vats. The Palazzo Corsi at Via de' Benci No. 6 (now the Horne Museum) is an example. The dyers' main drying-shed was the *Tiratoio dei Castellani* on the bank between the Piazza Mentana and the Piazza dei Giudici on the site of the present Stock Exchange. On the wharf in front of it timber which had come down the Arno from the Casentino forests was landed. The timber was used in quantity for the beams (*travi*) of the drying-racks and from this came the Piazza Mentana's original name: Piazza delle Travi. Mentana is the name of a Garibaldian battle near Rome.

So famous were the deep, rich dyes of Florence that finished cloth came all the way from France and Flanders to the Arno to be dyed. Also, Florence was closer to the Orient and the Mediterranean where the best dyes and fixatives came from. The colours often had names which smack of the affectionate sarcasm for which Florentines are famous; there were browns known as 'little monk', 'small beret', and 'lion's pelt' (*monachino, berrettino, pelo di leone*). A shade of pink was 'dry Turkish rose' (*rosa secca di turchino*) and blues called '*cilestrino*' and '*alessandrino*' (a pale blue with metallic lights).

The most admired colours were rare red dyes: vermilion which came from a crystalline substance obtained on the shores of the Red Sea; purplish-red from a lichen called *oricello* imported from Majorca; cochineal from a small, granular Mediterranean insect called *coccus ilicis*; and later, brazil which came from a West Indian tree *Caesalpina sappan*). These reds often went by the general name of *Grana* – the very best of which was reserved for a fine cloth called scarlet, with which a shade of red eventually became identified. *Grana* today, in Florentine slang, means Parmesan cheese or 'lots of cash'. One Florentine family owed its name to the famous red dyes; the Rucellai from *oricello*.

Some colours used by Florentine dyers lay close at hand such as the bright yellow used for silk which came from the fields of crocuses which were the speciality of S Gimignano. Aloes, on the other hand, which were essential for making all the dyes colour-fast, had to be brought from Constantinople, Smyrna, Aleppo and Alexandria.

Exotic colours and brilliant stuffs daily passed through the dyers' hands, but the dyers' lives were grim. The land around the Corso dei

101

Tintori was marshy and the wooden houses packed around S Croce were an infamous slum. The dyers had no guild of their own. They had the consolation of a religious brotherhood – the Company of S Onofrio – S Onofrio being a hermit who lived in the desert clothed only by a girdle of prickly vines. Once a year, on June 11th, they staged a horse race down the Corso dei Tintori in honour of their patron saint and the Florentine victory of Campaldino (1289) which happened to fall on his feast-day. In the Via de' Malcontenti along S Croce's northern flank they built themselves a little church, adding a hospital in 1339.

The cloth-makers and dyers got beggarly pay although Florentine power depended on their work. They were utterly at the mercy of the great merchant bankers' guilds – the Lana, Calimala and Seta. The exercise of the craft itself was a privilege which only the guild could grant. Infringement of its rules could mean expulsion from the guild for life, which was virtually a sentence to death by starvation. When Ciuto Brandini tried to organize a wool-workers' guild in 1345 for the S Croce quarter, he was promptly arrested by the officials of the Commune. The carders and wool-combers went on strike and a contemporary diarist tells us that they 'went to the prior and urged them to restore Ciuto safe and sound . . . and they also wished to be better paid. And Ciuto was then hanged by the neck.'

The cloth industry was simply too important to the prosperity of Florentine business to risk social experiment. This may be the reason why none of the ranks of specialized artisans (carders, shearers, weavers, dyers, etc.) had a guild of their own, while the less numerous butchers, hosiers, smiths and furriers did. The position of the painters was not much better; their lot was thrown in with the doctors, apothecaries and dealers in spices – the Arte dei Medici e Speziali.

Matters finally took a turn for the better in 1378 with the Ciompi Revolt.[1] The power of the conservative Parte Guelfa and the few all-powerful merchants' guilds was broken and at last the dyers and wool-workers were allowed to organize their own guilds.

PIAZZA SANTA CROCE AND THE FRANCISCANS. Italian life has

[1]*Ciompi:* a Florentinization of the French *compere* which gradually became the label of the labouring proletariat (or *popolo minuto*). The Florentines probably picked up the word from the French troops who occupied Florence in 1343 during the brief reign of Gualtiero di Brienne, the Duke of Athens, who gave vague approval to the idea of letting the disenfranchised wool workers organize independent guilds.

always had a gregarious, outdoor character; hence the importance of loggias and piazzas. No one here has patience to sit still indoors for long. Italian chairs of all periods are notoriously uncomfortable. There are more bars serving standing customers in a hurry to get outside again than *caffès* with tables and chairs. Almost the only thing Italians have patience for is a good talker. To this they are ready to listen for hours. Until a monument, posts and chains got in the way, Piazza S Croce was the city's main outdoor assembly hall after the Piazza della Signoria. When the early thirteenth-century church of the Franciscans became too small to accommodate the faithful, the preachers took to the Piazza.

The Franciscans, then a newly established order, were supposed to support themselves by manual labour, preaching and begging. It was no accident that they had chosen to settle in the middle of the city's largest slum. The chief aims of the Franciscans and Dominicans (whose orders were founded almost at the same time) were to combat heresy and to encourage clerical reform. To make the doctrines of the church intelligible to the ignorant, sermons were given in the vernacular which everyone could understand. The Franciscans pleaded for a sense of brotherhood, mercy and penitence. This was the time when the sermon became a regular part of the church service. Further, the sermon could now be delivered by any priest without having to obtain the bishop's permission first.

Popular preaching in the Piazza had an immense appeal. It was a comfort for the oppressed dyers and wool-workers to hear the Franciscans tell them that before God all men were equal and that there was honour in poverty. These preachers were not only edifying, they were often very entertaining. Their sermons were full of homely anecdotes, local gossip, lessons from the Gospels and astrological prognostications. S Bernardino of Siena, the most famous of these wandering Franciscan preachers, delivered a series of Lenten sermons which packed the Piazza in 1424 and 1425.

He would begin: 'Italy is the most intelligent country in Europe, Tuscany the most intelligent region in Italy, and Florence the most intelligent town in Tuscany . . . [but] where noble gifts are allied to malice, you get the most evil men.' Bernardino said that eloquence consisted of three things: to speak clearly, briefly and well. Brevity he compared to the speech of angels and as an example cited the message of the Angel Gabriel at the Annunciation. Nevertheless, Bernardino is known to have held his audience captive for as long as four hours. The Archbishop of Florence (who later became S Antonino) disapproved of this spellbinding talker and in 1425 had him tried for heresy. The moment he was acquited, the monks of S Croce had his sign of the Holy Name fixed to their facade.

The Piazza S Croce also served for the burning of heretics and heretical literature. In the summer the Inquisitor read out the convictions in the form of sermons from a pulpit set up in the square. Afterwards the guilty were burned or hanged. Bonfires of vanities – books, pictures, mirrors, wigs, cosmetics – were burned here too at the instigation of Bernardino and Savonarola. Book burnings continued as late as 1580.

The Piazza was known as *la piazza degli spettaccoli* as much for its cheerful sights. The Duke of Athens tried to mollify Florentine resentment by staging a joust there between competing teams from the city's wards. After the caputre of Pisa in 1406, annual tournaments were held. And it was here that Lorenzo and Giuliano de' Medici put on their splendidly costumed jousts, for which Botticelli and Verrocchio supplied the trimmings. Football games and wild animal fights were put on by the Medici Grand Dukes, who also ordered a 'War of Beauty' to celebrate a visit by Prince Federigo of Urbino in 1616. Now, like so many others, the Piazza has become a parking lot.

THE CHURCH OF SANTA CROCE: ITS PATRONS. S Croce has the most beautiful chapter-room (by Brunelleschi), the most handsome Novitiate (by Michelozzo), and the most refined cloister architecture (by Giuliano da Maiano?) in Florence. No other medieval church in the city has more of its original sculpture and murals still intact. All this ran counter to the intentions of St Francis, the Order's founder. The vow of poverty, the renunciation of worldy goods, was one of the rules of the Order officially recognized in 1223. Francis did not want the Order to be monastic, nor did he want it to have churches and chapels. His ideal for the friars was that they renew the Apostolic mission, travelling from town to town, earning their bread by preaching and manual labour. Francis told his *frati* to live in wooden huts when they had to. He once left Bologna because a house had been specially built to make him and his companions comfortable. As soon as Francis died this changed, and before long the great churches of the Order were built in every Italian city, the friars lived in magnificent convents and studied theology in Paris.

S Croce grew in size and splendour thanks to the patronage of the Commune and its rich mercantile families. Not only piety, but civic pride was involved. Just as cities competed for the preachers who would draw the largest crowds, so they competed in the size and splendour of their new town halls and churches. S Croce was deliberately planned to be one of the largest churches in Christendom: its measurements about equalled those of old St Peter's. It was begun in 1294 or 1295 – within a year of the Cathedral and the Palazzo Vecchio, and all three buildings are attributed to the same architect: Arnolfo di Cambio. The interior is spacious and a soft rosy light is diffused by the many windows and the pinkish-yellow stone. So high and wide are the arches that they do not interrupt the vast space. There is something Roman about the majestic scale, which has been compared to that of the Early Christian basilicae. S Croce's architect may have been thinking of these. If Arnolfo di Cambio really was S Croce's designer, it is known that before he came to Florence he worked in Rome and just when the Early Christian basilicae there were being restored.

It is clear from the documents of the time that S Croce and its Dominican counterpart on the other side of the city (S Maria Novella) were regarded as public buildings. They were built 'to do credit to the city', as well as 'to benefit the soul' (*ad utilitatem animarum et decorum civitatis expedit*). The government avowed its responsibility for S Croce by referring to it as 'founded by the Commune' or 'founded by the people of Florence'.

In return the friars of S Croce assumed various public duties. They were charged with the office of the Inquisition, which was a very useful instrument for persecuting Ghibellines, dead as well as alive. Once convicted of heresy, the property of a Ghibelline was confiscated; a third went for the building of city walls and the rest was used for building S Croce and S Maria Novella. The friars were also entrusted with part of the communal election procedure. Perhaps due to the city's alliance with the Guelph or papal party (of which the Angevin kings, who favoured the Franciscans, were the chief secular guardians) the election bags – or *borse* – were stored in S Croce's sacristy.

The Commune gave large sums for the new S Croce, but so did many private citizens of the neighbourhood. The Bardi, Peruzzi, Baroncelli, Cerchi and Alberti were all great banking clans who owed some of their wealth to usurious practices which, officially, were held to be sinful. To appease their consciences and divine displeasure, they turned over some of their ill-gotten gains to the construction and decoration of the Franciscan church. One *frate*, Ubertino da Casale, complained in 1310 about S Croce's magnificence and the great sums raised for it. In 1333 Fra Simone Fidati, an Augustinian, blamed the great Arno flood of that year on the luxurious new churches which had provoked God's punishment. Such criticism failed to inhibit S Croce's growth. The Franciscans succeeded in crushing the faction within their Order which held to the strict interpretation of the vow of poverty.

The families who gave large sums to the church were allowed the official patronage of chapels inside it. Their arms were set on the keystones of arches and they used the chapels as family burial sites. Before the thirteenth century, lay burials inside the churches were rare; usually this was a privilege reserved for monarchs and princes. Between 1227 and 1243 a series of papal bulls relaxed these rules. Until then, affluent parishioners were buried outside the church, either in cemeteries or in rows of grave niches known as *avelli*. A number of these are in the porches on either flank of S Croce. To maintain a family tomb, funds had to be specified in the donor's testament. The family then inherited the financial obligations of the tomb or chapel. If they failed to meet these obligations, their rights were forfeited. Sometimes there was trouble between the *frati* and patrons who wished to acquire fame for the family name at the church's expense. The Alberti, for instance, had since 1348 been patrons of the site occupied by the monks' choir and the main chapel. They wanted burial rights in the chancel. When the monks refused, the Alberti proceeded instead to build an oratory on the near-by Ponte alle Grazie. Although the Alberti did not succeed in burying their dead in S Croce's chancel, their arms, the crossed chains, span the width of its great vault and are set on the pillars at either side of its entrance. Then there was the dispute with Castello Quaratesi, who offered to pay 100,000 gold florins for decorating the still rough stone facade. But when he was refused permission to include the family arms in the scheme. Quaratesi withdrew the funds and used them instead for building S Francesco al Monte, the church of the Observant Franciscans, who were the ultimate descendants of the dissident faction at S Croce.

SANTA CROCE AS THE FLORENTINE PANTHEON. For an Order which made a point of disdaining riches and fame, it seems paradoxical that S Croce should have become the Florentine Pantheon. There are commemorative cenotaphs in the Duomo too: to learned theologians (Luigi de' Marsili and Cardinal Corsini), to military commanders (Niccolò da Tolentino and John Hawkwood), and even to artists (Giotto and the organist Squarcialupi). There were also images of famous men in the Palazzo dei Priori with labels in verse composed by Coluccio Salutati. Already in 1396 the Commune decreed that monuments should be raised in the Duomo to Dante, Petrarch, Boccaccio and several others. Of these only Dante's was ever realized – almost five hundred years later. Cities vied for the bones of famous Florentines; Dante's were never returned from Ravenna, nor were Fra Filippo Lippi's from Spoleto, despite all Lorenzo de' Medici's efforts. But the centre for the cult of famous men in Florence became S Croce. Until the fifteenth century portraits of laymen buried in the church were rare, and when they do appear, as in the Bardi di Vernio chapel, they are relatively inconspicuous, During the Quattrocento this changed.

The earliest examples of a new type of tomb monument in Florence celebrating a man's individual achievement are those raised in S Croce in honour of two of the city's chancellors: Leonardo Bruni and Carlo Marsuppini. Both were great scholars, humanists and patriots. Bruni's translations of Plato, Demosthenes, Aristotle and Plutarch were celebrated for their beauty and precision. He was the author of the most beautiful speech ever written in praise of Florence (the *Laudatio*). Marsuppini had been a diplomat and a teacher of Greek rhetoric and philosophy at the Studio. Neither, as far as we know, had any special Franciscan leanings and Marsuppini is believed to have died without benefit of confession or communion. Yet they were given places of honour at the head of either aisle. Their funerals and probably their tombs were paid for by Florence and by their native town, Arezzo. The funerals, in 1444 and 1453, were in the ancient Roman style. They were gowned in dark silk, a volume of their work was laid in their lifeless hands and the city's most distinguished citizens accompanied them to S Croce. After the funeral oration laurel wreaths were laid on their brows. This is the way both men are commemorated in the tombs by Bernardo Rossellino and Desiderio da Settignano. They are framed by a triumphal arch, guarded by the Madonna and Child, and supported by classical sarcophagi.

Compared to earlier Renaissance tombs, such as those by Donatello and Michelozzo for Baldassare Coscia in the Baptistery and for Cardinal Brancacci in Naples, Rossellino's Bruni tomb has greater unity and simplicity. Above all, it is the portrait of the man which for the first time dominates in a secular tomb. The figures of saints and virtues have disappeared, and the Madonna and Child are high up in the lunette. The Bruni tomb is the more severe, the more Roman, of the two humanist tombs in S Croce. On it were based later monuments by Desiderio, Antonio Rossellino and Mino da Fiesole. There is not a single detail which relieves the solemnity of death, but it is a solemnity without a trace of tragedy or mysticism. Despite the realism of the portrait, there is a barrier restraining the world of the living from the world of the dead.

How different in this respect is Desiderio's Marsuppini monument directly opposite. Desiderio was more light-hearted. In the face of death he gives us youth. The most bewitching children in Florentine sculpture timidly stand guard in front of the imposing Corinthian pilasters. These *putti* and the wonderfully varied carving of the surfaces invite one to touch and to smile. Every detail is to be enjoyed: the fluttering ribbons, hanging garlands, rich foliage, shimmering brocade, and the sleeping face of Marsuppini carved to tissue fineness. This is a virtuoso performance of marble sculpture, celebrating the elegance and grace of life.

THE MURALS. Nowhere does the Franciscan character reveal itself more clearly than in its murals. These are the pictorial counterparts to the Franciscan sermons – their sentiment appealed to the populace. Instead of the severe, symbolic figures usually associated with the style known as Byzantine, Franciscan murals represent the personages of sacred history and legend in a quite human way. That the doll in the Christmas crèche at Greccio became for St Francis the Infant Jesus was not just a miracle but an experience which all might hope to have.

Unlike the Dominicans, who overwhelmed their public with dogmatic spectacles, the Franciscans showed in the murals at S Croce their preference for straightforward narrative set in a scale which was never superhuman. Instead of panoramic views spread over entire walls (as at S Maria Novella), the stories are developed in tiers of scenes. The chapels were painted with the actions of saints rather than with doctrinal expositions: in the Castellani Chapel Anthony Abbot, the protector from illness, gives away his wealth to live a hermit's life; Nicholas of Bari, the patron saint of children, saves a poor man's daughters from prostituion and revives three murdered boys. And when the Crucifixion was painted in the sacristy and in the refectory, St Francis was always included as a witness and sharer in Christ's Passion. The image of Christ as the suffering man was for the Franciscans more important than that of Christ the merciless judge.

The disposition of murals was not haphazard. The main chapel tells the story of the *Finding of the True Cross*. This theme explains the name of the church, *Santa Croce*, or Holy Cross. The story had a special significance for the Franciscans because in 1333 they became the official custodians of the holy sites in Jerusalem. All the other chapels in the transept are devoted to favourite saints of the order. Not all of these have come down to us. The places of honour, on either side of the chancel, are occupied by Mary as the Queen of Heaven and by the Order's founder, St Francis. These are succeeded by the two SS John, St Michael, SS Stephen and Lawrence and St Sylvester. When viewing the transept chapels from the nave, it is clear that they were intended to be seen as a unified pictorial as well as programmatic scheme. The wall of the transept above them is painted as if it were an inlaid façade, into which are set scenes of the Virgin's Assumption and Francis's Stigmatization.

Never before did sacred history appear so vivid, so human, as in the murals painted by Giotto and his immediate followers. Giotto had a genius for selecting the most dramatic psychological moment in a story and devising compositions which would underline it. A classical example of this is his treatment of *St Francis renouncing his Worldly Goods* in the lunette of the Bardi Chapel. The tension between Francis and his enraged father is reinforced by the building behind them, which is set so that its projecting angle coincides with the Saint while its receding walls echo the father's movement of frustrated violence. Even the children placed symmetrically at either side of the scene repeat the gestures and the contrast of feeling: one is eager to join the central group, the other withdraws in angry tears. Then there is the group of hooded and turbaned bystanders in the scene of *Francis's Trial by Fire before the Soldan*; they register the emotions of doubt, fear and conversion. The group of grief-stricken *frati* mourning the *Death of St Francis* became a classic of Florentine painting. A century and a half later Domenico Ghirlandaio used it as the model for his own version of the scene in the Sassetti Chapel at S Trinita.

In the Peruzzi Chapel, Giotto's narrative is more restrained – perhaps because John the Evangelist and the Baptist were remote figures of ancient history compared to Francis, who had been alive less than a century before. But even so, certain groups were copied again and again by Tuscan painters. The two pensive servants watching Salomè ask for the Baptist's head turn up in a mural of an entirely different subject by Ambrogio Lorenzetti in Siena (*St Louis of Toulouse before Pope Boniface VIII* in S Francesco). The whole Salomè episode was the most copied scene of the Trecento – it reappears in predella panels and on the walls of the Bargello, as well as in a remote castle in the Casentino – that of the Guidi counts at Poppi. During the next century it was the monumental gravity of Giotto's figures and the dignity of their gestures which appealed to painters of the period: Masaccio used the figure of the Evangelist raising Drusiana several times in the Brancacci Chapel, and one of Michelangelo's earliest studies is of the two solemn spectators at the left of the Evangelist's *Ascension*.

In the Peruzzi Chapel the view of the action is larger than in the Bardi murals. Some of the buildings disappear behind the framework, implying a sense of continuity absent from the simple, box-like stage-settings in the Francis cycle next door. Taddeo Gaddi developed these features of the Peruzzi scheme still further in his murals representing the life of Mary in the Baroncelli Chapel. In fact no other Florentine painter of the century tried to reduce the barrier between the real and painted world more than he did. Thus in his scenes surrounding the window he painted the miraculous light in each event as if it continued the actual light streaming through the window. Beneath the scenes on the next wall he painted fictive cupboards containing the books and vessels used in the Mass. The same taste for realism and illusion recurs in his mural of the *Last Supper* in the refectory (now the church museum). Here he painted Christ and the Apostles as if they occupied the high table in the convent dining-hall. Behind them, like a mural within a mural, there is a Franciscan allegory of the Crucifixion, together with appropriate scenes from the lives of saints. At the very top are painted a row of foreshortened consoles which look as if they really supported the refectory roof.

Maso di Banco had his moments of realism too. In the Bardi di Vernio Chapel at the northern end of the transept he painted a member of the family rising from the top of his actual grave to meet his Maker. But on the whole Maso did not rely on illusionist tricks to engage his public. Of all the schemes in S Croce, his pictorial composition is the most intellectual. The story of St Sylvester, also in the Bardi di Vernio Chapel, is told in serene clarity. There is an internal geometry in Maso's compositions based upon shapes which repeat and echo each other: the tall arch of the wall with its round and square subdivisions is repeated in the design of the settings, the arrangement of the figures, and even in the ornamental patterns. Their like is only to be found a century later in intarsiae work and in murals by Piero della Francesca.

The S Croce murals were not only studied and copied in schemes elsewhere. Several times the same composition was repeated inside S Croce itself. Scenes from Giotto's Peruzzi cycle were copied in the chapel opposite it belonging to the Castellani family. Taddeo Gaddi's rich Gothic temple devised to receive the Virgin in the Baroncelli Chapel was also a great favourite. It was borrowed by the Rinuccini

Master in the sacristy chapel, as well as by the Flemish miniaturist responsible for the Duke of Berry's Book of Hours known as *Les Très Riches Heures* (Musée Condé, Chantilly).

THE PAZZI CHAPEL. Although there were plenty of individual monuments of the first quality raised in S Croce during the Quattrocento, the great age of its chapel decorations had passed. There are only two exceptions, which by coincidence were built by rival banking families – the Pazzi and the Medici. Cosimo de' Medici had Michelozzo build the novices a new chapel *ca* 1445 after a fire had destroyed an older one. About fifteen years earlier Andrea Pazzi had promised to build the convent a chapter-room with a chapel behind its altar in which his family were to have burial rights. By 1443 the building was far enough advanced for him to have Pope Eugenius IV to dine with him in a room over the chapel. When Andrea died two years later he left a sum in his will for its completion. In 1459 the cupola was complete and two years later the porch. But by 1478, the year of the Pazzi Conspiracy, the exterior of the chapel was still unfinished, and as far as is known none of the Pazzi was ever buried there. The documents concerning the chapel never cite the architect by name, but Brunelleschi's authorship of its design is undisputed. Its conception belongs to the period of the Old Sacristy at S Lorenzo. It too is based upon a harmony of the circle and the square. The interior is pure and serene – undisturbed by the accretion of later additions as is the Old Sacristy. Nothing in the structure is left unclear, unexplained. The columns of the porch and the entrance arch are echoed by the pilasters and cornices inside. Even the tall rounded windows are repeated in the form of blind arches. One of the beauties of the chapel is that it appears to radiate light from within, thanks to the predominance of its white plastered walls. It is from the inside that the lucid order of the chapel's structure and decoration is completely revealed.

THE CONVENT. Besides the living quarters for the monks, the convent also contained the Inquisitor's court-room and prisoners' cells. There was also a Studio which by 1277 already served as the university for the Franciscan Order. Two of its outstanding teachers were Pietro Olivi (*ca* 1248–98) and Ubertino da Casale (1259–*ca* 1338). Because of their outspoken views against the wordly possessions of the Church they were accused of heresy. St Francis escaped such accusation because he advocated poverty solely for himself and his friars. In the end Ubertino da Casale fled to France, where he found it expedient to change his Franciscan habit for a Benedictine one. Casale's influence spread through a treatise on the life and mystical sufferings of Christ and Mary called the *Arbor Vitae*. Dante was familiar with it, and it was also the basis for S Bernardino's sermons. So vivid was Fra Ubertino's discourse on Christ's Passion that once an audience of Franciscan tertiaries in Florence were persuaded that they themselves were imbibing blood from the Saviour's wounds.

Pope John XXII did his best to disperse the gathering of dissident Franciscans at S Croce. Some monks retreated to remote convents. Others were dispatched as missionaries to the Tartars. In 1317 the Spirituals, as this faction was called, were condemned and excommunicated. But the struggle within the Order so undermined the Studio of S Croce, that the school soon lapsed into insignificance. The only school at S Croce today is one devoted to the manufacture of leather goods. Many of the neighbourhood boys learn a useful craft here and turn out merchandise for the troops of tourists who are brought here after their visit to the church.

The old convent refectory is now S Croce's museum. Only a few years after it was opened, the flood of 1966 wrecked the interior and most of its contents. Here hangs Cimabue's great cross and opposite it, in a niche, stands Donatello's gilded *St Louis of Toulouse*. Near by was Domenico Veneziano's fresco of *SS Francis and John the Baptist* which once shared a chapel with Donatello's *Annunciation* (still inside the church). Taddeo Gaddi's *Last Supper* was stripped from the wall. Some of these works have already been reinstalled in the museum, others still await the completion of repairs.

STREETS AND PIAZZAS AROUND SANTA CROCE. During the thirteenth and fourteenth centuries many widows and maidens chose to live in the shadow of S Croce, assuming the grey gowns of the Franciscan tertiaries known as *Pinzochere*. A street is named after them. Apparently the virtue of the *Pinzochere* was not all that it might have been and Boccaccio has a number of bawdy tales about them. The whole neighbourhood between S Croce and S Ambrogio had (and still has) an equivocal reputation. The Via de' Macci used to be called Malborghetto (Street of Ill Fame). In the Via delle Casine, Borgo la Croce, Via S Giuseppe and Via del Fico there are ancient stone inscriptions set up by the magistrates banning harlots. Near by is Angel Street (Via dell' Angelo) and the Street of the Happy Ones – Borgo Allegri (*borgo* means a street outside the city walls). Here Cimabue, Lorenzo Ghiberti and Antonio Rossellino had workshops, Vasari says that when Cimabue finished his great Madonna (probably

Bronze head of *Salomè* by Vincenzo Danti, 1571, over the south door of the Baptistery

The Infant Christ from *The Adoration of the Magi* in the Uffizi, begun by
Leonardo da Vinci in 1481

the one now in the Uffizi) the neighbours carried the picture in triumph down the street. Today these streets, as well as the Via Pandolfini, are filled with carpenters and picture-framers.

The S Croce neighbourhood was also where Michelangelo lived as a boy. His father moved the family down from Settignano when he was eight or nine. The house they lived in, which belonged to an uncle, still stands on the south-west corner of the Via dei Bentaccordi and the Via dell' Anguillara. Like many young painters and sculptors of the time, Michelangelo learned by copying the great masters. One of his earliest drawings (now in the Louvre) is after two of Giotto's monumental figures painted in the Peruzzi Chapel at S Croce. A little over a decade later it was Michelangelo's turn to design a great mural: the *Battle of Cascina* for the town hall. To prepare the cartoons for it, he took over a room in the old dyers' hospital of S Onofrio, which was just behind S Croce. His earliest works in sculpture, the *Battle of the Centaurs* and the *Madonna of the Stairs*. are exhibited in the house on the Via Ghibellina which he bequeathed to his nephew, Leonardo. Though Michelangelo died in Rome in 1564, his body was secretly brought back to Florence where a magnificent funeral was given him in S Lorenzo by the Medici court. He was buried, however, in the parish church of his youth, at S Croce.

Around the corner from the house of Michelangelo's uncle is the Piazza Peruzzi. The great banking family had their palaces here and a loggia (since walled in) which was used for banquets and trading. The houses were built on the foundations of the old Roman amphitheatre and when, as after the battle of Campaldino in 1289, extra space was needed to hold the many prisoners, the Peruzzi rented out the basement rooms of their palaces. In May 1406 the officials of the Commune gathered in the Piazza for a ceremony honouring the great chancellor, Coluccio Salutati. After the funeral oration delivered by Fra Giovanni Dominici, a laurel wreath was laid on Salutati's brow. The Piazza today is calm, the only businesses being a printer's shop and several law offices.

Things are livelier in the piazza on the other side of the old amphitheatre – in Piazza S Simone, in Via dell' Isola delle Stinche and the Via Matteo Palmieri. There is an express laundry, an excellent bookshop, a *rôtisserie*, and several bakers. The only touch of authentic quaintness is the herb shop beside S Simone. In boxes worthy of *belle époque* hats are kept entire bushes of dried sage, camomile, rosemary and more exotic items. In jars are natural licorice (in twig form), poppy seed and cinnamon bark. Labels explain the contents of others: *Fieno Greco* (Greek hay) to help people gain weight; *Biancospino* (whitethorn) for heart complaints; and *Biondella* (pink centaury) – 'three rinses and the hair becomes golden-blonde' (*con tre lavature i capelli vengono biondo oro*).

Opposite the herb shop is the Teatro Verdi which has a capacity of four thousand. It is where touring vaudeville shows and light opera are given. These are popular occasions for which Florentines turn out in full force. Domenico Modugno, the singer and composer of sentimental songs, gets a larger audience here than would a performance of a Verdi opera sung by stars from La Scala. The Teatro Verdi occupies the site of the old debtors' prision known as the *Stinche*. Many distinguished Florentines languished here because of bankruptcy or ruinous taxes and many Stinche prisoners were used as scribes. Villani whiled away his time writing the famous *Chronicles of Florence*, and later Cavalcanti wrote his *History* here while serving a term because his family owed the Commune money.

The palaces of the neighbourhood are mostly concentrated along the edges – on the Via Proncosolo, Borgo degli Albizzi, Via Ghibellina and the Via de' Benci (where most of the houses of the Alberti were). Of these streets, the Borgo degli Albizzi remains the most imposing – the parade of façades runs from the rusticated medieval tower house of the Albizzi to the richly carved and stuccoed ones of the Altoviti and Ramirez-Montalvo. They are now crowded with law offices, clothing manufacturers and municipal auction-rooms. Few if any of the palaces are still occupied by their old owners. Not long ago the last surviving member of the Altoviti family moved out of their 'Palazzo dei Visacci'. The Altoviti had been papal bankers. One member of the family led the revolt against the Duke of Athens, another was painted by Raphael and befriended Michelangelo. For many years the last of the Altoviti presided over one of the few salons of Florence. To her rooms hung in red damask came intellectuals and anti-Fascist politicians, as well as a sprinkling of like-minded clerics. Then she moved to a modern flat with a faithful servant as her only companion. She remembered her friends on their name-days with the best mocha tarts to be had in the city (still to be found at Robiglio).

Chapter 5

From Santa Maria Novella to Ognissanti: The Hounds of the Lord

❧

SUMMARY OF THE CHIEF MONUMENTS

1. The Dominican Church and Convent of Santa Maria Novella

An older church and the lands around it turned over to the Dominicans in 1221. Present church (begun 1246) built in restrained Cistercian Gothic style by Dominican architects (Fra Ristoro da Campi and Fra Sisto), who were probably responsible for the great hall of the Bargello. Bell tower (*ca* 1330) was used as a watch tower for locating fires in the city.

A. Façade – lower part belongs to the 14th c.; the upper section above the level of the main portal as well as the great columns and pilaster strips are the work of Leon Battista Alberti, who finished the façade at the behest of Giovanni Rucellai between *ca* 1456 and 1470. The right volute was, however, inlaid only at the end of the last century. The sundial on the left side installed in 1572 by Cosimo I's court astronomer, Egnazio Danti. To the right of the façade and continuing round the corner: a low wall with grave niches known as *avelli*.

B. Interior – originally its walls had many murals. Under Vasari's direction the walls were whitewashed, the monks' choir and rood screen were demolished, and gabled tabernacles were installed between 1565 and 1571.

1. Rose window with *Coronation of the Virgin* – based on a design attributed to Andrea Bonaiuti (after 1365).
2. Lunette of the *Nativity* attributed to Botticelli (1476–7), moved here perhaps from the Lami Chapel.
3. Holy water font, 1412.
4. Tomb of the Beata Villana delle Botti (a Dominican tertiary, died in 1361) by Bernardo Rossellino and assistants (1451); in fragmentary condition commissioned by the Beata's nephew, Fra Sebastiano di Jacopo Benintendi.
5. Tomb of the Beato Giovanni da Salerno (d. 1242), carved by the shop of Vincenzo Danti – mid 16th c.

115

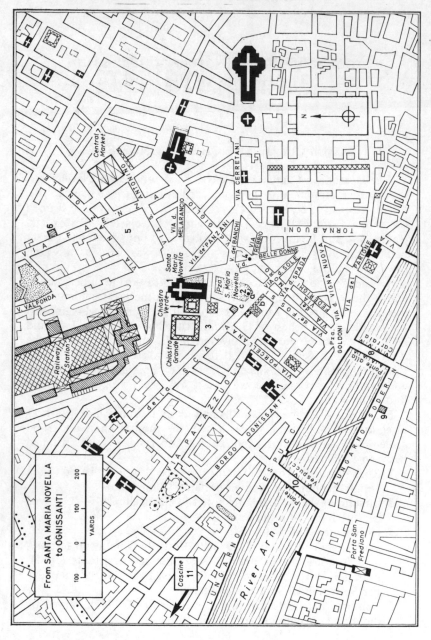

From SANTA MARIA NOVELLA
to OGNISSANTI

100   100   200

YARDS

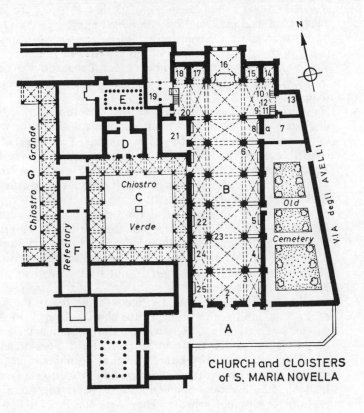

CHURCH and CLOISTERS
of S. MARIA NOVELLA

6. Holy water font in form of a ship, 1412.
7. Cappella della Pura – built between 1472-97 for a miracle-working mural (*a*) of the Madonna of Humility (*ca* 1380); chapel thoroughly restored in the last century.
8. Altarpiece of *St Raymond resuscitating a Child* by Jacopo Ligozzi (16th c.).
9. Terracotta bust of S Antonino (15th c.).
10. Above: tomb of Tedice degli Aliotti, Bishop of Fiesole (d. 1336), by a follower of Tino di Camaino.
11. Tomb of the Patriarch of Constantinople (d. 1440), a mixture of Renaissance and Gothic styles.
12. Above: polychromed tomb of Fra Aldovrando Cavalcanti, a prior of S Maria Novella, later Bishop of Orvieto (d. 1279).

13. **Rucellai Chapel** – built between 1303 and 1352; raised up in 1464. *Madonna and Child* by Nino Pisano (after 1348). On the north wall hangs Bugiardini's *Martyrdom of St Catherine* (early 16th c.); faint traces of early Trecento murals on the walls. Ghiberti's bronze tombplate for Leonardo Dati (died in 1425), general of the Dominican order. Originally the bronze plate was in front of the high altar.

14. **Bardi Ilarioni Chapel** – 17th c. wrought-iron gate. Murals dedicated to St. Gregory; lunettes are late 13th c., the rest is later and attributed to Spinello Aretino. Patronage of the chapel assumed by the sons of Riccardo de' Bardi in 1336. Their predecessor here was probably the *Società dei Laudesi* who commissioned Duccio's great altarpiece of the *Madonna Enthroned* now in the Uffizi.

15. **Strozzi Chapel*** – decorated at the behest of Filippo Strozzi with murals by Filippino Lippi of the lives of St Philip and St John the Evangelist (1487–1502) and tomb sculpture by Benedetto da Maiano (1491–5). The stained glass window designed by Filippino and carried out by Ingesuati monks of S Giusto fuori le Mura.

16. **The Chancel***, or Cappella Maggiore – dedicated to the Virgin of the Assumption, the titular of the church. Chapel originally painted by Orcagna in 1348, of which only the ornamental borders of the vault survive (now in storage at the Soprintendenza alle Gallerie). A century later, Giovanni Tornabuoni acquired the chapel's patronage from the Ricci and Tornaquinci families. In 1485 Ghirlandaio commissioned to paint the murals repeating the original scheme. They were finished by him and a team of assistants five years later. Left wall: *Scenes from the Life of the Virgin*. Altar wall: *Coronation of the Virgin* in the lunette; below, on either side of the window, *St Dominic burning Heretical Books*, the *Death of St Peter Martyr;* the *Annunciation*, *John in the Desert*, and the *Portraits of the Donors* (Giovanni Tornabuoni and his wife, Francesca Pitti). Right wall: *Scenes from the Life of the Baptist*. There are many portraits; the donor's sister, who was Lorenzo the Magnificent's mother, Lucrezia Tornabuoni, is the third lady on the right in the *Birth of the Baptist*. Ghirlandaio was also responsible for the design of the stained glass window carried out by Alessandro Agolanti. His altarpiece was broken up in 1809, sections now in the museums of Munich and Berlin. Recently, another panel from the altarpiece, *St Peter Martyr*, was auctioned

off at the Ruspoli–Talleyrand sale to a private buyer. Present altar, 1860. Choir stalls (incorporating some 15th c. intarsiae) designed by Vasari. Crucifix by Giambologna.

17. *Gondi Chapel* – marble décor by Giuliano da Sangallo (1503–8); wooden crucifix (1410–14) traditionally attributed to Brunelleschi. It is supposed to have been carved by him after his criticism of Donatello's cross carved for S Croce. Two stuccoed angels by Francesco Gargiolli (1602). Late 13th c. fresco fragments in the vault.

18. *Gaddi Chapel* – décor designed by G. A. Dosio (late 16th c.), murals by Alessandro Allori (1577). The altar-piece is Bronzino's last work. Bas-reliefs of *Mary's Presentation in the Temple* and the *Marriage of the Virgin* by Giovanni dell' Opera.

19. *Strozzi Chapel** – dedicated to St Thomas Aquinas; built *ca* 1340–50. Altarpiece signed and dated by Orcagna (1354–7): *Christ giving the Keys to St Peter and the Book of Knowledge to St Thomas.* The murals (*ca* 1351–7) are by Orcagna's brother, Nardo di Cione. They show the *Last Judgement* on the altar wall, *Paradise* on the left and the *Inferno* on the right. Dante is represented among the Blessed in the *Last Judgement* (third from left, second row from the top). The donor and his wife appear in the *Last Judgement* and again in *Paradise*, where St Michael leads them to the Heavenly Kingdom. The *Inferno* is based upon Dante's description in the *Divina Commedia* and upon an earlier painted version of it in the chapel in the Bargello.

20. Muralled *Coronation of the Virgin* (mid 14th c.), over a door.

21. *Sacristy* – originally built as the Chapel of the Annunciation (*ca* 1380) by the wife of Mainardo Cavalcanti, the Grand Seneschal of Naples. Over the door the great *painted cross** (finished before 1312), often attributed to Giotto. Originally it was set over the entrance to the monks' choir in the nave. To the right of the door: lavabo by Giovanni della Robbia (1498); to the left of the door: a Baroque lavabo by Gioacchino Fortini (1721). On the altar, *Crucifix* by Maso di Bartolomeo originally from the church interior. Wall cupboards: on sides (1743), at rear (early 17th c.) based on designs by Bernardo Buontalenti with ornament added by Guerrino Veneziani in 1693.

22. The *Trinity with Two Donors** by Masaccio (*ca* 1425). To the left hangs a panel painting of *St Lucy and Fra Tommaso Cortesi* by Davide and Benedetto Ghirlandaio (late 15th c.).

23. Pulpit planned by Brunelleschi (1443) and executed by Giovanni di Pietro del Ticcia and Buggiano in 1448, who was also responsible for the reliefs finished in 1452.

24. Panel painting of the *Annunciation* in the manner of Neri di Bicci (mid 15th c.).

25. Tomb of the jurist, Antonio Strozzi (1524); the black sarcophagus by Andrea Ferrucci da Fiesole, the reliefs of the *Virgin and Child and Angels* by Silvio Cosini and Maso Boscoli.

C. Chiostro Verde or Green Cloister because of the monochromatic green murals illustrating the Old Testament which once covered its walls (hours 09.00–16.00 weekdays; 09.00–12.00 Sundays and holidays; admission fee 100 lire) – built between 1330 and *ca* 1350 by Fra Giovanni Bracchetti da Campi and Fra Jacopo Talenti. Murals with scenes from the Old Testament filled the lunettes. All these paintings have been removed since the 1966 flood. Uccello's *Creation* scenes, originally on the east wall, have recently been detached and are usually exhibited in the refectory (*see* F). Murals by other contemporaries now in storage at the Soprintendenza alle Gallerie.

D. Spanish Chapel*, or chapter-room – built and decorated with funds provided by Buonamico di Lapo Guidalotti, who was allowed to use the chamber behind the altar as a family burial chapel. Andrea da Firenze (Andrea Bonaiuti) commissioned to paint the murals (documented between late 1365 and late 1367), but were not entirely executed by him. The altarpiece by Bernardo Daddi (1344) which involves the theme of Corpus Domini was moved here from another chapel inside the church. In 1566, the burial chamber behind the altar was, through the agency of Eleonora of Toledo – the Grand Duchess of Tuscany – transformed for use of the Spanish colony, hence the chapel's name. Murals by the school of Alessandro Allori.

Pictorial scheme based on Dominican concern with the cult of the Eucharist or *Corpus Domini*. Appropriately the culminating scene, the *Crucifixion*, occupies the site directly above the altar as well as over the entrance to the former Corpus Domini Chapel. On either side, below are the *Way to Calvary* and *Descent into Limbo*. On the entrance wall, opposite, are scenes from the life of the Dominican St Peter Martyr who died writing the words of the Creed in his own blood. The vault continues the Christological cycle: *Resurrection*, *Navicella*, *Ascension* and *Pentecost*. Allegorical panoramas fill both side walls. On the left, St. Thomas Aquinas (who wrote the liturgy for the feast of Corpus Domini) via divine revelation unifies all knowledge shown here through biblical and historical representatives. The wall opposite is a vision of Christian society; clergy and laiety are united in the *Corpus Christi Mysticum* identified with Ecclesia, or church, shown here in the guise of Florence cathedral. From it procedes the road to salvation with Dominican saints Thomas Aquinas, Peter Martyr and Dominic leading the way to Paradise. In the centre of this great panorama, the donor – Guidalotti – kneels at the feet of his confessor.

E. Chiostro dei Morti – murals from the circle of Maso and Nardo di Cione. At the rear: a small chapel with a glazed terracotta *Noli me Tangere* from the della Robbia shop.

E. Refectory (ask custodian for key) – built by Fra Jacopo Talenti (*ca* 1353); murals by Alessandro Allori. Here are exhibited some of the detached murals from the Chiostro Verde, including Uccello's *Creation** (1431) and *Flood** (after 1447). The costumes for the traditional football games played at the end of June in the Piazza della Signoria and Boboli Gardens are stored here.

G. Chiostro Grande – not open to the public; now part of the school for Carabinieri. Above it were the papal apartments built in 1419–20 to house Pope Martin V. A chapel was decorated for Pope Leo X's visit in 1515 with murals by Pontormo and Ridolfo Ghirlandaio and grotesques by Andrea di Cosimo Feltrini.

2. Piazza Santa Maria Novella – the limits of the actual piazza were established by communal decree in 1287. (*a*) Obelisks of Serravezza marble supported by turtles – all by Giambologna. (*b*) Loggia (1490–5) of the old hospital of S Paolo dei Convalescenti originally run by Franciscan tertiaries, with glazed terracotta décor by Andrea and Giovanni della Robbia. (*c*) Tabernacle of the Guild of Doctors and Apothecaries (Medici e Speziali); the mural is a copy of the original by Francesco d'Antonio (*ca* 1430–40) now in storage with the Soprintendenza alle Gallerie. The house behind the tabernacle was originally the guild house.

3. Pharmacy of Santa Maria Novella (Via della Scala No. 16) – all that remains of the old Chapel of St Nicholas, built by Fra Giovanni da Campi (1333). Murals by Mariotto di Nardo (*ca* 1400). The pharmacy has been here since 1612.

4. Croce al Trebbio – cross erected in 1308 to commemorate the militant Dominicans organized by St Peter Martyr to fight the Patarene heretics. (Trebbio) from *trivio* – or three streets, although now five meet here.)

5. San Jacopo in Campo Corbolini (Via Faenza Nos. 37–9) – the only Gothic church porch in Florence. The original church consecrated in 1206. It later belonged to the Knights Templars.

6. Cenacolo di Fuligno (Via Faenza No. 42) – formerly part of the Convent of S Onofrio (ring bell for custodian; tip). The *Last Supper* – a mural by Perugino and assistants (*ca* 1500) recently freed from grime and repaints by A. del Serra in 1969–70.

7. Church of Ognissanti – originally founded by the Umiliati, who moved into their convent which they built in 1256. Since the end of the 15th c. the church and convent have undergone many reconstructions. The façade is a faithful 19th c. copy of a façade by a pupil of Ammannati, Matteo Nigetti, in 1637. The campanile is a survivor of the 13th c. structure. The Franciscans from S Salvatore al Monte replaced the Umiliati here in 1561. Over the entrance portal: polychromed terracotta from an older façade – *Coronation of the Virgin with Saints and Angels* attributed to Giovanni della Robbia or Benedetto Buglioni (*ca* 1515). Inside: second altar on right – dedicated to St Elizabeth of Portugal by the Vespucci family, with a mural of the *Madonna of Mercy* with portraits of the donors painted by Domenico Ghirlandaio (one of his earliest works), *ca* 1473. Below it a *Pietà* painted not long afterwards by Domenico or his brother Davide, originally made for another decoration elsewhere in the church. In the sacristy: a muralled *Crucifixion* by Taddeo Gaddi or a close follower (*ca* 1340); *Annunciation*, an ex-voto of 1369 originally on the façade wall; and a large painted cross by a follower of Giotto. In the former refectory (since 1893 a museum): Ghirlandaio's **Last Supper*** (1480), which is very well preserved save for the head of Christ painted in by Carlo Maratta in the 17th c. On the walls: the *sinopie* for Ghirlandaio's *Last Supper* and for his *Pietà* from the Vespucci chapel. Detached from the monk's choir (demolished by Vasari in 1564) are Botticelli's *St Augustine** (also painted for a Vespucci) of 1480 and Ghirlandaio's *St Jerome*. At No. 2 Piazza Ognissanti – the **Palazzo Lenzi Busini** (later Quaratesi), one of the finest 15th c. palaces in the city. It is so good that it has sometimes been erroneously ascribed to Brunelleschi. There is also early 16th c. sgraffito work. Now the seat of the French Institute of Grenoble University.

8. Ponte alla Carraia – first built about 1220, rebuilt in 1269 by the monks of Ognissanti. This bridge collapsed in 1304 and was rebuilt, only to be swept away by a flood in 1333. Its successor, also destroyed by a flood, was rebuilt again by Ammannati in 1559. The present bridge was rebuilt after the war to replace the older one reconstructed in 1867.

9. Museo Arcivescovile di Cestello (Lungarno Soderini No. 19.) The works formerly gathered here from parish churches in the neighbouring countryside were withdrawn after the flood on 1966 and now await reinstallation in a new Museo Diocesano which will probably be located at the Certosa di Val d'Ema near Galluzzo. Included in this collection were: Ambrogio Lorenzetti's *Madonna** from Vico l'Abate (1319); Masolino's *St Julian* (from S Giuliano a Settimo); the *Adoration of the Magi* by a follower of Paolo Uccello sometimes identified with the Master of Karlsruhe; the C*odex Rustici* (1448) which contains one of the earliest illustrated accounts of Florentine churches; a *Crucifixion* by Giovanni di Francesco, a contemporary of Castagno's (from S Andrea a Brozzi); a painted *Crucifixion* by a follower of Lorenzo Monaco. In the present refectory, an *Assumption* by Jacopo da Empoli. In the cloister besides S Frediano, a ruined 15th c. mural of the *Virgin and Child Enthroned*, removed in the 19th c. from the tabernacle formerly on the Ponte alla Carraia.

The **Porta S Frediano** stands to the west behind one of the few surviving sections of the old city wall. The gate, also known as the Porta Pisana, was built between 1332 and 1334.

10. Ponte Amerigo Vespucci – a new bridge built in 1957 (architects: E. and G. Gori, E. Nelli, and R. Morandi) in honour of the great navigator who was born in the near-by parish of Ognissanti.

11. The Cascine – the public park outside the Porta al Prato which runs along the right bank of the Arno for 3 kilometres. It occupies the site of hunting preserves and farms once owned by the Medici which were turned into a public garden by the Grand Duke at the end of the 18th c.

THE HOUNDS OF THE LORD

S. Maria Novella has always stood somewhat aloof from the rest of the city. The present church was begun in 1246 outside the city walls on land then only recently brought under cultivation. Even today it is removed from the crowded streets of its parishioners. Unlike S Croce, whose architect was probably a layman, S Maria Novella was designed by friars from its own convent. Inside, the church has a forbidding character and the only cheerful incident ever connected with it, as far as I know, is that Boccaccio started his *Decameron* there. The reasons for the gloominess of S Maria Novella are several: the character of the Dominican order, the fact that many of the chapels and courtyards owed their existence to a calamity, and that from the 13th through the 15th century the church was the centre of religious orthodoxy and political conservatism in the city.

Each in their own way, the Dominicans and Franciscans popularized religion. Both orders relied on preaching and begging. Both established tertiary divisions and societies to encourage lay participation; the members gathered to sing lauds, stage miracle plays, comfort criminals and other charitable acts. Not only was preaching brought out of doors, so was religious imagery. Tradition attributes the idea of street tabernacles to the Dominican preacher St Peter Martyr. It was to accommodate his audiences that the Piazza in front of S Maria Novella was enlarged in 1244–5. Peter, the son of Patarene heretics, instituted the city's most popular religious company, *La Compagnia dei Laudesi*, which called itself a society for the defence of the faith. Later it was also responsible for the Bigallo orphanage.

THE DOMINICANS. The Dominicans, unlike the Franciscans, were from the very start a militant clerical order. The conquest of heresy was their initial task. Their very name means Hounds of the Lord (*Domini canes*). St Dominic, a Spanish fanatic, fought heresy not with love as the Franciscans did, but with the sword and fiery tirades. The Dominicans even led street fights against suspected unbelievers. The stone cross of Trebbio at the near-by cross-roads of Via delle Belle Donne and Via del Moro marks the spot of such a battle. It is one of the curious ironies of the time that the office of the Inquisition was in 1254 transferred from them to the Franciscans, who had the milder, less orthodox reputation.

As pillars of orthodoxy, the Dominicans contrived intellectual systems blending secular ideas with the theology of the Church Fathers. They were less interested in making sacred history popular than in impressing the faithful with the infallibility of a theological system. This explains the appearance of many of the large murals at S Maria Novella which are not so much illustrations of stories but dogmatic expositions. The same spirit ruled the convent and school of the church. Secular interpretations of the Bible were discouraged and vernacular translations were read with caution. The provincial chapter meeting of 1335 even forbade the monks to read Dante. In spite of this, the poet's portrait appears among the Blessed in the

Strozzi Chapel, while the vision of Hell painted beside it is largely based upon his description of it in the *Divina Commedia*.

The Dominicans encouraged acts of mass penitence. Their sermons could whip up feelings of guilt and fear, as well as incite violence against suspected heretics. This drove some into organized companies of Flagellants. Early in the 14th c. groups of these gathered at S Maria Novella on the first and third Sundays of every month to whip themselves and sing lauds. Once a troop of 10,000 from Lombardy, dressed in Dominican habits, stopped here on their way to Rome. A dove bearing a bough in its beak was sewn to their mantles. They arrived in groups of twenty-five, carrying the Cross before them, shouting 'Peace and Mercy'. Then they would go into the church, cast off their garments before the altar and whip themselves with their belts. Meanwhile the Florentines set up tables in the Piazza so that as many as five hundred could be fed there at a time.

The great plague of 1348 and the various economic disasters which coincided with it seemed to confirm what the Dominicans had always predicted. It was generally regarded as an act of divine punishment, a virtual triumph of death. Half of Florence was carried off by it. Workers, artisans, monks and businessmen were stricken alike. Unemployment, famine and political unrest followed. Many of the chapels and courtyards which give to S Maria Novella its solemn atmosphere were built with funds left by the victims or frightened survivors.

THE CHIOSTRO VERDE AND THE SPANISH CHAPEL. Turino Baldese gave a thousand florins for the painting of the 'story of the entire Old Testament from beginning to end'. Some eighty years later it was eventually carried out by Paolo Uccello and several contemporaries on the walls of the Chiostro Verde. Turino Baldese also gave money to start the revestment of the façade as well as the building of the altar of the Holy Sacrament on the other side of Florence at S Ambrogio. Buonamico di Lapo Guidalotti, whose wife perished in the plague, provided for the construction and decoration of a new chapter-room, the 'Spanish Chapel'. Its walls, painted by Andrea Bonaiuti and others between *ca* 1366 and 1368, propound Redemption through Christ via His Dominican agents. Christ's Passion over the altar faces the story of St Peter Martyr on the entrance wall. At the sides, the Apotheosis of St Thomas Aquinas confronts a view of Christian society wherein the Dominicans exhort, convert and minister to the penitent along the road to Paradise. It is a Paradise of unsmiling angels, stern saints and a Christ who sits aloof holding book and key. As a pictorial scheme, these murals were the largest, most ambitious piece of pictorial theology of their time. The room was often used as a clerical tribunal, and in 1374, not long after the murals were finished, St Catherine of Siena was brought here to defend her mystic visions and to justify her outspoken criticism of the Pope's exile in Avignon.

THE STROZZI CHAPEL. During the same period, the Strozzi Chapel had its altarpiece painted by Andrea Orcagna and its murals by his brother, Nardo di Cione. As in the Spanish Chapel, each wall is treated as a single overwhelming spectacle celebrating the immutable hierarchy of the divine order of things in the Last Judgment, Inferno and Paradise. The altar-piece has the same character. Instead of the conventional polyptych with its many subdivisions, all the protagonists appear on a single panel: a stony-faced Christ hands His book to St Thomas Aquinas and His key to St Peter. Neither in the face of Christ nor in any of His saints is there a flicker of tenderness or sympathetic human interest; the picture is not so much a devotional image as a declaration of authority, a ceremonial admonition.

The Strozzi, however, were not among the intimidated. They were proud of their place in the world and the Dominicans did not discourage their exhibition of it. Nor were the Strozzi over-anxious about their status in the hereafter. They had Nardo di Cione paint their portraits twice in the chapel: Strozzi and his wife (probably Diana and her husband, Jacopo di Strozza degli Strozzi) rank among the Blessed in the Last Judgment and an angel leads them by the hand into Paradise.

THE RUCELLAI CHAPEL. Another family of benefactors to the the church were the Rucellai. Their chapel faces that of the Strozzi at the opposite end of the transept. The Rucellai were also responsible for the completion of the marble inlays on the façade. To do the job, they hired Leon Battista Alberti, who had also designed the family palace. The Dominicans had no objection to having the donor's name inscribed in bold Roman capitals across the façade nor to the inclusion of his emblem, the Sail of Fortune, all over it. Apart from the Romanesque Baptistery and S Miniato al Monte, S Maria Novella's façade was the only one in Florence largely completed before the end of the fifteenth century.

QUATTROCENTO MURALS. After the painting of the Chiostro Verde was begun in the first years of the century, few great mural schemes were painted in the church. The greatest single mural was Masaccio's *Trinity* of about 1425. It was probably painted for one of the Lenzi family who had been *gonfaloniere di giustizia*. He and his wife kneel at the foot of the Cross and are equal in size to Mary and John, their intercessors. The theme is again a dogmatic one – the Trinity – which is here given a very tangible form. The Dominician calendar began with the Trinity and their favourite feast, Corpus Domini, had in 1425 been adopted by the Signoria as an official communal feast and this Lenzi was the city's chief magistrate at that time. As with Giotto, Taddeo Gaddi and Maso a century before, Masaccio once more tried to bring the real and sacred worlds closer together without, however, sacrificing anything of the wonder or dignity of the theme. All the figures are in a human scale and are given a setting which is an astonishing architectural illusion of the Holy Sepulchre.

During the next decades, the stern character of Dominican painting radically shifted to the bright and festive mood of Fra Angelico. At last the Dominicans had a painter of their own. (Oddly, the Fransicans never had one.) But it was S Marco, not S Maria Novella, that fostered his work. The only pictures Angelico did for S Maria Novella were some tiny panels for reliquaries which have since found their way back to S Marco.

Between 1485 and 1490, Ghirlandaio painted the lives of the Virgin and the Baptist on the walls of the main chapel. They repeated the same subjects painted there by Orcagna a century earlier which had been destroyed by a bolt of lightning. The new version was commissioned by Giovanni Tornabuoni who paid 1100 florins for the paintings devoted to the patrons of the church and the city of Florence. Conveniently, the Baptist also happened to be Tornabuoni's patron saint. However, the theme in Ghirlandaio's murals was no longer so very important. The holy story looks like a contemporary chronicle of prosperous Florentine life in the age of Lorenzo the Magnificent. The donor, who was an uncle of Lorenzo's, openly admitted that he had them painted in praise of his city and his family. In the scene of *Zacharias and the Angel* there is an inscription of 1490 which reads: 'Florence fair and noble through her victories, her great works, her crafts and houses, enjoys abundance, health and tranquillity.' The scheme has not the formal harmony or the ideological concentration of Ghirlandaio's murals painted for Sassetti at S Trinita. But its scenes are among the most reliable sources for costume and interior decoration of the period and they abound with contemporary portraits including the donor's family, the painters and such learned contemporaries as Ficino, Poliziano and Cristoforo Landino. However, much of this detail is lost in the vastness of the site. The tiered scheme was just the kind Leonardo da Vinci had no patience with. He hated the illogical piling of scenes one on top of another, landscapes and interiors pell-mell. And then it was all so petty and confused; the noble Florentine taste now preferred the broad view, the comprehensive statement. Filippino Lippi's murals in the chapel next door show the reaction.

THE CHAPEL OF FILIPPO STROZZI. Filippo Strozzi was a descendant of the family who occupied the chapel at the western end of the transept. Like his contemporary, Giovanni Rucellai, Filippo built himself a great palace and he intended to pay for a church façade (that of S Trinita). In 1486 Filippo acquired a chapel for himself to the right of the chancel. It was part of a commercial deal with the Boni family, who apparently ceded their rights to it together with a shop in the Mercato Vecchio. Filippino Lippi was immediately commissioned for the murals and Benedetto da Maiano for the sculpture for the tomb. Neither was finished in time for Filippo's burial in May 1491. Filippo Strozzi kept a firm hand on the choice of subject-matter and was very tight-fisted about what was to be paid to Filippino Lippi. The painter was to get 300 florins for his work; almost ten times as much was spent on his patron's funeral. But as the work progressed, Filippino found he would lose money on the job if work proceeded according to the original agreement. In the end, the painter won a suit against Strozzi's heirs and was awarded another 100 florins.

The chapel is a combination of Quattrocento Florentine tradition (the tomb sculpture by Benedetto da Maiano) and the new enthusiasm for ancient Roman ornament (Filippino's mural on the altar wall and his settings for the scenes on either side). The paintings were begun while Ghirlandaio was finishing the cycle in the next chapel. It was a frenzied affair which was often interrupted while Filippino went off to paint for a Dominican cardinal in Rome or to make a float for the festivities ordered by Savonarola to welcome the King of France to Florence in 1494. Filippino's scheme transformed the actual Gothic structure of the site with an illusionistic architectural framework of pseudo-antique style. The action of the story is contained in a few large views and the subject is exalted by

The Pazzi Chapel in Santa Croce, begun by Brunelleschi *ca* 1430

Detail of *S. Francis renouncing his Worldly Goods* from the murals by Giotto and his shop (*ca* 1315–20) in the Bardi Chapel in Santa Croce

allusions to antiquity instead of to commonplaces from everyday life. The figures seem consumptive, their movements fevered, and their surroundings cluttered with bizarre structures. Sheer visual entertainment via fantastic ornament and audacious brush work begins to loom more important than the communication of a specific theme. In this is already the kernel of Mannerism – the style favoured by the mystics as well as the courts of the next century.

THE PAPAL APARTMENT. Apart from its church and convent, S Maria Novella also maintained an apartment for the Pope. In 1420 the pilgrims' hospice was rebujlt at communal expense to accommodate Pope Martin V, who came to escape the factional strife of Rome. Ghiberti and Giuliano Pesello competed for the design of the staircase and Donatello carved the *Marzocco* (now in the Bargello) for its base. In the same year the Pope made Florence an archbishopric and at last consecrated Santa Maria Novella. This was the beginning of the renewed alliance between Florence and the Curia which led to the Medici becoming its bankers. Martin V's visit was followed by Eugenius IV's. Most of the sessions of the great Oecumenical Council of 1439 were held at S Maria Novella. This was the climax in the history of S Maria Novella's association with the high clergy. Kings sometimes lodged there too: the Emperor Frederick III in 1452 and Christian of Denmark twenty years later. Leonardo da Vinci used the apartment in 1504 to prepare his cartoon for the *Battle of Anghiari*, which was to be painted in the great council hall of the Palazzo Vecchio.

OGNISSANTI AND THE WOOL INDUSTRY. Five minutes' walk to the south of S Maria Novella brings one to Ognissanti. The foundations of Florentine wealth were built on wool and it was a colony of Lombard monks, the Umiliati, who first developed the industry. A pelt of fleece formed part of the habit of the female branch of the Order – *see* Pietro Lorenzetti's altarpiece of the Beata Umiltà in the Uffizi.

In 1239 the Commune leased the land to the Umiliati and by 1256 they had built their church and monastery of Ognissanti. In addition, the monks rented some thirty houses to families of wool-workers. They also had the custody of the nearby bridge, which in 1269 they replaced with a more solid structure. Ever since, this bridge has been known as the Ponte alla Carraia because of the *carri* or carts which carried raw and worked wool to and fro across the Arno between the parishes of Ognissanti and S Frediano where the wool-workers were concentrated. The first mills of Ognissanti which pumped water into the back canals were built by two feudal clans – the Tornaquinci and Frescobaldi – but by the fourteenth century the Umiliati had acquired them. At about this time the monks had Giotto paint a great picture for their high altar. This is the *Maestà* now in the Uffizi. Hardly fifty years passed and they replaced it with a richer altarpiece with more gold, more carving and more saints, painted by Giovanni da Milano. Like Giotto's altarpiece, many of these panels have since gone to the Uffizi.

Tuscany never had sufficient native wool of good quality. But Florence, besides the practical monks of Ognissanti, had capital, initiative and plenty of cheap, skilled labour. Every year Florentine agents bought up the annual supply of fleece sheared from prized flocks of distant monasteries in the Cotswolds of England and the Algarve of Portugal. Often the purchase was made sight unseen because competition among buyers was so great. Wool cloth was a costly item. Before the long process of manufacturing the stuff itself began, there was the very expensive matter of transport. Eighty-five kilos of long-haired English wool cost some 9 gold florins by the time it reached Florence via ship to south-west France, mule-back to Aiguesmortes, and by ship again to Pisa. But if either Pisa or Lucca chose to block Florentine access to the closest ports, the wool had to be shipped to Venice and sent overland from there.

The business of making raw fleece into cloth involved the labour of hordes of artisans for about six months. The wool was beaten, picked, greased, washed, combed, carded and spun (this was done mostly by farmers' wives in their spare time). Then it was woven, burled, shorn (while still damp), and stretched out to dry. At first the stuffs were hung out on the roof-tops and over the city walls by the riverside. Later, this helter-skelter was prohibited by law and the Wool Guild (Arte della Lana) built special barn-like sheds for the purpose called *Tiratoi*. One of these was called 'the Bird's' (*dell' Uccello*) and it stood until the eighteenth century near S Frediano on the bank opposite Ognissanti. These *tiratoi* had enough racks to hang thousands of yards of stuff. Labyrinths of stairs and terraces were sheltered by a huge wooden roof (*tettoia*). A locked gate guarded access to the *tiratoi* from the flight of steps leading down to the Arno where the stuffs were washed and rinsed. After the cloth was stretched out to dry, it was teasled and shorn again, dyed, napped, shorn once more, and at last pressed and folded. A full quarter of the population was involved in the industry. So important was the river to these artisans that the right to wash and rinse the fleece there was recognized as a fundamental civic right. This part of the process had to be carefully timed with the seasons for during the summer the Arno often went dry. Even then there was always the unreckonable; if, for instance, the river happened to be unusually muddy it meant disaster because then the wool and cloth could not be washed. For this reason the entire year's output of 1333 was given up for lost. That year a flood swept away most of the bridges. Only the building of an aqueduct and auxiliary wash-houses eventually brought security and relief.

In the face of all these difficulties Florence produced the world's best cloth and it was sold all over Europe and the Middle East. The wealth of the Arte della Lana and the Calimala (the two guilds who dealt in cloth of local make and who supervised the refining and sale of foreign wool) was such that they could afford the reconstruction and decoration of the Cathedral, the Baptistery and S Miniato. Because it was the centre of wool manufacture, there was greater industrial specialization in Florence than in any other medieval European city. Many of these specialized artisans and the places where they worked have left their names on the city's streets: *Lavatoi, Saponai, Tintori, Cimatori* (the wash-houses, soapers, dyers and shearers).

The industry was at its peak between 1338 and 1427. Early in the sixteenth century, for political reasons, the Medici had the Umiliati expelled from Ognissanti. The prosperous and practical monks were replaced by Franciscan mendicants. By 1537 wool manufacture was in decline. Wars in France and the Low Countries interfered with the supply of fine wool. Furthermore, the centre of the industry now shifted to England and Flanders. The end finally came with the industrial revolution, with which Italy has only recently caught up. Wool is still made in Tuscany, but now it is Prato instead of Florence which thrives on it. It is a sore point among the Florentines, who turn up their arrogant noses at the rich *pratesi*, calling them rag-picking parvenus.

THE VESPUCCI. Besides friars and wool-workers, Ognissanti also had the Vespucci. The quarter was a veritable hive for the 'Wasps' from Peretola – the town on the Prato road from which the family originally came. Silk was their speciality. But they also dealt in wine, wool, banking and the Orient trade. To the Medici they supplied loyal civil servants; to the New World they gave its name – from Amerigo, the navigator. The affairs of the Vespucci and Ognissanti often merged. They used the same mills and *tiratoi*. The friars built the church, the Vespucci built the nearby hospital (S Giovanni di Dio). The friars buried their dead in the convent courtyard, the Vespucci lay in their chapels inside the church.

The Vespucci were on the friendliest terms with a clan of tanners who also relied on the waters of the Arno and Mugnone – these were the Filipepi. It was only fitting that one of the Filipepi, whom we know as Sandro Botticelli, was engaged by the Vespucci to paint in Ognissanti. A picture of St George has disappeared, but the *St Augustine* of 1480 remains. This mural and its companion, a *St Jerome* by Domenico Ghirlandaio, were originally set on either side of the entrance to the monks' choir – an enclosure which rose from the middle of Ognissanti's nave. Both murals were probably the gifts of Giorgio Antonio Vespucci, a canon of the Duomo and Amerigo's tutor. He was a learned bibliophile who encouraged the new edition of St Jerome's *Martirologia*. His interests are reflected in the pictures of the two Church Fathers, who are shown closeted among books and lecterns. These show all the comforts of a well-furnished study: inkwells, spectacles, scissors, a shaker of sand for drying fresh ink, rotuli, some fruit, decanters and a Turkey carpet. On the margins of an open folio are geometrical doodles. There is even an astrolabe, an instrument which was then just coming into use by navigators and astronomers. Giorgio Antonio was probably familiar with a famous Flemish picture of *St Jerome in his Study* by Jan van Eyck, which was owned by Lorenzo the Magnificent. Ghirlandaio and Botticelli certainly knew it, for they based their two murals in Ognissanti on it.

Many of the Vespucci appear in other works by Ghirlandaio and Botticelli. Several generations are protected by a *Madonna of Mercy* painted about 1473 by the young Ghirlandaio for the family chapel in Ognissanti and a persistent legend has it that the beautiful Simonetta, the beloved of Giuliano de' Medici, is represented in Botticelli's *Venus* in the Uffizi.

It was characteristic of Florentine patrician families that they chose to live in the midst of the labourers who toiled for them. The Vespucci palaces have gone. But we know that along with the carts and mule trains which passed through the reeking streets littered with leather trimmings, straw, wool, and dust, came also poets, philosophers, and artists who were the Vespucci's friends and associates. Luigi Pulci and Poliziano came to the house of Piero, Ariosto and Vasari lodged at Niccolò's, Verrocchio for a time at Guido Antonio's, and Machiavelli often came to see Agostino.

Chapter 6

The Arno:
'La maledetta fossa'[1]

❧

SUMMARY OF THE CHIEF MONUMENTS

1. Palazzo de' Mozzi (Piazza de' Mozzi No. 2) – built between 1260 and 1273 and much restored. Now owned by the Bardini family.

2. Museo Bardini (Piazza de' Mozzi No. 1: open daily 09.00–14.00; Sundays 09.00–12.00; closed Wednesday; admission fee 100 lire). The Galleria Corsi, also housed here, is closed for restoration. The palace (built on the site of the 13th c. church of S Gregorio della Pace) together with its contents was given to the city in 1923 by Stefano Bardini. The gallery is especially good for architectural decoration (fireplaces, ceilings, fountains, sarcophagi, coats-of-arms, porticoes, tabernacles) from all over Italy ranging from classical times to the 17th c.; furniture, armour, pottery, musical instruments, sculpture and some painting.

On the ground floor is Tino di Camaino's *Charity*, a medieval Sicilian-Norman pulpit, Pope Leo X's (Giovanni de' Medici) coat-of-arms, and other stone emblems of the Guelph party and the Florentine guilds which were saved from the demolition of the city's centre at the end of the 19th c. In a room where musical instruments are kept, two pictures: one attributed to Lucas Cranach (a *Madonna and Child*), the other by Beccafumi (*Hercules at the Cross-roads*).

Upstairs: Room XVIII – terracotta bust of *Gian Francesco Gonzaga* (Mantegna's patron) by Gian Cristoforo Romano (*ca* 1470–1512). A fine portrait attributed to Salviati is in Room XIX. In this room also: a fragment of a *Madonna and Child* attributed to Ambrogio Lorenzetti, a polychromed tabernacle modelled by Benedetto da Maiano. Room XVI has a painting of the *Baptist* by Michele Giambono (active 1420–62) and a monumental painted cross by a close follower of Bernardo Daddi. In Room XI: drums and shields (including one painted by Taddeo di Bartolo of Siena for

[1]The cursed ditch.

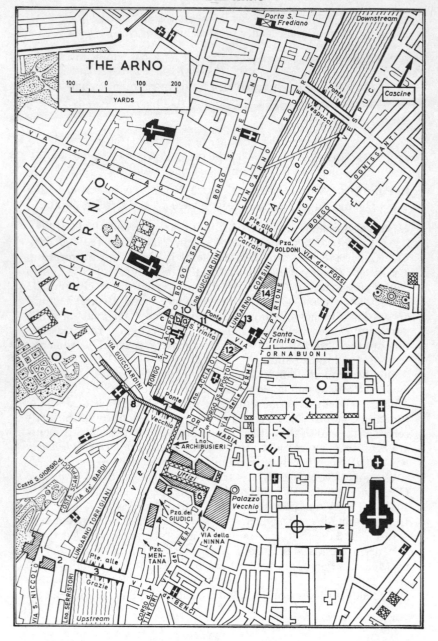

THE ARNO

100   0   100   200

YARDS

the Buonamici family *ca* 1400 which bears the arms of King Charles of Anjou, the first great leader of the Guelphs).

3. Ponte alle Grazie – spans the Arno at its widest point inside the city. The original bridge was built by the Milanese podestà Rubaconte (after whom it was named) in 1227. Later its name was changed to that of 'Grazie' after a little oratory dedicated to S Maria delle Grazie built on one of the piers.

4. The Stock Exchange and Chamber of Commerce (the *Borsa* – built early in this century by M. Majorfi on the site of the Tiratoio dei Castellani, which was a warehouse in which freshly dyed stuffs were stretched and dried.

5. Palazzo dei Giudici (formerly dei Castellani) – in it is the *Museo Nazionale di Storia delle Scienze* (The National Museum of the History of the Sciences and Natural History), open 10.00–13.00; 14.00–16.00 weekdays, 09.30–12.30 Sundays, admission fee 200 lire; ring for custodian. Its collections include celestial and terrestrial globes dating from the 8th to the 17th c., Galileo's telescopes, old maps, clocks and astrolabes; chemists' and apothecaries' equipment, typographers' instruments, and bicycles; optical illusions and a science library partly made up from the Medici–Lorraine collections. Here too is an optical device for burning crystals which was much admired by Sir Humphrey Davy and his assistant, Michael Faraday, during their visit to Florence in 1814. Also housed in the palace is the *Accademia della Crusca*, founded in 1582, which is still the arbiter of Italian speech. (The *Crusca* is the wheat in the sense that the academicians separate the wheat from the chaff.) The palace was built by the Castellani on top of the ancient castle of Altafronte which was ruined during the great flood of 1333. In 1574 the *Consiglio di Giustizia* or *Ruota* (the civil tribunal) was housed here and from this body the Piazza del Giudici takes its name.

6. The Uffizi
The site of the great art gallery, the state archives (*Archivio di Stato*) and the restoration laboratories of the Superintendency of Galleries. Built to house all the public offices, guilds and court artists between 1559 and 1580. The design is by Giorgio Vasari, who supervised the construction. After his death the work was finished by Bernardo Buontalenti and Alfonso Parigi. The bizarre doorway beneath the archway leading to the Via Lambertesca (called the *Porta delle Suppliche*) is by Buontalenti, *ca* 1580.

ITINERARY OF THE UFFIZI GALLERY (Hours: 09.00–19.00 weekdays 09.00–13.00 Sundays and holidays (closed Mondays): admission fee 250 lire). Visible in part of the ground floor and basement are remains of the Romanesque church of San Pier Scheraggio which Vasari absorbed into the new structure. Traces of some of the 12th and 13th c. murals of the church survive. This area has recently been converted into gallery space in which are exhibited Castagno's detached murals of *Famous Men and Women** (*ca* 1450) originally painted in the Villa Carducci–Pandolfini at Legnaia (and until the flood of 1966 exhibited in the Castagno Museum at Sant' Apollonia). Among the figures represented are such celebrated Florentines as Dante, Petrarch, Boccaccio, Nicola Acciauoli, Farinata degli Uberti and the mercenary captain 'Pippo Spano' – the nickname of Filippo Scolari. Among the female figures are the Cumaean Sybil, Queen Esther and Queen Thamyris (the latter two were included because they heroically defended their subjects).

In the room above the stairs and opposite the elevators is a detached mural: Botticelli's *Annunciation** from San Martino alla Scala.

On the mezzanine is the gallery of prints and drawings (*Gabinetto dei Disegni e Stampe*) which occupies the area once filled by the theatre of the grand ducal court.

The main galleries are located on the top floor. At present many of the rooms are undergoing reconstruction or rearrangement (especially Rooms 36–49). Thus the numbering of the rooms must be regarded as provisional. The gallery of artists' self-portraits assembled in Vasari's Corridor is open when custodians are available.

Room 1: (closed) contains antique sculpture including the *Hermaphrodite* and portraits of *Cicero* and *Demosthenes*.

In the loggia, aside from the many ancient marbles, are 16th c. tapestries – including the famous *Valois Tapestries** illustrating festivals held at the court of King Henry III of France and his wife, Catherine de' Medici.

Room 2: contains the three great **Maestà** by Cimabue, Duccio and Giotto – the great trio of Tuscan painters at the beginning of the 14th c. The large size alone of these altar-pieces is a clue to the broad, monumental vision which was then abroad. Cimabue (Cenni de' Peppi), the oldest master of the group, painted his *Virgin in Majesty** for the high altar of S Trinita (*ca* 1280). Although the composition is still in the relatively flat, hieratic style of the 13th c., all the angels and even the Virgin and Child turn their gaze appeal-

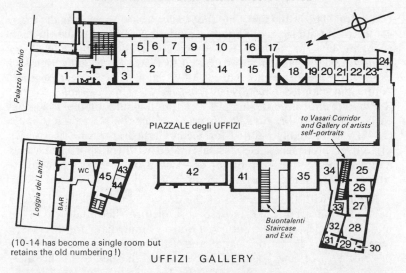

Palazzo Vecchio

PIAZZALE degli UFFIZI

to Vasari Corridor
and Gallery of artists'
self-portraits

Loggia dei Lanzi

WC

BAR

Buontalenti
Staircase
and Exit

(10-14 has become a single room but
retains the old numbering!)

UFFIZI GALLERY

ingly to the onlooker. This is not true of either Duccio's or Giotto's rendering of the same subject. **Duccio's picture*** was especially painted in 1285 for *La Compagnia dei Laudesi* of S Maria Novella. Duccio was the first of a series of Sienese painters who were active in Florence during the late 13th and early 14th c. Ugolino da Siena painted altars for both S Maria Novella and S Croce and the Lorenzetti brothers later painted altars for the churches of S Procolo and S Lucia dei Magnoli. Giotto's *Maesta*** from Ognissanti (*ca* 1310) shows the decisive break with the traditional rendering of the subject. The mood is more severe than that of either of its predecessors; nothing is conceded to sentiment. Only the Virgin looks solemnly at the spectator, but without a trace of the gracious bend of the head of Cimabue's and Duccio's Virgins. Even the colours are severe; instead of the soft pastels of Cimabue and Duccio, Giotto used white, olive green, dark blue and vermilion. Figures and setting are treated sculpturally. The setting and the volume of the figures explain depth and mass.

Besides these three pictures, there are older masters – including the dossal of Meliore Toscano and two Lucchese Masters.

Room 3: (The Sienese): proceeding from left to right are: Pietro Lorenzetti's rather Giottesque *Maestà* (*ca* 1340): Simone Martini's ***Annunciation with SS Giulitta and Ansana*** (1333)* from Siena

Cathedral. This is the first time the *Annunciation* appears as the main subject of an altarpiece. Simone's rendering of ideal grace through swinging line marks him as a precursor of Botticelli. The *Beata Umiltà* (*ca* 1330) altarpiece attributed to Pietro Lorenzetti originally came from the Florentine church of S Salvi. His younger brother, Ambrogio, painted *Four Scenes from the Life of S Nicholas* for the S Procolo altarpiece during a Florentine sojourn of the 1320's or early 1330's. Ambrogio's *Purification of the Virgin in the Temple* (1342) was probably painted for Siena Cathedral as one of a series of Marian altarpieces. He was fascinated with foreshortened views and long before the Florentines he worked out perspective compositions with a single vanishing point.

Room 4: with the exception of the dossal by the S Cecilia Master painted soon after 1300, most of the pictures here date from the middle decades of the century. Giotto's immediate followers are represented by Bernardo Daddi and Taddeo Gaddi. But the altarpiece of *St Matthew*, begun by Orcagna and finished by his brother, Jacopo di Cione, 1367–8, shows the hieratic reaction to Giotto's more humane, sculptural style in the period following the Great Plague of 1348.

Rooms 5–6: early 15th c. painting of the International Gothic style. Here are Gentile da Fabriano's **Strozzi altarpiece*** of 1423 from S Trinita and Lorenzo Monaco's *Adoration of the Magi*, *ca* 1420. Gentile's and Lorenzo's treatment of the same subject shows the two directions late Gothic painting took in Florence. Gentile's is a chronicle of an aristocratic cavalcade full of jewellery, brocades and loving descriptions of plants, animals, and soft flesh – all of which betray the influence on Gentile of Veronese masters such as Pisanello. Lorenzo's, by contrast, is very Florentine in its restraint. There is little naturalistic description and the colours are kept clear of ornament. The ornament here is in the drawing of draperies and postures which make the scene the pretext for a linear ballet.

Room 7: here are the works of the greatest of the early Renaissance masters of Florence. Masaccio's and Masolino's **Virgin and Child with S Anne*** of *ca* 1423 from S Ambrogio (Masolino was responsible for the St Anne and four angels; Masaccio for the Virgin, Child, and the upper angel on the right); Uccello's **Battle of S Romano*** (1456–7) which once hung in Lorenzo the Magnificent's bedroom; Domenico Veneziano's **St Lucy altarpiece*** (*ca* 1440); and Piero della Francesca's **Portraits of Federigo da Montefeltro and Battista Sforza*** (1460s?).

Room 8: many of the best known pictures of Filippo Lippi: the altarpiece ordered by the Medici for the Cappella del Noviziato at S Croce (The *Virgin and Child with SS Cosmas, Damian, Francis and Anthony of Padua, ca* 1450), and the famous *Madonna* with the fluttering veil and the laughing angel (*ca* 1465). Here too are Alesso Baldovinetti's *Madonna with Eight Saints* painted for the Medici chapel at Cafaggiolo (*ca* 1450–5), the *Annunciation* from S Giorgio sulla Costa (*ca* 1455–60) and Paolo Uccello's ruined *Nativity* fresco (before 1460) from S Martino alla Scala still shows the elaborate perspective construction reminiscent of Jacopo Bellini's experiments in Venice.

Room 9: contains five panels of the *Virtues* painted by the Pollaiuolo brothers for the Merchants' Tribunal (the Mercatanzia); the sixth of the series, *Fortitude*, is by Botticelli (1470). One can move the *Charity* panel (which hangs beside the door) to expose the beautiful drawing on the back. Near the window are Botticelli's small panels *The Discovery of Holofernes' Corpse* and *Judith's Return* (*ca* 1470). A century later they were presented to Bianca Cappello. In the corner is Piero Pollaiuolo's *Portrait of Galeazzo Maria Sforza*, who visited Florence in 1471.

Rooms 10–14: the room of the great Botticellis: *Primavera** (1477–8), the *Birth of Venus** (*ca* 1486), the *Madonna del Melagrano* (1487), the *Adoration of the Magi* (*ca* 1475–8), and *Pallas and the Centaur* (*ca* 1485–7). The three pagan subjects once hung in the Medici villa at Castello (*see* chapter 8). The *Adoration* panel from the Lami Chapel at S Maria Novella is full of idealized Medici portraits (*see* plate opposite p. 193). Cosimo il Vecchio kneels at the feet of the Virgin, Piero il Gottoso in the guise of a red-robed king kneels at the centre, Lorenzo the Magnificent stands on the right in a dark tunic, and his younger brother Giuliano stands beside the horse on the extreme left. The man in the ochre robe looking out at the beholder on the extreme right is generally thought to be Botticelli himself.

In the middle of the room: Hugo van der Goes' **Adoration of the Magi*** painted for Tommaso Portinari, the director of the Medici's Bank's Bruges branch, for the high altar of S Egidio in Florence. When it came to Florence in May 1483 the picture created a sensation. Its loving description of delicate flowers and even rough peasants had a strong influence on Domenico Ghirlandaio and Filippino Lippi whose altarpieces hang in the same room. Behind the Portinari Adoration is Roger van der Weyden's *Entombment* once in the collection of Cosimo il Vecchio's illegitimate son, Carlo.

Room 15: Leonardo da Vinci's *Adoration of the Magi** ordered in 1481 by the monks of S Donato a Scopeto and never finished due to the painter's departure for Milan. The picture was a mine of new expressive and formal ideas, of which Botticelli and Filippino were among the first to avail themselves. Near by is Verrocchio's *Baptism* (*ca* 1470) from the Convent of S Salvi. The kneeling angel on the left, the plants and part of the landscape are by the young Leonardo. The *Annunciation* (*ca* 1475), recently moved from the Sala delle Carte Geografiche, often attributed to Leonardo, was painted for the Convent of Monteoliveto on the slope below Bellosguardo. In the same room is Perugino's altarpiece (*Madonna between SS Sebastian and John the Baptist*) of 1493 from S Domenico at Fiesole, five Signorellis, and Piero di Cosimo's *Perseus and Andromeda* (*ca* 1515–20) painted for the Strozzi family.

Room 16: (*Sala delle Carte Geografiche*); Décor consisting of maps of Tuscany painted by Stefano Bonsignori and allegorical subjects on the ceiling by other artists; possibly all executed for the occasion of Ferdinando de' Medici's marriage to Christine of Lorraine in 1589.

Room 17: Contains Mantegna's triptych of the *Adoration of the Magi* (1466), *Madonna of the Quarry*, and *Portrait of Carlo de' Medici* (before 1466) then provost of what eventually became Prato Cathedral.

Room 18: (the *Tribuna* of Buontalenti, 1585–9; where the prize pieces of the Medici collection were installed; of the original décor, the intarsiaed pavement, *pietre-dure* table, and the vault inlaid with mother of pearl survive): the *Medici Venus*, a Roman copy of a Greek original found at Hadrian's villa at Tivoli was brought to Florence in 1717. On the walls are portraits of the Medici and their court. There is Pontormo's magnificent posthumous portrait of **Cosimo il Vecchio*** painted *ca* 1518–19. Beside it is portrait of Cosimo I's mother, *Maria Salviati* (*ca* 1543–5), dressed in the gown of a Dominican tertiary. The most interesting of the many portraits by Bronzino are those of *Bartolomeo and Lucrezia Panciatichi* (*ca* 1540). Like the portraits by Pontormo, who was Bronzino's master, these are psychological studies where the pose of a hand and the disposition of the setting are as telling as the analysis of the features of the face.

Room 19: portraits by Perugino and the followers of Raphael.

Francesco delle Opere (1494) is Perugino's best-known portrait.

Room 20: here are Dürer's *Portrait of his Father* (1490), *Adoration of the Magi* (1504), and *Calvary* (1505); and *Apostles* (1516). Dürer visited Venice in 1494–95 and 1505–7 where he greatly admired Giovanni Bellini. This Italian experience prompted his remark 'Here I am a lord but at home I live as a sponger.' In the same room are Lucas Cranach's portraits of *Luther and his Wife* (1543), and *Adam and Eve*.

Room 21: (Venetians): here is Giovanni Bellini's **Allegory*** (*ca* 1490), an idyllic view of autumnal light and serene order; one of the most beautiful pictures of Italian painting. There is also Bellini's *Pietà* – a grisaille, and a portrait. Giorgione continued Giovanni's warm lyrical style. Several pictures in the room are attributed to Giorgione but I do not think any of them are worthy of him.

Room 22: (Germans and Flemings): Holbein, Gerard David, Altdorfer and others.

Room 23: Correggio's *Madonna and Child* (*ca* 1518–20) and the *Holy Family* (*ca* 1515), which was the Duke of Mantua's gift to Cosimo II in 1617.

Room 24: (*Gabinetto delle Miniature* – often closed): this was formerly the gem cabinet of Francesco II of Lorraine; the pieces have since passed to the *Museo degli Argenti* in the Pitti. In their places are miniatures from the 15th to the 18th c.

Room 25: (door to right of entrance leads to the gallery of self-portraits and Vasari's corridor; open when custodians are available) (the High Renaissance): Michelangelo's **Holy Family*** (1504) painted for the marriage of Agnolo Doni and Maddalena Strozzi, whose portraits (now in the Pitti) were painted by Raphael. To the left: Rosso Fiorentino's *Moses defending the Daughters of Jethro* (*ca* 1520) a bizarre Mannerist rendering of nudes in violent action derived from study of Michelangelo.

Room 26: The *Madonna of the Goldfinch** was painted in Florence by Raphael in a Leonardesque mood (*ca* 1506) for Lorenzo Nasi. Raphael's **Portrait of Leo X*** with Cardinal Giulio de' Medici (later Clement VII) and Luigi de' Rossi was painted in Rome *ca* 1518–19. Andrea del Sarto's *Madonna of the Harpies* (1517) painted for the monks of S Francesco in Via de' Macci; it shows the strong influence of Michelangelo and Fra Bartolommeo. Pontormo's *St Anthony*

Abbot shows his interest in Michelangelo's draughtsmanship and in his psychological penetration.

Room 27: Pontormo's *Supper at Emmaus* (1525) from the Foresteria of the Certosa near Galluzzo, and his fine *Portrait of a Musician*. Rosso's *Madonna and Saints* (*ca* 1518) is flanked by two Bronzino's: a *Pietà* (*ca* 1528) and later *Holy Family*.

Room 28: (the room of Titian): the *Venus of Urbino**(1538) painted for Duke Guidobaldo II of Urbino, the later *Venus and Cupid* (*ca* 1560, painted with an assistant), and the portraits of *Caterina Cornaro* (1542) and the *Duke* and *Duchess of Urbino* (1538). The latter was painted at about the same time as the *Venus of Urbino* and the same little dog appears in both pictures. The *Flora* was painted *ca* 1515.

Room 29: dominated by Parmigianino's *Madonna dal Collo Lungo* painted in the late 1530s for the church of the Servi in Parma and never finished. Emilian contemporaries are in **Room 30**. In **Room 31** are Sebastiano del Piombo's Giorgionesque portrait known as the *Uomo mulato* and his (recently cleaned) *Fornarina;* portraits by Lorenzo Lotto and Dosso Dossi.

Room 32: Sebastiano del Piombo's *Death of Adonis* (*ca* 1511) with a view of Venice in the background. Near by are portraits by Romanino and a *Holy Family* by Lotto (1534).

Room 33: portraits by Allessandro Allori, Amberger and Clouet; leading into the corridor are small Biblical and allegorical pictures by the late Mannerists of Florence – Vasari, Ligozzi, Allori, Zucchi, Jacopo da Empoli, and Bronzino. These are all much in the same style as the *Studiolo* decorations in the Palazzo Vecchio to which the same artists contributed.

Room 34: Savoldo's *Transfiguration* and Veronese's *Holy Family with St Barbara*. Both the Veroneses are from the collection of Cardinal Leopoldo de' Medici.

Room 35: Barocci's *Madonna del Popolo* painted (1575–9) for the Pieve at Arezzo, Tintoretto's *Leda*, and his fine portraits of *Jacopo Sansovino* (1566) and a *Venetian Admiral*. A recent addition is El Greco's *Baptist and John the Evangelist*.

Vestibule leading to exit; Greek torso of a satyr (2nd c. B.C.) and Roman marble boar (based on a Hellenistic original), the model for Tacca's bronze in the Mercato Nuovo. The two Goyas were recently acquired from the Ruspoli – Tallegrand Collection.

Rooms 36–40 have been eliminated as a result of reconstruction work.

Room 41: three splendid Rubenses – the *Triumphal Entry of Henry IV, Herny IV at the Battle of Ivry,* and the *Portrait of Isabella Brandt* (the painter's wife) painted *ca* 1620. The two history pictures were done between 1628 and 1631 for Maria de' Medici, the French Queen and wife to Henry IV. The canvases were never finished, but they have all the vigour and freshness of the artist's smaller oil sketches.

Room 42: (**Sala della Niobe,** usually devoted to French and Italian masters of the 18th c.) – Watteau's *Flutist,* Chardin's *Girl with a Badminton Racket,* Liotard's *Portrait of Marie Adélaide of France,* and works by Magnasco, Piazzetta and Guardi. Room designed by Gaspare Maria Paoletti for the Niobe group, a Roman copy of a 3rd c. B.C. Hellenistic original which Grand Duke Pietro Leopoldo brought from Rome in 1775.

Room 43: (17th c. French and Dutch): Claud Lorrain's *View of the Sea* and landscapes by Poelenburgh, Jacob van Ruysdael and Hercules Seghers.

Room 44: Caravaggio's **Bacchus*** (*ca* 1589) and the **Medusa shield*** (*ca* 1590) painted for Cardinal Francesco del Monte. Other pictures by Caravaggio's contemporaries who were working in Rome during the same period: Annibale Carracci and Guercino. Here too are Rembrandt's *Self Portrait* (1658 or 1666) and *Old Rabbi.*

At the end of this wing of the gallery there are restrooms and a *caffè*. Room 45 is a lecture and special exhibits room.

7. The Ponte Vecchio* – built (on the site of the city's oldest bridge) in 1345, probably by Neri di Fioravanti. Opposite Borgo S Jacopo end, a fountain formed of late Roman sarcophagus and Bacchus by Giambologna.

8. Vasari's Raised Corridor connecting the Palazzo Vecchio and the Uffizi with the Palazzo Pitti. Built in 1565–6.

9. San Jacopo sopr'Arno – the portico is a Romanesque structure moved here in 1529 from the church of S Donato a Scopeto, a church which was once outside the Porta Romana. The church was dismantled and destroyed in an effort to clear the land outside the city walls so that the defence of the city wall might be easier. The portico is the sole example which survives of a type common to many Florentine churches of the 12th and 13th c.

10. (*a*) Palazzo dei Padri delle Missioni – built in the 17th c. by Bernardo Radi; Baroque façade adorned with busts of Medici Grand Dukes. (*b*) The remains of the 13th c. Palazzo Frescobaldi. (*c*) Fountain at the corner of the Borgo S Jacopo designed in the manner of Bernardo Buontalenti.

11. Ponte Santa Trinita* – originally built in 1252 by one of the Frescobaldi family. The present structure is a stone-for-stone reconstruction of Ammannati's bridge (built between 1567 and 1570) destroyed in 1944. The statues, from the garden of Alessandro Accaiuoli, were installed in 1608 for the marriage festivities between Cosimo II and Maria Maddalena of Austria. At the Piazza S Trinita end are *Spring* (by Giovanni Caccini) and *Summer* (by Pietro Francavilla); at the opposite end: *Autumn* (by Caccini) and *Winter* (by Taddeo Landini).

12. Palazzo Spini–Ferroni – built *ca* 1290 for the Spini family, great wool merchants, who with the Frescobaldi (whose palaces were on the opposite bank) dominated the medieval bridge.

13. Palazzo Gianfigliazzi (Lungarno Corsini No. 2) – originally built in the 14th c. and later given a Baroque façade by Gherardo Silvani in the 17th c. Here lived the Countess of Albany, the long-suffering wife of Charles Edward Stuart (the Young Pretender), and the poet Vittorio Alfieri, who died in the house in 1803. Chateaubriand, Canova, Byron, Stendhal and Foscolo were all guests here.

14. Palazzo Corsini, Lungarno Corsini No. 10 – entrance to the gallery is at Via del Parione No. 11. Seldom open. Built for the Marchese Filippo Corsini between 1649 and 1656 by Pier Francesco Silvani and Antonio Ferri. At the back, to the left, a splendid spiral staircase by Silvani, *ca* 1660. Paintings by Botticelli, Signorelli, Giovanni Bellini, Ridolfo Ghirlandaio, Sebastiano del Piombo, Rosso, Puligo, Bronzino, Domenico Feti, Luca Giordano, and others.

'LA MALEDETTA FOSSA'

For two miles the river Arno cuts its way through the breadth of the city – from the bridge of S Niccolò down to the Porta S Frediano at the beginning of the Pisa road. Upon this waterway depended the fortune of Florence from the thirteenth through the fifteenth centuries. Along its fortified banks the cloth finishers and dyers had their mills and drying-houses and the tanners cured their hides. Soap, tannin, dyestuffs and refuse discoloured and putrefied its course through the city. The Arno was – still is – a fickle river. Dry in summer, a raging torrent in winter, it was for centuries the only sewer, the source of flood, famine, pestilence and inter-communal strife. Even today, from June to September, Florence for days on end puts up with little or no water just because the still quasi-medieval hydraulic system relies upon the Arno's meagre supply. No wonder that for Dante too the river was a 'cursed and unlucky ditch' (*la maledetta e sventurata fossa* – *Purg.*, xiv, 51).

For this vital passageway to the sea, Florence throughout the fourteenth century fought Pisa and Lucca who tried to choke her off from the Mediterranean ports. By 1406 Florence finally succeeded in bribing and starving Pisa into her hands. The route to the sea was safe for Florentine commerce but the harbour at the river's mouth was silted up. In 1421 Florence purchased Leghorn for 100,000 florins from the Genoese. The Orient trade thus fell to Florence and to meet competition the city had to build her own fleet. During the 1420s the entire pine forest of Cerbaia, just south of Florence, was reserved for its construction.

Once the Arno was Florentine, her engineers tried to make it navigable. There was talk of digging a canal between Florence and Pisa. The Arno at Florence is 145 feet above sea level and fifty miles inland. To keep the river flowing in summer, it was proposed to dig more canals in the upper Arno valley so that streams such as the Chiana near Arezzo could be fed into the system. One of the last of these schemes was Leonardo da Vinci's He was familiar with the successful networks of artificial canals in Lombardy and a drawing at Windsor Castle shows how he explored the possibilities of using such a system in Tuscany, linking Florence with Prato, Pistoia, Lucca, Pisa and Leghorn. Machiavelli backed this scheme when it was officially accepted by the city council in 1504. But a few months later the plan was discarded as impractical. It was Leonardo's fascination with this canal problem that kept him for ever finishing his famous mural, the *Battle of Anghiari*, for the Sala del Maggior Consiglio in the Palazzo Vecchio.

THE GRAND VIEW. For a period from about 1560 to 1490 the Arno suddenly became a favourite subject for painters. Lyric views of the Arno valley filled the backgrounds of pictures of all kinds – sacred and profane. Baldovinetti used it for his *Nativity* in the courtyard of the Annunziata. Antonio Pollaiuolo chose the view of the river between Florence and Siena as the setting for his *Apollo and Daphne* and the *Martyrdom of St Sebastian* (both in the National Gallery, London), and Botticelli had the river as a foil for his *Portrait of a Young Man* now in the Uffizi (No. 1488). And there are many more examples.

The river began to be appreciated not only for its pictorial possibilities but also as something to be enjoyed from one's palace window or on leisurely walks. These were the years when the boulevards (or *Lungarni*) along the Arno were lengthened and paved. Palaces began to replace the grim family fortresses and the crenellated battlements. But more of this later. With the bird's eye view of the Arno valley which appeared in so many paintings, there appeared pictures of a new kind: maps for explorers and navigators of the coasts of Asia, Africa and America. A number of these maps are exhibited in the Palazzo dei Giudici, which is the Science Museum on the north bank of the Arno.

Among the early Florentine map-makers during the fifteenth century was Cristoforo Buondelmonte, who produced the first atlas of the Aegean Sea and its islands. What spurred astronomical and geographical studies in Florence was the revived interest in the works of Ptolemy. The man responsible for this was Manuel Chrysolarus, who in 1397 was invited to Florence by Coluccio Salutati. This Byzantine Professor of Greek, who had come earlier to Venice in the hope of securing allies against the Turks, brought along a library. Among the books was a copy of Ptolemy's *Geographia*. Thanks to Chrysolarus's move to Florence, the city became the centre where copies of the book were made.

ASTRONOMY AND GEOGRAPHY. The revival of Ptolemaic geography refreshed the study of atronomy. The first observations of a truly scientific nature were made by Paolo dal Pozzo Toscanelli, who was born in the very year Chrysolarus came to Florence. He recorded the paths and recurrence of comets. It was he who devised the gnomon beneath Brunelleschi's cupola (*see* chapter 3).

Meanwhile, the Turks had cut off the traditional overland routes to the East and Europe was forced to look for a safer, quicker route by sea. In 1474, Toscanelli prepared a map based upon his astronomical calculations by which he maintained that it was possible to reach Asia by sailing across the Western Ocean. The Portuguese at the time were the leading promoters of exploration and Toscanelli sent his map and a letter to Fernando Martins, a councillor to the

Portuguese king. In 1478 a shipwreck brought Columbus to Portugal, where he came upon Toscanelli's map and the famous letter. Copies of the map were made and Columbus used them on his first voyage across the Atlantic in 1492, exactly ten years after Toscanelli's death. By coincidence, it was a Florentine firm, that of Giannetto Berardi, who fitted out Columbus's second expendition the next year.

In order to confirm the claims of Columbus's discovery, the Spanish king turned to Berardi's partner in the firm, which also functioned as an agency for the Medici Bank in Spain. The partner was Amerigo Vespucci. Amerigo, who had grown up in Toscanelli's Florence was familiar with the talk of Asia from the travellers and scholars who had much to do with his family's affairs. But Vespucci made his own calculations, sifted for himself the stories of sailors and explorers, and gradually, all the time looking after the Bank's business in Seville, trained himself as a navigator – the most trusted navigator of his time.

The expeditions which Amerigo guided across the Atlantic proved that it was a new world and not Cathay which Columbus had discovered. The concept of the earth's geography had to be entirely revised. Maps had to be drawn anew. The year after 'America' appeared for the first time on a map of the Western Ocean (Waldsee-müller's map of 1507), Amerigo Vespucci was appointed as 'Pilot Major' to the Kingdom of Castile.

Loyal Florentine that he was, and aware of the possible commercial advantages to be gained, Amerigo kept the government at home minutely informed. His letters to Lorenzo di Pier Francesco Medici and to Soderini described what he saw. In 1504 some of these letters were printed in Florence as *Mundus Novus*, which was immediately translated all over Europe. The Florentine cartographers took advantage of this. Francesco Rosselli (who designed the scheme for the famous '*Catena*' map of Florence) and his son Alessandro had a business which produced terrestrial and celestial globes and *mappa-mondi*. As a side-line they made prints after Raphael's designs. When the elder Rosselli was informed of Columbus's fourth voyage in 1502, he immediately set about preparing and publishing on his own an oval map of the world.

There was one more famous Florentine navigator, Giovanni da Verrazzano. In 1524 the King of France sent him out to look for a north-west passage. Verrazzano sailed up the North American coast as far as Nova Scotia, naming the points he saw after places remem-bered in Tuscany: Vallombrosa, S Miniato, Bellariva and Impruneta. In 1542 a Florentine cartographer, Eufrosino della Volpaia, engraved these and other names on a bronze globe (now in the New York Historical Society) on which the American coast is rendered with fair accuracy for the first time.

The della Volpaia were a family which for several generations had specialized in mathematical and astronomical equipment. Of Eufrosino's father, Lorenzo (1446–1512), Cellini said that 'he knew the secrets of the heavens and the stars so well that it seemed he had lived up there a long time'. He made a clock for Lorenzo the Magnificent which had seven planets on it in the form of the spheres of the Medici arms which moved in orbits. Vasari praised him too, and tells us that it was he who was the keeper of the clock in the Palazzo della Signoria. Another son, Benvenuto, is famous for a relief map of Florence he made with Tribolo which was used by Pope Clement VII during the fatal siege of the city in 1529–30.

LEONARDO AND GALILEO. The two giants whom Florence gave to the development of science and cosmography are, of course, Leonardo (1452–1519) and Galileo (1564–1642) – the greatest amateur and the most brilliant professional. Some of Galileo's instruments are exhibited in the Science Museum. Of Leonardo there are models based on his manuscripts and drawings. Both men in time and the nature of their achievements spanned the transition between medievalism and modern science. The marvel is that Vespucci, Michelangelo, Machiavelli, Leonardo and Galileo were not isolated figures. They were representative of the life of their city – a city of 'mavericks' who quarrelled with kings and popes. They did what they pleased even when the lords of the earth wished otherwise.

Everyone knows of Leonardo's many marvellous inventions. Far more important was his intuitive perception, a century before anyone else, of the right experimental method. Leonardo said that only mathematics, arithmetic and geometry give absolute certainty within the realm of science. 'Those sciences are vain and full of errors which are not born of experiment, the mother of all certitude.' Leonardo's curiosity ranged too widely for the formulation of general laws. He preferred repeating the observations in all their minutiae again and again. His notebooks are largely filled with these. To those who tired of following these endless processions of detail, his reply was: 'Impatience is the mother of stupidity.'

Leonardo was the first in modern times to apply reason to everything in the universe: its past and future, and also to what lay within man. His discoveries in art are in the same spirit as his work on geology. It was Leonardo who first dared to say that the earth bears the marks of its past history – a history that reached far back beyond the records of books (including the Bible). Fossils found on mountains, though far inland, were none the less produced in sea-water and could not have reached their present position in the forty days of Noah's flood. This was not the sole occasion when Leonardo contrasted the certainty of scientific observation with the uncertainty of theological discussions.

For Leonardo the earth was a star like other stars; no more, no less. The 'heavenly bodies' were not divine and incorruptible; they were, like our own, subject to change and decay. In his dissections he worked out the structure and function of muscles. He saw that the blood circulated one hundred years before its rediscovery (and demonstration) by Harvey. Leonardo compared the flow of the blood to the circulation of water from the hills to the rivers to the sea, thence to the clouds and in rain again on to the hills. Like the poet he was, he told his vision in metaphors.

Leonardo made a model of the optical parts of the eye and with them demonstrated how an image is formed on the retina. He rejected the idea of his contemporaries that the eye saw by throwing out rays to the object it wished to examine. He saw nature as orderly, obeying rational (i.e. non-magical) immutable laws, which were universal and eternal.

Like the ancient Greeks, the educated Florentines learned about everything. And like the legendary heroes of Antiquity, the powers of the great men of Florence ranged far. Galileo came to mathematics and physics relatively late. Before that he had studied medicine. It appears that what he really wanted to be was a painter, but his father (a musician) discouraged this because there was no money in it any more in Florence and the Galilei had many mouths to feed.

As a student at the University of Pisa Galileo persistently challenged the assumptions propounded by his teachers as incontro-vertible fact. His easy way of assuming that he was always right provoked the hearty dislike of many. Throughout his career Galileo loved to show the other fellow was wrong. Even in small matters he had no patience for mere formalities or ceremonial mumbo-jumbo. As a young professor of twenty-five he antagonized many of his colleagues at Pisa by his refusal to wear the professional toga outside the classroom. All this plus his brilliant sarcasm are very Florentine. In this contumacious spirit he put on the demonstration of the speed of falling weights from the leaning tower: to show that a ten-pound weight and a one-pound weight dropped at the same time hit the ground at the same time.

Galileo soon became unpopular at Pisa and he resigned his professorship in 1591. Not long afterwards he accepted the chair of mathematics at Padua, where he spent the eighteen happiest years of his life. At Padua he carried out his first brilliant astronomical experiments, manufacturing hundreds of instruments with his own hands. He was not the original inventor of the telescope, but he was the most brilliant person first to use it. It was his discovery of the satellites of Jupiter that persuaded people to accept the Copernican view of the earth as a satellite of the sun. The book in which he first published these findings came out in Venice in 1610. The satellites of Jupiter he called *Medicea* in honour of Cosimo II, the Grand Duke of Tuscany, his former pupil at Pisa, who was about to become his patron.

The return to Florence meant the highest academic honours with none of the usual academic duties, and a salary double that at Padua. Within the span of just seventeen years, a scientific revolution had taken place within the confines of Medici patronage. In 1593 Ferdinando I lavished a thousand ducats on an armillary sphere of gigantic proportions; it was the most elaborate model of the Ptolemaic system of the universe ever made. Originally, a handle turned all the parts to demonstrate the harmony of the celestial spheres (was it merely coincidence that just this theme – '*L'Armonia delle Sfere*' – was also used for a memorable theatrical production celebrating the Grand Duke's marriage in 1589 to Christine of Lorraine?). The armillary sphere was also a statement of faith, defying Copernicus's heliocentric theory already set forth in 1543. This gilded construction made by Antonio Santucci still exists – filling up most of a room in the Science Museum. Galileo's publication of Jupiter's satellites (*Medicea Sidera*) in 1610 reversed all this. The next year he made a triumphal visit to Rome. where his astronomical discoveries were received with the greatest interest. Encouraged by his reception, he published in 1613 an essay in support of the Copernican theory. In 1616 the Holy Office ordered him to appear before the Inquisition. Galileo was so sure of his ground that he ingenuously supposed that he could persuade his opponents to see the light. Call it Florentine arrogance if you will, but Rome was not Florence. The outcome was that the papal court prohibited the dissemination of Galileo's ideas and forbade him to say or do anything further with the heliocentric theory.

The real quarrel with the Church was Galileo's refusal to accept theology as the queen of the sciences. He insisted that the truth of nature based on scientific demonstration had nothing whatever to do with the truth of revealed religion. For him the intellect and the senses were as much the gifts of God as faith was. For sixteen years more Galileo persisted in his theory and sought official recognition for it, despite the edict of 1616. The bitter story of his failure and the trial in Rome are so well known that they need not be retold here. He spent the last years of his life exiled to his villa at Arcetri and his house on the Costa S Giorgio, where Milton came to visit him in 1638. He went blind but continued dictating his studies to his devoted pupils, Viviani and Torricelli. Upon his death in 1642 the Church forbade any public monument to be raised in his honour. But Ferdinando II buried him in a Medici chapel at S Croce.

Galileo was the father of modern physics. He combined experimental observations with mathematical description and deduction. The deduction is of prime importance. Here Leonardo hesitated. Galileo's chief and most original work was the foundation of the experimental-mathematical science of dynamics and statics. His discovery and formulation of the laws of motion are the basis of all modern engineering, including space-craft.

Galileo was the professional scientist where Leonardo was the many-sided amateur. Galileo had students and published his findings quickly. Leonardo deliberately wrote his notes backwards so that they could only be deciphered in a mirror. Everything interested Leonardo. Galileo was the first specialist among the great scientists, confining himself to physics and astronomy. In Galileo, the last of the great Florentines, we meet science as we know it today.

THE PONTE ALLE GRAZIE. Until it was blown up by mines in 1944, the Ponte alle Grazie was the city's longest, strongest and oldest bridge. It dated from 1227, was built entirely of stone, supported by ten arches, and was the only medieval bridge to survive the catastrophic Arno flood of 1333. On its piers perched several chapels and oratories. Old photographs show how they looked before their demolition in the last century. One of the chapels was dedicated to S Maria delle Grazie, from which the bridge took its name. This votive tabernacle, venerated for the solace it gave to forlorn lovers, was built by the Alberti who had three palaces at the foot of the Via de' Benci end of the bridge. In one of them died Leon Battista Alberti, the great architect and theorist.

Another small building on the bridge was occupied by nuns who immured themselves for life. These were the *Murate*, who lived in solitary confinement in its tiny rooms until 1424, when the Benci built them finer quarters on the Via Ghibellina. The latter eventually became the municipal prison. Although the residents are now troglodytes of another sort, the building is still known as the Murate.

The Alberti lived at one end of the bridge, the Mozzi at the other. as loyal Guelphs, they had their houses destroyed after the Ghibelline victory at Montaperti in 1260. The Ghibelline triumph was short-lived; six years later at Benevento the power of their party and the imperial ambitions of the House of Hohenstaufen were finally crushed. On the site of their ruined tower houses the Mozzi built the grim fortress-like palace on the street leading to S Niccolò. By 1273 it was ready to receive Pope Gregory X and Charles of Anjou, the hero of Benevento. For several weeks they stayed as the Mozzi's guests. This was the occasion when the Pope's threat of excommuni-cation forced the Florentine Guelphs and Ghibellines to a reluctant kiss of peace. It was July and the Arno was dry; Pope, cardinals, Angevin court and Florentines assembled in the river-bed at the foot of the Ponte Rubaconte, as the bridge was then still called. A chapel, S Gregorio della Pace, was built to commemorate the Pope's efforts and the Mozzi added PAX to their coat-of-arms. The peace hardly lasted a year.

THE PONTE VECCHIO. Other bridges have had their tabernacles and pillories, such as those that stood on the Ponte alla Carraia and on the medieval predecessor of Ammannati's Ponte S Trinita; the Ponte alle Grazie even had its nunnery and a few tanner's shops specializing in goat-skins; but the Ponte Vecchio since time immemorial has been a bazaar. Today the Ponte Vecchio is restricted to pedestrian traffic; it serves as a bridge like the others, but it is pre-eminently a shoppers' goal. It was long the main thoroughfare between the two halves of Florence – between the old centre of the city and everything on the other side which goes by the general name of *Oltrarno* ('beyond the Arno').

The Ponte Vecchio spans the Arno's narrowest point. There has been a bridge here since Roman times. It was the only bridge spared in August 1944 by the retreating Germans. Its survival was purchased at the cost of the old neighbourhoods which were blown up at either end so that for several days all traffic across the Arno was effectively blocked. The bridge became known as the Ponte Vecchio, or 'old bridge', to distinguish it from the Ponte alla Carraia which was built around 1220. The present structure dates from 1345, when it replaced a twelfth-century bridge swept away by the flood of 1333. At its northern foot stood the equestrian statue of Mars which assassins used as the rendezvous for the murder in 1216 of Buondelmonte dei Buondelmonti, who was killed on Easter morning in revenge for the abandonment of his betrothed, a member of the Amidei and degli Uberti families. This personal vendetta was the pretext for a long political feud between two rival factions in the city. To further their ambitions they joined either the Guelph (the papal party) or the Ghibelline (the pro-imperial-Hohenstaufen party) cause and eventually involved Florence in a series of wars with the other towns of Tuscany.

At the other end of the bridge stood a hospital belonging to the Knights of the Holy Sepulchre. It was a stopping-place for pilgrims on their way to Rome. A fragment of the old hospital is tucked among the shops at the south-west end. Near the approaches to the bridge stood the fortified tower houses of the feudal lords, the Amidei and the Mannelli.

Already in the thirteenth century there were shops on the Ponte Vecchio. By 1206 the Commune had established a special agency, the Opus Pontis, for the bridge's maintenance and the renting of the shops. At first tanners and pursemakers were the chief tenants. Theirs was a particularly aromatic trade, for the hides were left to soak for eight months in the Arno and the chief curing agent was horse urine. (Today the tanners congregate further down the river at an isolated point in the neighbourhood of Fucecchio called S Croce.) Most of the shops were built of wood and were prey to fires. When the bridge was rebuilt in 1345 the shops became stone compartments built into a crenellated wall running along either side of the bridge. The rents were supposed to pay for the cost of the bridge's reconstruction in twenty years' time. In 1378 the Commune farmed out the rents to Alamanno de' Medici as a reward for his family's support of the Ciompi Revolt.

By 1422 the butchers had left their old haunts in the Via delle Terme and Borgo SS Apostoli and they gradually took over most of the shops on the bridge. After the expulsion of the Medici in 1494, the Signoria sold the shops in order to fill the depleted treasury. But the Ponte Vecchio, together with the other bridges, continued to be administered by a public agency called by the Gilbert and Sullivan name of 'The Officials of the Five Things' (gli Ufficiali delle Cinque Cose). The 'five things' were mills, bridges and walls, the offices of port officials and tax-collectors, and the property of expropriated rebels. Gradually, besides butchers, linen merchants, hosiers, greengrocers and blacksmiths moved on to the bridge. By 1593 the Grand Duke Ferdinando I could no longer tolerate these 'vile arts', as he called them, which continued to do a bustling business beneath the elevated corridor linking the two Medici palaces – the Palazzo Vecchio and the Pitti. Ferdinando decided to restrict the shops on the bridge to goldsmiths and jewellers. Forty-one goldsmiths and eight jewellers were forthwith installed and rents were promptly doubled, which may explain why these artisans went by the name of *banco rotti* – literally 'broken benches' or bankrupts. In spite of everything, the goldsmiths remained as permanent fixtures of the Ponte Vecchio.

ORFÈVRERIE. Florence was not famous for its jewellry and *orfèvrerie* until the fifteenth century. Venice was known for its filigree work. Siena for its reliefs and enamels, Burgundy for its jewellery. The craft began to develop among the Florentines during the Trecento, when the many new churches and rich merchants created a demand for ecclesiastical splendour and secular elegance. The statutes governing the Florentine goldsmiths date from 1335. They belonged to the *Arte della Seta* (the Silk Guild), probably because much gold and silver thread was used in shot silk. Before moving to the Ponte Vecchio, goldsmiths worked among silk merchants of Por S Maria, which is the northern approach to the bridge. The quality of the work was rigidly controlled by the officers of the guild, who promptly saw to the punishment of offenders. It was forbidden to use paste jewels in golden rings and artisans were not permitted to work at night or in places hidden from public view. The craft then involved the fashioning of precious metals and enamel work, leatherwork (if there was gold on it), sculpture and crystal-cutting. A wide variety of objects came from the goldsmiths' shops – buttons, chains, altar-frontals, leather boxes, book covers, vases, chalices, lamps and candelabra. Little of all this has survived outside church treasuries. Much was lost or dispersed through pillage, ransom, marriage, sale and loan. Often old pieces were melted down for cash, or they were refashioned to suit the changed tastes of the times. Cellini often did such work; he did to medieval jewellery what Vasari did to many old Florentine church interiors.

The goldsmiths' craft was many-sided and painters, sculptors, and architects often received their initial training here. Andrea Orcagna, Brunelleschi, Ghiberti, Donatello, Uccello, Gozzoli, Verrocchio and Pollaiuolo all served as goldsmiths' apprentices. Domenico Ghirlandaio owed his name to his father, a jeweller, whose speciality was wedding crowns or garlands (*ghirlande*). Later many of these artists supplied the goldsmiths with designs. Ghiberti made monumental statuary for Orsanmichele and the doors for the Baptistery but he also continued as a goldsmith. He was especially proud of the splendid golden mitre he made for Pope Eugenius IV set with gems valued at 38,000 florins and adorned with tiny angels surrounding images of the Virgin and Christ enthroned.

PIETREDURE WORK. The Medici from old Cosimo on took special interest in developing a sideline of the goldsmith's craft: the carving and setting of semi-precious stones. Their admiration of antique gems and vases probably started them off. Sometimes the Medici imported artisans to whom they could entrust the restoration of these ancient pieces. Jasper, sardonyx, porphyry, agate and chalcedony were the favoured materials, to which lids and bases of silver gilt and exquisite enamel work were often added. Lorenzo the Magnificent had his name inscribed in Roman letters on the jars and vases in his collection (now exhibited in the *Museo degli Argenti* of the Palazzo Pitti – *see* chapter 9). Even in large-scale undertakings, such as Verrocchio's tomb for Cosimo il Vecchio's sons in the Old Sacristy of S Lorenzo, the work is not so much sculpture as a monumental piece of *orfèvrerie*.

During the next century, *orfèvrerie*, sculpture and archaeology merged into a craft all its own. Benvenuto Cellini was its greatest virtuoso. There was also Bernardo Buontalenti, who designed villas and vases as easily as gardens and festival décor. To pump in fresh talent, Milanese and Flemings were hired to come to Florence. In 1599 pietredure work (or 'Florentine mosaic') was by Grand-Ducal decree established as a court institution housed in the Uffizi. The chief project was a Medici burial chapel in S Lorenzo which consists entirely of inlay work – a frightening monument of ostentation. The *Opificio delle Pietre Dure* still exists, although now it has moved from the Uffizi to Via degli Alfani No. 78, near the Annunziata. It contains a museum, workshops and one of the world's richest stock-piles of rare marbles, jaspers and chalcedonies – many of the pieces going back to the store accumulated by the Medici.

A VISIT TO A GOLDSMITH'S ATELIER. The Ponte Vecchio now has three landlords. The Ministry of Public Works owns the foundations. The city has the piers, the roadway and Vasari's corridor. But the merchants (at last) own their own shops. The shops hanging out over the river date from the seventeenth century. Until the flood of 1966, one of these belonged to the firm of Barocchi, which has for three generations specialized in antique jewellery, and contained one of the two ateliers remaining on the bridge. The little building had, incredibly, three storeys jammed beneath one of the arches of Vasari's corridor. On the ground floor behind the sales room sat an accountant and near him were scales for weighing gold and another pair for diamonds. The sales people are usually former craftsmen who can estimate corals, pearls and lapis at a glance from the tone of the colour. Up a spiral iron staircase were tiny workrooms, a veritable rabbit-warren, rented out to craftsmen who are proud of being specialists in one of four categories: *orafo* (goldsmith), *incassatore* (stone-setter), *incisore* (engraver), and *cesellatore* (chaser). The enamel-work was sent out to the Via Calimaruzza, near Orsanmichele. The goldsmith occupied the topmost chambers while the others worked in rooms beneath, so that when the piece finally emerged from the *cesellatore* it was finished and ready to go down to the salesmen. These rooms were so tiny that there were only a few in which one could stand erect. But each had a window overlooking the Arno. The view is always splendid, but during the summer the craftsmen had to cower behind paper shields to escape the scorching sun.

Most of the artisans had been here for generations. A younger son, nephew or cousin usually worked beside the master-craftsman. Bundles of drawings were crammed into drawers like old packs of cards – frequently studied and heavily fingered. Gold is bought by the kilo from Fiani's Precious Metals' Bank (*Società Italiana Metalli Preziosi e Affini*) nearby in the Piazza S Felìcita. The business of selling gold and silver is in Italy still mostly in private hands. Barocchi or the clients provide the diamonds, sapphires, rubies and emeralds which are usually purchased in Amsterdam. Turquoise and lapis come in from Persia, and coral from Torre del Greco, near Naples.

The tools, save for the welding equipment, have not changed much through the centuries. Lying about in odd corners, next to cages of canaries and robins, are ancient machines for rolling gold into wire and the finest thread. There are tiny crucibles of glazed crockery and a piece of hollowed charcoal used for melting silver into globules. This is how the florin was made and accounts for its characteristically irregular shape. The drop of soft metal was simply rolled on to a firm flat surface and given a hammer blow which printed the coin's mark upon it.

There is still plenty of opportunity for improvization. The real test of a workman's quality is his ability to make holes that exactly fit the given stones. Many brooches have as many as fifty holes.

Once a hole is the wrong size it is very difficult to correct it. Usually the gold has to be melted down again or a different stone has to be procured (the client's displeasure in such cases can be imagined). One *incassatore* relies on gramophone needles for this delicate task. When the setting is ready for the stones, it is fixed into a bed of red wax which gets very hard as it cools. It is then that the little prongs are made and bent round each stone.

The Ponte Vecchio jewellers display not only the domestic product but important pieces sent across Europe on consignment. Treasures from Cartier sometimes pass through Settepassi's and Barocchi's and then on to Bulgari in Rome.

VASARI'S CORRIDOR. For the occasion of Francesco de' Medici's marriage to Joan of Austria in 1565, Cosimo I had Vasari build a private corridor between the Palazzo Vecchio and the Pitti where the young couple were to live. It was built in only five months and five men lost their lives in the haste of the demolition work. The corridor, supported by an arcade, ran from the Uffizi along the river, over the eastern side of the Ponte Vecchio and on behind S Felicita to the Pitti.

Until the building of the corridor, the street along the Arno was called Via Pesciaiuoli because it was reserved for the fishmongers. During the thirteenth and fourteenth centuries the law prohibited the sale of fish elsewhere. In 1343 a woman was fined for selling her frogs near Orsanmichele instead of along the river bank. The name of Piazza del Pesce, just before one comes to the Por S Maria end of the bridge, is a reminder of the ancient fish-market.

Originally one could not walk through the arcade supporting the corridor on the Lungarno Archibusieri; until 1864, each arched compartment was occupied by a shop. Until recently the Ponte Vecchio section of the corridor was closed because bombardment badly shook both the bridge's foundations and the passageway. The weight of the corridor tended to pull the walls of the shops riverwards. The city engineers have embedded pieces of glass (called *spie*, or spies) in the walls of the workrooms to serve as strain gauges. Years of structural repairs have now been completed and the corridor is once more in use as the gallery of artists' self-portraits.

THE UFFIZI. The corridor was an architectural means of keeping the younger and older Medici households united. The Uffizi was designed to gather under close Medici control all the city's major guilds and the administrative and judicial offices. The independent character of these institutions had been fostered by their being scattered all over the city. Cosimo began to think of consolidating them in 1546 and turned the project of a general office building over to Vasari, who was his artistic superintendent. Work began about 1559 and was largely completed by 1574.

The site lay between the Piazza della Signoria and the river and included the *Zecca* (or Mint, which lay just behind the Loggia dei Lanzi), part of the Romanesque church of S Pier Scheraggio, and many houses owned by the Arte della Seta. The Seta complained that they could not afford to pay for the new quarters planned for them. Nevertheless, they and the other property-owners were obliged not only to sell what they had but to pay higher taxes to finance the construction of the new buildings. The doors of some of the old guild houses were incorporated into the Uffizi. Many humbler house-owners suffered too. When the Torre de' Girolami on the Arno was knocked down, masonry fell into a nearby house, destroying half of it including the best wine and kitchen utensils. Vasari listened to the unfortunate owner, a retired army captain, weep out his grievances but confessed that he was unable to console him.

The Uffizi consists of two matching palaces set along either side of a narrow piazza. It is the reverse of the Piazza della Signoria, which has a wide, open, unplanned look. The Piazzale degli Uffizi is like a private courtyard framing spectacular views at either end: the Arno and the soaring mass of the Palazzo Vecchio. The Uffizi is one of the few sixteenth-century buildings in which *pietra serena* was used in great quantity for an exterior. Usually it was reserved for ornament and inner courtyards – as in the Strozzi and Gondi Palaces. After the warm browns of the Piazza della Signoria, in the Uffizi one enters a precinct of reserved elegance – cool blue-green stone and a shade of yellow stucco which is like the colour of withered lemons.

Until the Uffizi assignment, Vasari had been employed as an architect only to remodel church interiors – Ognissanti and S Croce were among these. For the Uffizi, Vasari proceeded to prepare a very bold design, with Michelangelo's Laurentian Library in mind. He intended it as a faithful return to the principles of ancient architecture; instead of the ubiquitous round arches, his arcades have flat architraves. Niches were left in the piers for statues of illustrious Florentines. Most of these were empty until the last century. But the programme was initiated with a white marble bust carved by Giambologna of Cosimo I, sceptre in hand, lording it over the Piazzale from the Arno end.

The lower floors of the Uffizi were occupied by administrative offices and the celebrated theatre was located where the *Gabinetto dei Disegni* is today.

After Cosimo's death, the upper loggia of the Uffizi was transformed into a gallery. Here too were the studios of the court artists, armourers and *pietredure* workers. Nearby were laboratories where chemical experiments were performed. Originally, works of art were shown together with a vast accumulation of objects of all sorts – scientific equipment, furniture, crystal, ivories, exotic artifacts from the New World, and so on. Together they proclaimed the wealth and power of the Medici as well as their monarchical pretensions. At Carnival time the lower loggia at the piazza level was turned over to a masked parade, but for the rest of the year this space was usually left, as it is today, to vendors.

THE PONTE SANTA TRINITA. The Ponte S Trinita is the keystone of the Florentine panorama. Not only is it the main bridge connecting both sides of the city, it is the only one which was conceived as a work of art in itself. Like Brunelleschi's cupola, it is a miracle of aesthetic subtlety and engineering. Since the eighteenth century treatises have been written on its construction. The elliptical curve of the arches, like the structure of the cupola, has eluded mathematicians and architects who have tried to reconstruct them.

In 1557 Cosimo decided to build the bridge as a kind of triumphal arch after a flood swept away an earlier structure. Three years before he had led his troops over it to Siena, which he conquered after a long siege in 1555. The Capricorn, Cosimo's zodiacal sign, and the inscriptions on the white marble scrolls all honour him and his victories. As usual, it was left to Vasari to see to its construction. In 1560 he discussed the matter in Rome with Michelangelo, who was then busy on the cupola of St Peter's. It is believed that Michelangelo sketched out his idea for the bridge and that Vasari turned this over to Bartolomeo Ammannati, who eventually built it between 1567 and 1569.

Ammannati had already made a name for himself in Venice and in Rome, where he collaborated with Jacopo Sansovino and Vignola. On the death of Pope Julius III in 1555 he returned to Florence. Among the first things he carried out there was the completion of the staircase of the Laurentian Library designed by Michelangelo. After Vasari and Buontalenti, he was the busiest artist of the Medici court. Although the bridge was symbolically all Cosimo's, it was the people of Florence who paid for it; the cost was more than 46,000 *scudi*.

The plan was more than the construction of a bridge; it involved the reorganization of an entire neighbourhood and on a grand scale. The Lungarni approaching on one side from the Ponte Vecchio and on the other from the Ponte alla Carraia were raised to the level of the new bridge. The streets at either end were widened to give the bridge sweep as it swings into the broad avenues of the Via Maggio and the Via Tornabuoni. The two halves of Florence were thus united at its centre by a wide boulevard with grand vistas. 'Everyone was pleased,' wrote a diarist of the time, 'because of the beautiful views of the Arno's water.' Grandiose consolidations were the stamp of Cosimo's reign.

In profile the summits of the arches of the bridge seem so thin and delicate that from the beginning there were those who doubted its strength. In 1601 heavy traffic was prohibited on it, but early in the nineteenth century these doubts vanished when the French army sent its heavy artillery over it. The Germans did the same when they retreated in 1944, but the bridge was none the worse for this heavy wear before it was blown up.

The rebuilding of the Ponte S Trinita after its destruction involved the whole city and galvanized civic pride. For seven years the bridge's reconstruction was delayed, not by lack of funds but by violent arguments over how it should be rebuilt. The argument was whether the bridge should be rebuilt exactly as it was, using the same stones, the same plans (which were found), and the same tools; or whether the core should consist of reinforced concrete concealed by a pseudo-authentic mask. In the middle of the heated discussions, the Ministry of Works, which had no strong feelings about the matter, entered the fracas by foisting the pseudo-medieval Ponte alla Carraia on the city and tacitly approving a ferro-concrete project for the Ponte S Trinita. But the will of Florence prevailed. The money for the bridge had been raised by the sale of tickets for individual bricks and stones. One hundred and sixty thousand dollars were collected by a committee under Bernard Berenson. A third of the cost came from such contributions, another third from the Commune, and the remaining third from the central government.

Finally, popular feeling won and the bridge was rebuilt exactly as Ammannati had done it. The statistics, the mathematical calculations for the arches, were worked out through the co-operative labours of architects, engineers and archivists. The stones salvaged from the mined original were collected in heaps and piled up in the courtyard of Ognissanti and each stone was numbered. The additional stone needed was obtained from the original quarries in the Boboli

Gardens which were reopened for the purpose during the winter of 1954–5. The rudimentary kinds of tools used during the sixteenth century were distributed among the masons and stone-cutters. At last, in August 1957, the bridge was reopened. Everything was in place except the head of the *Primavera*, which had not been found with the rest of the rubble. There was an argument about the head. The Parker Pen Company offered a reward of $3,000 to its finder. The statues were not part of Ammannati's original scheme and, unlike the bridge itself, they were not universally beloved. They had been added as part of the festive décor for the wedding of Cosimo II and Maria Maddalena of Austria in 1608. One morning a poem ridiculing the *Primavera* and her head-hunters was affixed to the statue's base:

> *Questa è la Primavera*
> *che prima v'era*
> *e adesso è ritornata senza testa.*
> *La cosa è manifesta:*
> *mentre Firenze dorme*
> *s' è mutilata forse da se stessa*
> *per essere conforme*
> *a quelli che ce l'hanno ora rimessa.*

(This is Spring, who was here before and has now returned without her head. The matter is manifest: while Florence slept, she was mutilated – perhaps she did it herself – so that she could be just like those who set her up again.)

At last in 1961 a dredging crew turned up the head and, after a week's display on a red velvet cushion in the courtyard of the Palazzo Vecchio, it was firmly replaced on the shoulders of *La Primavera* and the bridge was once again complete.

THE LUNGARNI: PALACES AND FESTIVITIES. Until well into the fifteenth century the river front, like the rest of the city, was walled and towered. The Palazzo dei Giudici and the Palazzo Spini-Ferroni are relics of the grim facades which once lined the river banks. Originally the Palazzo Spini's facade rose sheer from the river-bed. There were only short stretches along the north bank where the Arno could be seen from the roadway. Since the second half of the thirteenth century there was a Lungarno between the Ponte alle Grazie and the Palazzo dei Giudici in order to provide access to the large drying-shed of the S Croce dyers. The steps which once led from the *tiratoi* to the river are still visible in front of the Borsa, the neo-classic

Stock Exchange. In 1472 a short stretch between the Ponte Vecchio and the Palazzo Spini-Ferroni was paved. For the rest, the streets parallel to the river were internal passageways. The present Lungarno Serristori was a canal known as 'della Mulina', and the Lungarno Torrigiani, also built during the last century, was a field with the little church of S Maria sopr' Arno at the Via de' Bardi end. By the second half of the Quattrocento, patrician palaces with open loggias and many windows began to replace the old tower houses. One of the loveliest of these is the small Palazzo Coverelli on the Lungarno Guicciardini. No one knows who the architect was. During the sixteenth century it was occupied by one of Cosimo I's cavalry officers. The little street beside it leading back towards the Via del Presto S Martino used to be known as the Via dei Pizzicotti (Pinchers' Alley) because of the local rapscallions who pinched the passers-by venturing into the passageway.

Opposite is the golden-yellow Palazzo Corsini, one of the few grandiose pieces of secular Baroquery in Florence. Its balustraded pavilions topped by romantic statuary were built between 1648 and 1656 by Pier Francesco Silvani and Antonio Ferri (the author of S Frediano's cupola). The Corsini are a family of feudal proprietors. They have produced cardinals, a pope, and even a saint. They went in for grandiose architectural schemes; the palace was the first of these and it whetted their appetites. Lorenzo Corsini, who in 1730 became Pope Clement XII, was responsible for the restoration of the Vatican, built the Trevi fountain and the facades of the Lateran and S Giovanni dei Fiorentini. It was this Pope's newphew, another Lorenzo, who began the great picture collection now housed inside the family palace on the Lungarno.

Since the Middle Ages the river and its bridges have been used for staging festivities of all kinds. There was the fatal spectacle of the *Inferno* put on by the ward of S Frediano in May 1304. It was performed on the river between the Ponte S Trinita and the Ponte alla Carraia. So many spectators packed on to the Carraia that it collapsed with a heavy loss of life. On New Year's Eve exactly three centuries later an ice festival was given on the same stretch of the Arno. Sleds were fashioned into ancient *quadrighe*. Madrigals and verses were composed for it and the nobility decked itself out in exotic costumes, Virginio Orsini appearing as a pasha. Probably the most elaborate spectacle of all was the *Argonautica* staged four years later for the marriage of Cosimo II. The Arno between the same two bridges was turned into a giant theatre. Grandstands were set up on the Lungarni to watch Jason capture the Golden Fleece and a personification of the Arno present the bride with six apples symbolic of the Medici *palle*. There were marvellous boats made into fire-breathing hydra, a peacock, a lobster and a dolphin. And in the middle there was an artificial island.

The last authentic festivity given on the Arno was the fireworks display set off on the Ponte alla Carraia on St John's Day. But in 1870 this was transferred to the new Piazzale Michelangelo built by Giuseppe Poggi. Today one can rent a rowing-boat near the Ponte S Niccolò and watch the display from the river. The bridges are now only for traffic, except the Ponte Vecchio. Frivolity has moved to other parts.

Chapter 7

The Centre:
'La più gioconda età'[1]

❧

SUMMARY OF THE CHIEF MONUMENTS

1. Santo Stefano al Ponte – lower part of facade, *ca* 1233, is the most important surviving example in Florence of the Pisan-Lucchese style of Romanesque architecture which once prevailed throughout Tuscany until *ca* 1250. *Interior:* rebuilt in the 17th c. by Ferdinando Tacca. Balustraded staircase framing chancel designed by Bernardo Buontalenti (1574) for church of S Trinita, but moved here in 1894. High altar by Giambologna (1591) comes from S Maria Nuova. Other items: painting of *St Peter* by Jacopo di Cione; opposite: *St Peter Martyr* (*ca* 1330–40) painted by the Master of the Horne Triptych. Also: a bronza altar frontal, the *Stoning of Stephen* by Tacca (1656); and a marble *Madonna and Child* by a follower of Verrocchio.

2. The tower house of the Amidei, 13th c.

3. Palazzo degli Acciaioli (Borgo SS Apostoli Nos. 3–10) – the house of Nicola Accaioli, the Grand Seneschal of the Angevin kingdom of Naples. Rebuilt in the 15th c. around a nucleus of 13th and 14th c. buildings. The Acciaioli had other houses on the same street (Nos. 7, 9, 17) as well as a great palace on the Arno once famous for its furnishings and its hanging gardens (blown up in 1944). The family made its fortune first in steel (*acciaio* – hence their name) and then in banking.

4. Church of SS Apostoli. *Façade:* despite many restorations, it is substantially the Romanesque structure of *ca* 1050–75. Main portal (*ca* 1512) by Benedetto da Rovezzano. *Interior:* one of the finest early church interiors of the city – roughly contemporary with the Baptistery (*ca* 1059–1100). Ground plan resembles that of the early Christian basilicae of Rome. The painted timbered roof, 13th and 14th c. Side aisles rebuilt during the 15th and 16th .Chancel by Dosio (1573–83). In the right aisle: second altar – *St Peter at the Temple*

[1]The Happiest Age.

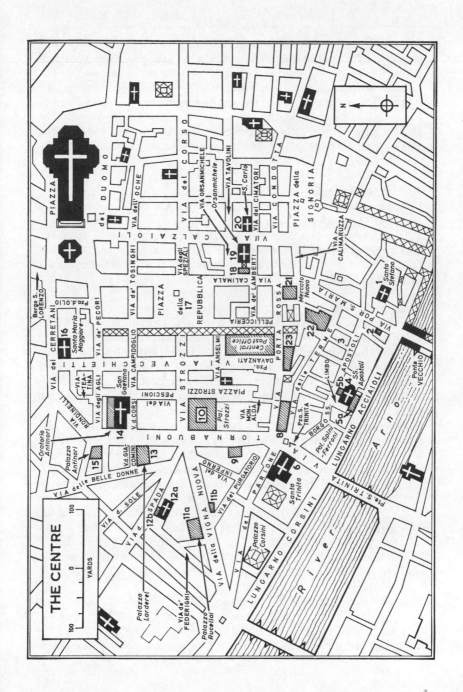

THE CENTRE

YARDS

100   100

N

PIAZZA del DUOMO

Borgo S. LORENZO

VIA dell' OCHE

VIA de' TOSINGHI

VIA de' PECORI

VIA degli SPEZIALI

VIA del CORSO

VIA ORSANMICHELE

Orsanmichele

VIA TAVOLINI

S. Carlo

VIA del CIMATORI

VIA CONDOTTA

PIAZZA della SIGNORIA

VIA CALIMARUZZA

Santo Stefano

20

18 19

VIA CALIMALA

VIA de' LAMBERTI

21

Mercato Nuovo

VIA PELLICCERIA

PORTA ROSSA

VIA POR S. MARIA

1

PIAZZA della REPUBBLICA

Pza. d.o. OLIO

16 Santa Maria Maggiore

VIA de' CERRETANI

VIA CAMPIDOGLIO

VIA VECCHIETTI

VIA ANSELMI

Central Post Office

17

Pza. DAVANZATI

22

23

VIA delle TERME

LIMBO

3

SS. APOSTOLI

5b

4

SS. Apostoli

LUNGARNO ACCIAIOLI

2

VIA POR

Ponte VECCHIO

Arno

VIA dei TEATINA

VIA degli AGLI

San Gaetano

V. d. CORSI

VIA del PESCIONI

VIA STROZZI

PIAZZA STROZZI

Pal. Strozzi

VIA MONALDA

10

8

7

Pza. S. TRINITA

Borgo SS.

5a

Pal. Spini-Ferroni

VIA TORNABUONI

VIA RONDINELLI

Oratorio Antinori

Palazzo Antinori

15

VIA delle BELLE DONNE

V.d.GIA. COMINI

13

14

VIA d. SOLE

VIA d.

12a

12b SPADA

11a

VIA del PARIONE

Santa Trinita

6

LUNGARNO CORSINI

Palazzo Corsini

Palazzo Larderel

VIA de' FEDERIGHI

Palazzo Rucellai

VIA del PURGATORIO

VIA del' INFERNO

VIA della VIGNA NUOVA

11b

River Arno

Pte S. TRINITA

Door by Pomarancio; third altar – *Immaculate Conception* by Vasari (1541); at the end of the aisle – *Madonna and Child* by Jacopo di Cione (*ca* 1375). On the high altar: *Madonna and Child with Saints* painted by an unknown follower of Orcagna, 1384, lent by the Academy (No. 8607); it was originally made for the Poor Clares of Monticelli. Left aisle: last monument – tomb of Oddo Altoviti, the great patron of the church, by Benedetto da Rovezzano (1507); at the end of aisle – fragments from the tomb of Donato Acciaioli by the shop of Giovanni della Robbia (*ca* 1500).

5. Piazza del Limbo – so-called because it is on the site once occupied by a graveyard for unbaptized infants. (*a*) On the south side: the *palace of Oddo Alroviti* built *ca* 1512 by Benedetto da Rovezzano. (*b*) To the left of the church facade: flank of *Palazzo Rosselli del Turco* (Borgo SS Apostoli Nos. 17–19), an early work of Baccio d'Agnolo (*ca* 1517). Immured in the wall is an early 16th c. relief of the *Madonna and Child*.

6. Santa Trinita
The mother church of the Vallombrosan Order founded in 1092 by the Florentine nobleman, S Giovanni Gualberto. Present church (*ca* 1258–80) built on top of two earlier ones which go back at least to the 11th c. *Façade:* by Bernardo Buontalenti (1593–4); the *Trinity* relief by Pietro Bernini (the father of the famous Lorenzo) and Caccini. Wooden doors carved in the 17th c. with saints of the Vallombrosan Order.

Interior: the Gothic interior built between *ca* 1250 and 1415. Its broad nave and aisles have been compared to Cistercian abbey architecture, its transept and raised choir to those of S Maria Novella.
1. On the inner wall of façade – remains of the Romanesque façade which itself bears the traces of a remodelling campaign (note the area around the oculus). For a view of how it looked on the outside, see Ghirlandaio's view of the Piazza S Trinita in the Sassetti Chapel (*see* below, 9). (*a*) Detached mural of the *Trinity* (*ca* 1390); (*b*) tomb slab of an abbot, 14th c.; (*c*) tomb slab of Antonio Amato, his head a skull, by an associate of Donatello (*ca* 1450); (*d, e*) holy water fonts attributed to the shop of Battista Lorenzi (late 16th c.).
2. *Gianfigliazzi Chapel* – remodelled *ca* 1630 in the manner of Gherardo Silvani; (*a*) miraculous crucifix (14th *c.*) popularly known as the *Crocifisso dei Bianchi* or *della Provvidenza*; (*b*) muralled niche with *St Mary of Egypt and S Zosimus* (*ca* 1400).

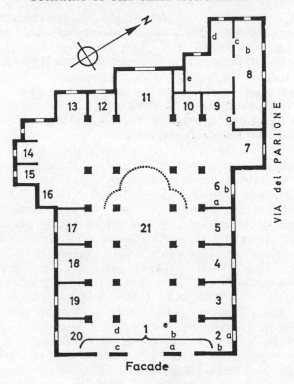

CHURCH of S. TRINITA

3. **Davizzi Chapel** – remodelled in the manner of Matteo Nigetti (*ca* 1642).

4. **Cialli-Seringi Chapel** – altarpiece of the *Madonna Enthroned with Saints* by Neri di Bicci brought here in 1890 from the Uffizi; on the aisle walls – the sinopia under-drawing and the finished mural of the *Mystic Marriage of St Catherine* by a follower of Spinello Aretino (*ca* 1389), moved here after their recent discovery beneath the *Meeting of Joachim and Anna* by Lorenzo Monaco in the chapel next door.

5. **Bartolini-Salimbeni Chapel*** (light switch on left) – one of the few surviving examples of a complete ornamental scheme of the early 15th c. – down to its wrought-iron gate and the frame of its altarpiece (the *Annunciation*). The murals illustrate *Scenes from the Life of the Virgin* and were painted by Lorenzo Monaco and assistants (*ca* 1423): over the chapel entrance – the

167

Assumption; inside on left wall, above – *Expulsion of Joachim*; below – *Meeting of Joachim and Anna*; on altar wall, below left – *Birth of the Virgin*; below right – *Presentation in the Temple*; above – *Miracle of the Snow*; on right wall, below – *Marriage of the Virgin*; above – *Dormition of the Virgin*.

6. **Ardinghelli Chapel** – (a) *Man of Sorrows* (*ca* 1430); (*b*) altar tabernacle by Benedetto da Rovezzano, *ca* 1505–13?, upper sections added *ca* 1552 from the unfinished monument commemorating S Giovanni Gualberto.

7. Exit passage to Via del Parione, lined with grave niches (*ca* 1394) called *avelli* which may once have lined the church's flank as at S Maria Novella.

8. **Sacristy (*the Chapel of Onofrio Strozzi*)** * 1418–23 – architecture sometimes attributed to Michelozzo or Ghiberti. (*a*) Portal frame in the style of Lorenzo Ghiberti. (*b*) The chapel is to the rear. On its altar once stood Gentile da Fabriano's *Adoration of the Magi*, now in the Uffizi. Beside it on the left (*c*) is the tomb of Onofrio Strozzi (d. 1418), thought by some to have been designed by Donatello but largely carried out by an assistant. (*d*) *Madonna, Child and Saints* by Francesco d'Antonio (*ca* 1430). (*e*) Ruined pietra serena lunette of *S Giovanni Gualberto* (*ca* 1480).

9. **Sassetti Chapel** * – murals of *St Francis and prophecies of Christ's birth* painted by Domenico Ghirlandaio (*ca* 1482–5); the altarpiece of the *Adoration of the Magi* (1485) is also by Domenico. The black marble sarcophagi attributed to Giuliano da Sangallo enclose the remains of Francesco Sassetti and his wife, Nera Corsi, the donors of the chapel, who are portrayed on either side of the altar. Over the entrance is a view of Rome with the sybil informing Augustus of Christ's coming. But all the scenes on the altar wall illustrate Roman events cast in Florentine settings – views of the Piazza della Signoria and the Piazza S Trinita. Florence is seen as the new Rome – the site of Christian renewal. In the upper picture, Sassetti stands between his young son, Federigo, and Lorenzo the Magnificent, for whom he acted as general manager of the Medici Bank. Opposite stand the three older Sassetti boys – Galeazzo, Cosimo and Bartolomeo. Up the steps come Lorenzo de' Medici's sons accompanied by their tutors – Luigi Pulci and Agnolo Poliziano. This scene combines *St Francis receiving the Rule from Pope Honorius III* and Florentine reconcilliation with the papacy. The entire pictorial program beautifully blends sacred, personal and civic ideas such as Christ's advent, gratitude to St Francis,

and confidence in the coming of a new golden age to Augustan Florence.

10. *Doni Chapel* – the mathematician Paolo Dagomari (known as dell' Abaco) was originally buried here – his tomb since moved to the Usimbardi Chapel (*see* 12). The Baroque décor was devised by Cigoli for the Doni family between 1608–40. On altar wall: the heavily repainted cross of S Giovanni Gualberto and remains of the Saint's garments.

11. *Chancel* (ex: Gianfigliazzi Chapel) – once painted with an Old Testament cycle by Alesso Baldovinetti (1471) famous for its many contemporary portraits (recent restoration has disclosed fragments on the upper walls, another fragment survives in the Accademia Carrara at Bergamo). Originally, Cimabue's *Maestà* (now in the Uffizi) served as the altarpiece. Later it was replaced by Baldovinetti's *Trinity* now in the Accademia. Today, its place is occupied by Mariotto di Nardo's *Trinity* (1406) on loan from the Academy.

12. *Usimbardi Chapel* – contains tombs of two brothers, both bishops, rebuilt by Cigoli soon after 1602.

13. *Scali Chapel* – on the walls fragments of a fresco cycle (*ca* 1434–5) devoted to St Bartholomew by Giovanni dal Ponte and Smeraldo di Giovanni. In the left wall: *Tomb of Benozzo Federighi*,* Bishop of Fiesole (d. 1450), by Luca della Robbia (1454–7), originally made for the Federighi Chapel in S Pancrazio but brought here in 1896.

14. *Chapel of S Giovanni Gualberto* – designed by Caccini (1593–4) with murals by Passignano. Tabernacle containing reliquary by G. B. Puccini (1584). In pavement, fragments of a Romanesque altar frontal.

15. *Chapel of the Madonna dello Spasimo* – *Christ on the Road to Calvary* in style of Cosimo Rosselli (*ca* 1470).

16. *Spini Chapel* – wooden statue of the *Magdalen* left unfinished by Desiderio da Settignano and finished by Benedetto da Maiano (*ca* 1464–5).

17. *Compagni Chapel* – the historian Dino Compagni buried here. Altarpiece: *Coronation of the Virgin* (*ca* 1400) by an unknown Florentine.

18. *Davanzati Chapel* – altarpiece by Neri di Bicci, *Annunciation*, *ca* 1450–60. Tomb of Giuliano Davanzati (d. 1444). His effigy carved *ca* 1450 reposes upon a 3rd c. Roman sarcophagus. In round niche, mural of the *Disputation of St Catherine* by the school of Maso di Banco.

19. **Bombeni Chapel** – remodelled by M. Nigetti (1629–35). Original pictures stolen. In their places hang: the *Mystic Marriage of St Catherine of Siena* by Antonio del Ceraiuolo, a pupil of Lorenzo di Credi; *St Jerome* by Ridolfo Ghirlandaio (*ca* 1550); and the *Annunciation* also by Ghirlandaio. The picture on the left has a handle beside it which, if pulled back, reveals a 14th c. mural of the *Man of Sorrows*.

20. **Strozzi Chapel** – rebuilt by Giovanni Caccini. Ruined murals by Bernardino Poccetti. Handle on left wall when pulled opens door concealing niche with a mural recently detached of the *Noli me Tangere* by a very good follower of Daddi (*ca* 1365) called the Fabriano Master.

21. Stairs leading to crypt, which also contains remains of an earlier Romanesque church recently excavated.

7. Column of Justice – the shaft from the Baths of Caracalla presented to Cosimo I in 1560 by Pope Pius IV. Raised in the piazza in 1565 to commemorate the battle of Montemurlo (August 2, 1537). Porphyry statue, probably by Romolo del Tadda, added in 1581.

8. Palazzo Bartolini-Salimbeni* (now Torrigiani) – built by Baccio d'Agnolo between 1517 and 1520, recently restored. Now the seat of the French Consulate.

9. Palazzo Giaconi (Via Tornabuoni No. 5) – built in the 17th c. by Gherardo Silvani for the poet, Giovan Battista Strozzi. The statues on either side by A. Novelli.

10. Palazzo Strozzi* – built at the behest of Filippo Strozzi (d. 1491). Begun 1489, probably based on model by Giuliano da Sangallo but largely carried out by Benedetto da Maiano and 'il Cronaca' (Simone del Pollaiuolo, 1457–1508). The courtyard was begun in 1493 but its loggia was not completed before 1533. By 1501 the façade on the Piazza Strozzi side finished. Halt in construction between 1507 and 1533. Wrought-iron lamps by Caparra based on a design by Benedetto da Maiano.

11. (*a*) **Palazzo Rucellai*** (Via della Vigna Nuova No. 18) – probably built late 1450s on a design prepared by Leon Battista Alberti and carried out by Bernardo Rossellino. (*b*) **Loggia de' Rucellai,** 1464–8, part of the same Albertian complex now used for exhibitions and as a public information office.

12. (*a*) **Former Church of San Pancrazio** – in process of restoration. Façade *ca* 1375 with additions by Alberti (the architrave). (*b*) The *Rucellai Chapel** by Alberti (1461–7), entrance on Via della Spada, get the key from the porter of the Palazzo Rucellai (tip). Contains replica of the Holy Sepulchre as it then was; inside it is a much damaged mural of the *Resurrection* attributed to Baldovinetti.

13. Palazzo Giacomini-Larderel (Via Tournabuoni No. 19) – begun *ca* 1580 by an unknown architect sometimes identified with Dosio.

14. San Gaetano – built between 1604 and 1649 on the site of the 11th c. church of S Michele Berteldi. The plan for the Baroque church probably prepared by Don Anselmo Canigiani and Don Giovanni de' Medici. Nigetti began to carry it out but most of the work was done under Gherardo Silvani. *Façade* (1645): ornamental detail by Alessandro Neri Malavisti. Statuary, *ca* 1680, by Balthasar Permoser, Francesco Andreozzi and Carlo Marcellini. *Interior:* Silvani's Baroque stated with Florentine restraint. Fine stucco work mostly by Foggini and his school. Left side: second chapel, *Martyrdom of S Lorenzo* (1653) by Pietro da Cortona. Door in left wall leads to Antinori Chapel or Oratory – which contains three 12th c. reliefs (St Michael and two Saints) from the old church of S Michele Berteldi – rare examples of Florentine figure sculpture of the Romanesque period; lunette of the *Madonna and Child* by a follower of Botticelli; *Crucifixion* painted and then cut out in silhouette by Pesellino (?) and framed by a handsome marble tabernacle.

15. Palazzo Antinori – nostalgic medievalry, built *ca* 1465 for the Boni family. Products of the Antinori farms sold on ground floor in the '*Cantinetta*'.

16. Santa Maria Maggiore – rebuilt *ca* 1300, remains of Romanesque bell-tower incorporated on left side of façade. The Gothic portions built *ca* 1360. Baroque remodelling: inside of façade by Buontalenti (1596) with altars by Gherardo Silvani; monks' choir by Cigoli (*ca* 1607). In chapel to left of choir: grave of Dante's teacher, Brunetto Latini; large altarpiece with the *Madonna and Child* in polychromed low relief surrounded by saints, angels and two scenes perhaps painted by Coppo di Marcovaldo, *ca* 1260. To see it, ask sacristan to open the curtains. In the choir: remains of a fresco cycle attributed to Spinello Aretino.

17. Piazza della Repubblica – built 1890–1917 after the city's medieval centre (including the Mercato Vecchio and the Ghetto) was demolished. For views of this old neighbourhood see the Museo di Firenze com' era (Via S Egidio No. 21). The figures of *Abundance* on top of the column is a copy of Foggini's original (1721) now preserved in the Palazzo della Cassa di Risparmio, Via Bufalini Nol 1.

18. (*a*) **Palazzo dell' Arte della Lana** – begun *ca* 1284 on the site of the tower house of the Compiobesi. Acquired in 1308 by the Arte della Lana as the headquarters of the wool guild which supervised the production of more than 200 ateliers of wool-workers. *Inside* (ring for custodian): in the Hall of Justice, mural of *Brutus as the Just Judge* (late 14th c.) surrounded by the four cardinal virtues assailed by the vices.

(*b*) The **Tabernacolo della Tromba**; the *Madonna Enthroned with Saints* by Jacopo del Casentino (*ca* 1334) and the *Coronation of the Virgin* by a close-follower of Niccolò di Pietro Gerini (late 14th c.).

19. Orsanmichele* – so named because it was built on the site of the 8th c. oratory of S Michele in Orto (St Michael's in the Garden). The present structure built at the order of the city council between 1336 and 1350 as a combination of communal granary and oratory. The architects may have been Neri di Fioravante, Benci di Cione and Francesco Talenti – all of whom were engaged in the construction of the Cathedral. The arcades were walled in soon after 1380. The oratory is dedicated to the cult of a miraculous picture of the Virgin on a pillar inside, which was replaced several times between 1292 and 1347.

Exterior: each pillar adopted by a guild:
1. For the *Calimala* (the importers of foreign cloth) – niche by Albizzo di Piero and others based on Ghiberti's design, bronze statue of the *Baptist** by Ghiberti, 1412–16.
2. Niche originally made for the *Parte Guelfa* by Michelozzo and Donatello, 1423–5; bronze group of *Doubting Thomas** by Verrocchio, *ca* 1465–83, after the niche was acquired by the *Mercatanzia* (the merchants' tribunal).
3. For the *Giudici e Notai* (judges and notaries) – niche by Niccolò di Piero Lamberti, 1403–6, bronze *St Luke* by Giambologna, 1601, which replaced an earlier figure by Lamberti now in the Bargello.
4. For the *Beccai* (butchers) – marble *St Peter* (probably by Ciuffagni), *ca* 1415–25.
5. For the *Conciapelli* (the tanners) – *St Philip* by Nanni di Banco, *ca* 1412–16. The niche also by Nanni.

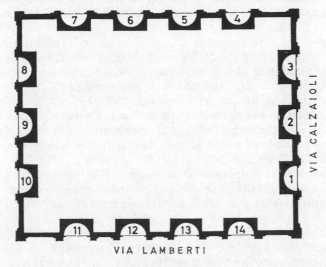

ORSANMICHELE

6. For the *Maestri di Pietre e Legname* (the masons and carpenters) – the **Quattro Coronati** (four Christian sculptors who were martyred for their refusal to make a pagan image for the Emperor Diocletian) by Nanni di Banco, *ca* 1413.
7. For the *Corazzai* (armourers) – a bronze copy of the original marble *St George* (now in the Bargello) and relief below of *St George and the Dragon* (this is the original) by Donatello, *ca* 1417.
8. For the *Cambio* (bankers) – tabernacle executed by Jacopo di Corso and Giovanni di Niccolò based on Ghiberti's design; bronze *St Matthew* by Lorenzo Ghiberti, 1419–23.
9. For the *Lana* (the wool guild) – the niche made 1339–40, the bronze *St Stephen* by Ghiberti, 1425–9.
10. For the *Maniscalchi* (the smiths) – tabernacle and the marble statue of *St Eligius** by Nanni di Banco, *ca* 1410–11.
11. For the *Linaiuoli* (linen drapers) – niche by Perfetto di Giovanni and Albizo di Piero, 1411, and marble *St Mark** by Donatello, 1411–13 – recently removed for repair.
12. For the *Pellicciai* (furriers) – statue of *St James the Great* attributed to Niccolò di Piero Lamberti, early 15th c.
13. For the Medici e Speziali (doctors and pharmacists) – niche attributed to Simone Talenti, marble *Madonna della Rosa*, 1399,

173

variously attributed to Piero Tedesco or to Niccolò di Piero Lamberti; above, *Madonna Enthroned* by Luca della Robbia, 1455–65.

14. For the *Arte della Seta* (silk guild) – niche, 1414–16, bronze *St John the Evangelist* by Baccio da Montelupo, 1515; replaced an earlier figure of the saint by an Orcagnesque master now in the museum of the Ospedale degli Innocenti; above – terracotta roundel by Andrea della Robbia, 1450–60.

Inside on ground floor: between 1336 and 1380 the guilds adopted pillars inside the loggia on which they painted images of their patron saints. The murals in the vault (1398–1401) followed a programme devised by Franco Sacchetti, the novella-writer, who was also an official of the Company of Orsanmichele. The programme consists of holy figures of the Old and New Testaments paired as counterparts in historical order proceeding from the western end eastwards. At the east end, *Orcagna's tabernacle* (1355–9) framing the miraculous *Virgin* painted by Bernardo Daddi (1347). To the left: marble group of *St Anne, Mary and the Christ Child* by Francesco da Sangallo (*ca* 1526), the result of a cult dedicated to St Anne which became especially popular after St Anne's Day 1343, when the Florentines expelled the petty Angevin tyrant, the Duke of Athens. Twelve stained glass windows (*ca* 1410) represent *Miracles of the Virgin* which were designed by Agnolo Gaddi, Niccolò di Pietro Gerini, Ambrogio di Baldese, and Lorenzo Monaco.

'Saloni di Orsanmichele' – entrance from Palazzo dell Arte della Lana (see n. 18 – p. 172); closed on Sunday; open weekdays 09.00–14.00. Recently the upper floors of the former granary have been opened. Though originally built for storage purposes, these great vaulted halls are among the most magnificent interiors of the Italian Trecento. Splendid views of the city and its environs. Temporary exhibitions often held here.

20. San Carlo dei Lombardi – begun in 1349 to accommodate the cult of St Anne. Built by the then architects of the Duomo – Neri di Fioravante, Benci di Cione and Simone Talenti. After 1380 it was supposed to replace the old church of St Michael on which the grain market of Orsanmichele rose. Behind high altar: *Entombment* by Niccolò di Pietro Gerini (*ca* 1385).

21. The Mercato Nuovo – built by Giovanni Battista del Tasso, 1547–51. Popularly known as the Porcellino (or piglet) because of Pietro Tacca's fountain (*ca* 1612) situated on the southern side. This bronze boar is a copy of the Roman marble once in the Grand Duke's possession and now in the Uffizi.

22. Palazzo di Parte Guelfa – a 13th c. structure, the headquarters of the Guelph Party, enlarged in 1359, 1370 and 1377 and then rebuilt between *ca* 1418 and 1458 largely on Brunelleschi's designs but probably carried out by an adjutant, Antonio di Domenico. The building was never entirely completed. See also the Brunelleschian audience hall inside with a fine lunette of the *Madonna and Child with Angels* by Luca della Robbia (from the former church of S Piero). Stairs and loggia on Via Capaccio side added by Vasari in *ca* 1589.

23. Palazzo Davanzati (Via Porta Rossa No. 9) – the most distinguished example of 14th c. palace architecture remaining in the city. The loggia is a 15th c. addition. The Davizzi owned it until 1516, when it was acquired by Onofrio Bartolini, a papal pronotary, who sold it to Bernardo Davanzati. Now a museum (frequently closed due to insufficient funds to pay custodians; admission fee 150 lire). Many of the rooms still have their original muralled decoration; the fine collections of furniture and pottery as well as pictures and sculpture by masters including Piero di Cosimo, Lorenzo di Credi and Francesco di Giorgio, all from the store-rooms of the Uffizi, Pitti and Bargello.

'LA PIÙ GIOCONDA ETÀ'

The city's ancient centre lies buried beneath its newest piazza. A Roman forum once took up about a quarter of the Piazza della Repubblica. Like any other respectable Roman community, Florence had its capitol or *Campidoglio*, temples, baths and theatres. To this day some of the neighbouring streets perpetuate the memory of the Roman past: the Via del Campidoglio – now a street of restaurants and cloth-merchants; the Via Roma – with its hotels, shipping agents and Fiat showrooms; the Via delle Terme and the old Corso. The main inter-section of ancient Florence was at the corner where UPIM, the ultra-modern department store, now stands. What is thought to be a pre-Roman Villanovan graveyard lies beneath the central post-office. Beside the Capitoline baths near the present Via Campidoglio was another establishment between what is now the Palazzo di Parte Guelfa and the Palazzo Davanzati. It was a large affair occupying some 12,000 square feet. The Via delle Terme takes its name from it and the Via Capaccio along the Palazzo di Parte Guelfa's eastern flank is probably a corruption of *caput aquae* – the conduit which supplied the water.

Villani and his fellow Florentines were heartened by the belief that the city was founded by the best people of Rome. But Roman Florence did not survive the barbaric invasions: the ancient buildings were abandoned and the ruins gradually sank into piles of accumulated rubbish. By Dante's time hardly a trace of ancient Florence was to be seen. The medieval town was built on a level from four to ten feet above the ancient remains. Dante blamed the disappearance of the city's classical heritage on the corrupting influence of the 'beasts from Fiesole'. The truth was less dramatic: ancient Florence owed its existence to the trade routes passing through it; with the disruption of the empire and its commercial network, the city withered into insignificance. Because Florence had so few visible reminders of a glorious Roman past and because until the eleventh century she was so unimportant, proud Florentines early on began to manufacture their tradition. Thus from Villani onwards the Charlemagne was hailed as the founder of medieval Florence. Up to a few years ago most guide books solemnly attributed to him such foundations as SS Apostoli, S Stefano al Ponte, and S Trinita.

Early in the eleventh century the city rose to importance, thanks to an ecclesiastical reform movement which happened to coincide with the transfer of the margravate from Lucca to Florence. During the reign of the *gran contessa* Matilda, the city's first walls were raised. They followed the course of the Via Tornabuoni, Via Cerretani, Via Proconsolo and Borgo SS Apostoli, which still hold the city as in a frame. Some of the gates in this wall have survived in street names: Porta Rossa, or the Red Gate, with its brick piers gave on to what is now the Via del Parione, and Por S Maria stood between Borgo SS Apostoli and the Ponte Vecchio.

THE MERCATO VECCHIO. The Mercato Vecchio, which was demolished only in 1890 to make way for the Piazza della Repubblica, already existed in Matilda's time. It was the city's chief food and produce market. 'Never was there a nobler garden,' wrote the fourteenth-century poet and town crier, Antonio Pucci. During Carnival there were hens and capons, and for Lent there were mountains of onions, garlic, shallot tarts and spicy herbs fried in batter. The favourite meat then, as now, was veal (it was probably not worth while to let cattle mature into beef). The best cuts were reserved for the priors' table in the Palazzo Vecchio. Good meat was expensive, which explains why the most substantial part of the meal was – and still is –

la minestra – either soup or pasta. The Trecento recipe for *lasagne* was the same dish we know: layers of green pasta interlarded with cheese and meat sauce, save that it was heavily sugared and spiced. Spices not only outshouted high meat, they also provided the necessary stimulant in the diet when coffee and tea in Europe were still unknown.

The medieval Florentine took no breakfast. The nearest thing to it was a prophylactic suggested during times of plague when 'a piece of toasted bread and half a glass of wine' were to be taken 'before leaving the house in the morning'. There were two meals: at nine or ten in the morning and at sundown. In the summer the sun set late so a snack or *merenda* was allowed between meals. 'Drink not save at meals and you will be much healthier,' advised Paolo da Certaldo, '. . . this is living like a man, while to eat all the time is like a beast.' Most Tuscans would still agree with this. Despite the great abundance of wine in the province, it is rare to see anyone drunk. But in the old days, instead of the refreshment bars which cluster around the Piazza della Repubblica full of their tempting piles of hot sandwiches and tarts, there were a number of taverns – La Spada, the Inferno and the Purgatorio, which are commemorated in the names of nearby streets. A relic of this remains in a combination wine-shop and *trattoria* in the Via del Purgatorio called The Filthy Cook's (*Dalla cuoca sudicia*) known for its excellent *baccalà alla Livornese* (cod Livorno style – i.e. with tomatoes and onions) served on Fridays.

Everyone came to the Mercato Vecchio: merchants, housewives, farmers, beggars, pickpockets. Women and girls of good family were carried about in closed litters. Vegetable sellers and vendors of junk of all kinds threaded their way through the loggias and stalls crying: '*Brucia Pistoia*' (Pistoia's burning) for red Pistoiese watermelons, '*Eccolo il vero medico*' (Here's the real doctor) for baked pears. Other criers were hired to call out lost property or help wanted (wet nurses, for instance). Above the crowd, communal heralds on horseback announced death sentences, exiles, war news and bankruptcies. With the exception of the heralds, the Commune levied either a rent or a tax on all these market folk.

A statue of Abundance, the *Dovizia*, by Donatello once looked down on the market-place. She was a striding nymph in the guise of Flora, with fluttering garments and a cornucopia. It was the first time since antiquity that a profane figure instead of the usual saint or Madonna guarded an Italian market-place. The Florentines must have known that a Roman deity occupied the very same spot and been proud of it. The ancient base lay beneath the Dovizia and now rests in the Museo Archeologico. In 1721, Donatello's goddess, worn by three centuries of weather, was replaced by a version of G. B. Foggini. Now only the column remains at the corner between UPIM and Gilli's *caffè*. Foggini's original has been replaced by a copy. Recently, a relic of Donatello's statue has been recognized as the head of '*Faith*' inserted at some time on Jacopo di Piero Guidi's figure in the Loggia dei Lanzi.

Near what was once the south-eastern corner of the Mercato Vecchio is the *Tabernacolo della Tromba*. Condemned criminals were obliged to kneel before it on their way to execution. The original image inside it is still there: a large painting of the *Madonna Enthroned* by Jacopo del Casentino, a contemporary of Giotto's. The *Coronation of the Virgin* above it was painted later in the century. The tabernacle was under the care of the guild of doctors and pharmacists (the *Medici e Speziali*). At some time between 1686 and 1859 the picture was moved to the nearby church of S Tommaso so that a sausage-maker could set up shop inside the niche. Only in 1905 was it brought back again.

ORSANMICHELE. Orsanmichele was the pride of the guilds of Florence. Its architecture was an elegant frame for business and devotions. Its sculpture accustomed the Florentines to placing the monumental expressions of their civic and personal ideals in the midst of the everyday bustle of the city. These statues are the work of a miraculous generation which came of age between 1406 and 1426. It was as if the preceding almost blank forty years of sculpture in Florence were a predestined wait for Nanni di Banco, Ghiberti and Donatello. The revival of the difficult technique of bronze casting was more than matched by an artistic inventiveness of unsurpassed boldness. As great a miracle was that the city's guilds also recognized the occasion and were ready to confide their commissions to these brilliant youngsters instead of to older, duller, but reliable men such as Ciuffagni, Niccolò Lamberti, and Giovanni d'Ambrogio, all of whom were very respectable sculptors known for their work on other communal projects.

On the site of the present Orsanmichele was originally the old grain market. It was a loggia for traders, money-changers and lenders, and beggars. The Commune rented out the grain sacks, stalls and storage facilities. The devout came to kneel before a miracle-working picture of the Virgin painted on one of its piers. Because of the miraculous image, a religious brotherhood was associated with the building. In front of the picture lauds were sung with organ and viol. Free singing lessons were given here every

Sunday. On the eve of important feasts involving the Madonna, the musicians were supplied at the Commune's expense. Since 1325 the brotherhood has been governed by six captains, high-standing members of the Guelph Party, who saw to it, long before New York's Tammany, that its charities went only to those who supported the Party. The brotherhood became very rich. After the great plague of 1348 it was showered with legacies which amounted to the prodigious sum (for those times) of 350,000 gold florins (more than the annual income of the Commune from taxes, etc.). The plague was regarded as a Divine punishment and these extraordinary gifts were a sign of the prevailing mood of guilt and penance. Much of the money was spent on charity, such as gifts to dowerless maidens. Some of the funds paid for Orcagna's glittering tabernacle built to house the miraculous Virgin. Ghiberti said that 86,000 florins were spent on it. Rich as the tabernacle looks, it is the earliest known instance of the quality of the craftsman's work being praised by his contemporaries above the mere value of the materials.

In 1336 the city council decided to replace the old hall with a building which combines the features of a market and an oratory; they referred to it as the *palatium Orti S Michaelis* because it was the place where a church of St Michael once stood. The guild of Por S Maria (which included silk merchants and goldsmiths) was entrusted with the task of its construction. The costs were to be defrayed by market dues and rents. Until 1380 the ground floor remained a loggia of open arcades while the upper floors served as a great warehouse.

From the first, decoration assumed a role of unprecedented importance in the new building. It was entrusted to the brotherhood run by the Parte Guelfa and to the guilds invited by Por S Maria. The inscription on a coin laid in with the masonry proclaimed that the structure was to show off the magnificence of the city's guilds and artisans (*ut magnificentia populi fiorentini artium et artificum ostendatur*). Each of the major guilds adopted a pillar as a kind of tabernacle on which their patron saint was painted and before which an altar was raised. At first these pictures were on panels but by 1402 most of them were replaced by the murals visible today. Not all the piers inside, however, were under the custody of the guild. One of them, that of the *Good Thief*, was painted in 1361 at the behest of a citizen condemned to death.

As early as 1339 the programme of monumental sculpture was already planned for the new loggia. Each of the outside piers was assigned to a guild which was to see that the niche was filled with its appropriate statue. Only the Arte della Lana met its obligation almost immediately with a stone figure of *St Stephen*. Another sixty years went by before further progress was made. By 1406, when most of the interior decor of murals and stained glass was complete, the city council sought to speed up the scheme of statuary by setting a ten-year deadline, after which the guilds would lose claim to their niches if they were still empty. There was an interesting clause in the communal decree: permission was given for bronze statues to be raised. In practice this privilege was reserved for the great guilds; the lesser guilds were obliged to use stone. The smaller guilds were first to respond to the Commune's directive. Between 1405 and 1412 the notaries, furriers and smiths had stone statues of *SS Luke* (now in the Bargello), *James the Great*, and *Eligius* carved for them by Niccolò di Piero Lamberti and Nanni di Banco. But late in 1412 there was a new development. Until then the great guilds had held off. But in that year, for the richest guild of all, the Calimala, Ghiberti began to fashion a *Baptist* to be cast in Flemish bronze. No statue as large as this had ever been cast in Florence before. Ghiberti himself had no previous experience with either modelling or casting on such a scale and he risked having to pay for the bronze himself should he fail. But Ghiberti succeeded in casting the figure in one piece (save for the second toe on the left foot!). The cost of a bronze statue was about ten times that of one in stone. But from then on competition between the great guilds was intense and all of them had their patron saints made of bronze. The Parte Guelfa, not content with bronze alone, had Donatello *gild* their *St Louis of Toulouse*, which originally occupied the central niche now filled by Verrocchio's *Doubting Thomas*. This extravagance was a final splurge recalling the Parte Guelfa's glories of the past. The *St Louis* was made exactly a century after the Parte Guelfa had assumed the guardianship of the confraternity of Orsanmichele. That theirs was the only gilt statue fanned bitter political rivalry and exacerbated the party's already great unpopularity. A few decades later the Medici did all they could to erase every trace of the Parte Guelfa and they banished *St Louis*, gilt or no gilt, saint or no saint, to S Croce. In 1463 even the niche, in what appears to have been a forced sale, was turned over to the Mercatanzia (the merchants' tribunal) and Verrocchio, a favourite Medici artist, was employed for the statuary.

FLORENTINE STATUARY, 1406–28. At Orsanmichele in the twenty-two years between 1406 and 1428 were set forth all the separate paths Renaissance sculpture was to take. Yet, for all their differences,

Nanni, Ghiberti and Donatello had two interests in common: to relate statuary to its setting and to express feelings and moral concepts in forms which are at once monumental and human. Nanni, Ghiberti and Donatello leapt forward where Giotto and Giovanni Pisano had paused a century earlier: they brought beholder and sacred image into a much closer relationship – physically and spiritually. To be sure, Nanni's *St Eligius* (*ca* 1410–11) and his *St Philip* (*ca* 1412–16) are still 'sentry-box' figures. But there is a new gravity which stirs them; Gothic stylishness is giving way to a ponderous classical bearing, Eligius's troubled countenance turns on a powerfully constructed neck and Philip's distraction is evoked by his open mouth, the shift of his body, and the way he unaccountably clutches his mantle. Both figures register physical responses to forces of mind and spirit which Nanni dignified with ancient Roman attitudes. This was carried further in the next few years in the *Quattro Coronati* (probably after 1413). These are the most self-consciously classical figures in Florentine sculpture. But if Nanni was here retrospective in the style of ancient Roman dress and facial type, his treatment of the niche and his disposition of the figures anticipate Verrocchio's *Doubting Thomas*. The world of saints in discourse is brought near; the front of the niche floor is scooped out, sandalled feet and even the knotted curtain protrude from the Gothic framework.

Donatello was only twenty-five when he began the *St Mark*. It was made only a few years before the *Quattro Coronati*. In no other statue did Donatello acknowledge so directly his study of Roman statuary. Yet compared to Nanni's saints, whatever is Roman here has been thoroughly transformed into Donatello's own highly personal style. There is no trace of a heroic Roman mask in the noble head nor is there anything rhetorical about the drapery. St Mark's head is burdened with thought, the gravity of which is felt through every finger and in the very slump of the cloth down the powerful torso and over the bent knee. The feeling of force is obtained by oppositions: of the body working through the cloth, of the verticals and horizontals in the gown, in the twist of the head, the setting of the hands, in the *contrapposto* of the stance. Despite its being placed in a Gothic niche which was ordered with the statue (Gothic because the linen drapers wanted to have a niche just like the one made for the Wool Guild some seventy years before), the *St Mark* has been justly called 'the earliest unequivocal instance of a Renaissance figure'. Its impact was enormous; it antedated Masaccio's famous *Apostles* in the Carmine by probably a decade.

Michelangelo said that he had never seen anyone, man or statue, who had more the bearing of an honest man than Donatello's figure.

Ghiberti's bronze *Baptist* (1412–16) belongs to another world altogether, although it was made in the same years as the *Quattro Coronati* and the *St Mark*. Ghiberti's *Baptist* belongs to the world of the so-called International style favoured then by the courts of Europe. Ghiberti's doors for the Baptistery are the supreme Italian examples. They are characterized by highly stylized schemes, technical virtuosity displaying elegant linear rhythms, and finely wrought detail cast in rich material. The bronze *Baptist* is essentially an enlargement to monumental proportions of a style best suited to miniatures. It was fitting that the Calimala, the richest and most aristocratic of the great Florentine guilds, should associate itself with a courtly fashion. In spite of the style, Ghiberti's hoary saint conveys something of the wild and feverish fanatic which goes beyond a merely modish formula.

Ghiberti's *Baptist* was the popular success, but Donatello's *St Mark* was the critical success. With the exception of Donatello's *St Louis*, all the other bronze statues at Orsanmichele during the Quattrocento were ordered from Ghiberti. Yet in the Cambio's *St Matthew* (1419–22) Ghiberti changed towards a classical conception: posture, gesture, and facial type recall figures of ancient orators and the niche is lined with Corinthian pilasters. Like Nanni and Donatello (the *Quattro Coronati*, the *St Mark* and the *St George*), Ghiberti now also assumed a dramatic posture as if to acknowledge the presence of an audience: the shifting stance, the oratorical gesture, the glance and the protruding foot.

Oddly enough, Ghiberti's last bronze for Orsanmichele, the *St Stephen* (1425–9), harks back to the sculptor's more Gothic moments. Perhaps the Arte della Lana's conservatism had something to do with it. The bronze replaced the stone figure of 1339 which was moved over to the Cathedral Works, also administered by the Lana. Compared to Ghiberti's other bronzes, the *Stephen* is inferior both in size and workmanship. It was the victim of the guild's penny-pinching policies and the artist's worries over the deadline for the Paradise Doors.

Donatello's *St George* (1415–17) is the first statement of the heroic ideal in Florentine art. He is the young warrior, proud and brave in his righteous cause, comely and touching. He is the direct ancestor of Michelangelo's *David* made almost a century later for the Piazza della Signoria. Donatello's *St George* in stone (the original is now in the

Bargello) was made for the smiths and armourers. Probably he once held a metal lance or sword in his right hand. The figure is still, action is implicit in the glance and in the readiness to spring into action. The *St George* is an early instance of a statue carved with more than a single main view in mind; a foretaste of what was to become the chief preoccupation of sixteenth-century sculptors.

The predella of *St George killing the Dragon* (1417) introduced even more novelties of technique and composition. Remarkably, it is Donatello's earliest known relief and the first example of *rilievo schiacciato* ('crushed relief'). This method lent itself to the finest nuances of light and shade, making possible representations of atmosphere which, when combined with linear perspective, allowed illusions of space vaster than had ever been imagined in stone before.

The Parte Guelfa chose *St Louis of Toulouse*, the mystic prince who renounced a crown for a friar's cowl, as their figure for Orsan-michele. Donatello's gilded bronze (1422-5), now in the S Croce Museum (*see* chapter 4), was deliberately conceived on a larger scale than its pseudo-antique niche, for which Donatello was also in large part responsible. The fire gilding required that the figure be cast in eight separate pieces. The great mantle of St Louis and not the body of the saint, which is completely obscured by it, is the dominating feature of the statue. Ghiberti, in his handling of drapery (as in the *St Stephen* begun a year or two later), was careful to have the figure beneath come through by sharp lines and accents. Donatello gave the drapery expression, meaning, a life of its own. He anticipated Verrocchio later in the century in Florence and even Bernini two centuries later in Rome.

OF BUSINESS, BANKS, AND THE MERCATO NUOVO. The merchants bankers and artisans who constituted the company of Orsanmichele (and were responsible for the building of the same name) conducted their affairs in the streets and guild houses clustered around it. The Wool Guild (*Arte della Lana*) even boasted a place which still stands directly behind Orsanmichele. The Lana controlled the domestic wool industry and was the great rival of the Calimala, who were the entre-preneurs of foreign cloth finished in the city. One flank of the Palazzo dell' Arte della Lana faces the Via Calimala, a corruption of *Cardo Major*, or *Calle Mayor* – the absolute north and south road of the Roman *decumanus*. At the beginning of the Trecento the Calimala was a tight club of old mercantile families: the Cerchi, Mozzi, Pulci, Canigiani, Bardi, Pazzi, Spini and Peruzzi. Only after the great plague of 1348 decimated the city were newer magnates permitted to join it.

To the Calimala was entrusted the control of the measure of cloth. It had a standard iron rod mounted in three different spots in the city and once a year every merchant's measuring-stick was checked against the official rod, or *canna*. The Calimala also ran the city's first postal service, with regular couriers and relay stations to which the guild's members could subscribe. For more than two centuries the Calimala was responsible for the financial administration of the fabric of the Baptistery, S Miniato and several hospitals. The Lana's patronage of this sort was concentrated on the Cathedral Works (the *Opera del Duomo*), which accounts for the frequent appearance of the flag-bearing lamb inserted in the Duomo's structure.

The bankers were concentrated around the Mercato Nuovo and Por S Maria. The neighbourhood is in fact still a banking centre. By two great commercial inventions, Florentines during the thirteenth and fourteenth centuries became the bankers of Europe. One of these was the international letter of credit, the other was the coinage in Florence in 1252 of the gold florin, which established the first stable international currency. No other city had the vast network of agents and branch banks maintained by the Florentines across Europe, North Africa and the Middle East. The Bardi and Peruzzi were the chief bankers to the kings of France and England, the Acciaioli to the Angevin kings of Naples and Sicily, and the Alberti to the Curia (after the collapse of the Bardi and Peruzzi). The Bardi and Peruzzi over-extended their credit to the Duke of Burgundy and King Edward III of England and a catastrophic chain of bankruptcies followed in Florence between 1339 and 1341.

The great risks caused interest rates on loans to go as high as 60% sometimes. This carried with it the stigma of usury. which was an occupational hazard of banking. A permanent guilty conscience provoked bankers to expiate their sins through good works. Ledgers of the time carried on their books *il conto di Messer Domeneddio* (God's account) as one of the regular creditors to whom money was given via alms and charities. The patron saint of the bankers was St Matthew, who had been a money-changer, and his image is painted on one of the piers inside Orsanmichele, but with no allusion to his former profession. Villani, once a partner in the Bardi bank, never refers to his occupation. Indeed, part of his chronicle was written in the Stinche, the infamous debtors' prison. Nevertheless, a guilty conscience did not get in the way of the bankers' defence of their rights even where the Pope and Curia were concerned. When in 1345 the papal Inquisitor, Piero d'Aquila, demanded that preference be given to Cardinal Sabina in the collection of a debt from the Bankrupt

Acciaioli Company, the Commune refused to yield up any of the bank's partners. An interdict was promptly laid on the city. The Commune forbade any layman or cleric to obey it. A delegation was dispatched to Avignon and in the end it was the Curia which backed down.

By 1421 there were seventy-two banks in the neighbourhood around the Mercato Novo. Nearby were the myriad retail shops of the silk guild. Their affairs and those of the Cambio (the bankers' guild) often overlapped. Por S Maria was the most subdivided of all the guilds; it included merchants and weavers of silk, goldsmiths, upholsterers, feather merchants, embroiderers and mercers. Their shops lined Via Por S Maria (completely destroyed during the war). Here, besides silks and jewellery, they sold table napkins from Cremona and veils from Perugia, scissors, needles, thread, hammers, metal clasps for books, and soft soap.

Early in the 1420s silk-worm culture was brought to Florence. Before this, silk thread or cloth was imported from the Middle East and the best cut-velvet brocades were sent in from Rumania and Anatolia. A decree of 1419 urged Florentine silk-makers to make their product the very best possible. The death penalty was instituted for those manufacturers who dared take their craft elsewhere. In 1422, the technique for weaving gold thread into silk was introduced. As the wool trade gradually declined, the silk industry increased (although it was never to have the predominant position which Florentine woollens had in the Trecento). Throughout the Quattrocento the silk industry was the staple of the expanding Levant trade. In exchange came jewels, pearls, and luxury goods in ever greater quantities. Much of this was re-exported from Florence and the influx of precious stuffs had much to do with the flowering of the courtly International style in art and in ladies' fashions during the first decades of the fifteenth century. Gentile da Fabriano's great altarpiece painted for the Strozzi belongs to 1423; it is a feast of precious brocades, embroideries, bejewelled headgear and harnesses. These were also the years of sumptuary laws and Bernardino da Siena's famous Lenten Sermons (1424–5): 'I know some women who have more heads than the devil: each day they don a new one . . . I see some who wear them in the shape of tripe and some like a pancake, some like a trencher and some like a flap, some folded up and some turned down. Oh, women, I bid you take them off! . . . You have made a God of your head.' We are told Bernardino had a pyre raised in Piazza S Croce for the burning of hats and other vanities – a foretaste of Savonarolism. Of course neither sumptuary laws nor sermons seriously inhibited the manufacture of luxury goods in Florence. Actually, the taste for such stuffs rarely ran wild among the sober Florentines because most of it was for export. By 1474, the silk guild had eighty-four shops.

The Mercato Nuovo, built in 1547, was intended by Cosimo I as the central market-place for silk and gold. It has become the straw market – an industry begun in Leghorn at the beginning of the last century. The demand for straw hats all over Europe provoked its development in Tuscany – and thus comes the name of 'Leghorn hats' familiar in English novels, and the *Florentiner* of Germany and Austria. The best grasses for this work are still grown in the neighbourhood of Signa, Brozzi and Carmignano, where towards sunset, with the day's labours in the fields done, farmers' wives and old women braid away to earn a little pocket-money – they usually get about 15 lire (something less than twopence) the metre.

Inside the loggia of the Mercato Nuovo is a round plaque for which there are two traditional explanations. The first has it that this was the spot where the Communal battle-wagon, or *carroccio*, was brought to celebrate a victory. The other associates it with the place where bankrupts were publicly disgraced by being tied to a rope hung from the strut above and bounced on the ground with their pants down.

By what code of behaviour did the Florentine businessmen who built the palaces in this neighbourhood live in the fourteenth and fifteenth centuries? One of the best early sources on the subject, besides Pegolotti and Francesco di Marco Datini, was Giovanni Frescobaldi. In 1278 King Edward I had called in a member of the Frescobaldi family to direct the new royal mint. Giovanni's advice to Florentine merchants bound for England was:

Wear modest colours, be humble, be dull in appearance but in fact be subtle in your dealings; if the Englishman [tries to] floor you, woe to him ...

Pay on the day [when payment is due and be] courteous in collecting, showing that need is driving you to the grave. Make no more demands than you are entitled to ...

It behoves you to club together with your nation, and see to it that your doors are well bolted early.

Pegolotti's handbook is filled with advice on how to judge merchandise: pepper should be dry and without trace of powder, if it should get damp in transit instructions are given for salvaging it; cinnamon should have a thin bark and be of a colour between red and grey; fresh dates should be large and reddish – a drawing of how all this should look accompanies the description.

The prosperity of the typical Florentine merchant was not founded on sharp practice. He was a realist with his wits about him, and though sometimes bold, he was content with a middle course in his affairs. It was in the fourteenth century that the great Florentine fortunes were being made. It was a time of financial booms and depressions, of great fortunes and great bankruptcies. In the scramble for money, power and security, some were 'perverse men, selfish and without charity', as the successful Florentine businessman Nicola Acciaioli wrote from Naples in 1363. Dante's opinion of his fellow Florentines was dyspeptic enough (*see* chapter 1); but he was in exile. In the next century the heirs of the great fortunes could afford the luxury of urbanity, the fine palaces and villas, poetry and philosophy. One of these, Giovanni Rucellai, could write that his city was 'the sweetest country of the universe . . . how thankful I am to have been born now in the happiest age (*la più gioconda età*) which our city has ever had since Florence was built.'

PALAZZO DI PARTE GUELFA. The Parte Guelfa was the political party under which the Commune's independence flourished. Early on, the Guelphs saw that their own and the city's liberty had a greater chance with the cause of the Pope in Rome than with that of the Emperor from beyond the Alps, with his old ideas of margravates and vassaldoms. Around 1250 the Parte Guelfa emerged as an association of nobles who were struggling against the Ghibelline faction for control of the city. The Ghibelines unluckily chose the losing side, that of the Emperor, and were finally crushed at Benevento in 1266 by the troops of Charles of Anjou. Then the Guelph era in Florence began. They fattened themselves on confiscated Ghibelline property, while their authority was guaranteed by the Angevin kings, to whom the papacy was also indebted. In this affair the Florentine Guelphs were not wards in chancery, they were the chief bankers to the House of Anjou and to the Curia, and we may surmise that they expected and received more in return than repayment of money lent. The Guelph connection with the House of Anjou is to be read in their emblem: the red eagle holding the Ghibelline dragon in its talons surmounted by a small red Florentine lily. The Calimala's sympathies with the Parte Guelfa are declared by their emblem, which has the same eagle but bearing a bundle of cloth instead of the dragon. The Guelphs adopted as their patron saint Louis of Toulouse, the elder son of Charles of Anjou, who became a Franciscan.

The party organization included representatives from all the guilds and wards of the city. But its real power lay in the hands of a small executive committee composed of the richest of the merchant bankers (Cerchi, Donati, Acciaioli, Alberti). At first the meetings were held in the little church of S Maria sopra Porta. Then around 1277 the committee acquired property next door to it on the Via delle Terme which was successively enlarged in 1359, 1370 and 1377. The Parte Guelfa was a state within a state and for many decades it controlled the city government. Its committees decided who was elibigle for office, disposing of opponents by labelling them as Ghibellines (even though Ghibellinism was long a dead issue, it remained a popular bogeyman). It also controlled the city's main charities: Orsanmichele, the Misericordia, and the hospital of S Maria Nuova. Like the Commune and the Calimala, it too sent out its own ambassadors to foreign courts. The party enjoyed this enormous moral prestige because it was a rallying-point for Florentine patriotism: the Parte Guelfa was regarded as the faithful ally of the Commune, as in fact it was. But eventually, after 1343, there was increasing objection to its conservative policies which reserved political power to a few rich families of commercial magnates. The old feud between Guelphs and Ghibellines rapidly became one between *magnati* and *popolani* (entrepreneurs and workers). Between 1343 and 1378 the Parte Guelfa was forced to cede room in communal affairs to representatives of the smaller guilds and to the labouring artisans. The Parte Guelfa, rigidly conservative, refused to bend with the times; it continued to side with the Church even when the Papacy began to pursue policies antagonistic to Florence. Out of this situation came the War of the Eight Saints (1371–5) – the Saints' being the eight members of the communal war committee. The Ciompi Revolt which came soon afterwards was not only an effort to free the city of the Parte Guelfa's yoke, it was also a movement of violent anti-clericalism. Houses of leading Guelphs were burned and plundered, including those of the Canigiani, Pazzi, Guadagni, some of the Strozzi, Alberti and Soderini, as well as the Palazzo dell' Arte della Lana. Thereafter the party's power was gradually chipped away. A few anti-Guelph magnates, first some of the Albizzi and then the Medici, succeeded in foisting their own government on the city with popular support. They promulgated legislation which permanently barred most of the other *magnati* and their descendants from office. The Parte Guelfa was allowed to administer its still considerable properties and to act as custodians of the city archives. But as a political institution it was now moribund. It remained prosperous for some time. When Pisa was captured in 1406 it paid for the first series of annual jousts in Piazza S Croce. Around 1418 it had its palace rebuilt and at a certain point, we do not know exactly when, Brunelleschi was called in on the project. Notwithstanding its political conservatism, the Parte Guelfa's palace is the earliest Renaissance palace in Florence. The style is at once simple and grandiose. Brunelleschi used the Trecento masonry on the ground floor as a dado for the second storey, which is almost a loggia. The smooth masonry is pierced by a procession of high arched windows. The window frames and the cornice consist of delicately profiled mouldings in the classical spirit. Inside, in the council hall on the first floor, Brunelleschi used for the first time giant orders of pilasters to articulate and frame the walls. For a while the building served as a firehouse, the fine council room became a dormitory. Now it houses the *Università Popolare* – a kind of night school.

PATRICIAN PALACES AND CHAPELS: THE PALAZZO DAVANZATI. The thirteenth and fourteenth centuries comprised the age of the great communal projects: the Palazzo Vecchio, the Duomo, Orsanmichele. Even the great churches of the mendicant orders, S Maria Novella and S Croce, were largely financed through public funds. The palaces built by the *magnati* of the fourteenth century such as the Palazzo dell'Arte della Lana, the Palazzo di Parte Guelfa and the Palazzo Acciaioli, still have the character of fortresses although by 1312 the great family feuds had ceased. The Palazzo Davanzati, built by the Davizzi around 1330, begins to show the shift in palace architecture towards a more leisurely way of life and a nobler style of building. As was the custom, the palace was divided between different members of the family; the building was really the headquarters of a clan. In the middle is an open courtyard bringing in light and accommodating a staircase. The entrance on the ground floor was once an open loggia where some of the family business was conducted. The store-rooms, servants' quarters and stable adjoined it. The bottom of the staircase leading to the living quarters is guarded by a small Marzocco and on a nearby wall a mural of St Christopher defended the family from violent or sudden death. Each floor has a broad high-ceilinged hall spanning the width of the building at its front brightened by many windows. The great studded wooden shutters are still intact. Until the fifteenth century, glass windows were a great luxury and had to be imported from Venice, France and Flanders. After the great flood of 1333 an angry friar listed glass windows among the vanities which had drawn God's wrath upon the city. Instead of glass, oiled linen or cotton panes (called *impannate*) were sometimes used.

189

Many of the smaller rooms in the Palazzo Davanzati were entirely painted late in the fourteenth century with muralled hangings adorned with parakeets and flowers. At the top, a common motif is an illusionistic arcade framing views of gardens and, in one instance, a chivalric story of the trials of fidelity and chastity. Many rooms have their own stone fireplace built into the wall. Such fireplaces were uncommon until about 1300. Hitherto the fire for cooking and heating had been in the centre of the room on an open hearth with the smoke escaping as best it could through the chinks and windows. There are also pulleys fixed inside some of the walls so that water could be brought up from the palace's private well. Most housewives of the time still had to fetch their water from the nearby piazza. The loggia crowning the facade was a fifteenth-century addition.

During the fifteenth century parts of the palace were rented out. The ground floor at one point was occupied by three wool shops. Until the Uffizi was built, several rooms were occupied by the officials of the *Catasto*, instituted in 1427 as a communal office which made tax assessments based on property and goods. Its records are a rich mine of Florentine social and economic history in the fifteenth century; there are declarations of family obligations, income, property and work in hand. From them we learn much more of what Ghiberti, Masaccio and Donatello were doing than from the records of contracts and payments. One can still see scrawled across the walls complaints and other uncomplimentary remarks of citizens who came to the Palazzo Davanzati to argue about their taxes.

THE BARTOLINI-SALIMBENI CHAPEL IN SANTA TRINITA. The Davizzi and the Davanzati were neighbours of the Bartolini-Salimbeni and both families as parishioners of S Trinita instituted family burial chapels there. About 1450 Guiliano Davanzati's heirs buried him in a late Roman sarcophagus, carving his effigy on top of it. The chapel of the Bartolini-Salimbeni is one of the few early fifteenth-century chapels of which the original decorations have survived in an almost complete state. The taste of the family, who had made their fortune in banking and were one of the pillars of the *Arte del Cambio*, was that of the courtly, late Gothic, International style. Around 1423 they had Lorenzo Monaco and his assistants paint the walls with tiers of scenes filled with elegant figures in ice-cream-sherbet colours. The altarpiece is a rich *fondo d'oro* of the *Annunciation* and a lacy wrought-iron gate screens the entrance.

THE CHAPEL OF ONOFRIO STROZZI IN SANTA TRINITA. The sacristy-chapel of Onofrio Strozzi boasted what was probably the apogee of the International style in Florence: Gentile da Fabriano's *Adoration of the Magi*, now in the Uffizi, commissioned by Onofrio's son, Palla. One would hardly guess from Gentile's altarpiece, which contains portraits of the Strozzi dressed in regal finery, that Onofrio as a communal officer promoted sumptuary laws against extravagant female dress. He was also responsible for legislation against dice-playing and advocated a scheme for raising monuments in the Duomo to Dante, Petrarch and Boccaccio, which was never realized. The chapel's architecture is one of the first monuments of the early Renaissance. Its style is a mixture of lingering Gothicism and graceful Classicism; a style between that of Orsanmichele and the Palazzo di Parte Guelfa. The interior is restrained. The walls are whitewashed and the floor is black and white marble. The steps leading to the altar are inlaid with family emblems: crowns, palm boughs and crescent moons. The first two symbols were given to the family by the Queen of Naples when she bestowed a knighthood on Palla, her court banker, in 1415. The moons were older; they were the symbol of Fiesole, whence the Strozzi claimed their origin. Onofrio Strozzi's grave is one of the earliest instances of a private monument raised in the classical style. A round lunette frames the sarcophagus, which has none of the conventional Christian symbology; there are only garlands and playful *putti* – perhaps by Donatello.

Six hundred tapers and candles burned at Onofrio's sumptuous funeral in 1417. Palla, his son, undertook to carry out the construction of the chapel by his father. He also served as one of the three overseers for the production of Ghiberti's Paradise Doors. He was the richest Florentine of his time. In one year, of the total annual tax declarations of 620,000 florins, more than 100,000 belonged to Palla Strozzi. Publicly he was very retiring and modest in manner. He never stopped to chat in the piazzas for fear of being conspicuous, and on his way to the Palazzo dei Signori he always took the narrow side-streets. He planned to build a great public library to be housed in the convent of S Trinita. His biographer, Vespasiano da Bisticci, says that it was Palla who was responsible for bringing to the West manuscripts of Plato, Ptolemy's *Cosmografia* and Aristotle's *Politics*. Politically he took a middle course, which eventually had fatal consequences. He refused to support a strong military force which would have quelled the Medici. When Cosimo returned to seize control in 1434 he sent Palla and all the male members of the

Strozzi family into an exile which lasted for decades. Their fortunes were ruinously taxed. Loyal citizen that he was, Palla went into debt to pay Cosimo and had to cede to him much of his property. Politics were not for Palla Strozzi; his great fortune thrust upon him the role of public figure. The congenial milieu for him was as an amateur among literary *cognoscenti*, which was the life he led in Padua until he died in 1462.

THE PALAZZO RUCELLAI. The first great Renaissance palaces were not begun until the middle of the century: the Palazzo Medici in 1444, the Palazzo Rucellai in the 1450s and the Palazzo Pitti after 1458. The delay was partly due to the great financial drain caused by the wars against Lucca and Milan. Of these palaces, that of the Rucellai on Via della Vigna Nuova was the first to be completed. Its builder, Giovanni Rucellai, was a political opportunist: he married Palla Strozzi's daughter and married off his own son to Cosimo de' Medici's granddaughter, Nannina. His character is stamped upon the capitals and entablatures of his palace; trios of Medici rings alternate with Fortune's sail. The design of the palace is generally accepted as Leon Battista Alberti's; he was also responsible for the rebuilding of S Pancrazio and the façade of S Maria Novella – all projects subvented by Giovanni Rucellai.

The rusticated masonry so typical of feudal houses survived in the palace architecture of the Quattrocento. But here it is flattened out and civilized, as it were, into regular courses. Classical pilaster strips and string-courses help to govern this tame rustication. The divided windows are relics of the medieval *bifore*, but the portals have flat arches in the classical manner. The medieval crenellation is now replaced by the classical cornice. As a scheme, every surface is squared off and tightly framed, each detail has its reciprocal; nothing floats, nothing is unexplained. In his treatise on architecture, written about 1450, Alberti said that only the tyrant's house should be like a fortress. Otherwise, palaces, he said, 'should be easy of access, beautifully adorned, and rather delicate and polite than proud and stately.' The Palazzo Rucellai is just this, but it was carried out to only two-thirds the width of its original plan.

THE RUCELLAI CHAPEL IN SAN PANCRAZIO. Alberti maintained that a funerary chapel should be a church in miniature. His client, Giovanni Rucellai, took the trouble to obtain the exact measurements of the Holy Sepulchre in Jerusalem for the replica to go inside the family chapel in S Pancrazio. In his barrel-vaulted chapel for the

Drawing by Michelangelo in the Uffizi

Portrait of Lorenzo the Magnificent as one of the Three Kings from
Botticelli's *Adoration of the Magi* in the Uffizi, *ca* 1475-8

Rucellai, Alberti – like Brunelleschi before him – kept to what had become the classical Florentine scheme of unadorned white walls articulated by blue-black stone pilasters. The replica of the Holy Sepulchre is a miniature basilica with black and white marble inlays in the tradition of the Florentine Romanesque such as the Baptistery and S Miniato, which were then thought to be classical buildings.

THE PALAZZO STROZZI. The descendants of Palla Strozzi had not been idle during their years of exile. Once more they became bankers to the kings of Naples. Filippo had amassed an immense fortune there. By 1480 Florence was in debt to the King of Naples and his son Alfonso, the Duke of Calabria. The Medici came to terms with them and Filippo Strozzi was involved in the arrangements. Thus the Medici family made their peace with the Strozzi and Filippo's palace proclaimed the family's triumphant return to Florentine life.

Already in 1474 Filippo had begun buying up property in the centre of Florence next to some the family had been able to keep. Later he acquired more through purchase from the Counts of Poppi. In May 1489 Lorenzo de' Medici, wishing to encourage building improvements, had the Signoria pass legislation exempting those who built new houses on empty sites from forty years of communal taxes (*gravezze*).

One of the best Florentine architects of the time was Giuliano da Maiano, who had been appointed court architect to the King of Naples on Lorenzo de' Medici's recommendation. Giuliano's Palazzo Spannocchi (1470) in Siena is closely related to the Palazzo Strozzi and he and Giuliano da Sangallo may in one way or another have been in on the early planning of Filippo's palace, even if only in an unofficial capacity. In any event, Filippo Strozzi turned to Guiliano's younger brother, Benedetto da Maiano. The plans for the palace were for a structure of unprecedented scale – free-standing with a garden stretching to the south down to the Via Porta Rossa. Filippo pretended that all he wanted was a simple, useful house devoid of pomp, suitable for himself, his family and his business. While the plans grew, feigning modesty, he complained that all the projects prepared so far by the architects were too grandiose and would be his ruin. At one point he said that on no account did he want to have any rustication because this would not be plebeian enough for his humble taste. Meanwhile Lorenzo de' Medici, himself an armchair architect, asked to see the plans and made several suggestions – rustication among them. Filippo cleverly proceeded to turn Lorenzo into the patron of the scheme and through him he acquired still more land:

the piazza in front of the Loggia de' Tornaquinci. Months were taken up by demolition crews to clear the site, which was so big that it straddled the parishes of S Trinita and S Gaetano. Landucci, the diarist and storekeeper, complained of the dust they raised and the difficulties of traffic. Finally, after consulting an astrologer, the date for laying the foundation stone was set for August 6th, 1489. It was in the sign of the Lion – signifiying strength and endurance and promising long residence in the building to Filippo's progeny. It was a great event. Tribaldo de' Rossi, who had tended Lorenzo de' Medici's wounds after the Pazzi Conspiracy, took his children to see it: 'I took Guarnieri in my arms and told him to look down there. I gave him a coin with a lily to throw down, also a bunch of little damask roses which I had in my hand. I said, "Will you remember this?" "Yes," said he. The children came with our servant Tita, and Guarnieri, who was on that day just four years old, had a new cloak made by Nannina of shot green and yellow silk.'

As it was finally carried out, the palace was probably based on a model prepared by Giuliano da Sangallo and revised by Benedetto da Maiano. By 1490, Cronaca was already involved in the work. It was he who was responsible for the loggia opening on the courtyard (1504–5; 1533–6) and the final cornice (1501–3). In May 1491 Filippo Strozzi died. His heirs were instructed to see to it that what with masons, manual labourers and stone-cutters, fifty people would be continually employed on the building so that it could be finished within five years. Then came the diplomatic master-stroke: if the building was not finished by 1496, he left the matter of its supervision to Lorenzo the Magnificent should he survive him. Should Lorenzo not wish to assume the task, it was to be left to the consuls of the Calimala and two members of the Strozzi family. He added that any of these might sell other properties in order to finish the building. The palace cost more than 200,000 florins before it was finished. Clearly it was intended as a colossal family monument.

At Filippo Strozzi's death, the construction had reached the height of the iron rings on the first storey. Thereafter the progress of the work was: April 1495 – the next storey begun

End 1495 – windows on top storey finished

1497 – death of Benedetto da Maiano

1501 – cornice finished on Piazza Strozzi side

1508 – death of Cronaca

1507 – 1533 – work slows down

1533 – 1536 – work taken up again, but cornice
remains incomplete.

The Palazzo Strozzi is the rusticated palace *par excellence*. Save for the square windows on the ground floor, the subtle scheme of classical articulations devised by Alberti for the Palazzo Rucellai was ignored. There is a contrast between the heavy masonry and the delicate windows embedded in it. All medieval coarseness is gone from the rustification. Each block was given a fine form, a clear biting profile, and not a stone projects further than its neighbour. There is a regularity of alternation between large and small blocks in each row. As it rises, the rustication gradually flattens, only to be finished off by the outward thrust of the terminating frieze and conrice.

But the greatest innovation is Cronaca's cortile. Gone is the spring-like freshness of the earlier Quattrocento. Here is the sombre magnificence, the massive grandeur of the High Renaissance. Cronaca turned away from Brunelleschi and Alberti; his style was based upon the ruins of ancient Rome with its implications of mass and power. Soon after he became *capomaestro* of the Palazzo Strozzi, Cronaca was invited to serve in the same capacity at the Opera del Duomo and the Palazzo della Signoria.

The Palazzo Strozzi also boasts some of the best Florentine wrought-iron work. The rings outside were used for tethering horses before the cortile's completion. Higher up are hooks which held rods on which caged birds or festive hangings were suspended. The great spiked lamps at the corners were a sign of dignity and rank granted by Communal decree. Among others granted this honour were Michele di Lando, the Medici, some of the Cerchi and Soderini. When news of Amerigo Vespucci's discoveries reached Florence, the Signoria sent torches to his house which were kept lit for three days and three nights. The lamps of the Palazzo Strozzi, designed by Benedetto da Maiano, are the work of Niccolò Grosso, called 'il Caparra' because he refused to give credit (the *caparra* is an advance down-payment on work to be done).

THE PALAZZO BARTOLINI-SALIMBENI, AND PIAZZA SANTA TRINITA. The Palazzo Bartolini-Salimbeni was the first palace in the centre of Florence carried out entirely in the new High Renaissance manner which Raphael and Bramante were then introducing to Rome. A crop of designs in the new style had already been seen in Florence in the monumental festival decorations for Pope Leo X's (Giovanni de' Medici's) triumphal entry into the city in 1515. Baccio d'Agnolo is said to have been one of the designers. Possibly because he showed himself versed in the architectural *dernier cri* from Rome, Giovanni Salimbeni gave him the commission to build his palace, which was carried out between 1517 and 1520. The façade caused a sensation. Public opinion held it more suitable for a church façade than for a private palace. Verses were read in public making fun of it and laurel garlands were hung between the windows to exaggerate its church-like appearance. According to Vasari, it was the first patrician house in the city to have square windows with frontispieces and its façade set the style of many a subsequent Florentine palace. The Duke of Retz (a Gondi and a peer of France) even had an exact copy of it built in Paris on the Rue Montmartre. The façade is an ideal balance, in proportion and detail, between classical Roman reserve and piquant Florentine elegance. What was new in the design was the deliberate tension created between mass and space, light and shadow.

Giovanni Salimbeni had as little regard for public opinion as he had for popular taste. He had inscribed across every window the arrogant family motto: *Per non dormire* (So as not to sleep). The story has it that once, in the negotiation of a great transaction, the Bartolini-Salimbeni invited their colleagues to a feast, where they drugged the wine with opium so that they could harvest all the profits for themselves while their victims slept. Proud of their trick, the Bartolini-Salimbeni had poppies crop up all over the palace as well as the motto across the windows.

During the second half of the century the Medici Grand Dukes imposed a certain unity of style and ideology upon the Piazza S Trinita. In 1565 the Column of Justice was raised between the Palazzo Bartolini and the church. It marked the spot where Cosimo I learned of the victory at Montemurlo (August 2, 1537), which once and for all established absolute Medici power. The granite column, which came from the Baths of Caracalla in Rome, was the gift of Pope Pius IV. It stands exactly on axis with Ammannati's Ponte S Trinita begun in the next year in honour of Cosimo's victory over Siena. In 1581 del Tadda's porphyry statue of Justice was set on top of the column. Florentines thereafter called it the Column of Infamy because Justice turned her back on the monument to Florentine Republicanism, the Palazzo Vecchio, preferring the view towards Montemurlo, the beginning of despotism. In 1589 the not-so-very ancient royal house had installed at the feet of Justice an elegant scheme of manufactured tradition triumphant: stucco statues of Augustus, Charlemagne, Cosimo Pater Patriae, and Cosimo the first Grand Duke were set up at the four corners of the Ponte S Trinita on the occasion of the marriage of Ferdinando I to Christine of Lorraine. The politics of the matter notwithstanding, and snicker as one may at Medici immodesty, these figures were more appropriate heroic characters for a triumphal arch than the statues of the four seasons taken from the Acciauoli gardens and installed on the bridge for another Medici wedding in 1608.

Through most of the sixteenth century the High Renaissance style in architecture had been changing the face of Florence. In the centre of it all, S Trinita still had its old Romanesque façade very much out of keeping with the rest of the piazza. At last the reigning Medici decided to do something about it and in 1592 commissioned the court architect, Bernardo Buontalenti, to put up a new façade. Buontalenti was the man of all talents for the Medici. He took over the building of the Uffizi on Vasari's death. He built floats and fireworks, the canal between Pisa and Leghorn, the trick fountains of Pratolino, and mechanical toys for the Medici princes. In 1587 he prepared a design for a new façade for the Duomo. This came to nothing, but he used several of its ideas for S Trinita.

FAMILY LIFE IN THE QUATTROCENTO. Giovanni Rucellai, like most Florentines of his time, was sure that his city was the most beautiful since ancient Rome. The nobility of its splendid churches, palaces, hospitals and villas was matched, so the Florentines thought, by the conduct and bearing of the people who lived in them. Alberti believed that a gentleman should be able to do three things perfectly: speak, walk, ride. In 1444 a relation who was Florentine ambassador at the papal court, Averardo degli Alberti, wrote that the beauty of Rome lay only in its ruins. But as for the 'men of the present day who call themselves Romans [they] are very different in bearing and in conduct from the ancient inhabitants . . . they all look like cowherds. Their women are generally handsome in face; all the rest is uncommonly dirty; the reason, they tell me, is that they all cook.' The Florentine feeling of superiority had not changed a quarter of a century later. There is Lucrezia Tornabuoni's famous report in 1467 on her prospective daughter-in-law, Clarice Orsini, who was about to be betrothed to Lorenzo the Magnificent: '. . . She does not carry her head erect, like our girls, but holds it a little forward, which I think is due to shyness. Her hand is long and graceful. Altogether, we consider that the girl is quite out of the common, but she is not to be compared with Maria, Lucrezia, and Bianca . . .' We may have a picture of her in Botticelli's portrait in the Pitti – a long-nosed, gawky girl, with lank red hair and no humour.

How were the ideal Florentine lady and gentleman raised? What kind of life was led inside those great palaces? The records show that the children were not spoiled. One of the handbooks on child education was prepared by Fra Giovanni Dominici. In order to make the child pious even when he was still in diapers, Dominici suggested that the house be filled with painting and sculpture of holy children and young virgins. Great as Dominici's faith was in pictures, he nevertheless warned against too much gold and silver ornament lest the children be made 'idolaters before they were Christians'. Children were not to presume to speak in the presence of their parents. In addressing them the child should use reverence and kneel at their feet on entering and leaving as in a kind of benediction. Filippo Strozzi addressed letters to his mother as *'carissima quanto maggiore Madre'* and *'savia e discreta donna mona Alessandra'*. The seven-year-old daughter of Lorenzo de' Medici wrote to her grandmother, Lucrezia Tornabuoni, 'My magnificent Grandmother'. Today it is only the rector of a university who is formally addressed as *'Magnifico'*.

One could never tell how a child's destiny would turn out and so it was best not to spoil him, to accustom him to fasting, to physical discomfort (by making him sleep once a week in his clothes on a bench with the windows open). 'Treat him as if he was the child of a farm labourer – who become fat, strong, handsome, healthy, and almost all grow old.' Children were usually nursed for two years and then, without transition, put on good Tuscan wine. Corporal punishment, however, was generally frowned upon. Dominici's admonitions against loving mothers tells us something about children's toys and their attire; all the following he advised against: 'Combing them often . . . curling their hair . . . making them embroidered little hats, silvered capes, little beribboned skirts, carved cradles, painted slippers, soled hose; giving them little wooden horses, pretty cymbals, counterfeit birds, gilded drums . . . holding them in your arms, kissing them, licking them, singing them songs and telling them lying tales.'

At six or seven, boys were taught to reckon with the abacus. Practical training for the family business took a large place in the curriculum. At eleven Matteo Strozzi was sent out to improve his handwriting to prepare him for the large correspondence he would later have to conduct. At fourteen he entered the family trading company far from home – first in Spain, then in Naples. Families of means usually maintained a scholar in the household to tutor the children in Greek and Latin. Luigi Pulci and Poliziano served Lorenzo the Magnificent in this capacity, teaching his children the classics and instructing them in philosophy and literary style. It was the type of education already advocated by Alberti but its ideal was rarely achieved. Alberti was no pedant. He did not advocate children chirping Latin in the nursery. Only the vernacular was to be spoken at home. But he rejected the common idea that writing and figuring were sufficient equipment for a useful life in a commercial republic. He believed that native intellectual curiosity was a divine gift though it needed nurture. He was convinced that a knowledge of letters bred gentle manners, gave dignity to the mind and grace and weight to the personality. A Palla Strozzi, a Lorenzo de' Medici, Alberti himself, were the exceptional graduates of such an education. Bernardo Rucellai, who certainly had similar opportunities, stubbornly refused to speak or write a word of Latin under any circumstances, even when he was invited in Venice to meet Erasmus who knew not a word of Italian. Erasmus said of the young Florentine: 'I told him he might as well attempt to speak to a deaf person as to talk to me in Italian, of which I knew no more than Indian, but still I could not get a word from him.'

It was only towards the end of the fourteenth century that girls even of good family began to be taught to read and write as well as to sew. Until then a girl was taught to read only if she was to be a nun. At the turn of the century the shutters were thrown open. Girls were taught to read and write Latin verse, to dance, and to play a musical instrument. Much attention was given to grace and gentleness of voice, honesty of glance and smile, dignity of behaviour. But all this was futile if the young lady was without a dowry. To get a husband, she had to have at least sixty lire. The daughter of a patrician, a Caterina Strozzi, had a dowry of one thousand florins when she married Marco Parenti. At the birth of a daughter, most Florentine fathers of even modest means took the precaution of investing cash in a communal fund established for the purpose of guaranteeing the subscriber a dowry when the girl became of age. If the daughter died or entered a convent, the father forfeited half his investment. Apparently the Commune made money on this system. Of Filippo Strozzi's seven daughters, for instance, only four ever needed their dowries. Widowed daughters always returned to their father's house, bringing back their dowries with them.

The search for the suitable husband or wife occupies a large space in family literature of the time. A patrician family's strength depended upon the variety of its alliances at home and abroad, in politics and commerce. The head of the family chose the wife or husband for his children as he chose the professions for his sons. The mother was often sent out to take a look at the prospective bride –

unnoticed at Mass, or formally surrounded by her family at home. Qualities admired were health, beauty, neatness, modesty and gentleness. Alessandra Strozzi's judgment of one shrew was to say that 'she goes about hunting for trouble, and hangs on to her soul with aching teeth.' Of a young Adimari girl she was considering for Filippo she said that although 'her manners were not very delicate, they were not rough, and from the way she walks and looks it seems to me she isn't asleep' (*addormentata* was her word for it). We know less of what was thought becoming behaviour in a suitor. Morelli's chronicle (1393–*ca* 1415) advised a young man to court a lady above his station and to play a lute beneath her window once a year but not to spend more than two florins in courting the girl. Michelangelo's advice to his nephew was not so calculating: 'When you find one well brought up, good, healthy, even if she has nothing, take her.'

The cost of the wedding was borne by the bride's family and it often amounted to more than the much sought after dowry. Caterina Strozzi's wedding hat made of 800 peacock's feathers adorned with pearls and little red and blue enamelled flowers came to 140 florins. Bernardino da Siena had a wonderful time comparing such elaborate headgear to 'castles with towers carrying the Devil's own banners, around which battles are fought', making their wearers look like 'barn owls' (*barbagianni*). Caterina's mother said that her daughter's wedding-dress of crimson velvet with wide fur-lined sleeves was made of material 'the most beautiful in Florence'. There were two other dresses in the bride's wardrobe, both of white wool with interchangeable sleeves, one pair being of green velvet. Sleeves, which were often richly embroidered and bejewelled, were usually the most precious item of the wardrobe. Other items included seventeen shirts, thirty handkerchiefs, three pairs of red hose, two pairs of shoes, two linen collars, a pair of scissors, a mirror, a prayer book, a strand of coral beads, and two ivory combs. It was the cloth and furs of the gowns which were so costly. Often jewels were cheaper than velvets and damasks. Tailors got very little for their work. In 1292 they and and the butchers belonged to the same guild; fifty years later they still ranked below dyers and shearers. Usually the tailor only cut the garment, which was then sewn at home. Buttons were procured from the goldsmith, embroidery was done by a specialist, and lining and fur were obtained from still other sources. Fur linings were indispensable for unheated houses when wool sweaters and underwear were unknown. Hose was a luxury and a sumptuary law forbade nurses and house-maids to own hose with leather soles. The footwear of humble folk were sandals and clogs. Gloves are rarely mentioned in the inventories of the fourteenth and fifteenth centuries. Apparently they were not very respectable garments, for in 1388 a law was passed requiring all prostitutes to wear them when they went out; the gloves and a little bell on their heads were the tokens of their profession.

To attend a fashionable wedding was a costly decision. On the occasion of Lorenzo de' Medici's marriage to Clarice Orsini in 1469, Filippo Strozzi's wife feigned illness so that she would not have to go. But in the end she did and an elaborate gown was made for her. A wedding celebration could last for several days. Sumptuary laws limited the number of courses served. A hundred and seventy people sat at the banquet table spread in the Rucellai loggia when Bernardo Rucellai married Nannina de' Medici in June 1466. The table was set with precious silver, some of it borrowed from friends. The piazza beside the loggia had a canopy to protect the dancers from the sun and was adorned with garlands and coats-of-arms. Wedding gifts included a pair of calves, baskets of pomegranates, marzipan, Greek wine, quails and hares. The Rucellai *contadini* of Carmignano sent as their present an olive tree in a cart.

Weddings and funerals were shows of public extravagance. But life at home was conducted with frugality. Once married, the running of the household devolved upon the bride, who had to have a practical knowledge of the economics of palace and villa because often her husband was gone for years at a time. Nevertheless, according to Albertian principles, she was not to gossip with the servants. Contessina de' Bardi, Cosimo de' Medici's wife, was a famous housekeeper who had her eye on everything: she saw to the sale of old cheese moulds, the proper cleaning of oil jars, and to the relining of a granddaughter's petticoat. She thought nothing of having one of her husband's old tunics turned into a garment for herself. Personal property was closely guarded. Clarice Orsini complained to Lorenzo de' Medici that the short black dress she wanted was kept in a cupboard to which only her husband had the key. To save a few pennies for the household of her son (who was lending money at the time to the Aragonese king), Alessandra Strozzi sent fennel all the way from Florence to Naples. While she exhorts Filippo to procure splendid jewels for his betrothed, she is content with twenty pounds of almonds and ten of capers sent in time for Lent. Among wives and mothers loneliness was the common lot. When the adolescent Marco Strozzi reached Naples, his widowed mother begged the older son, Filippo, to be patient and affectionate with him. It was a bitter blow when Marco died there despite all his brother and the best doctors

could do for him. Over and over again Alessandra's letters say
'comfort me and stay healthy . . . for without you I am dead.' One of
her main activities was to keep all the scattered members of the
family informed of events at home and of one another's doings.

Many servants were necessary to keep a patrician household going.
Many of these were slaves from North Africa or the Middle East.
The great merchants dealt in them as a sideline of international trade.
Thus Alessandra Strozzi wrote to Filippo in Naples to find her a good
one: '. . . ask for a Tartar, for they are the best for hard work, and are
simple in their ways. The Russians are more delicate and prettier, but
according to my judgment a Tartar would be best.'

When Filippo Strozzi came back to Florence he married as his
second wife Selvaggia (meaning either 'wild one' or 'extremely shy
one') de' Gianfigliazzi. We have already heard of Cosimo de'
Medici's wife, 'the little Countess' – Contessina de' Bardi. Girls'
names are a chapter in themselves. Despite all pieties and exhor-
tations against extravagance and immodesty, the Florentine sense of
humour and taste for the bizarre were not to be suppressed where
naming of daughters was concerned. Here is a string of them from the
fourteenth and fifteenth centuries: Altadonna, Almafida, Amica,
Belcolore, Bellatedesca, Berricevuta, Buona, Chiaragemma, Cortesia,
Dolcedonna, Finamore, Illuminata, Ringraziata, Ruvinosa, Soava
and Santa.

Chapter 8

Of the Medici and the World of Ideas:
'Luce intellettual, piena d'amore'[1]

❧

SUMMARY OF THE CHIEF MONUMENTS

1. Basilica of San Lorenzo*

Built between 1419 and 1469 on the site of two earlier churches dating from the 4th and 11th c. Designed by Brunelleschi, it was the first church in Florence to be built in the style of the early Renaissance. A committee of eight parishioners led by Giovanni d'Averardo de' Medici agreed to help the Commune finance the construction of the new church. Giovanni de' Medici (d. 1429) undertook the building of the sacristy chapel (the Old Sacristy), commissioning for the project Brunelleschi, who was in 1421 entrusted with the entire church. A long period of financial difficulties (1425–42) aggravated by the political situation prevented further progress in the transept and nave. Finally, in 1442 Cosimo de' Medici lent the Commune 40,000 florins, the interest of which was to pay for the construction of the nave. In exchange the Medici were given the privilege of mounting their arms here and in the crossing. The church thus virtually became a Medici property. The minor chapels of the nave and transept were left to other families. The bell-tower by F. Ruggieri was added in 1740–1.

The façade, like that of so many other Florentine churches, was never carried out. Between 1515 and 1517 many artists competed in preparing designs for it: Giuliano da Sangallo, Jacopo Sansovino, Baccio d'Agnolo and Michelangelo. In the end Michelangelo was awarded the commission after he dismissed Baccio d'Angolo's model (now in the Casa Buonarroti) as 'child's play'. But the project came to nothing and Michelangelo wasted two frustrating years (1517–19) at Carrara wrestling with technicalities – road construction, disgruntled quarry officials, and striking barge captains.

---

[1](Dante, *Paradiso*, xxx, 40) Light of the mind, full of love.

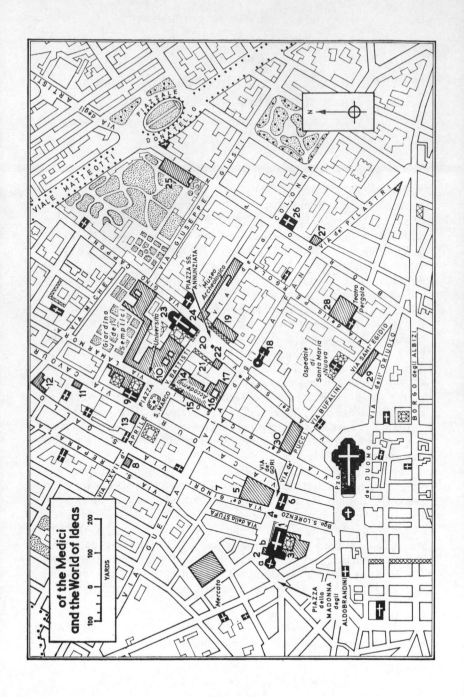

of the Medici
and the World of Ideas

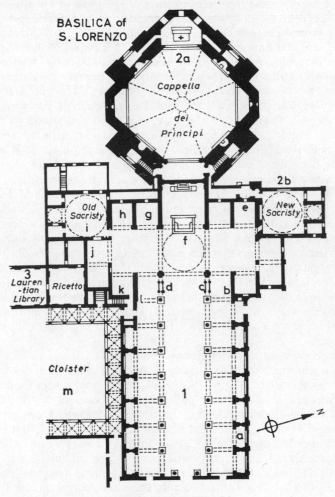

BASILICA of
S. LORENZO

2a

Cappella
dei
Principi

2b

Old
Sacristy
i

h g

e

New
Sacristy

f

j

3
Lauren
-tian
Library

Ricetto

k

d c

b

l

Cloister

m

1

a

z

PIAZZA SAN LORENZO

Interior:

(a) *Ginori chapel* – sepulchral slab of Francesco Landini (a musician), 1398; altarpiece: *Marriage of the Virgin* by Rosso Fiorentino, 1523.

(b) ***Marble altar tabernacle*** * – one of the finest works of Desiderio da Settignano (*ca* 1458–61). Moved at various times, it was in the

Neroni Chapel (in the right arm of the transept) and in the chancel. The *Pietà* relief below may once have served as the altar frontal.

(*c*, *d*) **Bronze Pulpits*** designed and partly executed by Donatello (*ca* 1455–66) and finished after his death by his pupils Bellano and, perhaps, Bertoldo. On pulpit (*c*) the following reliefs are by Donatello himself (who at least was responsible for the wax models although he left some of the chasing to his assistants): *Christ in Limbo*, *Resurrection*, *Christ appearing to the Apostles*, *Pentecost*, *Martyrdom of St Lawrence* (which bears the date 1465) and the *Maries at the Sepulchre*. The *St Luke* and the *Mocking of Christ* are bronzed wood additions of the 17th c. Donatello's participation in pulpit (*d*) is less strongly felt: the *Crucifixion*, *Lamentation*, *Christ before Pilate*, *Christ before Caiaphas*, *Agony in the Garden* and *Entombment*. The *Flagellation* and *St John the Evangelist* are bronzed wood additions of the 17th c. The pictorial programme of the reliefs must be understood in relationship to the high altar which is located between the two pulpits and in front of them. The pulpits are used only during Holy Week commemorating the events of Christ's Passion. On the southern pulpit the events proceed from the *Agony in the Garden* to the *Entombment* – from the Sacrifice to the promise of Salvation. The symbolic sacrifice of the eucharist performed at the high altar is the culmination of the programme. The reliefs on the northern pulpit show the fulfilment of Salvation in Christ's actions after the Crucifixion.

(*e*) Panel painting, *Annunciation and Saints*, *ca* 1385.

(*f*) Polychromed marble roundel in floor of crossing at foot of chancel by the young Verrocchio, marking the spot where Cosimo de' Medici is buried in the crypt below. The bones of his brother Lorenzo (d. 1440) are contained in the same sarcophagus. Donatello's are nearby. The rear wall of the chancel closed in 1860. Originally it was intended to open on the Cappella dei Principi (*see* 2(*a*)) where the Medici Grand Dukes are buried. High alter of inlaid marble (late 16th–18th c.) contains an inlay of the *Sacrifice of Isaac* designed by Cigoli (1607). This subject recalls the altar scheme in the Old Sacristy, which originally contained Brunelleschi's *Sacrifice of Isaac* made as the competition relief for the Baptistery doors. Altar and crucifix installed here now were made for the Cappella dei Principi.

(*g*) Polychromed statue of the *Madonna Bentornata*, mid-14th c.

(*h*) Altarpiece with *SS Anthony Abbot*, *Leonard and Julian* painted by a follower of Domenico Ghirlandaio (*ca* 1500).

(*i*) **Old Sacristy*** (Sagrestia Vecchia) – built by Brunelleschi

(1421–9). The architecture carried out under the patronage of Giovanni d'Averardo de' Medici who is buried with his wife in the sarcophagus by Buggiano (*ca* 1433) set under the marble table in the centre of the room. But the decoration was seen to by his sons: Lorenzo (d. 1440) and Cosimo (d. 1464). The sacristy dedicated to St John the Evangelist; four scenes from the Saint's life (the *Raising of Drusiana, John on Patmos, Martyrdom* and *Ascension*) represented in the polychromed stucco roundels by Donatello (1434–7) set into the pendentives of the cupola. The roundels of the *Four Evangelists* in the lunettes are also by Donatello.

Sacristy Chapel – the inlaid marble altar imitates the Romanesque one in the Florentine Baptistery. Brunelleschi's relief of the *Sacrifice of Isaac* was set into its front in 1432 (removed in 1800, now in the Bargello). The wooden crucifix dates from the second half of the 15th c. The astrological meaning of the cupola mural (painted *ca* 1440–50) has not so far been made out. Bronze doors on either side of the chapel by Donatello (1437–43). Pairs of disputing martyrs fill the left doors; apostles and church fathers the right. Here Donatello explores all the dramatic possibilities of discoursing figures: greeting, listening, arguing, agreeing, or running past one another. The rough and ready treatment of the bronze suits the spontaneous expression of the figures. Over the doors are painted stucco reliefs, also by Donatello (1434–7), of *SS Stephen and Lawrence* and *Cosmas and Damian*.

In the small chamber to the left of the chapel: a marble lavabo by the Verrocchio workshop (1464–9) bearing the Medici devices of the griffon, the diamond ring, and the motto: '*Semper*'. Returning to the main room of the sacristy: to the left of the entrance – tomb of Piero il Gottoso de' Medici and his brother Giovanni – the father and uncle of Lorenzo the Magnificent and his brother Giuliano, who commissioned Verrocchio to make the splendid tomb of serpentine, porphyry, marble and bronze completed in 1472. Set upon one of the intarsia cupboards is a terracotta bust of S Lorenzo (or St Leonard?) probably by Desiderio da Settignano.

(*j*) **Chapel of the Relics** ('delle Reliquie', 1421–29, also known as the Chapel of SS Cosmas and Damian, or of St Zenobius) – inserted into the Baroque altarpiece by Francesco Conti (1714) is the early 14th c. *Madonna of St Zenobius* by a follower of the S Cecilia Master (heavily repainted).

(*k*) **Martelli chapel** – on the right: cenotaph to Donatello (d. 1466); altarpiece of the **Annunciation*** by Fra Filippo Lippi (*ca* 1440) – the predella with *Scenes from the Life of St Nicholas of Bari* added later (*ca* 1447). The donor of the altarpiece, Niccolò Martelli, is buried in the marble-basket style sarcophagus on the right (*ca* 1450) by the shop of Donatello.

(*l*) Mural of the *Martyrdom of S Lawrence* by Bronzino (1565–9). To the left, over the door leading to the cloister, a choir-loft (*ca* 1480) imitating Donatello's now in the Museo dell' Opera del Duomo (*see* chapter 3).

(*m*) Cloister by Brunelleschi's successor Antonio Manetti, after 1457.

2. (*a, b*) **Mausoleum of the later Medici** (16th–17th c.) – entrance to both the *Cappella dei Principi* and *Michelangelo's New Sacristy* on Piazza Madonna degli Aldobrandini (hours: winter: 9.00–16.00; summer: 09.00–19.00 weekdays; 09.00–13.00 Sundays and holidays; closed Mondays; 200 lire).

(*a*) *Cappella dei Principi* – the ground-plan was based on that of the Florentine Baptistery. Conceived by Cosimo I as a dynastic mausoleum for himself, his wife and descendants. Involved in the planning were the illegitimate son of Cosimo I (Don Giovanni de' Medici), Buontalenti, and the younger Giorgio Vasari (nephew of the artist and biographer). Built by Matteo Nigetti and others (1605– 1737); the cupola décor by P. Benvenuti (1828–36.) The decoration of the chapel kept a large team of pietredure workers busy for more than three centuries. Over-lifesize gilded bronze portraits of *Cosimo II* and *Ferdinando I* by Pietro Tacca (1626–34). The pavement in front of the sarcophagi contains the arms of the subject cities of the Grand Duchy inlaid in polychromed marbles, mother-of-pearl, coral, and lapis-lazuli. Great pieces of porphyry and fragments of fine antique marbles were dragged to Florence, where captured Turkish slaves were put to work sawing up the stone into manageable pieces.

(*b*) *New Sacristy** (or Medici Chapel); dedicated to the Resurrection. Architecture and sculpture by Michelangelo (1520–34). The work was commissioned by Cardinal Giulio de' Medici (later Pope Clement VII) as a mausoleum for his father and uncle (Giuliano, the victim of the Pazzi Conspiracy, and Lorenzo the Magnificent) and his recently deceased cousins (Giuliano, the Duke of Nemours, d. 1516, and Lorenzo, the Duke of Urbino, d. 1519). Lorenzo the Magnificent and his brother Giuliano are buried near the Madonna on the entrance wall; to the right is the sarcophagus of the Duke of Nemours upon which *Day* and *Night* (*Il Giorno* and *La Notte*) recline at the feet of the allegorical portrait of Duke Giuliano in the guise of a captain of the Roman Church. Opposite is the tomb of the Duke of Urbino with *Dawn* and *Dusk* (*Aurora* and *Crepuscolo*) at the feet of

Detail from the Neroni tabernacle by Desiderio da Settignano in San Lorenzo, *ca* 1458-61

Detail from the entrance vestibule of the Laurentian Library by Michelangelo

the pensive warrior who stands for Lorenzo. The sculptural scheme has a unity if viewed from behind the altar: both the allegorical portraits are turned towards the *Madonna and Child* on the entrance wall. The statues of *SS Cosmas and Damian* are the work of Montorsoli and Raffaele da Montelupo, who used Michelangelo's models. Further sculpture was intended beneath the sarcophagi (river gods?), for which wax and clay studies exist in the Academy and the British Museum. Other figures were to go in the niches beside the allegorical portraits. Michelangelo left the decor unfinished when he left Florence for ever in 1534. The cupola was once painted and stuccoed by Giovanni da Udine (1532–4). The pavement is by Vasari. Recently, architectural sketches by Michelangelo uncovered on the chancel walls. Other drawings in a basement chamber.

3. Biblioteca Laurenziana* (the Laurentian Library; open weekdays 09.00–13.00) – built on designs prepared by Michelangelo,1523–59, for Cardinal Giulio de' Medici (later Pope Clement VII). It was finished in Cosimo I's time. The great Medici collection of books and MSS. begun by Cosimo il Vecchio was eventually inherited by Clement VII (the illegitimate son of the murdered Giuliano). In 1532 the books were returned to Florence by papal bull. The entrance vestibule (the **Ricetto**) with the staircase leading from the cloister to the library is one of the most dramatic architectural conceptions ever realized. The central flight of stairs was already carved in 1533–4 following a clay model prepared by Michelangelo. The rest of the Ricetto was built in the master's absence by Ammannati (1555–9) following Michelangelo's instructions. The date 1571 over the entrance door refers to the year the library was opened to the public. In deliberate contrast to the entrance vestibule, the lines and proportions of the library are calm and harmonious. On the desks (known as *plutei*, also the name accompanying each manuscript's number because the books were originally chained to the desks) are exhibited some of the library's treasures: the 4th or 5th c. Virgil, the *Pandects of Justinian*, the 9th or 11th c. codex of Greek tragedies, the only early copy of the *Annals of Tacitus*, Petrarch's copy of Horace, and choral books illuminated by Lorenzo Monaco and Attavante.

4. Piazza San Lorenzo – the piazza is the beginning of the central market of Florence which winds on to the north-west via the Via dell' Ariento to the Via Nazionale. Everything can be found here: country bread brought down from the Consuma Pass, prepared pastry dough to be taken home and baked, honey from the monks at Vallombrosa, spices, old prints, toys, house-slippers, handbags and petticoats, kitchen utensils, cheeses, tailors, cloth, books. On a corner just in front of S Lorenzo is Baccio Bandinelli's ugly monument to Giovanni delle Bande Nere (1544), the mercenary captain and father of the first Medici Grand Duke, Cosimo I. Originally it was intended to go into the right transept of S Lorenzo. Instead, the base was set up by itself in 1543 and used as a market fountain, while the portrait was installed in the Palazzo Vecchio where it remained until 1851.

5. **Palazzo Medici-Riccardi*** (now the Prefecture; open to the public: weekdays 09.00–13.00; 15.00–18.00; Sundays 09.00–12.00; closed Wednesdays – built for Cosimo de' Medici by Michelozzo (but probably based on a plan by Brunelleschi) between 1444 and *ca* 1460. Originally the arches on the south-east corner were open. These were later closed (1517) and the 'kneeling' windows were inserted, based upon Michelangelo's design. The main façade on the Via Cavour was lengthened by seven windows (*ca* 1715) when the palace was enlarged by the Riccardi family. Inside on the ground floor is an arcaded courtyard adorned with eight roundels based upon gems in the Medici collection. The palace served as the family residence and as the administrative headquarters of the Medici's commercial interests. The first staircase on the right leads to the *chapel* (consecrated to the Epiphany on January 6th 1444) painted with murals by Benozzo Gozzoli (1459–60). The murals may have been ordered as a substitute for tapestries. The *Procession of the Three Magi* winds around the chapel towards the altarpiece, which is an old copy of the original *Nativity* painted by Fra Filippo Lippi now in Berlin. The inclusion of portraits of the Medici and their household in the procession is probably an allusion to the religious *Compagnia dei Magi* to which several of the Medici belonged. The inlaid seats are probably the work of Giuliano da Sangallo. Both the richly inlaid floor and ceiling are original, making the chapel one of the few decorated interiors of the period which remain complete.

The second staircase in the courtyard leads to a large room with ceiling murals by the Neapolitan, Luca Giordano (1682–3), of the *Apotheosis of the Medici Dynasty* and a cycle of human life.

The rooms leading off the courtyard to the left of the entrance constitute the **Medici Museum** – until recently an excellent, well-labelled exhibition of the history of the family containing facsimiles of letters, portraits, photographs of the works they owned or commissioned, as well as a beautiful *Madonna* by Fra Filippo Lippi (*ca* 1442). Now this area is being used for temporary exhibitions of material relating to the Medici family.

6. San Giovannino degli Scolopi – built on the site of an oratory dedicated to St John the Evangelist. Rebuilt between 1579 and 1661 by Ammannati, Giulio and Alfonso Parigi. At one point, in 1526, a project was afoot to build a round church as the burial site for the two Medici Popes, Leo X and Clement VII. In 1537 the corpse of the murdered Duke Alessandro de' Medici was brought here. Ammannati and his wife, the poetess Laura Battiferri, are buried in the first chapel on the left.

7. Via de' Ginori – a street lined with fine palaces of the 15th and 16th c. No. 7 – *Palazzo Donati* (formerly Neroni); No. 9 – *Palazzo Barbolani di Montauto*. At No. 10, the *Biblioteca Riccardiana,* founded by Riccardo Riccardi *ca* 1600 and opened to the public in 1715. In 1812 it was sold to the city. It contains a 10th c. Pliny MS., the Villani chronicles, the account books of the Peruzzi Bank and the most complete copy of Dante's *Divine Comedy* with notes by Cristoforo Landino (1481). Open weekdays 08.00–14.00; Saturdays until 13.00; entrance free. No. 11 – *Palazzo Ginori* (formerly Masi) – Baccio Bandinelli lived next door. The Ginori came to Florence from Calenzano early in the 14th c. In the 18th c. they established the porcelain works which continues manufacture at the nearby Sesto. No. 19 – *Palazzo Taddei* by Baccio d'Agnolo (1503–4); Raphael lived here in 1505. No. 23 – *Palazzo Garzoni* (formerly Tolomei).

8. Cenacolo di Sant' Apollonia *(the **Castagno Museum** in the former refectory of Benedictine nuns; Via XXVII Aprile, No. 1; ring for custodian). Here are some of the major works of Andrea del Castagno (*ca* 1423–57). The *Last Supper, Crucifixion, Entombment* and *Resurrection* (1445–50) were painted for the refectory. The upper scenes have been detached to save them from moisture. The sinopia under-drawings discovered beneath them show how the master prepared the work for painting; the more detailed drawings of the angels were painted by helpers. Castagno prepared cartoons which are full-scale drawings for both the sinopie on the *arriccio* and the final layer of plaster (called *intonaco*). These were transferred to the fresh plastered patches on the wall (which gradually concealed the sinopia) via coloured powder flicked through the holes pricked into the lines of the cartoon. Also in the museum is Castagno's *Cruxifixion* from S Maria degli Angeli (*ca* 1453) and other works by Paolo Schiavo and Raffaele da Montelupo. Formerly exhibited here were the detached murals from the Villa Carducci-Pandolfini near Legnaia illustrating *Famous Men and Women* (*ca* 1450) – these are now provisorily installed in the Uffizi. A Madonna and Child and the figures of Adam and Eve still remain at the villa.

9. Church and Convent of San Marco – built on the site of two earlier medieval convents inhabited first by Vallombrosan and later Sylvestrine monks. By the 15th c. the old cloister was in a ruinous state. In 1436 Pope Eugenius IV allowed the Dominicans of Fiesole to take over the convent. A year later Cosimo de' Medici began to assume the financial burden for the construction of a new church and convent designed by Michelozzo. Church and first cloister largely finished by 1443 when the buildings were consecrated on Epiphany Day 1444 to SS Mark, Cosmas and Damian (the latter two were the Medici's patron saints). Façade – 1780 by Gioacchino Pronti.

Interior: the apse by Michelozzo (1437–43); nave modernized by Vasari; wooden ceiling by Pier Francesco Silvani (1679). On façade wall over entrance – painted cross by a Giotto follower. Second altar on right: the *Madonna del Baldacchino* by Fra Bartolommeo (1509). Over the next altar: a fragment of a Roman mosaic of A.D. 706 from an oratory of Old St Peter's. At the apex of the triumphal arch: *St Zenobius* by Giambologna (1580). At the beginning of the left side: Chapel of S Antonino with the statue of the saint by Giambologna with murals in the cupola by Pocetti and the altarpiece of the *Descent into Limbo* by Alessandro Allori (1588). Near the third altar on the left are the tombstones of three companions of Lorenzo the Magnificent: Pico della Mirandola and Poliziano (who both died in 1494) and of Girolamo Benivieni (d. 1542). Fourth altar on the left: *Exaltation of the Cross* by Cigoli. Sacristy (walk through vestibule at end of right side of church) by Michelozzo.

*San Marco Museum** (hours: 09.00–14.00; holidays and Sundays 09.00–13.00; closed on Mondays; admission fee 150 lire). Here are assembled many of Fra Angelico's major works: the tabernacle painted for the guild house of the linen drapers (the Linaiuoli) in 1433 with its frame designed by Ghiberti; the Annalena altarpiece of *ca* 1437; the high altar of S Marco (1438–40) with the Medici patron saints, Cosmas and Damian, kneeling on a Turkey carpet; the altarpiece from the Franciscan church of Bosco ai Frati (*ca* 1440–5), also a Medici commission; and the *Deposition* painted for S Trinita (*ca* 1440) with pinnacles by Lorenzo Monaco. Other works by Baldovinetti, Zanobi Strozzi and others follower of Angelico.

In the **chapter-room** (on opposite side of cloister) muralled *Crucifixion* by Angelico (*ca* 1445). Room to right of chapter-room contains Fra Bartolommeo's preparatory drawing of the *Virgin*,

Child, and St Anne with Saints (1510–13). In the adjoining **refectory:** murals by Franciabigio (*Adoration of the Shepherds*, 1510), Fra Bartolommeo and an assistant (tondo of *Madonna and Child*), Fra Bartolommeo and Albertinelli (*Last Judgment*, 1499–1501, which influenced Raphael's composition for the *Disputa* in the Vatican); and at the end of the room Sogliani's *Vision of S Dominic* c. 1536).

Leaving the chapter-room, walk round through the corridor on the right to the **small refectory** with the mural of the *Last Supper* (1480–90) based on a composition by Domenico Ghirlandaio. Walk up stairs beside the door to the **Dormitory** (1437). At the top is Fra Angelico's justly famous **Annunciation***. Each cell has its own muralled scene by Fra Angelico and his helpers. Off the corridor on the left is the splendid **library** by Michelozzo (1444); exhibited here are illuminated MSS. At the end of this corridor is the double-chambered cell used by Cosimo de' Medici. At the end of the western corridor is Savonarola's cell containing relics and pictures of his stormy career.

10. Università degli Studi (the University of Florence) – founded as the 'Studio' in 1321. The present building on the corner of the Piazza S Marco formerly served as the Grand Ducal stables. Behind it (entrance on Via Lamarmora No. 4) the **Giardino dei Semplici** or Botanical Gardens, founded by Cosimo I in 1545. On the Via Battisti side of the university is the **Istituto Geografico Militare** with one of the largest collections in Italy of maps and map-making – unfortunately without an adequate catalogue or library filing system.

11. The Chiostro dello Scalzo (Via Cavour No. 69; ring bell for custodian, gratuity expected – contains scenes from the *Life of the Baptist* and the *Four Cardinal Virtues* painted in grisaille by Andrea del Sarto and Franciabigio (1511–26). The murals, detached in 1960 and 1968 have now been re-installed. The architecture rebuilt by Pietro Giovannozzi in 1722. Lunettes over the murals added by Giovanni Panaiotti. The cycle begins to the right of the entrance: *Faith* (1523), *Annunciation to Zacharias* (1523), *Visitation* (1524), *Birth of the Baptist* (1526), *Baptist taking leave of his Parents* and the *Meeting of Christ and the Baptist* (both painted by Franciabigio in Sarto's absence, 1518–19), *Baptism of Christ* (*ca* 1511), *Charity* (*ca* 1513), *Justice* (4515), *Preaching of the Baptist* (1515), *Baptism of the Multitude* (1517), *Baptist taken Prisoner* (1517), *Dance of Salome* (1522), *Decollation* (1523), the *Feast of Herod* (1523), *Hope* (1523).

12. Palazzo Pandolfini* (Via San Gallo No. 74, still owned by the family) – based on a design by Raphael – the only example of his architecture in Tuscany. Commissioned *ca* 1520 by the Archbishop of Troia, Giannozzo Pandolfini. Probably executed by Francesco da Sangallo. At Via San Gallo Nos. 66–70 **San Giovannino dei Cavalieri,** originally founded in 1323 as a home for girls of easy virtue and dedicated to St Mary Magdalen. Acquired present name in 1551 after the patron saint of the Knights of Malta. Rebuilt between 1553–1784; the façade –1699. Inside: a 15th c. *Annunciation* by the Master of the Castello Nativity; in the apse a painted cross by Lorenzo Monaco; the Baroque murals in the vault by Gherardini. At the end of the right aisle *Coronation of the Virgin* by Neri di Bicci.

13. Palazzo della Corte d'Appello (the former **Casino Mediceo**) – built by Buontalenti in 1574 and remodelled in 1804. Here were once the Medici gardens where the collection of ancient statuary was installed. Tradition has it that Bertoldo, Granacci and Michelangelo as a boy came here to study and to work. The statue of *Diana* in the courtyard fountain is by a follower of Giambologna.

14. Accademia di Belle Arti (Via Ricasoli No. 54) – founded in 1563 by Cosimo I to replace the old *Compagnia di S Luca* – the painters' brotherhood. The school, devoted entirely to drawing, moved here in 1764. The loggia dates from the 14th c. and was part of the Hospital of S Matteo.

15. Museo dell' Accademia* (the Academy; Via Ricasoli No. 60; galleries containing pictures of the 13th through 16th c, as well as those containing Michelangelo's statuary, have been re-opened since the flood; 09.00–14.00; Sundays and holidays 09.00–13.00; closed Monday; admission fee 150 lire) – contains the collection originally assembled for the study of the pupils of the Accademia di Belle Arti. The museum was enriched by works from the monasteries and confraternities suppressed in the 18th and 19th c. The gallery contains Michelangelo's **David*** (originally his hair and the band across his chest were gilded – *see* chapter 1), and the **Slaves*** (*ca* 1518) from the unfinished tomb for Pope Julius II, and the **St Matthew*** (*ca* 1504) from the Duomo. In the other rooms of the gallery are assembled Florentine paintings of the 13th to the 18th c., including works by Taddeo Gaddi, Lorenzo Monaco, Baldovinetti, Cosimo Rosselli, Filippino Lippi, Perugino, Fra Bartolommeo, Albertinelli, and many others.

16. Conservatorio Musicale Luigi Cherubini – the music academy founded early in the 19th c. One of the best music libraries in Italy housed here (MSS. by Monteverdi, Rossini, and others) and a collection of musical instruments begun by a son of Cosimo III.

17. Opificio delle Pietre Dure (Via degli Alfani No. 78; hours: weekdays 09.00–13.00; closed Sundays; admission free. *See also* chapter 6) – the gallery and ateliers of the craftsmen-working in semi-precious stones. These craftsmen were housed in the Casino di S Marco, then in the Uffizi, and in 1796 they were moved to their present home in the former monastery of S Niccolò. They carried out commissions and repairs for the courts of Europe. Among the directors of the Opificio were Bernardo Buontalenti, Matteo Nigetti and Pietro Tacca. Now run by the state, it still trains youngsters in the craft. Exhibited are vases, portraits, tables, cupboards, pictures, models and drawings – many of them from the Grand Ducal Collections.

18. Rotonda di Santa Maria degli Angeli – octagonal chapel begun in 1434 by Brunelleschi for the heirs of Filippo Scolari ('Pippo Spano'). Work on it stopped about 1437, the funds being spent instead on the war against Lucca. Its plan influenced by ancient Roman centralized structures such as the Minerva Medica. The Convent of S Maria degli Angeli (since absorbed by the Hospital of S Maria Nuova) was famed for its embroideries and its manuscript illuminators – among whom was Lorenzo Monaco.

19. Ospedale degli Innocenti* – the foundling hospital named after the Innocents of Herod's massacre. Established in 1419 by the *Arte della Seta* not as an institute, but as a home for foundlings much as the present day 'Madonnina del Grappa'. The 'Istituto degli Innocenti' is now maintained by the province. Designed by Brunelleschi, who directed its construction between 1419 and 1426 but largely carried out by his adjutant, Francesco della Luna. The original Brunelleschian nucleus is a U-shaped plan with church and residence of the Innocenti facing each other. In the crypt of the church was once the site of the Confraternity of St Lawrence – some of its white-hooded members are frescoed on its piers. Underground passages reached the crypt as well as all other parts of the building. Around 1432 the loggia was raised together with that around the men's cloister (Chiostro degli Uomini) to accommodate more rooms. Of the loggia facing the piazza, only the middle nine arches are original, the rest were added in the 16th and 17th c. The medallions of swaddled infants added *ca* 1487 by Andrea della Robbia. *Chiostro degli Uomini* (adjoining the entrance) adorned with painted decorations of the 17th c. – they include the ladder and rooster symbols of the *Ospedale di San Gallo* in Via della Scala with which the Innocenti were combined during this period. The long graceful *Chiostro delle Donne* (women's cloister) to the right has only recently been freed from later accretions. On the first floor: a small picture gallery, the *Pinacoteca*, contains works by Domenico Ghirlandaio (*Adoration of the Magi*, 1488, once on the high altar of the hospital's church), Piero di Cosimo, and the young Botticelli.

20. Piazza Santissima Annunziata – the piazza's form dates from

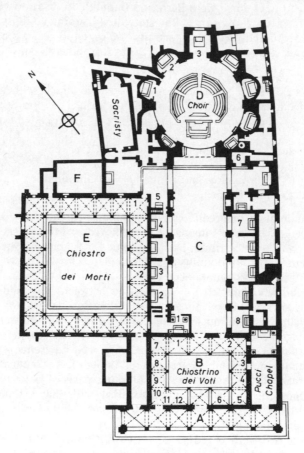

CHURCH and CLOISTERS of SS. ANNUNZIATA

1519 when Antonio da Sangallo the Elder cleared the area and built (together with Baccio d'Agnolo) the *Loggia of the Confraternita dei Servi di Maria* (21) between 1516 and 1525. The *Palazzo Grifoni* (22) 1557–63, was built by Ammannati for Monsignor Ugolino Grifoni, one of Cosimo I's secretaries. The palace was not only a private residence, it was also the headquarters of the 'Altopascio', a charitable order of which Grifoni was the knight-commander. Between 1601 and 1607 the motif of the loggia was continued across the head of the piazza screening the façade of SS Annunziata. The equestrian monument to Grand Duke Ferdinando I was begun by the seventy-eight-year-old Giambologna and finished by his disciple, Tacca, in 1608. The bronze came from Turkish cannons captured by the Knights of S Stefano. The ornament on the pedestal was finished in 1640. The two fountains made by Tacca in 1629 for Leghorn were installed here by Ferdinando II in 1643.

23. Church and Convent of SS Annunziata

The mother church of the Servite Order (called the *Servi di Maria*, or Servants of Mary) founded by seven aristocratic Florentines in 1234. Built on the site of an earlier monastery abandoned by the Franciscans when S Croce was built. Between 1444 and *ca* 1455 the church and convent were rebuilt by Michelozzo, who happened to be the brother of the prior. Since 1314 the church dedicated to the miraculous image of the Annunciation – a much repainted mural. The legend is that the picture begun by a monk in 1252 was finished by an angel. It is one of the most celebrated shrines in Italy. Already in the 14th c. visiting celebrities left lifesize effigies of themselves in wax (*voti*) which were hung from the rafters of the nave or set up in the atrium (still known as the *Chiostrino dei Voti*). In the 17th c. more than 600 lifesize *voti* packed the atrium, including a figure of Lorenzo the Magnificent by Verrocchio. These are all lost. The Annunziata was always a popular gathering-place, not only for its miraculous image but also because the Florentine year until the end of the 18th c. began on Annunciation Day (March 25th). This is still observed by the officials of the Commune, who assemble here in homage on Lady Day, when there is also a gay fair in the piazza.

A. Antiporto – the central arch by A. Manetti (1447–52); the rest of the porch completed by G. B. Caccini (1599–1601) for the Pucci family.

B. Chiostrino dei Voti* (1447–52) by Michelozzo. Murals illustrating *Scenes from the Life of the Virgin and S Filippo Benizzi* (one of the founders of the Servite Order). Since detachment, many of the following have not yet been returned.

1. *Nativity* painted (directly behind the holy image of the Annunciation) by Alesso Baldovinetti, 1460–2.
2. *Voyage of the Magi* by Andrea del Sarto, 1511.
3. *Birth of the Virgin* by Sarto, 1513–14.
4. *Marriage of the Virgin* by Franciabigio, 1513.
5. *Visitation* by Pontormo, 1516.
6. *Assumption* by Rosso, 1517 (the artist's earliest work, painted when he was 17 years old).
7–12. *Scenes from the Life of S Filippo Benizzi* – (7) by Cosimo Rosselli, 1476, the rest of the series by Sarto, 1509–10.

C. Interior of the church built between 1444 and 1460 by Michelozzo, Pagno di Lapo Portigiani and Antonio Manetti. On its design were based Alberti's S Andrea in Mantua and Vignola's Gesù in Rome. The Baroque décor added between 1644 and 1790. The ceiling by Pietro Giambelli (1664–9) based on a design by Volterrano, who was responsible for the painting of the *Assumption* at its centre.

1. Tabernacle of the Annunziata by Michelozzo and Pagno di Lapo Portigiani, 1448–52, commissioned by Piero de' Medici. The image of the Annunziata painted *ca* 1350 based upon an earlier version; it served as the model for other copies in the churches of S Lucia, S Marco and Ognissanti. Usually visible on feast days honouring the Madonna.
2. Feroni Chapel – décor by G. B. Foggini, 1692; mural over the altar: the **Vision of St Julian** by Castagno, *ca* 1455.
3. Mural over altar: the **Trinity with SS Jerome and Two Saints*** by Castagno, 1454–5.
4. *Assumption* by Perugino and an assistant, formerly on the high altar, 1506. The *Deposition*, once on the back, now in the Academy.
5. *SS Ignatius, Erasmus and Blaise* by Raffaellino dei Carli.
6. *Pietà* by Baccio Bandinelli, 1559, who is buried here with his wife.
7. Monument to Orlando de' Medici by Bernardo Rossellino, 1456.
8. Altarpiece of the *Madonna in Glory* by Jacopo da Empoli and murals by Matteo Rosselli.

D. Tribune*, or Choir, also known as the Rotonda – begun in 1451 by Michelozzo and modified by Alberti (1470–*ca* 1477).

1. *Madonna with Saints* by a follower of Perugino.
2. *Resurrection* by Bronzino, 1548–52; in a niche a wooden statue of *S Roch* by Veit Stoss(?), early 16th c.

3. Adorned by Giambologna, 1594–8, for his own grave and those of other Flemish artists resident in Florence. He was responsible for the Crucifix and the reliefs. The statues of the active and contemplative life by his pupil, Francavilla. The saints and angels by Pietro Tacca. Murals by Poccetti.

E. Chiostro dei Morti
1. The *Madonna del Sacco** by Andrea del Sarto, 1525.
2. Tombstone of Guglielmo Durfort, the lieutenant of Amerigo di Narbona, who fell at the Battle of Campaldino in 1289.

F. Cappella di S Luca (ask sacristan to open, tip) – since 1563, the seat of the artists' confraternity. Buried here are Cellini, Pontormo, Franciabigio, and others. Crucifix in entrance vestibule attributed to Antonio da Sangallo; inside: Pontormo's *Holy Family* (*ca* 1514, transferred here soon after 1823 from the church of S Ruffillo), and other murals by A. Allori (*Trinity*), Vasari (*St Luke paints the Madonna*) and Santi di Tito (*Solomon directs the Construction of the Temple of Jerusalem*, 1571). The ten large stucco figures by Vincenzo Danti, Montorsoli and others.

24. Museo Archeologico (Via delle Colonne No. 38; 09.00–14.00 weekday (until 19.00 Tuesdays); 09.00–13.00 Sundays and holidays; closed Mondays; 150 lire) – the largest archaeological collection in Italy north of Rome. Contains many of the antiquities owned by the Medici. The palace built for the Grand Duchess Maria Maddalena of Austria, perhaps by Giulio Parigi; it is known as the Palazzo della Crocetta. The vast collections, well labelled and explained, range from ancient Egypt, Etruria (arranged according to sites of discovery), Greece and Rome. Here it is advisable to invest in the guide printed in English which is sold at the entrance. All the galleries on the ground floor are being re-organized as a result of the havoc caused by the flood. Most of the sarcophagi and fragments of ancient architecture were installed on the ground and first floors. Among the exhibits are the fragments of the old Florentine amphitheatre, the Temple of Isis, and the Capitoline baths. Of the ancient bronzes, there is the celebrated Etruscan *Chimera** (the tail is a 16th c. reconstruction) discovered in Arezzo in 1555 and brought to Florence by Vasari; also the bronze statue of an orator known as the *Arringatore** (3rd c. B.C.) – both on the first floor. Nearby is the *Idolino* (6th c. B.C. Greek) found in Pesaro in 1530; the base is 16th c. and probably of Mantuan workmanship. Among the vases is the magnificent *Francois Vase**, a 6th c. B.C. Attic vase, probably a wedding present. It was found near Chiusi in 1845 by Alexandre François.

25. Palazzo of Bartolomeo della Scala (Borgo Pinti No. 97) – built between 1472 and 1478 by Giuliano da Sangallo. Scala, a miller's son, rose under Lorenzo the Magnificent to be secretary of state in the Republic. The courtyard adorned with allegorical stucco reliefs attributed either to Sangallo or Bertoldo. In 1585 the palace was acquired by the Archbishop Alessandro de' Medici, who became Pope for 26 days in 1601. For him, Stradano decorated the chapel and Volterrano painted the ceiling of the Salone.

26. Santa Maria Maddalena dei Pazzi (entrance beside Borgo Pinti No. 58; hours: 09.00–12.00, 17.00–19.00) – named after a nun of the Pazzi family canonized in 1669. Originally built for the Cistercians, today occupied by French Augustinian monks. Present structure by Giuliano da Sangallo (1480–92) but thoroughly restored after the flood of 1966. Entrance corridor from street; on right: *Cappella del Giglio* with murals by Poccetti and his shop of SS Filippo Neri, Bernard, Nereo and Achilleo; altarpiece by Passignano. Atrium by Sangallo begun in 1492. *Inside the church*: 4th chapel on right has stained glass window by Isabella Rouault, daughter of the painter; 5th chapel, founded by Francesco di Chirico Pepi in 1500 dedicated to St Francis, stained glass window by the workshop of the Ingesuati monks who also made the St Lawrence window (designed by a late 15th c. follower of Filippo Lippi) in the 4th chapel on the left. The sacristy (entrance towards end of right aisle) finished in 1767 is a rare example for Florence of a late Baroque interior of fine quality. The 6th chapel on the right contains the *Crucifix* attributed to the young Buontalenti. The choir chapel, which originally contained a mural by Domenico Ghirlandaio, was entirely rebuilt (1685–1701) in order to receive the remains of the titular saint. Cirro Ferri and Pier Francesco Silvani were responsible for its design; Ferri painted the high altar while Luca Giordano did the pictures on either side. Statues of *Penitence* and *Faith* on right by Innocenzo Spinazzi, *Innocence* and *Religion* on left by Giovanni Montauti. Fine bronze reliefs by Soldani who also designed the pavement of pietre dure. Entrance piers with *verde antico* and *breccia africana* taken from ancient Roman monuments. One reaches Perugino's *Crucifixion* fresco (1493–96) commissioned by Dionisio Pucci in the chapter room by way of the crypt (ask sacristan for admission). Of the other works belonging to the church, the following are still in restoration: Puligo's *Madonna and Child*, several saints by Raffaellino dei Carli, and a predella by Lorenzo di Credi.

27. Former church of *Santa Maria dei Candeli* (open Sunday mornings only) – one of the most complete late Baroque churches in Florence, by G. B. Foggini, 1703. Further down the Borgo Pinti at No. 26, the *Palazzo Bellini,* the house Ferdinando I gave to Giambologna. The Grand Duke's bust is over the door. Giambologna had his foundry here. From it came the equestrian monuments in the Piazza della Signoria and the Piazza SS Annunziata, and others for Henry IV of France and Philip III of Spain. After Giambologna died here in 1608, his disciple Tacca moved in.

28. Teatro della Pergola (Via della Pergola No. 12) – first built in 1656 by Ferdinando Tacca for the *Accademia degli Immobili.* The present structure by Bartolomeo Silvestri dates from 1828. During the 17th and 18th c. court operas were staged here.

29. Museo di Firenze com' era (the historical museum of the city; Via S Egidio No. 21, ring for custodian; hours: 09.00–14.00 weekdays; 09.00–12.00 Sundays; closed Thursdays; 100 lire) – housed in the former *Convento delle Oblate.* Drawings, prints, paintings, photographs of Florence as it looked in the past.

30. Palazzo Pucci (Via de' Pucci Nos. 2–4) – façade by Paolo Falconieri, 1650. The loggia inside and the windows on the ground floor by Ammannati. On the corner of Via dei Servi, a handsome coat-of-arms of Leo X by Baccio da Montelupo.

'LUCE INTELLETTUAL, PIENA D'AMORE'

North of the Piazza del Duomo is the neighbourhood of the Medici – of Cosimo il Vecchio, Piero the Gouty and Lorenzo the Magnificent. Here is Cosimo's palace built by Michelozzo. Nearby is S Lorenzo, the Medici parish church, rebuilt by Brunelleschi and enlarged by Michelangelo. Further up is S Marco, also rebuilt at Medici expense, with architecture by Michelozzo and murals and altarpieces by Fra Angelico. Next door is the University, which the Medici at first supported and later undermined. Then there are the Annunziata and the Academy of Fine Arts, both of which enjoyed Medici patronage.

The neighbourhood is not particularly beautiful, nor even quaint. Yet many of the buildings and the objects in them are of a perfection. The Medici and these works were what made Florence a great city. The Medici were moved by ideas and many of their commissions gave visible form to intellectual abstractions. These Florentines had a marvellous optimism; they believed that intellect united with beauty

221

could set the world to rights and acted accordingly. Dante's phrase: *'luce intellettual, piena d'amore'* (the light of the mind which reveals, clarifies and warms with love) perfectly describes their fresh, lucid style. This wonderful union of head and heart was unique to Florence at that time. For three generations sculptors, architects and painters were of the company of poets and philosophers. Architectural ground-plans and structural proportions were informed by a harmonious view of the cosmos; divine intentions were seen in mathematical proportions. Pictures of Venus and Spring were contrived for the moral and intellectual instruction of a Medici boy. All represent a miraculous coincidence of men, ideas and talent. If, therefore, we linger over the Medici, their character and some of the ideas that interested them and their contemporaries, it is because the buildings and their furnishings are not otherwise to be understood. When it is said that Florence in essence is a city of the mind, it is the minds of these men and their works that is meant.

THE MEDICI: THE MAKING OF PRINCES. Between 1434 and 1492 the Medici ruled Florence unofficially. In this they shrewdly bowed to the deeply ingrained republicanism of Florentine public opinion. Republicanism took a long time to die in Florence. From generation to generation the Medici reinforced their position as a dynasty. As it turned out at the end of the century, events outside Florence made the republican system obsolete. Just as Machiavelli had foreseen, of necessity the city was saddled with a prince – but when this happened the Medici had long been prepared to supply one.

COSIMO PATER PATRIÆ. For thirty years, without holding any office, without changing the form of government and always preserving the outward appearance and manner of a private citizen, Cosimo was practically the absolute ruler of a republic jealous of its liberty. The political power of the Medici family was built on the favour of the working masses and on opposition to the power of the oligarchy of *magnati* who dominated the great guilds and shared the rule of the city. The Medici motives were the mixture one finds often enough: self-interest, money, power and pride; money to get power, power to protect the money. But in the Medici these motives were tempered by a genuine love of Florence and ambition to glorify her.

The first Medici of any prominence in politics appears to have been Salvestro di Alamanno, who, although he belonged to the greater guilds, joined the lesser and worked to be their chief. He supported the Ciompi Revolt, that rising of the woolworkers in 1378, the brief success of which was crushed and its nominal leader, Michele di Lando, banished in 1382. Salvestro, however, remained with a popular following that succeeded in keeping the *magnati* from office until he died in 1388. Then the opposition led by the Albizzi family again took over the government and the Medici lay low.

Meanwhile another branch of the family, led by Giovanni di Averardo de' Medici (1360–1429) founded the immense family fortune through trade, a network of international banks, and the purchase of political favours. The motto of the bank was *Col Nome di Dio e di bona Ventura* (With the Name of God and of Good Fortune). Giovanni's greatest legacy was the training of his son, Cosimo, in business, in the policy of friendly relations with the papal court and how to turn this relation to great profit. Giovanni de' Medici kept out of politics, but he openly sympathized with the populace against the *magnati*; he favoured taxing the rich to spare the poor and lent money liberally. He built up a kind of Florentine Tammany organization, while his son Cosimo travelled throughout Europe on ambassadorial missions.

Giovanni and Cosimo were admired by the populace for their humility of manner and their simple ways; they would take no part in the fashionable aristocratic festivities such as the annual joust in the Piazza S Croce, although it was theirs for the taking. Medici participation in the Ciompi Revolt was remembered and father and son became the hope of the discontented working-classes and small tradespeople. When Giovanni died in 1429, Cosimo stepped into the leadership of the family and of the popular political party. Years of war and a series of defeats had brought Florence to the verge of economic ruin: 70,000 florins a month were being spent on military operations. Taxes were heavy and business was bad because Florence depended on international trade and banking, which needed peace. For the labouring classes work was scarce. A colleague of Masaccio, one Mariotto di Cristofano, groaned: 'In my craft there is no work – it needs peace not war, and I have six mouths to feed – I just can't manage any more. I'm going out like a candle.' Twenty-five of forty-three master craftsmen at work on Brunelleschi's cupola for the Cathedral had to be laid off for lack of funds. Adding insult to injury, Rinaldo degli Albizzi had guild participation in civic affairs reduced by half and dissolved popular lay confraternities to realize funds by expropriating their property. Cosimo was banished for his opposition. But popular feeling against the government rose to a boil during Cosimo's year of exile in 1433 because it was feared that Albizzi was going to establish himself as a tyrant with Milanese backing. Pope Eugenius IV, then resident in Florence, sympathized with the Medici faction and his support encouraged the Signoria to invite Cosimo back from Venice the next year to occupy the town hall.

In the thirty years of his unofficial rule, the only office Cosimo held was that of *Gonfaloniere di Giustizia* (the communal minister of justice, the most important civil authority in the city) for three separate terms of two months each. Cosimo was probably the greatest city political boss in history. He ruled through committees whose election he controlled. He overcame his rivals by seeing to it that they were ruined by taxes. This is what happened to Palla Strozzi. Just as the communal committees made sure that neither Medici money nor Medici votes went for measures which might go against the family interests, they also refused to support anything which might bring public disfavour to the family. By lending the Signoria vast sums of money, Cosimo put the government morally as well as financially in his debt, thereby avoiding the crippling taxes levied on other rich citizens. For Cosimo it was a capital investment, as it were, for it was tacitly understood that he never really expected to be paid back. 'States,' he once said, 'are not maintained on paternosters.'

Just as the family fortune served as a public treasury, so Cosimo's palace became a second town hall. The entertainment of visiting dignitaries was one of the civic duties assumed by Cosimo and his heirs. For Florence the style of these entertainments was splendid propaganda, and again Cosimo neither expected nor received any public reimbursement. Not only were guests lavishly entertained in Cosimo's palace, but the bills for housing the Byzantine Emperor and his retinue during the Oecumenical Council were paid by Cosimo too. When Pope Pius II came to Florence, Cosimo staged a joust, a ball in the Mercato Nuovo, and a hunt in the Piazza della Signoria with lions, wolves and wild boars.

COSIMO AND THE PRESTIGE OF FLORENCE. Cosimo had a genius for choosing the right men to act for him and to build up the international importance of Florence and the Medici family. He used philanthropy with boldness or discretion according to political necessity. When Pope Eugenius IV granted permission to the Dominicans of Fiesole to take over the convent of S Marco in 1438, Cosimo agreed to undertake the cost of the new buildings in return for official recognition of his patronage. Later in the same year at Ferrara, Pope Eugenius helped Cosimo persuade the delegates of the

Oecumenical Council to move to Florence instead of to Venice. As a result, Florence became the centre of Christendom for six months. The Pope, the Byzantine Emperor, and the highest clergy of the Eastern and Western churches provided a daily spectacle of ritual splendour. The foreigners admired the unrivalled quality of Florentine painters, sculptors and architects (Brunelleschi, Ghiberti, Masaccio, Uccello and Donatello). In July 1439 the union between the Greek Orthodox and Roman Catholic Churches was declared in the Duomo.

Just a week before the Council's end, Cosimo consolidated his authority in Florence by the victory at Anghiari against the allied forces of the exiled Albizzi faction and the Milanese. It was the hope of these allies so to intimidate the Florentines that they would rise against the Medici. Neither the great army nor Niccolò Piccinino, the most feared *condottiere* of the time, succeeded in shaking confidence in the Medici. It was this victory that gave Florence the Casentino and Borgo S Sepolcro in the upper Tiber Valley.

One of Cosimo's astute choices in backing the right man led to the acquisition by the Medici of the papal bank account. When the cardinal who later became Pope Nicholas V needed money badly, Cosimo gave it to him without asking for guarantees of repayment. On his accession to the tiara, the curial account was confided to the Medici Bank. As the Curia's official bankers, the Medici collected papal revenues abroad. A candidate for a bishopric who did not meet his payments could expect an unfavourable report to be sent off to Rome. If, on the other hand, the candidate was successful thanks to Medici recommendations, the Bank got commercial preferences. Cosimo devoted much time to the Bank's affairs, keeping very close check on all its branches (Milan, Venice, Pisa, Rome, Avignon, Lyons, Geneva, Bruges and London), delegating little authority and avoiding risky speculations.

COSIMO AT HOME. The Palazzo Medici, begun between 1444 and 1446, was originally intended to be the headquarters of Cosimo's business as well as the family residence. It seems unlikely that he actually lived there until 1459, five years before his death. Instead of the classicizing style of Alberti's Palazzo Rucellai, Cosimo's house was in the tradition of the rusticated palace. The arcaded courtyard (in which Donatello's bronze *David* stood, now in the Bargello) smacks of the cloister. Only in the ornament does the taste for antiquity crop up – in the Corinthian capitals and in the ornamental *tondi* taken from ancient gems in the Medici collection. Cosimo was never really at home in the new house. When Giovanni, his second son,

225

died in 1463 and he himself was already ailing, he sadly muttered, 'Too large a house for so small a family'. He was happy in his villas close to his vines and olive orchards. With the city's cares behind him there was time to read in his magnificent library. Here is Cosimo at his leisure in 1462, writing from Careggi to his young friend Marsilio Ficino, the brilliant son of the Medici's family doctor who had been educated at Cosimo's expense (the original text is in Latin): 'Yesterday I arrived at Careggi – not so much for the purpose of improving my fields as myself – let me see you, Marsilio, as soon as possible, and do not forget to bring with you the book of our favourite Plato – which I presume, according to your promise, you have now translated into Latin; for there is no employment to which I so ardently devote myself as to discover the true road to happiness. Come then, and fail not to bring with you the Orphean lyre.'

Cosimo had another country house in the Mugello at Cafaggiolo, which he preferred to his son Giovanni's new villa at Fiesole. 'From there,' he said, 'everything I can see is ours, which is not the case at Fiesole.'

Cosimo's library contained hundreds of volumes. In his study were the *Epistles of Ovid*, Livy's *Decadi*, a fifth-century tract on the hermit's life which had belonged to Salutati, and the *Morals* of St Gregory – the books of a man with ascetic taste. At first, collecting manuscripts of the classics proved to be highly competitive. Palla Strozzi, Roberto de' Rossi and Niccolò d'Uzzano were Cosimo's rivals. According to Vespasiano da Bisticci, Cosimo spent more on books and on the furnishing of S Marco's library and sacristy than he did on his own palace. Cosimo's agents searched the monasteries of Europe and the Middle East for ancient texts to enrich his library. Those which were unpurchasable were patiently copied by Poggio Bracciolini, Niccoli, and Vespasiano's team of scribes. To catalogue his books, Cosimo hired the future founder of the Vatican library – Tommaso Parentucelli, who became Pope Nicholas V.

Thanks to the Oecumenical Council, which brought so many learned prelates to the city together with their precious books, Cosimo's library acquired rare Greek texts. While the Council met, Vespasiano da Bisticci kept forty-five scribes busy copying two hundred codices for Cosimo. It was this fresh nucleus of classical literature and a delegate from Trebizond, George Gemistos Plethon, which gave the initial stimulus to Platonic studies in Florence. This was the only lasting achievement of the Council, for the union proclaimed in the Duomo as eternal endured but one year. Fourteen years later Constantinople fell to the Turks.

Cosimo dreamed of going himself to the Holy Land with the learned monk, Ambrogio Traversari, in pursuit of rare manuscripts. In the end, he sent Ciriacus of Ancona and Aurispa instead, paying them handsomely for manuscripts, medals, ancient sculpture and inscriptions. Sometimes treasure lay closer to hand. There is the charming story, a compliment to the innate classicism of the Florentines, of how Niccoli found the most precious antique gem in his collection hanging as a talisman round the neck of a Florentine street urchin. Eventually it wound up in Lorenzo the Magnificent's collection.

But it was not only money and power which gave Cosimo's library and his collections their superb quality. He inspired devotion and affectionate regard. Cosimo gave Poggio and Ficino houses and land. When Niccoli died, he left two hundred volumes to Cosimo. Mention was made earlier of Cosimo's fondness for Donatello. During the financial crisis of the 1420s and '30s, he saw to it that Donatello had enough work and continued to give him commissions to the end of his life. For S Lorenzo, Donatello made the stucco roundels and the bronze doors of the Old Sacristy, which was the first of the great Medici chapels. Later he made the bronze reliefs for the pulpits in the nave. For the Medici palace he made two fountains: the *David*, now in the Bargello, and the *Judith*, since moved to the *ringhiera* of the Palazzo Vecchio. In his old age Cosimo gave Donatello a pension. There must have been more to their association than the respect of a patron for a great artist, for when Donatello died two years after Cosimo, Piero the Gouty buried the sculptor near his father.

A few years before Cosimo's death, Pope Pius II visited Florence. Here is his memoir of the grand old man in his seventies: 'He was of fine physique and more than average height; his expression and manner of speech were mild; he was more cultured than merchants usually are and had some knowledge of Greek; his mind was keen and alert; his spirit was neither cowardly nor brave; he easily endured toil and hunger and often passed whole nights without sleep. Nothing went on in Italy that he did not know ... He was a king in all but name and state.' For a lack of a better name to fix on Cosimo, Pius called him 'Florence's paramour'.

When Cosimo died his prestige was enormous. Even if his family political machine had not controlled the government, Florence would almost certainly have wished to honour his memory. The Florentines liked to speak of themselves as transplanted Romans of the old noble stock. Camillus and Cicero had been cited as *patres patriae*, and so the Signoria decided to follow the example of ancient Rome and officially added *pater patriae* to Cosimo's name. It was the only permanent official title Cosimo ever had.

PIERO THE GOUTY. When Cosimo's only surviving legitimate son, Piero, took over his father's former duties, the Medici as a dynasty began. He adopted *Semper* (Forever) as his motto. The old Florentine fear of hereditary rulers was used as a pretext for a conspiracy to overthrow him. The plot was led by one of Cosimo's former henchmen, the unscrupulous Luca Pitti. Piero was an invalid bedridden with gout. But he did not lack courage; he had himself carried from his villa in the country to Florence, snuffed out the conspiracy, and settled all uncertainty about the endurance of Medici rule and power. The conspirators were condemned to death in 1466 but Piero pardoned them, thereby increasing public affection for the Medici and reassuring the Florentines of his magnanimous intentions. Piero's public duty was even acknowledged in his own house. He had the following inscription made on Donatello's *Judith severing the Head of Holofernes*, which once stood inside the Palazzo Medici: 'Kingdoms fall through luxury, cities rise through virtues; behold the neck of pride severed by humility. Piero, son of Cosimo de' Medici, has dedicated the statue of this woman to the liberty and fortitude bestowed on the republic by the invincible and constant spirit of the citizens.' Piero's statement of faith in the republican spirit in the face of his dynastic ambition was not hypocritical. So far, the Medici were able to demonstrate that their paternalistic control of the republican system was the only successful means of governing the city. If not all the *magnati* agreed, most of the working classes did.

It was Piero who really saw to the furnishing of his father's palace. Even during Cosimo's lifetime, many of the dealings with painters were apparently left to him. When pleading their cases, Domenico Veneziano and Fra Filippo Lippi wrote to Piero. Gout kept him from being as active in business and politics as his father; he sought 'to while away the time and give recreation to the eye' with the beautiful objects he collected. This description is Filarete's, who dedicated a treatise on architecture to Piero. Compared to Cosimo's austere taste, Piero's was extravagant. Filarete compared him to a famous collector of the first decades of the century – the Duke of Berry. It was in fact the old courtly style which Piero loved – the style of Gentile da Fabriano's Strozzi altarpiece, then in S Trinita. When it came to decorating the chapel of the Palazzo Medici in 1459, Piero had Benozzo Gozzoli paint the same subject, the *Adoration of the Magi*, in a manner recalling Gentile's. Piero kept a close watch on its progress. 'I understand,' wrote Gozzoli, 'that you think the seraphim are out of place . . . two little cloudlets will take them away.' Piero's study was decorated with a glazed terracotta floor and ceiling by Luca della Robbia, of which the *Labours of the Months*, now in the Victoria and Albert Museum, was a part. Agents in Flanders tried to supply him with tapestries but Piero would complain of their quality or of the bad taste of the designers in including corpses. For the audience hall, Antonio Pollaiuolo and his seventeen-year-old brother, Piero, painted a set of three large canvases of the *Labours of Hercules* – a memory of these survives in two tiny panels in the Uffizi.

In 1441 Piero and Leon Battista Alberti staged a literary contest in the Duomo. The entrants were to compose a poem in the vulgar tongue 'On Friendship', which was to be read before the Signoria, the archbishop, and the Venetian ambassador. The high altar was transformed into a tribune. The judges were the leading humanists of the day: Poggio, Flavio Biondo, Carlo Marsuppini and Giovanni Aurispa. Among the contestants were Alberti, Leonardo Dati, Ciriacus of Ancona and the seventeen-year-old Cristoforo Landino. The fact that the verses had to be written in Italian spoke for the Medici's respect for the *volgare* as a language worthy of lovers of the classics, and their respect for public opinion – they wanted as many as possible to understand what was said. The popular reaction proved to be enthusiastic and the verses were widely copied.

PIERO'S CHILDREN: THE CONSOLIDATION OF A DYNASTY. Piero's wife, Lucrezia Tornabuoni, unlike her mother-in-law the good housewife Contessina de' Bardi, was something of a blue-stocking. She encouraged Luigi Pulci to polish up his improvised verses on Carolingian knights and mythical giants into what became *Il Morgante Maggiore*, which was dedicated to her. Piero and Lucrezia saw that their boys, Lorenzo and Giuliano, were given an education based on the classics. First Landino and later Ficino were their tutors. These studies were balanced by exercise in sports and games. In 1468 Piero allowed the twenty-year-old Lorenzo to put on an entertainment which the retiring Cosimo might well have frowned on – for it was all show and extravagance. This was the celebrated joust in Piazza S Croce, given not to celebrate a victory or to honour a visiting dignitary, but for the reigning beauty of Florence, Lucrezia Donati. It was also an occasion to celebrate Lorenzo's forthcoming marriage to Clarice Orsini, in whom he apparently took less interest. She, in fact, stayed in Rome praying for his safety. Lorenzo's own account of the joust is cool; he apparently did it because it was expected of him: 'To follow the custom and do like others . . . I find that about ten thousand ducats were spent on it. Although I was not a vigorous warrior, nor a very hard hitter, the first prize was adjudged to me, namely, a helmet inlaid with silver with a figure of Mars as the crest . . .'

Lorenzo wore a red and white surcoat with a scarf bearing the motto *'Le Tems Revient'* embroidered with roses, some full-blown and some withered. Rubies, diamonds and pearls were sewn into his black velvet cap and there was a feather of gold thread spangled with more precious stones. His horses and armour were presents from the King of Naples and the Dukes of Ferrara and Milan. For another entrant, Antonio Pollaiuolo made a harness rich with enamels and reliefs. Seven years later, Giuliano became the central figure of a joust honouring another inaccessible beauty, Simonetta, the wife of Marco Vespucci. Officially the occasion celebrated an alliance with Venice and the Pope. Giuliano wore silver armour wrought by Verrocchio and bore a standard painted by Botticelli. The banner represented Simonetta in the guise of Pallas Athena in a flowery meadow. Within three years both Simonetta and Giuliano were dead and the joust became immortalized in Poliziano's beautiful verses. These chivalric pageants were in the style of the late medieval courts and in them we can see how Piero's sons carried on their father's nostalgia for the brilliant spectacles of a bygone age. They also led the public to associate an ancient aristocratic style with the Medici name.

The decision to marry Lorenzo off to a daughter of a noble Roman house was the first step towards the Medici's dynastic aspirations. It was the first time that a scion of the family married a foreigner. Piero saw the need of important ties beyond the walls of Florence and Clarice Orsini had cardinals, archbishops and a clan of military captains among her relations. The bride's arrival in Florence was greeted with days of sumptuous feasting. Tables were set up inside the cortile of the Palazzo Medici and Donatello's *David* on top of a column stood at its centre. Upstairs in the Sala Grande where Pollaiuolo's *Labours of Hercules* hung, Clarice in a gown of gold brocade ate with two hundred of her attendants and guests. Each day more than a hundred barrels of wine were drunk.

LORENZO THE MAGNIFICENT AND HIS CHILDREN: EXPANDING AMBITIONS. By contrast, the private entertaining of the Medici was simple. Once a son-in-law (Franceschetto Cibò) who was visiting Lorenzo confessed the fear that his Roman companions might take a poor impression of Medici hospitality away with them. For Florence then as now had a reputation for parsimony. Lorenzo replied that while it was the custom to entertain guests and strangers in a splendid manner, a member of the family, like Franceschetto, was treated without ceremony.

Lorenzo was ambitious for his children but at home he tried not to spoil them. After the Pazzi Conspiracy he sent his family first to Pistoia and then to Careggi and Cafaggiolo. Poliziano, who adored Lorenzo and was his closest friend, was the family's reluctant companion. Poliziano found it a trial to put up with the dull and haughty Clarice, who treated him like a servant. The two got on each other's nerves. Clarice never sympathized with Lorenzo's learned companions (she herself knew no Latin) and both she and Poliziano missed the life in Florence. Poliziano did his best, teaching the boys their Latin and the rudiments of a good literary style. But Clarice would take them away to read the Psalter. Finally Clarice threw Poliziano out of the house. Here is a letter written to Lorenzo (in Latin) from the seven-year-old Piero at Pistoia:

Magnificent Father mine, etc. . . . to let you know how well we are I write you this letter even though I don't know how to write very well yet. I will do now what I can. I will strive and exert myself to do much better in the future. I have already learned many verses of Virgil and I know almost the whole first book of Theodorus by heart, and understand it too, I think. The master [Poliziano] has me decline verbs and examines me every day. Sometimes Giovanni [Piero's younger brother, the future Leo X] comes to Mass with the master. Madonna Clarice and the others are well. We commend ourselves to you.

The next year Piero in the country wrote to remind his father of a promise:

Magnifico padre mio. As for the pony, I am afraid he has met with some ill or other; because if he were healthy I know you would have already sent him to me, as you promised. I beg you therefore, as a grace, to relieve me of this worry because day and night I can think of nothing else. Until the pony arrives I shall have no peace. If by chance that one can't come, would you please send me another. For as I wrote you the other time, here I am on foot and I really need now and then to go [on horseback] with the gang (in brighata con questi miei compagni) . . . I am studying hard (gagliardamente) and everyone here is doing his job. It remains that you protect yourself carefully from the plague and all other mortal perils and that you come here sometimes to see us. God save you. Your son Piero.

In the end Piero got his pony, together with sweetmeats from his doting grandmother, Lucrezia Tornabuoni.

When little Giovanni was only seven he was given clerical orders and the benefices of Fonte Dolce and Passignano were conferred on him. Lorenzo was already scheming to obtain the highest ecclesiastical post for him. In order to recommend him to the Pope, Lorenzo sent the fourteen-year-old Piero to Rome in 1484, accompanied by Bartolomeo Scala and Poliziano. A letter full of fatherly advice was sent to guide the boy on his mission. Piero is to speak naturally, without affectation; he should not be anxious to display his learning; he should use expressions of civility, and address himself with seriousness and yet with ease to all. On his arrival in Rome, he is cautioned not to take precedence over his countrymen who are his superiors in age, 'for though you are my son, you will remember that you are only a citizen of Florence like themselves'. Despite all Lorenzo's cautions, Piero grew up an arrogant young man. He resembled his mother, Clarice Orsini, more than Lorenzo. It seems only fitting that he was married off to another Orsini – Alfonsina, the clever daughter of the Grand Constable of Naples. The couple was heartily disliked, and two years after Lorenzo's death Piero was exiled for ever.

Piero's younger brother, Giovanni, was already a cardinal at the unprecedented age of thirteen. When the boy took up residence in Rome, Lorenzo shortly before his death dispatched a letter to guide the child's conduct there: '. . . silk and jewels are not appropriate to persons of your station. You will be better served by antiques and fine books and by your household being gifted and well bred rather than numerous. Invite others to your house oftener than you receive invitations. Practise neither too frequently . . . you should be the link to bind this city closer to the Church and our family with the city . . . I doubt not but this may be done with equal advantage to all, observing however that you are always to prefer the interests of the Church.' Giovanni had a strong character like Lorenzo and similar interests. With him the legendary Roman-ness of the Florentines became reality. As Pope Leo X, he saw to the political and allegorical reunification of Florence and Rome. At his assumption of the papacy in 1513, he had his brother Giuliano and his nephew Lorenzo made citizens of Rome on the Capitoline Hill. The reunion of Florence and Rome was also the theme of the elaborate theatricals performed on this occasion.

LORENZO THE MAGNIFICENT: HIS TASTE. Of all the Medici, it is
Lorenzo the Magnificent who is the most fascinating. His interests,
his mind, his manner, were magnificent in an entirely unostentatious
sense. His clothing was of a restrained elegance. From the inventories
we learn of his preference for dark colours: gowns of dark brown,
dark red (*pagonazzo*), and black. Many of his jackets were black –
taffeta, quilted velvet and damask. He was not handsome, nor was
he as agile as Giuliano. His complexion was swarthy, his voice high-
pitched and raucous, and his flat nose deprived him of the sense of
smell. In a crisis he was often heroic (the Pazzi Conspiracy, the
mission to Naples); but he could be unscrupulous (the difficulties of
the Medici Bank). In his poetry he was a fine romantic.

No one had a finer sense of the Tuscan landscape than Lorenzo,
who preferred country meadows to the piazzas of Florence and the
life of the villa to the pomp of the city:

> *Cerchi chi vuol le pompe e gli alti onori,*
> *Le piazze, i templi, e gli edifizi magni,*
> *Le delizie e il tesor, qual accompagni*
> *Mille duri pensier, mille dolori,*
> *Un verde practicel pien di bei fiori,*
> *Un rivo che l'erbetta intorno bagni,*
> *Un augelletto che d'amor si lagni,*
> *Acqueta molto meglio i nostri ardori ...*

(Let him who wants them seek pomp and honour, public squares,
temples and grand buildings, pleasures and treasures which bring
with them a thousand worries, a thousand pains. A green meadow
full of lovely flowers, a stream which moistens the grass on its banks,
a little bird that makes its plaint of love, these soothe our passions
much better.)

Then there is his unsurpassed picture of the Florentine countryside
in winter near his villa at Poggio a Caiano, which he named after a
nymph called *Ambra*. Here is the lone bird sheltered in the tall
cypress, the shivering leaves of the olive trees tossed now green, now
white, by the wind, the flight of cranes over the bare fields:

> *Tiene il cipresso qualche uccel secreto;*
> *E con venti combatte il più robusto:*
> *L'umil ginepro con le acute foglie*
> *La man non pugne altrui, chi ben le coglie.*
> *L'uliva in qualche dolce piaggia aprica,*
> *Secondo il vento par or verde or bianca ...*
> *Stridendo in cielo i gru veggonsi a lunge*

233

L'aere stampar di varie e belle forme:
E l'ultimo col collo steso aggiunge
Ov'è quella dinanzi alle vane orme:

(The cypress shelters a secret bird, and the strongest battles with the winds. The humble juniper with its sharp leaves does not prick the hand of him who gathers them carefully. The olive on its gentle, open slope appears green or white according to the wind.

Shrieking through the sky, the cranes streak out their flight, imprinting various beautiful patterns on the air; and the last one, with neck outstretched, follows on the track of the next through the ethereal void.)

Both in what he collected and in his literary insight, Lorenzo was preoccupied with beauty of form. He chose vases for their harmonious lines as well as for their richness of material. A certain conformity and proportion, he said, should dictate the choice of the object loved – one must discard the perishable and the fleeting. He understood love as *'appetito di bellezza'* (appetite for beauty). He praises the *volgare* of Cavalcanti, Dante, Petrarch and Boccaccio for its 'balance, sweetness, and gravity'. Lorenzo saw in the Italian language, and above all in the Florentine achievement of the previous century, 'the brightest star . . . visible in the west'. He was aware that the first great age of Italian literature was over, but like the death of the beloved lady celebrated in his sonnets, he believed that its spirit would live on in new forms of art and inquiry. 'The life of love,' he said, 'springs from death.' Criticism and philosophy were its fruit. Lorenzo's poems have a double edge; they are as elusive as the character of their author. The sonnets are more than beautiful evocations of a beloved person or place. They are also a vehicle for Lorenzo's philosophy of the humanist ideal. Angelo Lipari has shown how Lorenzo used a beautiful young woman as the personification of divine perfection. Perhaps the beautiful Simonetta somehow embodied this ideal for the popular imagination and Lorenzo may have drawn on his own memory of her when he composed the sonnets. His ineffable lady was *gentilezza umana* (an untranslatable phrase meaning all that is noble, courteous, and civilized in mankind) who taught, inspired, humanized and civilized. Learning, for Lorenzo, became poetry; knowledge was but a means to human perfection. It was only later that classical humanism abandoned Lorenzo's fair lady for the pedants and fanatics.

LORENZO AND THE NEO-PLATONIC ACADEMY. Lorenzo's ideas were

based on neo-Platonism. Years before, Lorenzo's grandfather, Cosimo il Vecchio, had encouraged the revival of Platonism in Florence by commissioning Ficino to translate Plato's *Dialogues* into Latin. Lorenzo the Magnificent was one of Ficino's pupils and he became the pillar of what eventually was called the Platonic Academy.

As a young man of nineteen, Lorenzo and his brother Giuliano with a group of neo-Platonic companions (including Ficino, Alberti, Landino and Alamanno Rinuccini) took a trip to Camaldoli, where they were the abbot's guests. There the Medici boys, their teacher, the great architect, the famous wool merchant and the professional scholars talked philosophy for four days. This circle with Ficino at its centre was the Platonic Academy. Eventually the group included Poliziano, Pico della Mirandola and others. As long as Lorenzo lived it was the centre of the intellectual life of Florence.

The Academy was never a formal institution. It was an informal fraternity dedicated to the discussion of Platonic ideas. The members of the group referred to themselves as *Platonica familia*, and to each other as *frater in Platone*, and to Ficino as *pater Platonicae familiae*. They often gathered at Ficino's house next door to the Medici villa at Careggi. The house had been one of Cosimo il Vecchio's gifts. On other occasions the group assembled at the Badia Fiesolana, where Lorenzo kept most of his famous library. At Lorenzo's suggestion Plato's birthday was honoured by a banquet each year. Nine guests were invited, the *Symposium* was read aloud, and every guest made a commentary upon it. A lamp was always kept lit before Plato's bust and hymns were sung to him, often accompanied by Ficino playing on his lyre.

For the neo-Platonists religion and philosophy were sisters. They believed that the active and contemplative life went hand in hand. Lorenzo had the habit of saying that without Platonic philosophy one could neither be a good citizen nor penetrate the mysteries of Christianity. For Ficino, Lorenzo was the personification of the Platonic prince who governed the state as a philosopher-poet.

Lorenzo's temperament, like his interests, was varied and intense. He was gay as well as serious and his favourite companions shared his enthusiasm for philosophy, wit, poetry and the chase. The longest of Lorenzo's close friendships was with Poliziano, who came to Florence after the murder of his father, a prosperous citizen of Montepulciano. While still a schoolboy, Poliziano was a brilliant classical scholar. He was quick, ambitious, frightened and poor. In 1469, in search of a protector, the sixteen-year-old Poliziano sent the twenty-one-year-old Lorenzo a parcel containing the translation from Greek into Latin of the second book of Homer's *Iliad*. Carlo Marsuppini, a chancellor of Florence, had already translated the first book. A letter accompanying the manuscript concluded in this way:

'If you welcome it I propose to offer you all the *Iliad*. It rests with you, who can, to help the poet. I desire no other muse or other gods, but only you; by your help I can do that of which the ancients would not have been ashamed. May it please you, therefore, at your leisure to give audience to Homer . . .'

Lorenzo's response was immediate, and from then until the end of his life he maintained his friendship and protection of him. Poliziano was Lorenzo's companion at table and on the hunt. He became the tutor of his children and his private secretary. Before the time of his quarrel with Lorenzo's wife, Poliziano would keep Clarice informed of her husband's doings while away from home:

Yesterday, after leaving Florence, we came as far as San Miniato, singing all the way, and occasionally talking of holy things so as not to forget Lent. At Lastra we drank *zappolino*, which tasted much better than I had been told. Lorenzo is brilliant and makes the whole company gay: yesterday I counted twenty-six horses which are with him. When we reached San Miniato last evening we began to read a little of St Augustine, then the reading resolved itself into music, and looking at and instructing a certain well-known dancer who is here. I will finish another time. At San Miniato. April 8 (1476). Servitor. Your Angelo.

In town Lorenzo often took Poliziano with him on his nocturnal rambles through the city. Then they would often make up the songs and jingles which were used in the richly decorated, bawdy processions staged during Carnival and Maytime. One of Poliziano's songs begins with:

> *Ben venga maggio*
> *E l'gonfalon selvaggio . . .*

(Welcome May and the wildly waving banner.)

One of his ballads in rollicking vernacular expresses the same nostalgia for the country as Lorenzo's sonnet cited earlier:

> *I' mi trovai un dì tutto soletto*
> *In un bel prato per pigliar diletto . . .*

(One day I found myself all alone in a lovely meadow to take my pleasure.)

It speaks well for Lorenzo that his most intimate companions were not jealous of each other or of their patron's favours. In the last decade of his life Pico della Mirandola became one of his closest friends. He was brilliant, handsome, noble and virtuous. Poliziano loved him too, and after Lorenzo's death they would visit each other at home in Fiesole savouring wine, literature and each other's company. Unlike Poliziano, Pico was an aristocrat. He was Count of Mirandola, had studied in Paris, was said to know twenty-three languages, and was also a poet. Although the youngest of Lorenzo's circle, Pico made old Ficino reconsider the Hebraic writings, which the venerable Platonist had hitherto disdained. Pico came to Lorenzo after his bold and inquiring mind had provoked papal disfavour. Yet Pico was a pious man. He was among the first to turn to Savonarola.

So long as Lorenzo lived, Florence was bright with optimism. Every day something new and wonderful happened. Only a restricted circle, of course, appreciated the rediscovery of the classics. One day Poliziano would find four lost books of Cicero. But the whole city revelled in the parades of decorated carts that wound through the streets with their spectacles of pagan gods and goddesses, devils, imps, renegade nuns, satyrs chasing nymphs, clowns, fools, wild beasts and gipsies. The Sultan of Egypt sent a giraffe – an animal never seen before which delighted the whole town. During the winter it was kept in a stable on the Via della Scala. In the spring it was taken out – the nuns gave it refuge, the children fed it, the painters included it in their pictures. Eventually the beast died of over-attention, but its memory lives on in paintings by Piero di Cosimo, Andrea del Sarto and Franciabigio.

Everywhere in Florence there was the spirit of free inquiry and discovery. Toscanelli produced a map suggesting that the world might after all be round and not flat. Michelangelo turned up in the Medici gardens of S Marco and admired the antique sculpture there. Lorenzo invited him to the palace and Poliziano suggested the theme of the Battle of the Centaurs, which the boy probably carved when he was only sixteen. In every line of thought and endeavour, nothing seemed impossible. As long as Lorenzo lived it was a headlong pursuit of intellectual inquiry and delight. The humanists, as Alan Moorehead says, felt they were free to worship Plato as well as Christ. Once Lorenzo was dead, all this changed. Within two years of his death Florence had become a sombre place. Piero de' Medici was chased from the city. The Medici library was dispersed. The pyre of vanities burned in Piazza S Croce. And both Pico and Poliziano in 1494 requested and found burial in Savonarola's convent of S Marco.

LORENZO AND ART. Compared to his father and grandfather, Lorenzo commissioned few works of art. He had less money to spend and his taste was on different lines. His monastery in Via S Gallo is lost, so his is villa at Arezzo. He acquired another villa at Poggio a Caiano (originally the property of the Cancellieri family of Pistoia, and later of Palla Strozzi who was forced to give it up when exiled) but did not live to see its decoration. He advised others on their building projects, raised monuments to Giotto and Filippo Lippi, contributed a design of his own for the Duomo's façade and bought books, gems, vases and small bronzes. His bedroom in the Palazzo Medici contained six pictures. At one end hung Uccello's three battles (now in Florence, Paris and London) illustrating episodes of a Florentine victory won at S Romano in 1432. At right angles to these were two more pictures by Uccello – a combat of dragons and lions and a scene from the legend of Paris. There was also a hunt by Pesellino. Botticelli's *Adoration of the Magi* and *Pallas and the Centaur*, both in the Uffizi, may have been painted for him, as well as Signorelli's *Feast of Pan* destroyed in Berlin during the war.

Botticelli's *Birth of Venus* and *Primavera*, so often associated with Lorenzo, Giuliano and Simonetta Vespucci, were painted for another Medici – a second cousin, Lorenzo di Pierfrancesco. This young cousin had acquired the villa at Castello in 1477 and this is where Botticelli's *Birth of Venus* and *Primavera* originally hung. Lorenzo di Pierfrancesco was also given the best classical education available. Giorgio Antonio Vespucci (Amerigo's uncle) and Ficino were among his tutors. In a letter to the fourteen or fifteen-year-old lad, Ficino said that Venus signified Humanity and described her figure in terms of virtuous qualities:

... Humanity herself is a nymph of excellent comeliness, born of Heaven and more than others beloved by God all highest. Her soul and mind are Love and Charity, her eyes Dignity and Magnanimity, the hands Liberality and Magnificence, the feet Comeliness and Modesty. The whole, then is Temperance and Honesty, Charm and Splendour. O, what exquisite beauty! How beautiful to behold. My dear Lorenzo, a nymph of such nobility has been wholly given into your hands. If you were to unite with her in wedlock and claim her as yours she would make all your years sweet.

Botticelli's pictures served as the illustration of this and other related sermons. Indeed, as Professor Gombrich further points out,

Botticelli's Venus is as grave and serious as his Madonnas. The commission probably came to Botticelli through Giorgio Antonio Vespucci, who had already ordered pictures from him for Ognissanti. Later, Lorenzo di Pierfrancesco had Botticelli illustrate a Dante. Michelangelo worked for him too, and he corresponded with Amerigo Vespucci about the New World.

Lorenzo the Magnificent's passion for literature led to further enrichment of the Medici library, including some of the prototype manuscripts of the classics – Thucydides, Virgil, Terence and Seneca. When King Christian I of Denmark and Norway came to Florence in 1474 he requested his hosts in the Palazzo Signoria to let him see the celebrated copy of the Greek Evangelists obtained some years earlier in Constantinople and the *Pandects of Justinian* brought to Florence via Amalfi and Pisa.

LORENZO AND POLITICS. Lorenzo succeeded Piero the Gouty in 1469. A committee of six hundred citizens begged him, when he was just twenty, to carry on the family's unofficial rule of the city. His wry comment on accepting was: 'If one is rich one lives badly in Florence without control of the state' (*a Firenze si può mal viver ricco senza lo Stato*). Lorenzo shouldered all the family's traditional obligations to the republic but with diminished means. The affairs of the Bank were going into rapid decline. In a desperate effort to salvage the situation Lorenzo did not hesitate to dip his hand into public funds to serve the family's interests – something which Cosimo and Piero had managed to avoid. But the defrauding of the public dowry fund (the *Monte delle Dote*) thereby postponed the inevitable bankruptcy. The monopoly of the Tolfa mines acquired in 1461 from the Pope produced the alums essential to the dyeing industry and a fresh source of income. Ironically, it was the alum monopoly which eventually undermined the Bank. The Medici were promised the monopoly in the Low Countries if they would agree to make a huge loan to Charles the Bold, Duke of Burgundy. Portinari, the Medici agent (whom Cosimo had rightly distrusted), over-extended the Bank's credit and the loan was never repaid. Lorenzo was forced to mobilize all his personal resources in order to realize the necessary cash. He took over the portions of his young cousins Lorenzo and Giovanni, the sons of Pierfrancesco, who were not yet of age. Taking advantage of the situation, Pope Sixtus IV in 1476 withdrew the papal account from the Medici Bank and turned it over to the rival firm of the Pazzi. By 1485 Lorenzo, still unable to refund the debt to his cousins, was forced to hand over to them the villa at

Cafaggiolo and all his land and farms in the Mugello.

The Pazzi Conspiracy of 1478 was plotted by the rival Florentine banking family and Pope Sixtus IV. The Pazzi wanted to seize control of the city and the Pope wanted docile rulers so that his own family might expand their territories in central Italy without Florentine interference. The best known account of the plot is Poliziano's. The conspirators decided to make their attack in the Duomo just when Lorenzo and Giuliano were kneeling before the altar at High Mass. At the raising of the Host the assassins were to strike. Neither of the Medici suspected anything; they wore no armour as they had come to church from a banquet at which the Pazzi were their guests. At the last minute Giuliano, who was indisposed, had not arrived. Two of the conspirators went off to persuade him to come. As they entered the Cathedral they affectionately put their arms round Giuliano's shoulders to make sure he was not armed. Mass began, the Medici knelt, the Host was raised. Immediately Giuliano was struck with a dagger. He rose, only to be struck again and again by Francesco Pazzi, whose vehemence was such that he wounded himself deeply in the thigh. Lorenzo, meanwhile, was struck in the neck. He succeeded in jumping up and wrapped his cloak round his left arm as a shield and pulled out his sword. Then, with a few companions, including Poliziano, he fought his way back to the new sacristy and the heavy bronze doors were bolted behind them.

The public did not rise to the Pazzi's defence. And the Pazzi's effort to take possession of the town hall during the murder in the Cathedral failed too. Many of the conspirators were immediately hacked to pieces, Jacopo Salviati, the Archbishop of Pisa, was hung in all his vestments from a window of the Palazzo Vecchio. Another conspirator, Bernardo Bandini Baroncelli, managed to escape to Constantinople. But a year later the long arm of Medici authority caught up with him too; he was sent back to Florence in chains and hanged in the Bargello.

After the failure of the Pazzi-Papal plot, the armies of the Pope and his Neapolitan ally gathered around Florence. The situation was critical and it was then that Lorenzo performed his diplomatic master-stroke. As the noose of papal states tightened, Lorenzo secretly went to Naples in December of 1479 in order to turn his old enemy into a friend. After three months of negotiation, in 1480 he succeeded in drawing Naples away from the Pope. So charmed with Lorenzo were King Ferrante and his son, the Duke of Calabria, that they sought his advice for their private building projects. Lorenzo complied by sending the best Florentine architect available –

Giuliano da Maiano. A few months later (August 1480) the Turks captured Otranto on Italian soil. Then the frightened Pope found it expedient to make peace with Florence. Out of a seemingly hopeless situation Lorenzo had made peace with honour. When he returned to Florence he was received as the city's saviour and from then on he became the leading political figure in Italy.

Lorenzo was well aware of the growing threat beyond the Alps of French intervention in Italy on the pretext of pressing old claims on the Duchy of Milan and the Kingdom of Naples. So long as there was peace, the pretexts for intervention were weaker. For the last twelve years of his life Lorenzo was kept busy consolidating Florentine security and healing the quarrels of neighbouring Italian states, all the while maintaining the goodwill of the French king. The old ghost of Guelph loyalties and the large French market for Florentine goods nursed this friendship along. Already in 1465 one of the balls on the Medici escutcheon had been changed from red to blue to accommodate the *fleur de lis*, an honour bestowed on Piero the Gouty by the French king. Louis XI even sought Lorenzo's help in arranging a marriage with the King of Naples's daughter. Such an event would hardly have been in the interests of Lorenzo's dream of an alliance of Italian states which would be strong enough to keep out imperial powers. So without openly obstructing the King's designs, he let the matter come to nothing. Amid this precarious political situation, Lorenzo wrestled with an unresolvable dilemma. Apart from Venice, Florence was the only strong Italian state which still ruled itself as a free republic. All around her the ancient medieval communes had collapsed into the hands of tyrants. Lorenzo had all the responsibilities of a prince without actually being one. His title, *il Magnifico*, was purely honorary; the Florentines simply liked calling him by this title, which was usually conferred upon captains or lesser princes. Much as a permanent office would have strengthened his hand at home and abroad, he dared not press the Signoria for it lest this destroy the tacit dynastic claim which the Medici had as the unofficial ruling family.

COURTIER VS. PRINCE. Lorenzo's politics, like Florentine humanism, depended on his presence. Once he was gone, both became a shambles. The crisis of the Renaissance was that the cult of the individual, which had flourished in the isolated city states, came into conflict with international power politics based upon impersonal national interests. Twenty years after Lorenzo's death two works were written which present the two sides of the problem: the vanishing cult of the individual and the impersonal demands of state survival. The two works were Castiglione's *The Courtier* and Machiavelli's *The Prince*, composed within a few years of one another.

The Courtier was written in Rome at the courts of Pope Julius II and Leo X, where Castiglione recalled happier days at the remote court of Urbino, ruled by the bookish Guidobaldo da Montefeltro and Elisabetta Gonzaga. Like Lorenzo the Magnificent, Castiglione was primarily interested in style, in formal beauty. The appearance and manners of his courtier receive as much attention as his personal conduct and civic obligations. *The Courtier* is a blend of late medieval chivalry and Renaissance pride in the individual. Castiglione explains how speech, gesture, expressions, posture should be in harmony with one another. His ideal courtier is a figure of effortless elegance and ease of bearing, which he called '*sprezzata disinvoltura*'. This is the style of Andrea del Sarto's muralled figures in the atrium of the Annunziata and of Raphael's in the Vatican Stanze. The pictorial parallel was already noted years ago by Wölfflin. Like Lorenzo de' Medici, Castiglione's ideal gentleman wore dark colours. He admired 'pure and appealing simplicity'. Affectation in posture and dress, rigid carriage or clothes that fit too tightly, were censured. But this courtier was not to be an obsequious servant; he remained a noble individual who was to rely on his own judgment and discretion. He was to serve his prince only in honourable things. If the prince asked him to commit a betrayal or some ignoble act, he was morally obliged, said Castiglione, to disobey him because to concede to dishonour would be to do his master a disservice.

For Machiavelli, the interest of the state surpassed any private considerations and his Prince commanded absolute obedience. *The Prince* was dedicated to a Medici Duke of Urbino, the nephew of Leo X. It was written while its author was exiled to his farm at S Casciano. Its tone of moral seriousness, its confidence in the power of men to control events, belong to the 'civic humanism' of the Quattrocento. Machiavelli wrote as a politician deeply troubled by the sight of his beloved state falling to pieces. He bitterly learned what it was for Florence to be a mere pawn for the competing empires of France and Spain. Two years after Lorenzo's death he saw Charles VIII, the King of France, march into Florence with the biggest standing army Europe had ever seen. He saw the King lodged in the Palazzo Medici fitted out with special decorations by Perugino. Savonarola subsequently guided the republic for three more years. After Savonarola's execution on 23rd May 1498, Piero Soderini became the last *gonfaloniere* of the Florentine republic and Machiavelli served in his administration.

Machiavelli and Savonarola belonged to those who, late in the Quattrocento, reacted against the paganism and epicureanism which to many Lorenzo and his world represented. Savonarola railed against the great prelates and bookish clerics, who instead of devoting themselves to the saving of souls, occupied their time with poetry and the art of oratory, clutching their volumes of Virgil, Horace and Cicero. (But even Savonarola was accustomed to prepare his sermons in Latin, although he preached in Italian.) Disdaining the fancy allegorical language of many intellectuals of the time, Savonarola used direct simple phrases. The preoccupation with stylistic refinements was often associated with those whose veneration for antiquity verged on paganism. The time had passed when men such as Cosimo il Vecchio, Alberti and Ficino believed that pagan philosophy and Christian faith were reconcilable. On this score, there were those of Lorenzo's old circle who had a guilty conscience: Giorgio Antonio Vespucci, Pico della Mirandola and Botticelli were among them. They gave up their dream of the neo-Platonic ideal to follow Savonarola.

Like Savonarola, Machiavelli cared little for literary graces of the kind Lorenzo and Castiglione enjoyed. He preferred to make his points with harsh clarity. He advocated a life of hard work, courage and ceaseless struggle. Unlike Lorenzo the Magnificent and Castiglione's *Courtier*, Machiavelli's *Prince* was not a man of many talents, he was asked to be a master – a specialist – in but one thing: politics.

THE ARRIVAL OF THE PRINCE. After eighteen years of exile, the Medici returned to Florence in 1512 under the wing of a Spanish army. But now the old system of half-concealed authority while preserving republican institutions was frankly abandoned. Florence became an annex of the papacy. From now on, save for the brief interlude of 1527–30, the Medici had the official title of Duke, and later Grand Duke.

The first prince of Florence was Pope Leo X – the former Giovanni de' Medici, Lorenzo the Magnificent's son. For a while he used his younger brother, the Duke of Nemours, as the figurehead. Leo adopted the yoke (*il giogo*) as his insignia, and it exactly fitted the new style of Medici rule. It had a pacifying motto: *Jugum enim meum suave est* (For my yoke is easy). Despite Leo X's regime, which had been the cause of his exile, Machiavelli was a patriot and in *The Prince* he tried desperately to define how a wise ruler might maintain the strength of his state so that it would not fall prey, as Florence had, to foreign invaders. Instead of basing one's power on public affection as the earlier Medici had done, Machiavelli deemed it wiser for a ruler to be feared (though not hated!). He never went so far as his haughty friend, Francesco Guicciardini, who spoke of the 'people' as a 'crazy animal'! If expediency necessitated acts injurious to some, it was better to do these injuries all at once so that there was not a long period in which to nurse accumulating resentments. As for conferring benefits, it was wiser to give these little by little so that they could be savoured all the more. Perhaps remembering the virtues of the Medici and the vices of the neighbouring tyrants, Machiavelli advised the prince to keep his hands off others' property 'because men forget the death of the father much more quickly than the loss of their patrimony'. Austere as he was of mind, Machiavelli prized action, decision. It was better, he said, to be impetuous than over-considerate, and he explained with biting humour that 'Fortune is a woman ... more friendly to the young because they are less respectful, more ferocious and order her about with greater audacity.'

Alas for Florence, no messianic prince came to rescue her from the Spanish in 1530. After the sack of Rome in 1527, Pope Clement VII (Giulio de' Medici) fell prisoner to the Emperor Charles V. Florence, taking advantage of the situation, threw off the Medici yoke and for three years revived the republic under the pious Niccolò Capponi. All was lost when the Pope and the Emperor came to terms. Clement married off his bastard son, Alessandro, to Margherita, the illegitimate daughter of Charles V. To re-establish the Medici in Florence an army was sent to the Arno. After a hopeless but heroic defence, Florence was betrayed by its mercenary captain, Malatesta Baglioni (how Machiavelli had warned against traffic with mercenaries!). Seven years later Alessandro was murdered by his cousin, Lorenzino, who justified himself as a second Brutus. Then an eighteen-year-old Medici, who belonged to a cadet branch of the family, was installed as Cosimo I. Stable rule was established in the form of a petty principality which, under Spanish protection, was allowed to swell itself up with monarchical trappings.

OF LEARNING AND POLITICS. Great brilliance and shabby decline is also the story of learning and the university in Florence. The finest moments were those when scholarship served a vital function in public life. During the fourteenth and fifteenth centuries it was traditional that the Commune's permanent officials, the secretary and chancellor, be scholars of the first rank. The official correspondence with foreign states and the writing of important public speeches were their tasks. Dante, Salutati, Poggio, Bruni, Carlo Marsuppini, Accolti, Bartolomeo della Scala and Machiavelli were all holders of these offices. Such men were judged by their skill in rhetoric; their eloquence could be a powerful instrument for rallying public sentiments – the speeches of Salutati and Bruni were cherished for their heroic spirit couched in beautiful Latin prose. These chancellors were a sort of combination of foreign secretary and propaganda minister. The Duke of Milan, Giangaleazzo Visconti, is supposed to have said that Coluccio Salutati's pen did him more harm than thirty troops of Florentine cavalry. Vespasiano da Bisticci, the bookseller, was convinced that the fame of Florence was largely due to the writings of Bruni and Poggio.

The official language of diplomacy was Latin. For Italian jurisprudence was, and is to this day, based on the laws of ancient Rome. Because Justinian's code was the mainstay of Roman law, Florentine humanists were always on the lookout for ancient codices which might give less corrupt versions of the original texts. The eagerness of their search was spurred on as much by their practical desire to make the law more accurate as by their antiquarian interests. Thus Poggio, trained in civil law, sat in Swiss and English monasteries eagerly copying rare manuscripts. Later, Poliziano, on Lorenzo the Magnicent's order, set about correcting the *Pandects of Justinian*.

It was in the Commune's best interests to have well-lettered citizens. Yet in Dante's time Florence was still without a university. The teaching of the classics was for the most part left to the monastic schools. During the early fourteenth century the proportion of the populace who frequented schools was higher than in any other European city: out of a population of 90,000, 10,000 Florentines received at least some instruction in letters. About six hundred attended schools of higher learning directed by a master who paid the Commune a tax. Dante went to such a school, but for his professional legal training he probably went to Bologna.

THE UNIVERSITY OF FLORENCE. Thanks to a teacher's strike in the University of Bologna, the Florentine *Studio Generale*, as the university was called, was founded by communal decree in 1321. Taking advantage of the excommunication which had provoked the crisis, Florence offered posts to some of the rebellious professors. As elsewhere in Italy, the Commune was the ultimate authority of the Studio. It procured the teachers, built the schoolrooms, and saw to the students' board and lodgings. A ceremony inside the Duomo officially opened the term on October 18th. After reaching eighteen years of age and attending the Studio for three months, a student – native or foreign – had the same rights as a Florentine citizen, save that he had to wear a black gown, pay taxes on certain feast days, and was not allowed to play or even watch dice games except in the rector's own house on May Day. A public and a private examination terminated the pupil's study. Then the successful graduate was paraded through the streets to his lodgings. Trumpets and pipers accompanied him and played on for the rest of the day.

The Studio's development during the fourteenth century was slow and sporadic. Wars, pestilence and famine inhibited the regular flow of communal funds for teachers' salaries and lodgings. Several times the Studio was closed down altogether. This may be the real explanation for Petrarch's refusal to accept a chair in 1351 and again in 1365, despite all Boccaccio's powers of persuasion and the incentive of lucrative papal benefices. The most highly paid professors were those of civil and canon law; the most poorly paid were those of philosophy, logic and astrology. The professor of medicine got middling pay. Cadavers for the medical students were obtained from the podestà or from the chief of police in charge of the Bargello prison. Only the cadavers of men born at least two miles beyond the city walls were allowed for medical studies. The doctors had to fetch the body fresh from the gibbet and promise it decent burial after seeing that appropriate masses for the soul were said. Each student present at the dissection had to pay a tax, and a pair of shoes was given to the student in whose lodgings the dissection took place.

Salutati considered research in the natural sciences a hopeless waste of time, and we shall see how, early on, science and mathematics were allowed to be the specialities of the rival University of Pisa. Music, as one of the Seven Liberal Arts, was more important to Salutati than medicine. As for jurisprudence, he regarded it as divinely inspired. Before the end of the fourteenth century the first chairs established in Florence for Greek grammar and letters were founded by public decree. Either native Greeks or learned Italians occupied the chairs. In 1395 Emanuel Chrysolarus was invited to teach for a term of ten years with an annual salary of one hundred florins, and Salutati took time off from his duties as chancellor to attend his lessons.

A typical career of an early Florentine chancellor was that of Leonardo Bruni, 1369–1444 (for his tomb *see* chapter 4). He studied Greek and civil law at the Studio, followed by several years, practical experience as a papal secretary, from which post he was called to the

Florentine chancellery. According to Vespasiano da Bisticci's biography, Bruni was very dignified though not tall, he wore a red hat and a red gown with wide sleeves which hung to the ground. He was a conspicuous figure, often seen disputing informally and volubly in the Piazza dei Signori or walking along the Arno with his friends. In his *Laudatio*, Bruni likened Florence to Athens as the saviour of independent city states, as opposed to the Milanese under Giangaleazzo Visconti, whose policies he compared to the evil expansionism of the ancient Persian monarchy. Bruni made Florentines aware of their intellectual vigour and, in a time of crisis, he bolstered their spirits by pointing to their political greatness. He reminded them that from provincial narrowness Florence had become a great power and the cultural rival of Athens and Rome.

During the period of the Milanese wars the Studio suffered one of its declines. Communal funds were withdrawn for the defence of Florence. In 1418, for instance, two hundred florins were subtracted to build a bridge across the river Pesa and to pay for embassies to Genoa and Naples. In that year the Studio's finances were in such a critical state that Cosimo de' Medici, then the Florentine ambassador to Pope Martin V, asked and got benefices to ensure the professors a salary. Ten years later, during the rule of the Albizzi faction, the Commune appointed Francesco Filelfo to revive the Studio. At the same time, as a result of Niccolò da Uzzano's encouragement, the *Sapienza* (or House of Knowledge), founded by the Signoria in 1429, was built next to S Marco on the site of the present university to lodge about fifty poor students from outside Florence. Filelfo had a great reputation for science and ancient languages and at first Cosimo de' Medici and Niccolò gave him their support. Filelfo occupied the chair of rhetoric and was paid a salary of two hundred and twenty-five florins. But he was an arrogant trouble-maker and soon alienated his sponsors, the Albizzi party, as well as Cosimo de' Medici's faction. Finally, in 1432 Filelfo was denounced to the rector of the Studio as disloyal to the state because he favoured the Visconti. The charge was justified, for during his exile Filelfo wrote invectives for the Duke of Milan. Many other well-to-do Florentines had always tended to prefer unofficial academies like Ambrogio Traversari's at S Maria degli Angeli and that of Petrarch's friend, Luigi de' Marsili, in the Augustinian Convent of S Spirito. To this group also belonged Franco Sacchetti, Carlo Marsuppini, Bartolomeo Valori and Matteo Palmieri.

Under Cosimo de' Medici communal support of the Studio was undermined. Its bell was given to Michelozzo to use for the clock at the Palazzo Vecchio, and a thousand florins formerly allotted to the Studio was transferred to the *frati* of S Croce for their chapter-meeting. The Sapienza was dissolved under Lorenzo. The building became first a draper's shop, then a lion seraglio, and still later a Grand Ducal stable. The Studio continued to exist but it was not allowed to grow into a great university comparable to Padua, Bologna or Pavia. Ancient letters were, however, consistently encouraged. Thus, Cosimo called Giovanni Argyropoulos to teach Greek for fifteen years and among his pupils were Poliziano, Lorenzo the Magnificent, and John, Duke of Gloucester. In 1473, Lorenzo decided to reduce the number of chairs in Florence and to limit its teaching to the humanities. While deliberately thwarting the growth of the Studio, Lorenzo began to build up the University of Pisa which was reformed under him in 1472. The Studio was reduced to a debating society for philosophers and *letterati*. Science and law were taught seriously only in Pisa.

SCHOLARSHIP AND PRIVATE PATRONAGE. There were shrewd political motives behind these academic arrangements. For the subject town of Pisa, the establishment of a good university served as a sop to humiliated civic pride. The rearing in Florence of a flock of experts in civil law could have nourished opposition to the Medici. It was much safer to control brilliant minds through patronage – either by offering them posts in the Studio or the civil service, or as private scholars and family tutors. Ficino never held a chair in the Studio and was content as a private tutor and adviser with plenty of time left for the pursuit of his own studies. Always an ascetic, he eventually took holy orders and added to his duties that of a parish priest. Another type was Niccoli. Although he twice served a one-year term as a trustee or director of the Florentine Studio, he refused both academic and civic posts, saying brutally that such jobs were for those who went to beer halls and ate like poor men. In the tradition of Petrarch, Niccoli was not a teacher but a gentlemen-scholar. He had none of Petrarch's, Salutati's or Bruni's civic sense, however. He was handsome, gay, elegant, and had fastidious tastes. He insisted on the finest linen and set his table with crystal cups and antique vases. He was devoted to Cosimo de' Medici and collected for him statuary, inscriptions, paintings, manuscripts and medals from a world-wide network of contacts. Niccoli marks the beginning in Florence of the split between men of learning and men of state.

Under the Medici from Cosimo onwards, erudite conversation moved away from the unofficial monastic academies to the homes of learned private patrons – the Medici villas at Careggi and later Castello; and to the Rucellai gardens (the Orti Oricellari). With the exception of the latter, which for a while was a meeting-place for political malcontents, humanism in Florence gradually changed from an intellectual movement to a kind of literary club devoted to erudite diversion rather than, as it had been earlier, a source of practical public usefulness. The arts as well as learning were organized into official academies subject to court patronage. For the painters, the *Accademia del Disegno* founded by Vasari in 1563 took the place of the old guild. Other academies were invented for the humanists and scientists. Membership in these was more important than holding a chair in the Florentine Studio. An academician signified social dignity roughly equivalent to that of a courtier. Only the Accademia del Disegno eventually became a teaching academy. It froze the canons of style into a rigid programme of instruction based upon copying Roman models and Michelangelo (who was held up as the modern equal of the ancients).

Since Leo X's return to Florence in 1515, artists and scholars had grown accustomed to work on elaborate allegorical schemes in praise of the Medici contrived for triumphal entry processions, carnival or private family occasions. It was good propaganda for both domestic and foreign consumption. Glorification of the ruling family dominated learning and the arts for the rest of the sixteenth and seventeenth centuries. The Medici encouraged the myth of their responsibility for a Golden Age.

OF IDEAS AND THE ARTS. The beauty of the Florentine Renaissance was that its leaders in learning and the arts succeeded in giving visible expression to their belief in man as the measure of all things. The theory and practice of perspective composition, the ground plans and proportional of churches and chapels, were all based upon an ideal concept of the human figure. Man, it was believed, belonged to a clear, geometrically ordered universe. Perspective explained human vision and gave artists a practical method for organizing their compositions. Following the example of Vitruvius in antiquity, the proportions of the human body were rationalized into those ideal figures – the circle and the square which formed the basis of Quattrocento architecture. The faith in the human intellect and the joyous celebration of the human figure were all understood as the best way of expressing divinity. This constituted the optimism of the Quattrocento. It was an anthropomorphic view which was shattered in the next century.

In Michelangelo the Renaissance reached its culmination and its end. For no one was the human figure more important. But he saw that it could no longer serve as the model for order and harmony which were in themselves unattainable. For him, man was creator and destroyer; sometimes hero, sometimes beast; capable of equilibrium as well as chaos, and governed only by mysterious, irrational forces. It is interesting that he almost ignored perspective – it might well have hindered his dramatic expression. Just as in politics, the reasoning private intellect gave way before absolute arbitrary authority. The genius of Michelangelo was that he continued to strive for an unattainable harmony, knowing that the outcome would be defeat. However unreasonable, he made the struggle appear necessary, glorious, heroic.

The changes in the view of man and the cosmos are to be seen in many of the buildings by Brunelleschi, Micheolozzo, Alberti and Michelangelo which were commissioned by the Medici and their neighbours. This architecture of humanism set the style for the rest of Italy. 'Who wants to build in Italy today,' wrote Luca Pacioli towards the end of the century, 'must soon turn to Florence for architects.' This was as true of the Pope in Rome as of the courts of Rimini, Mantua, Milan and Naples. It even applied to the Sultan in Constantinople!

THE IDEAL CHURCH: THE BASILICA AND THE CENTRALIZED PLAN. Florentine architects always had a speculative turn of mind. They were amateur archaeologists who set out to rediscover the magic laws of harmony by which they thought the ancient Romans built. The philosopher's stone for them was composed of antiquity and mathematics. From their buildings, remarks, treatises and sketches we know that Brunelleschi, Michelozzo, Alberti, Leonardo and Michelangelo concentrated their thoughts about architecture on two types of building: the classical basilican scheme and the centralized plan. In theory and practice these became the two types of ideal church. The architecture of ancient Rome sanctioned both types of temple. For the centralized church there were the Pantheon, the temples of Vesta, and the Minerva Medica. Renaissance architects mistakenly included in this list the Florentine and Lateran Baptisteries. The type preferred by the early Christian church, however, was the basilica – the meeting-hall of the faithful.

SAN LORENZO. The original church of S Lorenzo was an early Christian building. Early in the fifteenth century it was decided to rebuild the old Romanesque church. Cosimo de' Medici and his father provided the necessary funds and Brunelleschi had an ideal opportunity to demonstrate the principles of classical architecture as he had worked them out. We are told how he measured and drew copies of ancient buildings in Rome. His admiration of the Florentine Romanesque (which he believed was ancient Roman) is evident in his choice of the dark-grey and white colour scheme, and in many of the ornamental motifs. But compared to the gloomy interiors of SS Apostoli and S Miniato, S Lorenzo is bright and spacious. In its planning Brunelleschi resorted to his own system of perspective composition to organize the parts into a harmonious whole. From the entrance, the view down the nave is like a perspective drawing, the lines of which are the mouldings, string-courses, columns, grooved pilaster strips, and profiled chapel steps, which all echo one another's forms and ripple serenely towards a common vanishing-point. Even the lateral views – from the nave towards each chapel off the aisles – were conceived as perspectives, for the ratio of the arches of the nave to the arches of the chapel-entrances is five to three.

Brunelleschi's perspective system subjected all the architectural members to a rational order. The *raison d'etre* of perspective was to make natural laws tangible – to render what we see coherent and explicable. According to Vespasiano da Bisticci, Giannozzo Manetti, a contemporary Florentine, used to say that 'our faith should not be called faith but certainty, because all the articles of this religion . . . are as true as a triangle is a triangle . . .' The church of S Lorenzo and its Old Sacristy demonstrate this sentiment; order was an act of reason and not the caprice of abritrary authority.

S MARCO AND THE ANNUNZIATA. Brunelleschi was engaged by the Medici only once – at S Lorenzo. Cosimo had inherited him from his father, Giovanni d'Averardo, who had launched the work there with the Old Sacristy. But for all the other churches and chapels he ordered, Cosimo turned to Michelozzo, the architect of his own palace and villas. Cosimo had the old convent of S Marco rebuilt by him, as well as the novices' chapel at S Croce. Piero the Gouty also commissioned tabernacles from him in the Annunziata and S Miniato al Monte. Interested as Michelozzo was in antiquity, he was a much less venturesome planner than Brunelleschi. So far as we can tell, his church interiors at S Marco and SS Annunziata (now hidden under a layer of baroquery) were not conceived according to any thoroughgoing rationale. They are simply up-to-date versions of a Gothic sceheme. His architecture is gracious and sober but not particularly intellectual. The intellectual church is S Lorenzo, and it seems only fitting that Donatello and Michelangelo should have worked there and that Fra Angelico kept Michelozzo company at S Marco. Michelozzo had his classical intellectual moment too – in the rotunda of the Annunziata, later finished by Alberti, of which more will be said later.

CENTRALIZED PLANS: ACCORDING TO BRUNELLESCHI. In many respects the story of the centralized plan during the Renaissance opens and closes at S Lorenzo – in the two sacristy chapels built for the Medici by Brunelleschi and Michelangelo. Brunelleschi's Old Sacristy set out the plan in its simplest form: a circle inscribed in a square. These two shapes, the circle and the square, are repeated in the lines of the structure and in the ornament. The repetition of these shapes and the way they frame each other confer upon the whole design the serene appearance and absolute lucidity of a geometrical figure.

After Brunelleschi worked on the Old Sacristy for Giovanni de' Medici, he began another centralized chapel for the heirs of Filippo Scolari at S Maria degli Angeli. Because of the Lucchese and Milanese wars, the family was never able to pay for its completion. This is a more complex structure in which a scheme of radiating chambers is framed by an octagonal plan. Compared to the Old Sacristy, volumes and curves become more important than lines and flat planes. The dominance of curves in the profiles, surfaces and volumes contributes to the sense of movement – contracting and expanding space and mass.

CENTRALIZED PLANS: ACCORDING TO MICHELOZZO AND ALBERTI. Finally, in 1451, a completely round, domed structure was conceived by Michelozzo for the monks' choir of SS Annunziata. The Minerva Medica and the Pantheon were his points of departure. There was strong criticism. Not because people objected to Michelozzo's classicism, but because the absolutely round plan, it was said, was not used by the ancients for temples but for imperial tombs and was therefore unsuitable as the model for a Christian structure. The real objection was probably that people were suspicious of the the association of this type of private imperial monument with the Annunziata's rotunda which was being financed by a foreign prince – a Gonzaga of Mantua. Added to all this, structural defects emerged. For fifteen years work on it stopped. It was finally taken in hand in 1470 by Alberti, an old advocate of the round plan, who developed it further in his own centralized schemes for churches in Mantua. For Alberti the round form was an ideal. About the time Michelozzo was beginning the rotunda, Alberti noted that nature herself preferred the round form above all others: in globes, stars, and the nests of animals. As a symbol of the cosmos it was the most perfect shape – and thus it appears in the domes and cupolas of ancient and modern buildings. Alberti and Cardinal Nicholas of Cusa maintained the Platonic view that a mathematical symbol was the best means of representing God. For apart from the reasoned harmony of geometrical figures which mirrored the cosmic order, such symbols were permanent, universal, and indestructible.

VITRUVIAN INTERPRETATIONS AND THE FURTHER DEVELOPMENT OF THE CENTRALIZED PLAN. This philosophy translated into artchitecture was not really so divorced from human reference. Vitruvius's classical treatise on architecture had demonstrated that the perfect geometrical figures of the circle and the square exactly corresponded to the symmetrical proportion of the human figure with limbs outstretched. Much was made of this idea during the Renaissance. One of Alberti's younger contemporaries, Francesco di Giorgio, drew the ground-plan of a basilica around such a man. Leonardo illustrated the Vitruvian figure of the man circumscribed by the circle and the square for Fra Luca Pacioli's treatise, *Divina Proportione*. Alberti and Pacioli were chiefly responsible for the revival of Vitruvian principles and their practical applications. The ancients derived the proportions of their architecture, said Pacioli, from the human body – 'in it is to be found all and every ratio and proportion by which God reveals the innermost secrets of nature'. Pacioli went so far as to maintain that divine services are of little value if the church has not been built with correct proportions!

In Florence the centralized plan was used only for chapels, sacristies, and one chancel. Entire churches based on this scheme were realized elsewhere by the younger followers of the Florentine masters. There is Giuliano da Sangallo's S Maria delle Carceri (1485) in Prato, S Maria della Consolazione at Todi (1504), and Raphael's S Eligio degli Orefici and Bramante's Tempietto of S Pietro in Montorio in Rome. They were exceptions in the church architecture of the Renaissance. The centralized plan is another example of Florentine optimism of the Quattrocento, for it sought to combine an anthropomorphic aesthetic with a religious-philosophical ideal. Apart from its unorthodox features, there were practical disadvantages to the scheme: there was the question of where the altar should

253

go and how to dispose the clergy and the congregation in accordance with the hierarchical distinctions between them. These difficulties notwithstanding, Bramante, Raphael and Michelangelo all tried to apply features of the centralized plan to the rebuilding of St Peter's.

MICHELANGELO, SAN LORENZO AND THE MEDICI CHAPEL. In 1516, while Raphael had his turn at the task, Pope Leo X sent Michelangelo back to Florence to complete the family church of S Lorenzo. Michelangelo was first occupied with its façade – his plan for it was a vast affair bristling with statuary. Michelangelo should have been forewarned about the chances of realizing it because in a much smaller project also requiring many statues, Pope Julius II's tomb, he had been making very slow progress. After two years of frustration only some of the marble for the façade was quarried. In the spring of 1520 Leo X's cousin, Cardinal Giulio de' Medici, had Michelangelo switched to build the New Sacristy as a family mausoleum. This was to contain the tombs of the Pope's father and uncle, Lorenzo and the murdered Giuliano (called the *Magnifici*), and his brother and nephew, Giuliano, the Duke of Nemours and Lorenzo, Duke of Urbino (known as the *Capitani*) both of whom had died a few years before. Michelangelo laboured on the chapel and its statuary for the next fourteen years, even though at one point he was in defiant political opposition to his patron, Giulio de' Medici, who in 1523 became Pope Clement VII.

Structurally, the problem for Michelangelo was to make an up-to-date pendant for Brunelleschi's Old Sacristy where the founders of the dynasty were buried. He kept the same colour scheme of white walls and dark grey-green articulations. But the serene relationship of the membering to the structure was deliberately disrupted for dramatic effect. Blind portals develop incoherently on top of open doorways, broken lunettes push against the first horizontal cornice. The cornice above and the windows float inexplicably and the dome hovers without visible means of support. All this is consistent not with the Brunelleschian aesthetic of geometrical lucidity, harmony and equilibrium, but with a mystical idea: the vertical movement underlying Michelangelo's scheme corresponds with the theme of Resurrection to which the chapel is consecrated.

Michelangelo's scheme defies definition as a system of architecture, it makes sense only as sculpture. At the end of his life Michelangelo wrote that 'there is no question but that architectural members reflect the members of Man and that those who do not know the human body cannot be good architects.' In Michelangelo's hands the old

Vitruvian concept suffered a bitter fate; the idea of man as the rational basis for a harmonious architecture was wrecked. Until Michelangelo, sculpture maintained an ornamental role in architecture. With him this situation was reversed. Not only was architecture treated sculpturally but even then it became only an armature for statuary. Furthermore, architecture for Michelangelo was subject to the same stresses and strains, moodiness and unreasonableness, as human beings – just as it was capable of elegance, repose and nobility. Michelangelo left the chapel incomplete. More statuary was planned for the niches beside the *Capitani*, river gods were to go at the feet of the two sarcophagi, and the cupola was to be painted and stuccoed. But the character of his intentions is already clear from the first storey. Almost all of the available wall space is carved in depth and and in relief so that the plane of the wall dissolves and the effect produced is one of uneasiness and melancholy. The literature interpreting the chapel and its style is vast. The emotional-mystical response is common to almost all accounts. Some have justified the illogical architecture by saying that as a burial chapel it is the airless realm of departed souls where earthly laws no longer apply. All Michelangelo's work is so varied and so profound in feeling that it drives those who stand before it to speculation. Never before or since has the *raison d'être* of religious art been more perfectly realized.

Just as Michelangelo turned Vitruvius upside down, so he treated antique sculpture. The Belvedere torso in the Vatican and various river gods are recalled in the two *Capitani* and the reclining figures at their feet. But the motive for Michelangelo's study of these classical statues was not the search for a canon of posture, proportion or decorum, but a means of settling on a monumental scale and a generalization of natural forms sufficiently universal to express his own intense emotions and ideas. The scale and proportions of the chapel's statuary and architecture are superhuman because the degree of grief and idea of after-life are also superhuman. The identity of the individuals for whom the mausoleum was built was only of secondary interest. The captains are not portraits but types. Instead of representing them lying down to remind us of their demise, as so many Quattrocento sculptors did, Michelangelo has them sit up. Both captains brood on the only hope of eternity – the melancholy Virgin nursing the Saviour – as time in the form of Day and Night, Dawn and Dusk, passes on at their feet.

In many respects Michelangelo is a culmination of the Florentine character. His interests were wide, his technique prodigious, his mind was bold in aspiration and comprehensive in its grasp. He was straightforward, loyal, hard-working and abstemious. He was also aloof, crabbed, ever critical, never content, and had a caustic humour. His personal will and convictions were always in conflict with the authoritarianism of the Church, to which, as a good Christian, he felt a servant. As if his nature and temperament were not enough to make him melancholy, political events and a long series of frustrated commissions added to the burden of his sorrows.

Michelangelo Buonarroti was descended from a minor house of the feudal nobility. As a boy, he was taken to see the antique statuary assembled by Lorenzo the Magnificent in the gardens of S Marco. It is uncertain who were his masters. Apparently he was apprenticed for a while to Domenico Ghirlandaio. His talents were recognized very early and from then on patrons competed for his work. His doings became an affair of state. We have seen how he was torn between the republic and the papacy for work in the Piazza della Signoria and the Vatican. Later he was torn between obligations to the heirs of one pope and the demands of two others. Like Machiavelli, he sympathized with Savonarola (although for different reasons perhaps) and committed himself to political ideals in his life and moral principles in his work. Again like Machiavelli, he had no patience with what for him passed as dandyism – hence his disdain for Leonardo and Raphael. He also disliked collaborating with other artists. He refused to share, for instance, the commission for the S Lorenzo façade with Baccio d'Agnolo. For all his high seriousness, in his youth Michelangelo was capable of a *Drunken Bacchus* and gentle Madonnas, but his austerity and moral tone were characteristic of the Florentine giants for two centuries from Giotto onwards.

Michelangelo embarked on projects of a vastness without prececent: the Sistine ceiling, the tomb of Julius II and the S Lorenzo façade. But vastness for its own sake did not appeal to him. In the middle of the labours for the Medici Chapel, Clement VII suggested that he carve a statue roughly twenty feet high to be set beside the Palazzo Medici. Michelangelo sent a laconic reply to the papal agent proposing a seated colossus hollow inside so that the head could serve as a belfry for S Lorenzo and the cornucopia might be the chimney for the near-by barber's shop, with plenty of room left over for a dovecote. It is just possible that Baccio Bandinelli's seated giant of Giovanni delle Bande Nere, which now occupies the corner between S Lorenzo and the Palazzo Medici, is a phantom of Clement VII's colossus.

Michelangelo's energy was proverbial. He painted the Sistine ceiling almost single-handed, and according to his letters, worked on all six of the tomb statues for the Medici Chapel at the same time. He said that he wanted to carry out these and the Madonna by himself, implying that he would only allow the secondary figures to go to the chisels of assistants. It was Michelangelo's practice to leave the roughing out of the figures to the experienced masons at the Carrara and Pietrasanta quarries, who followed his specifications. This is the state of the slaves intended for Julius II's tomb now exhibited in the Accademia; the master himself probably barely touched them.

Despite the great physical effort which his work required, we are told that Michelangelo ate and drank little – usually some bread and wine at the end of the day's work, records Condivi. Though a rich man, Michelangelo lived like a poor one. He was generous to his many relations and made presents of his drawings, pictures and sculptures to servants and princes alike. His life was solitary, filled by his work, and a few intense friendships (Tommaso Cavalieri and Vittoria Colonna). Condivi says that in his leisure he was fond of reading Dante and Petrarch, and we have a volume of his fine sonnets. In his old age he often worked on far into the night with a candle fixed to his cap to guide his hands.

During his lifetime awed contemporaries already regarded him as *divino* – as the prince of all the arts, surpassing not only nature but the great artists of antiquity. One of the first duties of the newly founded *Accademia del Disegno* was to stage his magnificent funeral in S Lorenzo in 1564. The church was adorned with pictures and statuary alluding to the master and Varchi's oration used the figure of Michelangelo to glorify Florence and Medici rule.

THE ROLE OF PAINTING AND SCULPTURE IN THE IDEAL CHURCH. Each in his own way, Brunelleschi and Alberti conformed to Alberti's dictum on the decoration of the ideal church: 'I would desire to have nothing either on the wall or pavement of the temple but what savours entirely of philosophy.' Like Cicero and Plato, Alberti thought white the most suitable colour for churches because it was chaste and did not distract the senses. 'Whichever way we may turn our eyes,' Alberti continued, 'we may be sure to find employment for our minds.' Thus he preferred edifying inscriptions and sculpture to murals and pictures. His own treatment of the Annunziata rotunda was even more Spartan than Brunelleschi's and Michelangelo's schemes. Originally it was completely white; only an inscription girdled the dome.

257

DONATELLO AND THE OLD SACRISTY. In all Brunelleschi's and Alberti's church interiors, painting and sculpture were given minor roles. Although both architects were much concerned with pictorial composition and perspective theory, which were of immense importance to the painters of the time, they never allowed such pictures in their churches. For while in their architecture they were striving to emphasize the opaqueness and structural clarity of walls, the painters were bent upon dissolving them with views of landscapes, loggias, niches, or whatever their fancy (spurred by perspective) contrived. In fact, all the great fresco cycles of the century were painted inside older Gothic interiors. The only murals in Brunelleschi's chapels are of astrological signs in the little domes over the altar of the Pazzi Chapel and in the Old Sacristy.

But in the Old Sacristy Donatello's sculpture challenged the subordinate role of pictorial decoration. Brunelleschi finished the interior in 1429. Donatello's sculpture – the roundels in the pendentives, the saints over the doors, and the bronze portals – were all carried out between 1434 and 1443 after Cosimo de' Medici's return from exile. In their youth Brunelleschi and Donatello were friends and they went to Rome together, measuring and studying the remains of the ancient city. Brunelleschi's biographer, Manetti, said that they were known in Rome as 'those of the treasure' because it was assumed they were searching for precious objects buried beneath the ground. Manetti adds that Donatello, however, never paid any attention to the architecture. Apparently there was some kind of a falling out between the two friends. There is Vasari's story of Donatello's Crucifix for S Croce. When Donatello asked Brunelleschi for his opinion of it, he was told it looked like a peasant whereas Christ's body was perfection. Another story concerning the Old Sacristy itself occurs in Manetti. It seems that Brunelleschi was so disgusted by the projecting gabled porticoes framing Donatello's bronze doors that he broke off his long-standing friendship with the sculptor.

At the time Donatello was commissioned to carry out the sculpture for the sacristy, Michelozzo had replaced Burnelleschi as the favourite Medici architect. Between 1425 and 1432 Donatello shared a studio with Michelozzo. They had collaborated on a number of projects – the tomb of Pope John XXIII in the Baptistery (installed there at the instigation of Cosimo de' Medici) and the tomb for Cardinal Brancacci which was shipped in pieces to Naples. Cosimo had rejected Brunelleschi's plan for the Palazzo Medici and probably the architect was not consulted about Donatello's additions to the

Sacristy. There were several reasons why Donatello may have been given so much work here. Its bare style could stand some decoration. Also, during the years of the Milanese wars when many artists lacked commissions, Cosimo did not want Donatello to be out of work.

Neither the stuccoed roundels in the pendentives nor the bronze doors disturb the harmony of the chapel, although there are unconventional features in both. The roundels contain the only narrative scenes in the chapel and are located, as far as convenient visibility is concerned, at the furthest distance from the observer. Each roundel contains a scene full of figures and the most dramatic perspective compositions yet seen in Florence. So far, neither elaborate scenes nor perspectives had ever been associated in Florence with vaults – the cycle in the Baptistery is simply a coiled ribbon of diagrammatic events. In an effort to make the action clearer to the spectator below, Donatello painted these stuccoes. The only cognizance he took of the archiecture was to co-ordinate the perspectives in the four scenes towards a common vanishing-point corresponding to the centre of the cupola. Indeed, there is open discord with the architecture in the pair of projecting gabled doorways framing the bronze doors and the two pairs of polychromed saints jammed between the doors and the cornice. It has been recently suggested by Professor Janson that the door frames are the work of Michelozzo. The combination of the doors and the profiled arches above them is the ancestor of Michelangelo's curious blind portals developed on top of the doors of the New Sacristy. In both cases the effect is to challenge the wall's solidity and to negate the existence of structural logic and the surface plane.

Donatello was not content with a minor role for sculpture in architecture. His feeling anticipates Michelangelo's in that he saw architecture as a foil as well as a vehicle for dramatic expression. His attitude clearly irritated Brunelleschi, who in a satirical poem told Donatello to stick to his knitting:

> . . . work in peace;
> Then you will gather laurel by the handful
> The most coveted praise of all,
> For by remaining your true self
> You will serve your own good.

FRA ANGELICO AND SAN MARCO. The aesthetic puritanism of Brunelleschi and Alberti never had a universal appeal. Critics of the time complained of the lack of ornament in their churches, which made the interiors seem 'poor and desolate'. Popular taste liked colour and dramatic stories, which contemporary painters and sculptors could provide with greater vigour and charm than ever before.

Fra Giovanni Dominici, the Dominician reformer, and after him the first priors of S Marco (Fra Cipriano and S Antonino) all thought devotional pictures in abundance were to be recommended because this was one more good reason why the faithful should come to church often. They might have added that beautiful paintings were a happy attraction – a promised feast for the eye not only for a rich collector like Piero the Gouty to savour in the privacy of his study, but for every Florentine who wanted to enjoy them. Thus both the cells and public rooms of the newly built convent contain murals by Fra Angelico and his helpers. In Angelico's work is a serene recognition of the divine qualities of the Tuscan scene. He rejoices in the sparkling light of spring and autumn warming the slopes, the faceted houses and arcaded corridors. He has a superb sense of tone – catching the subtle nuances of canted walls and the crisp profiles of delicate cornices. He is also a poet of spring colours and of soft, musically trailing garments. Nothing in his pictures ever shrieks, rarely is there a strident note. There is even a youthful grace to the movements of his venerable saints. The worldly life has left no mark upon them. On the other hand, Angelico's compositions take cognizance of Brunelleschi's perspective experiments, of Michelozzo's architecture, and the new heroic figure style evolved by Ghiberti, Masaccio and Donatello. He shares with the architects of his time a keen architectonic sense. His predellas are symmetrical and the accents of action and colour always coincide with the main divisions of his altarpieces. Ernesto Rogers, a Milanese architect of our own day, has compared the Tuscan countryside to Fra Angelico's pictures, saying: 'Those natural landscapes seemed prodigious intellectual inventions: every object – the cypresses placed within the golden section, the perfectly sloping hills, the exquisite valleys – seemed transfigured in the harmony of numbers . . .' and one wonders if Fra Angelico 'is a realistic painter or if the Tuscan landscape is a miraculous invention of aesthetic will-power.'

CASTAGNO. For the murals in their refectory the Benedictine nuns of S Apollonia turned not to their gentle neighbour, Fra Angelico of S Marco, but to the more robust, less refined Andrea del Castagno. His *Last Supper*, *Crucifixion*, *Deposition* and *Resurrection* have the rustic solemnity also found in Donatello's late reliefs for the S

Lorenzo pulpits. Since the early fourteenth century, the Last Supper had been the conventional subject for a refectory mural in Florentine convents. As in earlier versions, the *Crucifixion* appears as the tragic fulfilment of the sacrifice of Christ's flesh and blood, symbolized in the bread and wine of the Eucharist at His last meal. But by adding the *Entombment* and the *Resurrection* to the conventional scheme, Castagno's is a more humane interpretation: the *Resurrection* instead of the *Crucifixion* is the final episode.

Castagno was the first to exploit sharp contrasts of light, colour and pattern to express mighty events. There is, for instance, the radically different key in colouring between the upper and lower halves of the mural, which is explained neither by a change of style while the project was under way nor by the admitted fading of the pigments above and the addition of a dark waxy varnish to the section below. The dark rich colours in the *Last Supper* are those one might expect in a long room lit by only a few narrow casements at one end. The upper scenes all take place out of doors in a continuous landscape and the colours are appropriately bright: rose, jade green, vermilion and sky blue. When the two windows which once separated the scenes were thrown open, the light streaming in diffused a warm glow over them all. The tense drama of the *Last Supper*, its feeling of imminent disaster, is conveyed by the stillness of the regular sequence of friezes and inlays, and by the seating arrangement which is suddenly disrupted by Judas, who breaks the clear white bar of the table. His satyr-like profile is perhaps an allusion to John's remark that the Devil entered Judas the moment he took the piece of wine-soaked bread at the Last Supper; for throughout the Middle Ages the physical characteristics of antique satyrs inspired representations of the Devil. Directly behind his head, a veined marble slab with sinister red, grey and black flares draws Judas and the heads of Peter and Christ into the confines of the same square. Thus Castagno expressed the air of foreboding, of which the Disciples are as yet unaware.

The refectory of S Apollonia was a Gothic structure, but Castagno also contributed to a church built in the new classical style. For Micheolozzo's nave of SS Anunziata he painted two muralled altarpieces: a delirious *Vision of St Jerome* with a violently foreshortened Trinity, and a brooding *St Julian*. Another muralled altarpiece commissioned by Orlando de' Medici on the opposite of side the church is lost. Castagno's close to brutal realism made him a logical choice for the effigies of traitors and exiles on the walls of the Bargello, which earned him the name of '*Andreuccio degli Impicaati*'

(Rough old Andy of the Hanged).

He also painted a picture of the Baptist which in Lorenzo the Magnificent's time hung over the door to the Sala Grande in the Palazzo Medici. For a villa near Florence (the former Villa Carducci at Legnaia), Castagno painted the walls and the main room with heroes and heroines of sacred and profane history – including Dante, Petrarch, Boccaccio and Pippo Spano. These have since been transferred to the Uffizi.

OTHER DECORATIONS OF THE LATE 15TH AND EARLY 16TH CENTURIES. Most of the great new churches of Florence were built by the end of the fifteenth century. But save for the walls of S Marco, the courtyards and cloisters remained unpainted until the first decades of the sixteenth century. The atrium walls of the Annunziata had only Baldovinetti's *Nativity* and the opening scene of a cycle by Cosimo Rosselli. The murals which were being painted by Ghirlandaio, Filippino Lippi and Signorelli were carried out in Gothic churches. Alberti had said that courtyards and porches were the only suitable places for elaborate history scenes, of which the public were so fond. In such places there was less danger of pictures interfering with harmonious architectural schemes. For other reasons Leonardo complained about the old Gothic convention of piling tiers of scenes on top of one another which still persisted in the schemes of his contemporaries. Thus Andrea del Sarto, the great muralist of the early sixteenth century, developed his narratives horizontally in the courtyards of the Annunziata and the Scalzo. He tactfully contrived architectural settings for his scenes which echo the shape and proportion of the actual architecture. It has been said that there is something routine about Sarto's work; all is solemn, decorous, dignified, but without surprises. Nevertheless, he was recognized as the best draughtsman in Florence. Further, the heroic scale of his figures and their stately manner suited the new style of architecture which Baccio d'Agnolo and Sansovino were then developing. In their architecture, monumental statuary was allowed to play an ever greater role. Such was the temporary façade devised by Sarto and Sansovino for the Cathedral on the occasion of Leo X's triumphal return to Florence in 1515.

The Medici dynasty became extinct in the eighteenth century. But their endowment of S Lorenzo was such that even today the Medici tombs receive a special benediction once a year known as the *Uffizio della Porrea*. The name commemorates the annual feast which the Medici gave the canons, which included leek (*porri*) pies. Besides the *Porrea*, the *Palle* are perpetual reminders of the Medici benefactions. The famous red balls probably derive from the coins appearing on the shield of the bankers' guild (the Cambio) with which the Medici were associated. Later, because of their name (Medici means 'doctors') the *palle* were allegorically interpreted as pills. Leo X was flattered as Italy's Doctor. The festivities and commissions in which he was involved delighted in complex intellectual schemes, full of classical allusions and political allegories. But in Florence faith in the intellect was shaken. Gone was the faith of Dante's '*Luce intellettual, piena d'amore*' expressed in the works Cosimo, Lorenzo and their contemporaries commissioned. A song of Savonarola's speaks for the change of mind as well as the change of heart:

> *Ciascun purghi l'intelletto,*
> *La memoria e volontate*
> *Del terrestre e vano affetto;*
> *Arda tutto in caritate,*
> *Contemplando la bontate*
> *Di Gesù Re di Fiorenza;*
> *Con digiuni e penitenza*
> *Si reformi dentro e fore.*

(Purge the intellect, the memory and the will, of every earthly and futile passion, burn everything for the love of Jesus King of Florence; with fasting and penitence one reforms within and without.)

Chapter 9

The Oltrarno:
'Popolo e principi'[1]

❦

SUMMARY OF THE CHIEF MONUMENTS

1. (*a*) **Church of Santa Felìcita**
Since early Christian times there has always been a church on this
site. Until 1821 the Benedictines occupied the convent. Between 1736
and 1739 the Gothic church was entirely remodelled by Ferdinando
Ruggieri, who, however, left some of the post-Gothic chapels and
adjuncts intact.

Façade – remodelled in 1564, porch added by Vasari to support
the corridor connecting the Palaazzo Vecchio with the Pitti Palace.
Inside the porch – marble tomb of Cardinal Luigi de' Rossi (d. 1518
or 1519), who Raphael painted as one of the companions to Pope
Leo X (now in the Uffizi); the marble effigy on the tomb is by
Raffaele da Montelupo.

Interior – to right of entrance, the *Capponi Chapel**. Originally built
by Brunelleschi, or a close follower, for the Barbadori family. In 1487
their patronage was ceded to the Paghanelli who, in turn, in 1525
ceded the rights to Lodovico di Gino Capponi who had returned to
Florence in 1521 after a banking career in Rome. (If closed, ask
sacristan for key to open this chapel; tip expected). Between 1525
and 1528 the chapel adorned with paintings by Jacopo Carrucci
(known as Pontormo), masterpieces of the Mannerist style: the
muralled *Annunciation* on the west wall, the *Entombment* altarpiece.
Originally the vault, which was a half dome, was painted with God
the Father and Four Patriarchs (destroyed in the 18th c.); in the
pendentives: roundels of the *Four Evangelists* by Pontormo and his
pupil, Bronzino. The stained glass window by Guglielmo da Marcillat
which also represented the Entombment (an appropriate subject for
a burial chapel), now in the Palazzo Capponi in Via de' Bardi.

To the left of the entrance: the *Canigiani Chapel* built and painted
in 1589 as a pendant to the Capponi Chapel. Fresco of the *Miracle*

[1]Commoners and princes.

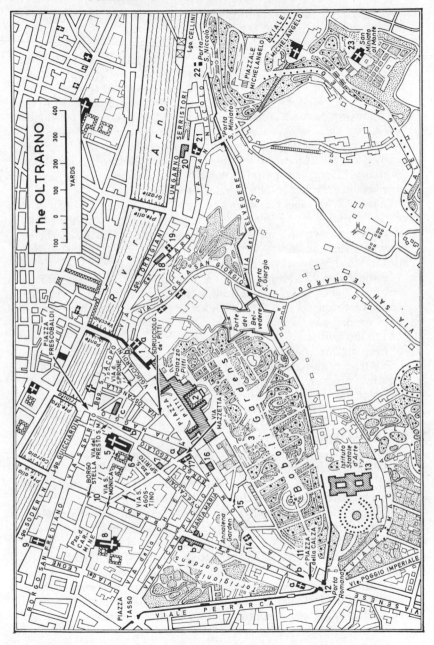

of the Snow by Bernardino Poccetti; altarpiece of the *Assumption of the Virgin* by Andrea del Minga.

Chancel designed by Lodovico Cigoli (1610–20).

Sacristy (entrance from right arm of transept) – architecture in Brunelleschian style of *ca* 1470. Pictures on the walls: altarpiece of the *Madonna and Saints* painted by Taddeo Gaddi at the end of his life (1353–5); *Madonna and Child* by Giovanni del Biondo (*c*) 1372; the following pictures are still being repaired as a result of the flood: *St Felicity and her Seven Sons* by Neri di Bicci (*ca* 1460) – the pre-della is in the chapter-room; painted cross by Pacino di Bonaguida (early 14th c.); *Adoration of the Magi* by a follower of Gentile da Fabriano. Detached murals: *Nativity, Annunciation,* and several prophets (attributed to Niccolò di Pietro Gerini).

Gothic Cloister and Chapter-room (ask sacristan to show the way; all that remains of the Benedictine convent, *ca* 1380) – in the vaults of the chapter-room: murals of the *Virtues* by Niccolò di Pietro Gerini; over the altar: *Crucifixion* by the same artist (finished March 6th, 1388).

In the **Palco Reale,** upstairs, over the porch, a collection of 17th and 18th c. reliquaries (some from S Jacopo sopr' Arno). The Palco Reale was built for the Grand Duke, who could enter it to attend Mass on his way to and fro in Vasari's Corridor leading from the Pitti to the Uffizi.

(*b*) **Piazza Santa Felicita** – granite column erected in 1381. At one time a terracotta figure of St Peter Martyr stood on top of it, which fell and broke in 1732. On the Via Guicciardini, the Machiavelli had their houses on the west side and the Guicciardini still maintain their palace on the south-east end.

2. Palazzo Pitti*

Originally built by Luca Pitti. From the mid 16th c. until the Napoleonic occupation, the palace was the residence of the Grand Dukes of Tuscany. After the Risorgimento it was occupied by members of the Italian royal family (the House of Savoy) until the establishment of the Republic in 1946. The Quattrocento nucleus of the palace consists of a central span of seven windows built between 1457 and 1466. Vasari thought Brunelleschi was the architect; but it was probably the work of Luca Fancelli (1430–95). In 1549 the Pitti family sold the property to Eleonora of Toledo, wife of Duke Cosimo I. Ammannati was charged with enlarging and embellishing the palace. By 1562 the great courtyard was finished and the façade remodelled. This was when the kneeling windows were added on the ground floor. The façade was widened by Guilio and Alfonso Parigi during the 17th c. The two wings designed by Giuseppe Ruggieri were added in 1764 and 1783–1819. The neo-classical structure on the south facing the Boboli Gardens, known as the Palazzina della Meridiana, was begun by G. M. Paoletti and finished early in the 19th c. by Pasquale Poccianti.

The Cortile* (1550–62) is one of the high-points of 16th c. Florentine architecture. Built after Ammannati's return from Rome. The dramatic scheme of imprisoning columns in rusticated blocks is the development of a Michelangelesque idea. Inherent in its design is the theme of conflict represented by the disciplined classical orders (the columns) and the forces of uncontrolled nature (the rusticated blocks). The theme was particularly appropriate to the site, which includes the garden façade of the palace. The garden end of the cortile was carved directly into the hillside. The grotto with the porphyry statue of *Moses* (the torso is antique, the rest is the work of Curradi and Cosimo Salvestrini) alludes to Ferdinando I's construction of aqueducts. Other allegorical statues represent *Law*, *Zeal*, *Magnanimity* and *Strength* by A. Novelli, G. B. Pieratti, and D. Pieratti. In niches on the garden façade are various antique statues. At the end of the northern corridor of the cortile is a late 16th c. relief of a mule which was commemorated for its long service in hauling materials for the palace.

Off the south side of the cortile is the **Cappella Palatina** (ask porter to open it, tip expected), which is a neo-classical remodelling of the original Baroque chapel; the murals are by L. Ademollo. It contains a magnificent altar of inlaid pietradura work (17th c.) which was originally intended for the Cappella dei Principi in S Lorenzo. Above it: an ivory crucifix by Balthasar Permoser with a gilded bronze *Magdalen* attributed to G. B. Foggini (*ca* 1700).

Interior – the Pitti today houses six separate museums: (1) the Museo degli Argenti on the ground floor; hours subject to change; (2) the Galleria Palatina; open every day except Monday from 09.00–13.00; and (3) the Royal Apartments, open even days except Tuesdays; (4) the Galleria d'Arte Moderna on the second floor has the same hours as the Palatina; and (5) the Collection of Coaches on the ground floor of the south wing of the palace. To see the coaches, apply to the porter's lodge at the entrance to the Cortile; (6) The *Meridiana* (the Contini–Bonacossi Collection) including paintings by Giovanni Bellini, Castagno* and Sassetta.

(1) THE MUSEO DEGLI ARGENTI north side of central courtyard (*Cortile*), recently reorganized in exemplary fashion. On the ground floor facing the piazza are the former state rooms and the summer apartments of the Grand Dukes. Here and in the rooms of the mezzanine are gathered the Medici collections of crystal, cameos, works in semi-precious stones (*pietre dure*), jewellery, gems, ivory, as well as the silver treasure of the archbishops of Salzburg brought to Florence in 1815 by Grand Duke Ferdinando of Lorraine. Nowhere can the character and scope of Medicean taste be better seen. Included are many of the virtuoso pieces of European craftsmanship.

From the entrance room, left to large reception room known as the *Sala di Giovanni da San Giovanni* with murals constituting a nostalgic piece of dynastic propaganda. Giovanni da San Giovanni began the scheme in 1634–36 with the *Allegory of the Union of the Houses of Medici and della Rovere* on the ceiling and on the east wall – *Satyrs and Time destroy Books, Mohammed destroys Greek Culture, Satyrs invade Parnassus while Harpies drive the Muses Away, Poets and Philosophers flee towards Refuge in Tuscany*. On the south wall painted by Cecco Bravo (1638–1642): *Lorenzo the Magnificent receives Apollo, the Muses and the Virtues and secures Peace for Italy;* between the windows, by Ottavio Vannini: *Lorenzo surrounded by Artists* and an *Allegory of Faith and Prudence*. On the north wall, by Francesco Furini (1638–42): *Lorenzo and the Platonic Academy at Careggi* and *Allegory of Lorenzo's Death*.

In the adjoining room on the south side are gathered *Lorenzo the Magnificent's Collection of Vases** including Roman, Byzantine, Persian and Venetian vessels inscribed with his name in beautiful Renaissance capitals: LAVR. MED. Many of these carved in jasper, amethyst, chalcedony and sardonyx were embellished during the 15th century with gold and silver mounts and the finest enamels.

North of the Sala di Giovanni da San Giovanni are further reception rooms frescoed with magnificent pseudo-architecture by two Bolognese painters – Agostino Mitelli and Angelo Michele Colonna (1636–41). In the first of these is a splendid *stipo* (or cabinet) made in Augsburg and presented to Grand Duke Ferdinando II by Archduke Leopold of Austria in 1629 at Innsbruck.

Behind these rooms and in the mezzanine above are concentrated the collections organized according to medium. First come the marvellous turned ivories with work by Eisenberg and Marcus Heiden looted by Prince Mattias de' Medici from Coburg Castle during the Thirty Years' War. Next is a room of more ivories and reliquaries followed by the amber collection in the Grand Duke's former bedroom. Then comes a room full of treasures: pietra dure vases from the 16th and 17th centuries, the engraved crystal casket by Valerio Belli which Pope Clement VII (Giulio de' Medici) presented to Francis I in 1533, crystal by the Saracchi of Milan, the lapis lazuli vase designed by Buontalenti and executed by Bilivert, and the engraved crystal vase made for Henry II of France with the enameled initials of the King and his wife Catherine de' Medici.

In the mezzanine: the Salzburg and Wurzburg treasure; cameos, intaglios and jewels. Here too is the pietre dure *Votive Image of Cosimo II* (1617–24) based on designs by Giulio Parigi originally intended for the church of San Carlo Borromeo in Milan. Further on are exotica (objects made of featherwork, coral and sea shells), oriental porcelain and casts of silver ceremonial plates.

(2) THE GALLERIA PALATINA. From the cortile, go up the staircase on the right to the first floor. (The gallery is closed on Mondays. Otherwise the hours are: 09.00–14.00 weekdays; 09.00–13.00 Sundays; admission fee 200 lire). The Galleria Palatina is the picture gallery of the Palazzo Pitti. It was first opened to the public in 1833 but it still has the character of a private collection. Such a mass of pictures may be discouraging to some. Here is a short tour of the rooms where the finest pictures are hung.

Room I; Titian's *Portrait of Pietro Aretino* (1545) was sent by the sitter as a gift to Cosimo I. The *Portrait of Pope Julius II* is a splendid copy by Titian of the same subject painted by Raphael now in the National Gallery in London. *The Concert** (1510–13) is variously attributed to Giorgione or the young Titian. There are also two of the finest landscapes by Rubens.

Room II; Titian's popular mawkish *Magdalen* (*ca* 1530–40) was painted for the Duke of Urbino. But his **Portrait of an Unknown Man*** probably painted during the same period is one of the most splendid Renaissance portraits. Rosso's *Madonna and Child with Saints* (1522) comes from the nearby church of S Spirito. Like Raphael's *Madonna del Baldacchino* (also painted for the Dei family), Rosso's scheme is based on Fra Bartolommeo. But the colours and the frenetic lines and gestures are all Rosso's own bizarre vision.

Room III; Ruben's *Four Philosophers* (*ca* 1611) recently cleaned, includes portraits (from left to right) of the artist himself, his brother Philip, the classical scholars Justus Lipsius and Hans van Wouver seated beneath the bust of Seneca. Rubens's **Consequences of War***

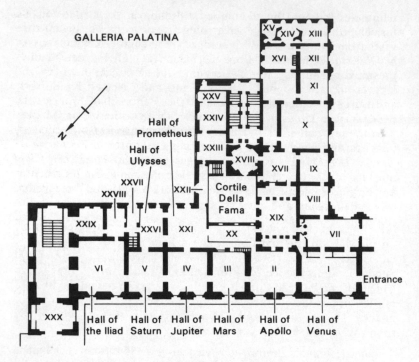

GALLERIA PALATINA

Hall of Prometheus	
Hall of Ulysses	

Cortile Della Fama

Hall of the Iliad — Hall of Saturn — Hall of Jupiter — Hall of Mars — Hall of Apollo — Hall of Venus

Entrance

(1638) was acquired by Ferdinando II through the court painter, Sustermans. In a letter Rubens explained the allegory: Mars eludes Venus's embrace to follow Discord while Plague and Famine sweep through the air and Europe grieves before the open doors of the Temple of Janus as Love, Industry and the Arts are trodden under-foot. In the same room is Titian's *Cardinal Ippolito de' Medici* (1533) in the plum-coloued uniform of a Hungarian officer. Near by is Van Dyck's brilliant **Cardinal Guido Bentivoglio*** (*ca* 1623), and Veronese's *Portrait of Daniele Barbaro.*

Room IV: Raphael's **Donna Velata*** was painted at the same time as his *Madonna della Seggiola.* The sitter was the Trastevere baker's daughter, La Fornarina, who was also the model for the *Sistine Madonna.* Fra Bartolommeo's *Deposition* (*ca* 1516) was left un-finished at his death in 1517 and was completed by Bugiardini. Fra Bartolommeo, a monastic painter, succeeded in formulating schemes for religious imagery which made simplicity seem grandiose. With him the delicacy and the trivialities of the Quattrocento were

SUMMARY OF THE CHIEF MONUMENTS

banished once and for all; his massive figures are ponderous, and his compositions consist of sweeping gestures and powerful contrasts of movement. Also in the room are Bronzino's fine portrait of *Guidobaldo di Montefeltro* and the *Three Ages of Man* attributed to the late Giovanni Bellini in a Giorgionesque mood.

Room V; contains Raphael's earliest Florentine works: the *Madonna del Granduca** (1505) and thr *Portraits of Agnolo and Maddalena Doni** (*ca* 1506). Here the influence of Raphael's master, Perugino, is giving way to the overriding influence of Leonardo da Vinci, whose *Mona Lisa* and *St Anne with the Madonna and Child* must have been in Florence then. The *Madonna del Baldacchino* painted for the Dei Chapel in S Spirito (1507-8) shows the development of his own monumental style, which paralleled that of Fra Bartolommeo. Raphael left the altarpiece unfinished when he left for Rome in 1508. The saints on either side are by another hand and the cupola is a Baroque addition by G.A. Cassana. The portraits of *Inghirami* and *Cardinal Bernardo Dovizi da Bibbiena* (both are thought to be early copies of originals in Boston and Madrid) were painted during Raphael's first years in Rome. Inghirami was secretary to Pope Julius II and organizer of the Vatican Library. Raphael changed the convention of portraiture from a general, impersonal statement to one which concentrated on the sitter's character and state of mind. Backgrounds were eliminated; everything was focused on the man. Although the *Madonna della Seggiola** (1514–15) developed a favourite Florentine scheme (the Madonna and Child in a roundel), Raphael's interest in tightly packed sculptural forms and the feeling for luminous flesh and materials came from his contact with Michelangelo and Venetian painters in Rome.

Room VI; two versions of the *Assumption* by Andrea del Sarto in 1526 and 1531 – two exercises in a complex formal problem where a severe monumental style is combined with increasing concern for strong emotions. Among other masterpieces in this room are Titian's *Man in Black* on the east wall and Raphael's *Donna gravida* on the north wall. The *Portrait of Queen Elizabeth I of England* on the west wall was presented to the Medici when, as newly created grand dukes, they began to make a collection of portraits of the crowned heads of Europe. The *Equestrian Portrait of Philip IV of Spain* from the shop of Velazquez was sent to Florence so that the sculptor, Pietro Tacca, could use it as a model for the bronze monument ordered by the King.

In **Room VIII,** allegorical murals by Volterrano, containing pictures by him and Giovanni da San Giovanni. Works by Cigoli, another fine master of the early Tuscan Baroque, are in **Room IX.** Examples of the late Florentine Renaissance (Jacopo da Empoli, Lorenzo Lippi, and Boscoli) hang in **Room XI.** In **Room XII** is the beautiful *Martyrdom of St Cecilia* by Orazio Riminaldi, a Pisan follower of Caravaggio. Here too are works by other Tuscan court artists of the 17th c. such as Furini and Bilivert. **Room XIII** (Sala di Berenice) entirely devoted to the work of Salvatore Rosa is often shut. **Rooms XIV–XV** include the handsome rotonda and bath by Cacciali (1808). **Room XVI** (Stanza della Fama) contains pictures by foreign artists such as Franz Floris's *Adam and Eve*, Pourbus's *Orpheus*, and six fine landscapes by Vanvitelli (Van Wittel) recently acquired from the Colonna Collection.

Room XXI; *Profile Portrait of a Lady in a Brown Gown* (perhaps Lorenzo de' Medici's wife, Clarice Orsini) by Botticelli, and Filippo Lippi's tondo of the **Madonna with Scenes from the Life of St Anne*** (1452).

Room XXII; (Corridoio delle Colonne): filled with small cabinet pictures by northern painters – a great fashion in Italy during the early 17th c.

Room XXIV; *Adoration of the Magi* (*ca* 1523) by Pontormo Puligo's *Portrait of Pietro Carnesecchi* (1527) was copied by Degas.

Room XXVI; Raphael's **Madonna dell' Impannata*** (1514) was designed by the master but largely carried out by assistants. Originally it was painted for the Florentine banker, Bindo Altoviti, then living in Rome. A few decades later it was installed in Cosimo I's chapel in the Palazzo Vecchio.

Room XXVIII contains Caravaggio's *Amorino* acquired by Cardinal Leopoldo de' Medici and pictures by 17th c. Florentines.

Room XXIX (Sala della Stufa)*; the best Baroque murals in Florence. Ceiling by Matteo Rosselli (1622) of *Fame and the Four Cardinal Virtues*. Above lunettes: ruler famous for their virtue (Cyrus, Alexander of Macedon, Julius Caesar, Suleiman, Charles V). Personifications of *Justice* and *Commerce* over the doors. The murals on the walls by Pietro da Cortona (1637, 1640–1) represent the *Ages of Gold* (youth), *Silver* (buculic life), *Copper* (the rewards of the active life), and *Iron* (violence and death). The maiolica pavement, a rare example of such Tuscan work, also has an allegorical subject

The east aisle of Santo Spirito by Brunelleschi. Vasari commented that if Brunelleschi's original plans had been adhered to, Santo Spirito would have been 'the most perfect temple of Christianity'

The Via Toscanella in the Oltrarno

which was restored earlier in this century by the Cantagalli factory at Florence.

(3) THE FORMER ROYAL APARTMENTS. These rooms were entirely remodelled and refurnished by the House of Savoy in the last century. Victor Emmanuel III gave the palace to the state.

The only relics of the Medici reign are the dozens of family portraits by Sustermans which lurk in almost every room. The prettiest rooms in the apartments are the Gabinetto Ovale (built during the second half of the 18th c., probably by the architect of the Meridiana, G. M. Paoletti), and the Gabinetto Tondo by the same architect, which was built to accommodate Canova's *Venus*, now in Room XXIV of the Galleria Palatina. There are two fine *stipi* (or tall cabinets) in the apartments – one of ivory, in the chapel, and the other of *pietre dure* work in the Sala Verde. Both are late 17th c. products of the grand-ducal workshops.

(4) THE GALLERIA D'ARTE MODERNA. The collection was founded in 1860 at the moment of Italy's unification. Its pictures (mostly by Tuscan painters of the 19th and 20th c.) are spread through 41 rooms all carefully labelled. Among these are the work of the Italian Impressionists known as '*I Macchiaioli*', the chief of whom was Giovanni Fattori. There are also pictures by two friends of Degas: Telemaco Signorini and F. Zandomeneghi. The two landscapes by Camille Pissarro were the gift of another of Degas' Florentine friends, Diego Martelli.

(5) THE MUSEUM OF COACHES is located on the ground floor of the south wing of the palace (ask porter for entry).

3. The Boboli Gardens (the gardens of the Palazzo Pitti: hours 14.00–16.30 in Nov., Dec., Jan., Feb.; 09.00–17.30 in Sept., Oct., Mar., Apr.; 09.30–18.00 in May, June, July, Aug.). As soon as the Medici acquired the Palazzo Pitti in 1549, they also bought up the terrain behind it belonging to various families, among them the Bogoli (or Bogolini) from whom the name Boboli probably derives. The gardens stretch from the slopes of S Giorgio down to the Porta Romana. The laying out of the Boboli went on concurrently with Ammannati's remodelling of the Pitti and the building of the Forte di San Giorgio (or di Belvedere). Already in 1549 Tribolo had designed the central axis from the cortile up the hill, including the amphitheatre and the pond above it. Tribolo died in the summer of 1550, and after him Buontalenti and Giulio and Alfonso Parigi developed the

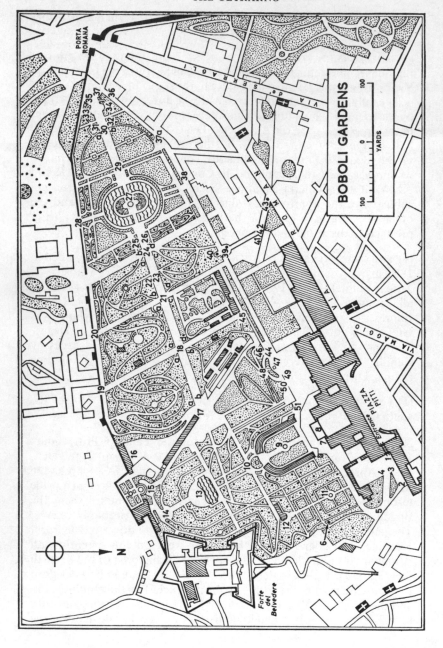

BOBOLI GARDENS

gardens. Bandinelli began work on a grotto for Eleonora of Toledo. A few years later Ammannati's unfinished Water-Cycle Fountain (originally intended for the Palazzo Vecchio) was set up above his cortile on the site now occupied by the Carciofo Fountain. Giambologna's Oceanus Fountain was set in the centre of the amphitheatre. All these pieces have since been shifted. Other pieces came to the garden from the villa at Pratolino late in the 18th c. The keyed diagram is a guide to the Boboli's sculpture.

1. Fountain of the dwarf Morgante – in the guise of Silenus riding a turtle, by Valerio Cioli, after 1560. The face recently reworked. Morgante was the name of a giant made famous in the poem Luigi Pulci dedicated to the mother of Lorenzo the Magnificent.

2. **'La Grotta Grande'** – lower half by Vasari, upper section by Bernardo Buontalenti (1556–93). On the façade: reliefs of *Peace* and *Justice* by Giovanni del Tadda with Capricorn, the symbol of Cosimo I; in the niche on either side: *Apollo and Ceres* by Baccio Bandinelli (originally intended as Adam and Eve for an altar). Interior: first chamber – murals by Poccetti (1586–7), stucco décor by Piero Mati (1587); at four corners, copies of Michelangelo's slaves (originals now in the Accademia) which were once installed here in 1585; second chamber – the Nymphaeum with Vincenzo de' Rossi's *Paris and Helen* as the central group; third chamber – the *Grotticella* with Giambologn's *Venus* (*ca* 1573) cringing before leering imps clutching the rim of the basin (1592) which was probably based on Giambologna's design. The room once had trick water jets.

3, 4. Two marble and porphyry statues – which stand on very fine bases, fragments of a triumphal arch (late 3rd c.). The statues represent Dacian prisoners: they were brought here in 1785 from the Villa Medici in Rome.

5. Seated deity – mid-16th c., originally made for a monumental complex to go inside the Duomo; this figure was rejected, reworked as a Zeus and taken to Pratolino. After Pratolino's destruction the statue was brought to the Boboli.

6. *Grotticina* – rustic grotto by Baccio Bandinelli (1553–4) with *putti*, nibbling goats and stalactites. She-goat over basin by Bandinelli. Some of the figures by Giovanni Fancelli. Original oval basin decorated with *putti* and capricorns now installed beneath one of the windows on the façade of the Palazzo Pitti (schoolchildren recently broke the basin!).

7. Fountain of the dwarf Pietro Barbino – by Valerio Cioli, after 1560. Vasari called Barbino clever, learned, and very kind.

275

8. Fountain of the Artichoke (*Fontana del Carciofo* by Susini and Francesco del Tadda (1639–41); it replaced an earlier Fountain of Juno by Ammannati.

9. *Amphitheatre* – shaped after an ancient Roman circus, often served as an outdoor theatre. Its present form dates from the 17th and 18th c. In in the centre: granite basin (from the Baths of Caracalla in Rome) and part of an Egyptian obelisk originally from Luxor. In the niches around the balustrade: terracotta urns and copies of antique statuary.

10. Statue of *Ceres* – Roman copy after a Greek original attributed to Alcamene; between statues of a Roman magistrate and Septimius Severus.

11. Ganymede Fountain – unknown sculptor, 17th c.?

12. *Coffee House* – by Zanobi del Rosso (1776), built for Pietro Leopoldo of Lorraine.

13. *Neptune Pond* – with rustic island of the 17th c.; the bronze statue of Neptune by Stoldo Lorenzi (1565–8) originally belonged to a formal cylix fountain installed in another part of the garden to the left of the amphitheatre.

14. Colossal statue of *Abundance* – begun by Giambologna and finished by the shop of Pietro Tacca (1636–7); originally it was conceived as a portrait of the Grand Duchess Giovanna d'Austria and was intended to go on top of a column in Piazza San Marco. When the column broke, the project for raising the statue collapsed too and the figure after its transformation into *Dovizia* by Tacca was installed in the Boboli instead.

15. *Giardino del Cavaliere* – its upper portion built on the site of a bastion constructed by Michelangelo in 1529 for the defence of Florence. The terrace was cleared for a botanical garden by Cardinal Leopoldo de' Medici. Early in the 18th c., Cosimo III had the casino built for his son, Gian Gastone, who was supposed to take his French lessons there. It now houses the *Porcelain Museum* (Museo delle Porcellane). The fountain ('*Fontana delle Scimmie*') with cupid and monkeys is by Tacca.

16. *La Lavacapo* ('The Shampoo') – by Valerio Cioli (1599); colossal figure of a woman washing a boy's head carved as a fountain, once occupied a place near the rim of Neptune's pond above the amphitheatre. Ask custodian to open gate.

17. Entrance to the *Viottolone* or cypress alley; beautiful view of Bellosguardo. To the left and right (*a*, *b*) ancient copies of the Greek tyrannicides, reworked in the 17th c.

18. (*a*) Lady with grapes on her head (*Prudence* by G. Caccini?);

(b) *Aesculapius and Hippolytus* by G. Caccini; (c) *Summer* by G. Caccini; (d) *Youth symbolic of Autumn* by G. Caccini (late 16th c.).

19. *Hippocrene*, goddess of the spring of Parnassus – by Ammannati (1556–79), from the incompleted Water-Cycle Fountain originally planned as a wall fountain for the Salone dei Cinquecento in the Palazzo Vecchio.

20. Colossal bust of *Jupiter* – by Giambologna, *ca* 1560.

21. (a) Bearded Roman figure; (b) bald Roman philosopher; (c) *Bacchus*; (d) *Andromeda*, 17th c.?

22. *Hermes with Infant Bacchus* – Roman copy of Praxiteles's lost original.

23. Youthful pagan deity with tree-stump and bird, 17th c.?

24. (a) *Andromeda*, Neapolitan, late 16th c.; (b) Pagan goddess making gesture of silence; (c) *Aesculapius*, Roman copy after Greek original; (d) ancient Roman goddess.

25. *Gioco del Sacco Mazzone* – by Romolo del Tadda based on a model by Orazio Mochi early 17th c.

26. *Gioco della pentolaccia* – by G. B. Cappezzuoli, 18th c.

27. *Piazzale dell' Isolotto* – island fountain designed in 1618 by Alfonso Parigi with modifications made later under Pietro Leopoldo. At entrances to the bridges leading to the island: paired pillars surmounted by Cosimo I's capricorns flanked by triton fountains. At either end of the other axis to the pool: cylix fountains surmounted by cupids by Domenico Pieratti and Cosimo Salvestrini. In the water: two small islands with *Perseus* and *Andromeda*. At the centre: the *Ocean Fountain* (1567–76) by Giambologna, the nucleus of which is a round granite basin already brought to Florence in 1567 from Elba, where it was quarried by Tribolo before 1550. At Ocean's feet are personifications of the Nile, Ganges and Euphrates rivers, symbolizing youth, maturity, and old age. The Oceanus is a copy of the original now in the Bargello. Originally, the fountain was set up in the amphitheatre.

In the hedge surrounding the piazzale are niches containing figures of bird hunters, collectors of fruit, a server of wine, a *David*, and a weary *Neptune*. This is a good place for a picnic in the summer (there are plenty of stone benches).

28. *Venus and Adonis* – by Cosimo Salvestrini, 18th c.

29. Left: *Saturn* by Gherardo Silvani; right: *Vulcan* by Chiarissimo Fancelli, both 17th c. Two red granite columns; around the

Hemicycle installed in niches of the hedge are colossal antique busts.

30. (*a*) Seated deity; (*b*) *Aesculapius* by Tribolo, originally part of a fountain at Pratolino.
31. Three grotesque figures (based on designs by Callot) by Romolo del Tadda, early 17th c.
32. Two figures of bird hunters, 17th c.
    Seated *Venus with Cupid*, 16th c.
34. Muse, 17th c.
35. Peasant emptying a cask into an antique sarcophagus – by Giovanni Fancelli (1550s, perhaps based on a model by Baccio Bandinelli).
36. Youth with a satyr, 17th c., unknown sculptor.
37. *Perseus and the Dragon* (begun as an allegorical portrait of Cosimo I), 16th c., fine antique sarcophagus of the labours of Hercules. The group was originally made for Pratolino.
37a. Young peasant with a spade – by Valerio and Simone Cioli (1599–1608).
38. *Fountain of the Vintage* – by Valerio and Simone Cioli (1599–1608). Two pink marble mastiffs (by Romolo del Tadda?) sit glumly opposite it. Near the fountain there was once a small zoo. In the 18th c. Cioli's Morgante Fountain (No. 1) stood nearby.
39. Seated shepherd playing bagpipes, 17th c. Behind the wall is an 18th c. building used as an orangery and sometimes as a stable. At one time it served as the grand-ducal seraglio.
40. *The Arno* – by Ammannati from the Water-Cycle Fountain (*see* No. 19).
41. *Adam and Eve in a Grotto* – a mawkish group by a pupil of Giambologna, Michelangelo Naccherino (1616), in which even the serpent is reduced to tears.
42. *Bacchus*, 17th c.
43. The Annalena Entrance to the gardens.
44. Roman captain.
45. Bacchic figure and fountain, 17th c.
46. *Judith*, 17th c.?
47. Granite basin; ancient?
48. *Pegasus*, 17th c.?
49. Roman captain, much restored (Augustus?).
50. *Apollo* – by Domenico Poggini, late 16th c.
51. Seated goddess with infant on knee, 17th c. restoration of antique?

4. The Via Maggio – corruption of the original Via Maggiore. Since the late 13th c. a street famous for its palaces. Most of those standing today date from the 15th and 16th c. (*a*) *Casa Guidi,* on the corner of Via Maggio and Via Mazzetta, built late in the 15th c. for the Ridolfi family. Elizabeth Barrett Browning lived and died here in 1861. (*b*) *The House of Bianca Cappello* (Nos. 24–6), rebuilt 1570–4 in the manner of Buontalenti as the residence of Francesco I's mistress who eventually became his Grand Duchess in 1579. Sgraffito work based on designs by Poccetti – much restored. (*c*) *Palazzo Ricasoli-Firidolfi* (No. 7), built early in the 16th c. in the manner of Baccio d'Agnolo with a beautiful courtyard in the style of Cronaca. Elsewhere on the Via Maggio lived Giulio Parigi (No. 36) and the sculptor G. B. Foggini (No. 48).

5. The Church of Santo Spirito*
Since the middle of the 13th c. the Augustinians have maintained their convent here. Their school was one of the best in Florence. Its most famous teacher was Luigi de' Marsili, whose cenotaph was painted in the Duomo early in the 15th c. A group of students gathered round him to discuss dialectics, physics and metaphysics. The subject of the day's debate was posted on a column. Boccaccio left his library to the convent.

The present church, largely based on a plan by Brunelleschi, was built between 1434 and 1487. It preserves much of its original decoration and thus has one of the most harmonious interiors in the city. Since 1397 the monks had wanted to replace the old Gothic church with a new one; for half a century they sacrificed a meal each day to help finance the church. In 1428 Brunelleschi was asked to prepare a model and in 1434 the building committee approved the plans. Before Brunelleschi's death in 1446 the foundations had been laid and the north end of the choir was largely finished. Twelve days before his death the first column shaft was on the site. For the next forty years construction continued under Antonio Manetti, Giovanni da Gaiole, Salvi d'Andrea and others. A fire in 1471 destroyed almost every trace of the medieval church and convent which still stood (only the refectory survived, *see* No. **6**). Between 1483 and 1486 there was dispute over how the façade should be built. Brunelleschi's original plan called for a façade with four doors. He also planned that the curved walls of the chapels should be expressed on the exterior too. Giuliano da Sangallo protested against the changes made in Brunelleschi's plans and tried to invoke the aid of Lorenzo the Magnificent, but to no avail. Vasari commented that

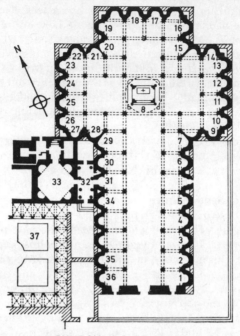

CHURCH of S. SPIRITO

if it had not been for those who thought they knew better and changed Brunelleschi's plans, S Spirito would have been 'the most perfect temple of Christianity'. The façade was never finished. The bell tower is by Baccio d'Agnolo (1503–17) and the cupola is by Cronaca (Simone del Pollaiuolo) and Salvi d'Andrea (1479–82).

Interior: the façade wall by Salvi d'Andrea (1483–7) with a stained glass window, the *Descent of the Holy Spirit*, designed by Perugino (*ca* 1500). The fictive coffered ceiling in the nave was painted in the 18th c. Originally the thirty-eight semi-circular chapels had low altars, which were later replaced by the pompous ones we see now.

1. *Disputa* by Pier Francesco di Jacopo Toschi (mid 16th c.).
2. Copy of Michelangelo's *Pietà* by Nanni di Baccio Bigio (1549).
3. *S Nicola da Tolentino* – polychromed wooden statue attributed to Nanni Unghero; angels on either side by Franciabigio, *ca* 1517–18.

4. *Expulsion of the Money-Changers from the Temple* by Giovanni Stradano (1572).
5. *Coronation of the Virgin* by Alessandro Gherardini (*ca* 1694).
6. *Martyrdom of St Stephen* by Passignano (1602), who was also responsible for the frame.
7. *Tobias and the Angel* by Giovanni Baratta (1698).
8. High altar and monks' choir by Giovanni Caccini (1599–1608), aided by Gherardo Silvani and Agostino Ubaldini. The two candelabra by Cosimo Merlini (1708). The inlaid pavement, the gift of Cosimo II (1609).
9. *Transfiguration* by Pier Francesco di Jacopo Toschi, mid 16th c.
10. 15th c. panel painting of the *Madonna protecting a Child from the Torments of the Devil* ('*Madonna del Soccorso*').
11. Architecture and altar by B. Buontalenti (1601); the 14th c. Crucifix formerly belonged to a religious confraternity known as the Compagnia dei Bianchi.
12. **Altarpiece of the Nerli Family***, *Madonna and Child with SS John the Baptist, Martin, Catherine of Alexandria, with Tanai de' Nerli and his wife* by Filippino Lippi (*ca* 1488). In the background a view of Porta S Frediano.
13. Copy of Perugino's *Apparition of the Virgin to St Bernard* by F. Ficherelli (17th c.); the original picture is now in Munich at the Alte Pinakothek.
14. Behind a bronze grille; marble sarcophagus made for Neri Capponi by Antonio Rossellino (after 1457). The portrait bust of a Capponi cardinal at the left was made in 1659.
15. *Madonna with SS John the Evangelist and Jerome*, attributed to an unknown artist with similarities to both Lorenzo di Credi and Piero di Cosimo, early 16th c.
16. *Madonna and Child with Four Saints* by one of Giotto's best followers – Maso di Banco (*ca* 1340).
17. *Martyrdom of the Ten Thousand* by Alessandro Allori (1574) – a 15th c. predella containing a view of the Palazzo Pitti before its enlargement. Altar frontal of *St Lucy with Two Angels* attributed to Neri di Bicci (*ca* 1460).
18. *Christ and the Adultress* by Alessandro Allori (1577); in the predella: portraits of the da Bagnano family.
19. *Annunciation*, late 15th c.
20. *Nativity* by a follower of Ghirlandaio.
21. *Madonna and Child and Angels and SS Bartholomew and John the Evangelist* attributed to Raffellino dei Carli

22. *St Monica establishing the Rule of the Augustinian Nuns* attributed to Botticini (1483).
23. *Madonna and Child Enthroned with SS Thomas and Augustine* (later altered to represent St Peter), by Cosimo Rosselli (1482); altar frontal with *Doubting Thomas* attributed to Neri di Bicci (*ca* 1460).
24. Corbinelli Altar carved by the youthful Andrea Sansovino (1492). Balustrade added in 1642. This is the earliest instance of a type of altar which later became very popular: the sacrament aediculum framed within a triumphal arch.
25. *Trinity adored by SS Catherine and Mary Magdalen* by Francesco Granacci (*ca* 1485).
26. *Madonna Enthroned with Angels and SS Bartholomew and Nicholas* by Raffaellino del Garbo (also known as R. dei Carli), early 16th c.
27. *Madonna Enthroned with SS Lawrence, John the Evangelist, Stephen and Bernard* by Raffaellino dei Carli, 1505; altar frontal with *St Lawrence distributing the Treasure of the Church* by Jacopo del Sellaio.
28. *Way to Calvary* by Michele di Ridolfo (*see* No. 34). Above: stained glass window of *Doubting Thomas* (1485–90) attributed to an assistant of Domenico Ghirlandaio known as Bartolomeo di Giovanni.
29. *Madonna Enthroned with SS Lawrence, Giovanni Gualberto, Catherine and Bernard* by a follower of Fra Bartolommeo.
30. Stained glass window, *Virgin appearing to St Bernard*, 15th c.
31. Entrance to the sacristy beneath the organ.
32. *Vestibule* (1492–4) with coffered vault, built by Cronaca after a design by Guiliano da Sangallo. Door to cloister on the left.
33. *Sacristy** (1488–96) – the model for the sacristy was prepared by Giuliano da Sangallo at the order of Lorenzo the Magnificent. The form was supposed to be based upon the Florentine Baptistery, of which Sangallo was the first to make a careful drawing. It was the architect's hope that he would be given the supervision of the completion of the entire church of S Spirito; in this he was disappointed. The cupola, based on a model by Simone del Pollaiuolo and Salvi d'Andrea, collapsed in 1496 two months after its completion and had to be rebuilt. The sacristy cupboards made in 1584, with a wooden Crucifix, by a follower of Giambologna. Altarpiece of *S Fiacre curing the Sick* by Allori (1597).
34. *Madonna, St Anne and Other Saints* by Michele di Ridolfo

(Michele Tosini, who was the pupil of Lorenzo di Credi and Ridolfo Ghirlandaio, is sometimes known as Michele di Ridolfo Ghirlandaio).

35. Copy of Michelangelo's *Christ* in S Maria sopra Minerva (Rome) by Taddeo Landini (1579).
36. *Resurrection* by Pier Francesco di Jacopo Toschi (mid 16th c.).
37. Cloister by Giulio and Alfonso Parigi (early 17th c.) with murals by Cosimo Ulivelli.

6. Former Refectory of Santo Spirito, now the Fondazione Salvatore Romano – a museum owned by the city (open weekday mornings; admission fee 50 lire). This is the sole surviving room of the Gothic convent of S Spirito. It contains a muralled *Crucifixion* and *Last Supper* (*ca* 1360) by close followers of Andrea Orcagna and his brother, Nardo di Cione. This is the most monumental Crucifixion of the Florentine Trecento and was commissioned by the Cambi di Napoleone family. The museum contains two fine 13th c. marble sea-monsters from the altar of S Restituta, Naples (No. 3), figures by Tino di Camaino, *ca* 1322 (Nos. 38, 44) and some relief fragments from Padua (No. 21) in the manner of Donatello.

7. Palazzo Guadagni (Piazza S Spirito Nos. 7–9) – one of the city's most elegant early 16th c. palaces built for Rinieri Dei soon after 1503, probably by Cronaca. It was this Dei who commissioned Raphael's *Madonna del Baldacchino* for the family chapel in S Spirito. Andrea del Sarto was responsible for the sgraffito work on the façade (*ca* 1506). Wrought-iron lamps probably by Caparra. The last member of the Dei family left the palace in 1683 to the Buonuomini di San Martino (*see* chapter 4 – No. 4 in Summary of Chief Monuments), who sold it the next year to Donato Guadagni. Round the corner in the Via Mazzetta, S Filippo Neri was nursed as a child.

8. Santa Maria del Carmine* – begun for the Carmelites in 1268 but not consecrated until 1422. This occasion was commemorated by a mural in the cloister painted by Masaccio which was famous for its crowd of contemporary portraits (since demolished). In 1771 a fire destroyed most of the church – only the chancel, part of the transept, the Brancacci Chapel and the sacristy were spared. The present church is the work of Giuseppe Ruggeri and Giulio Mannaioni (1771–5).

Interior: at the southern end of the church, to the right, is the **Brancacci Chapel***, famed for its cycle of murals begun by Masaccio and Masolino (1423–8) and finished by Filippino Lippi (*ca* 1484–5). Best light: 11 a.m., 4–5 p.m. Automatic lighting device installed to right of chapel entrance (insert 100 lire coin). Murals concern redeemed sinners: Adam and Eve at the entrance with the story of St Peter within. Progress on the paintings, begun *ca* 1423, were interrupted by Masaccio's trips to Pisa in 1426 and to Rome in 1428, and by Masolino's absences in Hungary from 1426 to mid-1427 and in Rome from 1428–31. The murals were left incomplete after Masaccio's death in 1428 and the exile of the Brancacci in 1436. Fifty years later they were finished by Filippino Lippi. The murals in the vault and in the lunettes (which were probably the work of Masolino) were destroyed or concealed in 1748 when Vincenzo Meucci painted the Baroque décor visible today. The subjects of the scenes and their authors are (proceeding from left to right and from the top downwards): on the entrance piers, on the left: *Expulsion of Adam and Eve* by Masaccio, *St Peter in Prison visited by St Paul* by Filippino; on the right: the *Temptation of Adam and Eve* by Masolino; below: an *Angel liberates St Peter* by Filippino. Left wall: the *Tribute Money* by Masaccio; below; the *Raising of the King of Antioch's Son* and the *Chairing of Peter*. Masaccio painted most of the right third of the picture and the figure of Peter raising the boy, as well as some of the crowd. Filippino painted the group on the left and completed the crowd – his figures are somewhat larger than Masaccio's. Note the Carmelites kneeling at the feet of St Peter: this was part of the Carmelite legend which claimed that the prophet Elijah founded their order on Mount Carmel and that his monks were already present when Peter came to Antioch. Legend had it that Peter instituted the tonsure during his visit there. Altar wall: upper scenes – *Peter preaching on Whitsunday* by Masolino and an assistant; *Peter baptizing the Neophytes* by Masaccio; lower tier; *Peter healing with his Shadow* by Masaccio and an assistant (this scene was damaged by fire the of 1771, as was the entire corner of the chapel), and the *Distribution of the Goods of the Church after the Death of Ananias* by Masaccio. Right wall: *Peter cures a Cripple and raises Tabitha* by Masolino; *SS Peter and Paul before the Proconsul* and the *Crucifixion of Peter* by Filippino Lippi. The Madonna (framed by the Baroque altar) was a famous miracle-working image painted during the second half of the 13th c.

In the apse: monument of Piero Soderini (who died in exile in Rome in 1522) by Benedetto da Rovezzano.

At the. end of the left arm of the transept: the **Corsini Chapel** dedicated to S Andrea Corsini (1302–73), Bishop of Fiesole. The architecture by Pier Franscesco Silvani (1675–83); in the cupola, mural by Luca Giordano of *S Andrea in Glory* (1682); silver relief by Foggini. To the right, behind a door in the chapel (ask sacristan to open, tip expected); remains of murals by Gherardo Starnina (1404). *Sacristy* built in 1394: in the chapel, early 15th c. murals by a follower of Agnolo Gaddi (sometimes thought to be Bicci di Lorenzo) illustrating the *Life of St Cecilia*; altarpiece by a follower of Jacopo del Sellaio with a predella illustrating the *Battle of Anghiari*. Also in the sacristy; a stucco *Madonna and Child* by a follower of Desiderio,a polyptych by Andrea Bonaiuti. *Cloister;* detached murals by Starnina and Filippo Lippi and refectory fresco by Francesco Vanni.

9. Church of San Frediano in Cestello – *Cestello* from the Cistercians who came here in 1628. Church rebuilt in 1680–9 on the design of a Roman architect, Cerutti. The cupola and bell tower were added in 1698 by Antonio Ferri. Inside: polychromed wooden *Madonna and Child* by a follower of Nino Pisano, *ca* 1350. *A Crucifixion with Saints* (late 15th c.) by Jacopo del Sellaio in the sacristy.

10. Via de' Serragli – the last of the Serragli died in 1648 but the street bearing their name remains. At its lower end near the Arno is the former *Palazzo Ferroni* (formerly del Pugliese, No. 8) – a mid 15th c. building enlarged in 1778 by Zanobi del Rosso (the architect of the Boboli Coffee House) with a splendid Baroque courtyard (one can walk in). At the corner of Via S Monaca is a tabernacle of the *Virgin and Child with SS Paul, Jerome and a donor* by Bicci di Lorenzo (1427). At the corner of the Via del Campuccio is (*a*) the former church of *Santa Elisabetta delle Convertite* (between No. 122 and 124) built *ca* 1330 and enlarged at the behest of Grand Duchess Maria Maddalena of Austria in 1624 for the convent of Augustinian nuns. Near the church at No. 102 is a large muralled tabernacle of the *Crucifixion and Saints* by Poccetti. (*b*) The former convent of S Elisabetta is now the Istituto Pio X, which contains a youth hostel and a theatre (the Teatro degli Artigianelli), where comedies in Florentine dialect are given on Wednesday evenings. (*c*) *Santa Chiara,* the former church of another cloister of nuns, founded in 1356, rebuilt in 1457, now the Galleria Pio Fedi. Its late 15th c. apse is now housed in London at the Victoria and Albert Museum.

11. Piazza della Calza – the name refers to the order of *frati Ingesuati* (founded by the Beato Giovanni Colombini of Siena) who wore a grey mantle with a long, white sock-like hood (*calza*). The order was suppressed in 1668. Their church since 1529, (*a*) *San Giovanni della Calza,* founded by Bindo Benini in the 14th c., stands on the west side of the Piazza. The convent is now run as a home for old ladies.

In the refectory is the mural of the *Last Supper* by Franciabigio (1514); to see it, ring the bell at No. 6 on the Piazza. The house facing the Porta Romana occupying the corner between the Via de' Serragli and Via Romana (*b*) once belonged to the Serragli family. Around 1617 Giovanni da San Giovanni painted a mural on its façade with allegorical figures of Florence seated between Pisa and Siena receiving gifts from Flora. In its place today is a mural by Mario Romoli illustrating Florentine artisans with portraits of their patrons (including Cosimo I and former Mayor La Pira).

12. The Porta Romana – the gate between Florence and the high road to Siena and Rome. Built between 1326 and 1328. In the lunette facing the Piazza della Calza is a late 14th c. mural of the *Madonna and Child with Saints*. Outside, on either side of the central arch, are two inscriptions commemorating the triumphal entry of Pope Leo X (Giovanni de' Medici) in 1515 and the visit of the Emperor Charles V in 1536, who came to install his son-in-law, Alessandro de' Medici, on the ducal throne of Florence.

13. Istituto Statale d'Arte – housed in the former royal stables. The city's best school for the arts and crafts: graphic arts, architectural design, painting, sculpture, textiles, ceramics, metal crafts, woodwork, mosaics, and photography.

14. San Pier Gattolino (ring bell for custodian at door to right of church portal) – the favourite church of the servants of the Medici Court. The painter Giovanni da San Giovanni is buried here. Present building rebuilt *ca* 1571 in the manner of Santi di Tito. The street beside the church, Via Ser Umido, bears the nickname of the workman who collected funds and materials to rebuild the old church destroyed in 1552 for Cosimo I's fortifications.

15. The Annalena Gate to the Boboli Gardens.

16. The former Palazzo Bini (Via Romana, No. 17) – now occupied by the Istituto di Zoologia of the University – also known as 'La Specola'. Built *ca* 1520, the handsome courtyard is in the style of Baccio d'Agnolo. Leopoldo I of Lorraine acquired the building from the Torrigiani family and deposited there a collection for a natural history museum, to which he appended a chemical laboratory, botanical garden, and astronomical observatory. Also a remarkable collection of anatomical models in coloured wax of the 17th c. Open on Sunday mornings, Monday through Wednesday 09.00–12.00.

17. Church of San Felice in Piazza – one of the oldest churches in the Oltrarno. In 1413 the Camaldolese monks took over the church. Funds for the façade left by Mariotto Stephani de Lippis in 1457. Soon afterwards this façade and chancel were rebuilt in the manner of Brunelleschi – perhaps by Antonio Manetti.

Interior: the front half consists of arcades supporting a gallery for nuns (late 16th c.?). Murals on façade wall to right of entrance, first half of the 15th c. in the style of Neri di Bicci. Right side of church, first altar: muralled *Pietà* attributed to Niccolò di Pietro Gerini (*ca* 1400). After the fourth altar: painted cross by a close follower of Giotto; *Pietà* group in terracotta attributed to Cieco da Gambassi (early 17th c.); above it, fragment of a 15th c. *Baptism.* Fifth altar: *Madonna and Child with SS Peter, Sebastian, Paul and another Saint* by Michele di Ridolfo (Michele Tosini), *ca* 1540. The lunette with God the Father is 17th c. Sixth altar: mural of the *Assumption of the Virgin* attributed to Bicci di Lorenzo, *ca* 1430. Below: *Madonna and Child* by a follower of Jacopo della Quercia.

Left side of church, first altar: triptych with *SS Anthony Abbot, Roch, Catherine of Siena* by a follower of Botticelli (*ca* 1500); the predella has an *Annunciation* with charming landscapes reminiscent of Jacopo del Sellaio. Fourth altar: *Calling of Matthew* by Matteo Rosselli (1619). Fifth altar: the *Virgin appearing to SS Hyacinth and Peter Martyr* by Jacopo da Empoli, 1595 (the church was taken over by Dominican nuns in 1557). Sixth altar: triptych by Neri di Bicci of *Resurrection with SS Nicholas, John the Baptist, Julian and Sigismund,* 1467; the mural in the lunette painted *ca* 1400. Seventh altar: belonged to the Parigi family; the tabernacle by Giulio Parigi, *ca* 1635–9; the mural of *St Felix resuscitating St Maximus of Nola* by Giovanni da San Giovanni (a neighbour of the Parigi family who, like them, was employed for years in the Palazzo Pitti).

18. Palazzo Canigiani (Via de' Bardi, Nos. 28–30) – a 14th c. façade built on the remains of a 13th c. hospital. The courtyard was built in the style of Michelozzo.

Palazzo Capponi, (Via de' Bardi, No. 36) – 15th c. façade. Inside; beautiful porphyry lion (probably ancient Roman) at bottom of staircase.

19. Santa Lucia dei Magnoli – next door to No. 22 Via de' Bardi. Founded in 1078 but rebuilt several times since. Over the door: polychromed lunette of *St Lucy flanked by Two Angels* by Benedetto Buglioni (1510–20). *Inside:* to the left, the *Annunciation* by Jacopo

287

del Sellaio (1473); first altar on left: *St Lucy* by Pietro Lorenzetti (*ca* 1332), only the face and hands are original; third altar on right: copy of Andrea del Sarto's *Disputà* in the Pitti. This picture occupies the place originally held by Domenico Veneziano's *St Lucy* altarpiece (*ca* 1440), now in the Uffizi. On the high altar: a painting of the *Virgin and Child flanked by SS John the Baptist, Sylvester, Martin, and Filippo Benizzi* (*ca* 1500) originally from the nearby monastery of S Giorgio sulla Costa.

20. Palazzo Serristori – built in 1515, rebuilt in 1873. At present an object of dispute between the city and the heirs of its former owner. The famous art collection has been largely dispersed.

21. Church of San Niccolò – one of the city's earliest churches (founded *ca* 1050), rebuilt early in the 15th c. with funds given by the Quaratesi family. On the façade about fifteen feet up is a marker commemorating the height reached by the flood of 1557. Most of the objects of worth are now collected in the sacristy to the rear of the church on the right. The sacristy, or Chapel of the Assumption (also built with Quaratesi funds), contains a pietra-serena tabernacle *ca*, 1510, a muralled lunette by a follower of Castagno representing the *Virgin giving her Belt to St Thomas*, *ca* 1480. Below: a triptych of *ca* 1390 with the *Virgin and Child with Four Saints;* in the predella, *Scenes from the Life of St Martin*. To the left of the mural: *Virgin and Child flanked by Six Saints* attributed to Bicci di Lorenzo, *ca* 1440. To the right: *Crucifixion-Trinity* by Neri di Bicci, 1463. Also a *Tobias and the Angel* by Francesco Morandini (called 'il Poppi').

22. Porta San Niccolò – built in 1324. It is the only remaining city gate which conserves its original height. On its eastern face were once statues and four coats-of-arms (among these were the *stemmae* of the Parte Guelfa and the Lily of the Commune). On the side facing the city: a muralled lunette of the second half of the 14th c. – the *Virgin and Child Enthroned*, flanked by SS John the Baptist and Nicholas of Bari and two angel musicians playing a viol and a portable organ.

23. San Miniato al Monte*
Take bus No. 13 from Piazza della Stazione; or walk from the Porta S Niccolò up a steep cypress alley. An easier route to walk up or drive is by way of the road issuing from the Porta S Miniato or via the Costa S Giorgio (or Costa dei Magnoli). The latter road follows the Via S Leonardo at the top, after which turn left into the Viale dei Colli and continue on to the stairs beneath S Miniato.

Angel by Luca della Robbia from the Cardinal of Portugal's Chapel in San Miniato al Monte, 1466

The porch of the Badia Fiesolana built by a follower of Brunelleschi, *ca* 1456

San Miniato – the present structure rebuilt after 1018 on the site of an earlier church. Originally the church was Benedictine, but in 1373 it was taken over by the Olivetans, who are still there.

Facade: marble inlays *ca* 1070–*ca* 1270; mosaic with *Christ, Mary and S Miniato* (*ca* 1260). Surmounting the gable is a gilt copper eagle (1401), the symbol of the Calimala – the guild which administered the church fabric since 1228.

Campanile begun by Baccio d'Agnolo in 1518. During the siege of 1529 Michelangelo saved it from destruction by covering it with mattresses to protect it from the stone cannon-balls.

Interior: of the original 13th c. décor, there remain the famous inlaid pavement of 1207 in the nave with its patterns of lions, doves, and Signs of the Zodiac; the inlaid choir and pulpit; and a few fresco fragments just to the right of the sacristy entrance. The timbered roof dates from 1322; its ornament is repainted. The fictive black and white inlays painted on the clerestory belong to a 19th c. restoration, which perhaps used a few original fragments as a point of departure (one such fragment is in the eastern end of the left aisle).

At the end of the nave is the *Cappella del Crocifisso* – a tabernacle originally built in honour of the painted cross of S Giovanni Gualberto (since removed to S Trinita). The structure probably designed by Michelozzo was commissioned in 1448 by Piero de' Medici, whose arms (a falcon in flight holding the Medici diamond ring with three feathers) are inlaid in a marble medallion on the back of the tabernacle. Terracotta décor by Luca della Robbia. The reassembled panels on the doors of the cupboards painted by Agnolo Gaddi (1394–6) and illustrate *SS Miniato, Giovanni Gualberto*, the *Annunciation* and *Scenes from the Passion*.

Right aisle: murals from the 13th through the 15th c. The *Madonna with Six Saints* set inside a pink pseudo-architectural framework is attributed to Paolo Schiavo (1436). The giant *St Christopher* is of the 13th c. Left aisle: detached murals of the *Crucifixion* and *Coronation of the Virgin* by Mariotto di Nardo (*ca* 1400).

*Cardinal of Portugal's Chapel** (if gate is locked, ask sacristan to open) was built to commemorate a young Portuguese prince, Cardinal James of Lusitania, who died in Florence in 1459. Brunelleschi's best pupil, Antonio Manetti, drew up the plan. After Manetti's death in 1460, construction was supervised by Giovanni Rossellino. Antonio and Bernardo Rossellino were responsible for the Cardinal's tomb and all the surrounding sculpture finished by

1466. Luca della Robbia made the terracotta decor for the vault representing the Holy Spirit surrounded by the Four Cardinal Virtues (1462–6). The tomb and the sculpture finished by 1466. Murals were begun in 1467 and probably completed by 1468. Antonio and Piero Pollaiuolo painted the angels drawing aside the curtain on the altar wall. They also painted the altarpiece (the original now in the Uffizi) of *SS James of Compostella, Eustace and Vincent* (1467–8). All the other painting in the chapel is by Alesso Baldovinetti. His *Annunciation* is painted on a panel, the lunette is a mural. The gate at the entrance is modern.

Crypt: 11th c. but heavily restored; murals of Saints and Prophets by Taddeo Gaddi (1341–2). The altar containing S Miniato's bones built in 1013. Wrought-iron gate by Petruccio di Betto of Siena (1338).

Raised Choir: inlaid wooden stalls by Giovanni da Gaiole and Francesco di Domenico, called Monciatto (1466–70). Apse: mosaic of *Christ blessing Mary and S Miniato* (1297) restored by Baldovinetti in 1491. Altarpiece on right of *S Giovanni Gualberto* (*ca* 1370); altarpiece on left of *S Miniato* by Jacopo del Casentino (*ca* 1340).

Sacristy: built in 1387 with funds donated by Benedetto di Nerozzo Alberti. Murals by Spinello Aretino of the *Life of St Benedict*. Inlaid cupboards by Jacopo Legnaiuolo (*ca* 1472). To see the cloister loggia upstairs, ask the sacristan.

Cloister: double-tiered loggia (1442–7) with murals illustrating the life of St Benedict, already attributed to Paolo Uccello in 1510, but documents and recent scholarship indicate that they are the work of two painters – one of whom was Giovanni Schiavo.

Palazzo dei Vescovi, joined to the southern flank of the church: begun in 1295 by Andrea dei Mozzi. Until 1553 it was the summer residence of the bishops of Florence. Later, Cosimo I used it as a garrison. Now it is part of the convent.

Cemetery founded in 1854. Here are buried the historian Pasquale Villari, and two Englishmen who left property in Florence: Frederick Stibbert and John Temple-Leader.

On the slope between S Miniato and the Piazzale Michelangelo is **San Salvatore** (or **San Francesco**) **al Monte,** named after the Franciscan church on Mt. Zion in Jerusalem. Built under the auspices of the Calimala with funds provided by Castello Quaratesi in 1449 (after his offer to provide S Croce with a façade was refused). The original model made by one of the monks. Delay in work caused by objections to its splendour. Finally Lorenzo the Magnificent approved the project in 1475, and in 1487 Cronaca became the supervising architect. In 1504 the church was finished. *Interior:* some 16th c. stained glass windows; on façade wall, lower left, bust of Marcello Adriani (d. 1524) who signed Savonarola's death-warrant; polychromed terracotta Deposition group (late 16th c.).

'POPOLO E PRINCIPI'

PIAZZA SANTO SPIRITO. The neighbourhood of Piazza S Spirito is my favourite. It is the heart of the Oltrarno. To the east squats the Pitti, aloof on its asphalted rise; to the west the Carmine faces a waste land of bare walls and paving stones. But the unfinished façade of Brunelleschi's stately church of S Spirito shelters a piazza which is always busy and is just about the right size. A slowly dripping fountain is there for children to sail home-made boats in and to splash each other up. Until recently there were stone benches for the old ladies to gossip on and do their knitting in the shade. Mornings, the piazza accommodates a market. At seven the farmers start coming in from near-by hills bringing the freshest of lettuce, herbs, fennel, bunches of flowers, tomatoes, or whatever is in season. Until a few years ago, this was all brought in on red wagons by small donkeys who filled the piazza with the clop-clop of their arrival and departure and hours of their braying conversation. Most of the farmers are motorized now and only one or two wizened beasts are to be seen parked at the northern end of the piazza, resigned to silence and nuzzling their feed bags. Beside the donkeys and small trucks, there is often an enormous ramshackle lorry from Naples bulging with loot from impoverished churches and villas. Old cupboards, discarded confessionals, a rustic reliquary, ceramics, brass bedsteads and tiles are disgorged on the piazza to be haggled over by swarms of local antiquaries.

In rainy weather the *contadini* raise enormous green umbrellas. Their competitors, the middlemen who have the stalls on the east side of the Piazza, have instead magnificently aged sail-like awnings of rusty red and old gold which are tilted at rakish angles to sluice off the rainwater. Here are the crates of standard fruits and vegetables bought in gross before dawn at Nòvoli. During the winter there is a frantic race from stall to stall for the best of the Sicilian oranges at the cheapest price which go by the name of *'Tarocchi'* or *'Mori.'* The market is the site of the daily convention of the neighbourhood's maids and housewives. Family gossip is exchanged and seller and buyer renew the daily game of needling each other (the produce is never good enough, the price never right). Signora Irma comes with Flick, her small black poodle, girded for battle. The custodian of the coach museum in the Pitti comes to pick up bread and fruit for his wife. Itinerant Sicilian pedlars wheedle odd lire out of reluctant pockets for a handful of lemons and garlic. A bizarre figure in high boots and a weather-beaten hat from which trail long pheasant feathers sells fish from the river when he is sober enough to navigate through the crowds. Otherwise he sits alone feeding the pigeons on the steps of S Spirito, quietly muttering obscenities at the passers-by (nobody ever bothers to react). The tripe-seller keeps his white wagon near the Borgo Tegolaio to catch the cooks on their way to the butcher, poulterer, and fishmonger on the Via Mazzetta. In the spring he also sells lilac in great bunches.

Opposite the fountain, in a narrow room no bigger than a closet, sits a cobbler amid a sea of the neighbourhood's worn-out shoes. He quotes prices in 'francs' (an unconscious survival from the era of French dominion). The value of the lire may rise and fall but '*un franco e mezzo*' remains the stable fee for a pair of new leather heels. The cobbler has the courtesy and dignity of other times. An engraving of the view of the Piazzetta in Venice after Canaletto hangs in a corner over his head. When he happens to be out, his family let down a basket to take in more shoes and he has never been known to mistake their owners.

Around the corner from the cobbler, on the Via S Agostino, is the baker, Signor Papini, whose speciality is a bread called '*Trionfo*' which has won him prizes. His ovens accommodate the pies and cakes of his ovenless neighbours and for Thanksgiving he even takes in my turkey and surrounds it with green apples to lubricate the roast and add snap to the flavour. The only fee for this (and he has to be pressed to accept) is a sample of the roast and a bottle of *vin santo*.

Besides the museum installed in the former Augustinian refectory of S Spirito, there is another institution on the piazza. This is Sor Gino's bar. Aside from dispensing refreshment, in summer it provides an unofficial communal ice-box: milk for the babies and meat for their parents' Sunday dinner are tucked into the refrigerator, which also holds the ice-creams. Postage stamps, cigarettes, and spaghetti are sold. There are also two public telephones, a billiard room in the back and a television set in front. The bar hardly ever closes and at night stays open until one or two in the morning.

S Spirito's great *festa* is on May 22nd – the day of S Rita of Cascia. Everyone, beggar or princess, emerges from the church bearing a beautiful long-stemmed yellow rose which has been blessed and sold by the friars in the cloister. The doors on the façade are all thrown open, framing a vista of rich red hangings and hundreds of twinkling candles. But even without a holiday the church is magnificent. Its forest of blue-green columns, its lofty proportions, its rose-coloured pavement, the perfect profile of every base and cornice make it an exalting place to wander idly in as well as to pray. Here and in the Pazzi Chapel is the Florentine character at its freshest and noblest. It is neither outspokenly Christian nor pagan. But it instils in the beholder a sense of lofty pride and dignity which the ancient Romans must have felt when they strolled through the *thermae* wrapped in their togas.

A HOUSE ON VIA MAGGIO. The S Spirito quarter is like a little kingdom. Everything one needs for oneself and one's household is here. Sor Eugenio knows just the quality of cheese, pasta and *baccalà* each of his clients prefers and goes out on his bicycle to deliver them. Sor Angiolo and Mimma will do one's hair, and the nervous electrician (a victim of liver trouble) knows how to tame any obstinate machine. All this is to be had in one block on the Via Maggio. But there are even kingdoms within the domain of S Spirito. One of these is the splendid palace at No. 7. Its feudal lord is the Barone Ricasoli, owner of the celebrated Chianti vineyards. Financial reverses have forced him to cede the controlling interest to an American corporation. Part of the ground floor of the palace, until recently, housed the administrative offices of the Brolio wines. Now a dancing-school has moved in. The rear rooms are occupied by a colony of chinchillas. Their complicated cages are kept immaculately clean by Renata, the porter's wife. The moustachioed breeder roars in and out every day in a gleaming blue-black Maserati. Nearby a shiny old-fashioned bicycle is kept in a rack should the Barone choose to ride to his palace on the opposite bank of the Arno. It has not been ridden in years, but it is ready just the same.

A room off the main staircase is seldom opened save for dusting. Here are stored the family archives going back to the thirteenth century, old globes and musical manuscripts. On the floor below are large vaulted halls with gay eighteenth-century frescoes on the ceilings.

The Barone's office is tucked away in another corner of the palace at the top of a series of tortuous staircases. The porter is awed by the apparition of his master's long thin figure, with its shock of snow-white hair and the slow nasal commands. To outsiders, however, the

Barone is shy and kindly and the last thing he seems to be interested in is the wine bearing his name. But his quiet manner, the wine and chinchilla businesses aside, he will not have either bicycles or Maseratis spoil the harmony of his magnificent courtyard. The palace, however, is so cavernous that it can swallow almost anything. A dozen families and more live up in its higher reaches, but never a sound leaks out. The walls are so thick that a lift-shaft is built inside one of them. Signora Irma and her dog live in one of these apartments. Since her own tower house on the Borgo S Jacopo was destroyed during the war, she has made her home with the family of a distinguished Florentine lawyer, who comes of a long line of specialists in canon law. Signora Irma is small, compact, full of energy, possessed of a peppery tongue and a kind heart. She is every bit as much an autocrat of the kitchen as the Barone is of his palace. Further, she is the most fervent monarchist and follows the doings of the royal families of Europe (the House of Savoy in particular) as if she were one of them. No one knows exactly how old she is and she tolerates no help – not even Sor Eugenio, the benevolent *pizzicagnolo*, is allowed to carry a package for her. When she cooks, she always wears black with a spotless white apron and red felt slippers, a cigarette is clamped in the corner of her mouth, and her brown hair is done up in a net with a bow at the top. She is an inexhaustible source of proverbs and rhymes, grumbles if one asks her questions, and whistles when she brings the breakfast tray. Every week she religiously enters the *Totocalcio* lottery (based on guessing soccer scores). On her annual holiday to play canasta with her relations, she leaves the palace in state, dressed in hat, veil and elegant coat, to catch the train to Turin, for which she always takes a first-class ticket.

NEIGHBOURS. To cross the Arno from this domain is to cross into alien territory. Indeed, the rest of Florence looks on the Oltrarno as a city within the city. Its residents are the only ones who have acquired a name of their own: the 'San Fredianini' – the name coming from the church to the west of S Spirito. As if to prove just how clannish they are and how rooted they are in their neighbourhood, the San Fredianini have a dialect and a salty slang all their own.

What the wool industry was to medieval Florence, the manufacture and repair of antique furniture is to the city today. The carpenters, carvers, gilders and stucco experts congregate in the very same streets – around S Felice, S Spirito, the Carmine and S Frediano What gondoliers are to Venice, the virtuoso riders of bicycles are to this quarter: handlebars are laden with racks of frames with a bedstead miraculously balanced on the back – all on its way to the gilder's or to the packer's.

In the Via delle Caldaie, just off Piazza S Spirito, which was a dyers' street during the Quattrocento (the *caldaie* being the dyers' vats), until recently were Signor Gucci's leather ateliers. The Palazzo Settimanni was entirely devoted to the production of hand-made leather bags, belts and suitcases, bound for Bond Street and Fifth Avenue. Leather was stacked in rolls and hung on racks, each piece having been specially cured down the Arno at S Croce. The medieval apprentice system is still in force here, although the state requires that the boys go to school for four hours each day. Each bench has its older master in either designing, moulding, glueing or stitching, with a row of boys watching and copying beside him.

No neon sign or plaque announced the presence of either Gucci or any other firm in the neighbourhood. One must hunt through a row of brass buttons to find the right bell and the inconspicuous name of its owner engraved no bigger than that of the private residents next door. In the midst of these buildings is the shop of 'Ciccione' the Modenese pastry-maker who makes the quarter's best country-style bread (*pane casalingo*) and ravioli. Around the corner, in the Via della Chiesa, is the hostel for the homeless poor where many of the more eccentric members of the neighbourhood regularly put up for the night (including the pheasant-feathered feeder of the S Spirito pigeons).

THE CARMINE AND THE BRANCACCI CHAPEL. The church of S Maria del Carmine has always been a working-man's church. Even a patrician chapel such as that of the Brancacci reflects the neighbourhood. There are the familiar bare stone houses and the poor but proud inhabitants: the mother and child receiving St Peter's alms, and the frequent sight of the sick and crippled. Contemporary portraits and contemporary events may also have been commemorated here. *The Tribute Money* may be a reference to the institution in 1427 of the Catasto or universal tax law encouraged by Cosimo de' Medici, who perhaps is portrayed below sitting at the feet of the King of Antioch. Masaccio discerned virtue in the commonplace; in the familiar he recognized what made men dignified and humane. All his paintings have the gravity and straightforward honesty of the Florentine artisan. This is not to say that rich merchants such as the Brancacci did not share the same qualities. But the appearance of these moral traits, raised in Masaccio's murals to a heroic degree, constitutes one of the great achievements of Italian art. It is the merest chance that the chapel survived the great fire which swept the church in the eighteenth century.

The murals were carried out for Felice Brancacci on his return from a diplomatic mission to Egypt in 1423. Masaccio and Masolino were a curious pair of collaborators. Their only bond appears to have been that they came from the same neighbourhood in the Val d'Arno. Masolino, eighteen years Masaccio's senior, was a court painter, while Masaccio worked almost entirely for monks and parish priests. Their styles were almost diametrically opposed; Masolino is essentially late Gothic, Masaccio belongs to the Renaissance. One has only to compare Masolino's graceful curvilinear rendition of Adam and Eve in the *Temptation* to the massive power of Masaccio's grief-stricken couple in the *Expulsion* on the opposite wall. The same difference appears in Masolino's dandies chatting in damasked garments in the middle of the *Raising of Tabitha*, and the solemn mien of Masaccio's apostles in *The Tribute Money*, who have the gravity of Roman senators whose garb disdains adornment

In spite of their very different outlook, the painters collaborated over a period of at least four years at the Carmine after they worked together on the *Virgin and Child with St Anne* (now in the Uffizi). In the Brancacci Chapel, the innovations were all Masaccio's. Yet the younger man acknowledged Masolino's seniority. In *The Tribute Money* Masaccio left the face of Christ to be painted by the older man. On the other hand, Masolino in one of his pictures left a minor detail such as the background of the *Raising of Tabitha* to his junior partner. Although here Masaccio's part may be accounted for by one of Masolino's frequent absences from Florence.

What was so new about Masaccio's contribution was that he brought back and developed the grave, monumental style introduced a century before by Giotto and Giovanni Pisano, which after them had been abandoned. Masaccio assumed the sculptor's approach; for him, mass and light were more important in his compositions than line and colour (so beloved by late Gothic painters). Indeed, his work is closer to the statuary of Nanni di Banco and Donatello than to the work of any contemporary painter. Masaccio was also the first painter of his time to apply the new principles of perspective composition and proportion worked out by sculptors and architects such as Donatello, Ghiberti, and Brunelleschi. The passion for perspective is to be explained by the Renaissance conviction that what was truthful and life-like was subject to rational laws. Masaccio's *Tribute Money* is an episode composed so that space, distance and the objects in it are all distinct and measurable. The vanishing-point or horizon line coincides with the heads of the figures. Masaccio assumed that the spectator's point of view corresponded with the eye-level of the protagonists in the scene. The imagery makes no concession to the beholder standing far below; instead, Masaccio asked the beholder to adjust his sight to the loftier realm of the representation. For more than a century afterwards, the Brancacci Chapel was the schoolroom of Florentine art. The postures, gestures and draperies of Masaccio's figures were studied and copied by such diverse artists as Fra Angelico and Castagno, Filippino Lippi and Michelangelo.

THE PALAZZO PITTI. In the twelfth century the S Spirito quarter was open countryside dotted with a few churches and convents. The first private residences to go up here were built by the Corsini, Pitti, Capponi and Ridolfi along what is now the Via Maggio. It was then called the Via Maggiore – and it has remained the widest, most handsome avenue in the Oltrarno. When Luca Pitti decided to build himself a palace in the middle of the fifteenth century, he was not content to have one in the middle of Florence as Cosimo de' Medici and Giovanni Rucellai were, nor did he want to add one more to the formidable cluster already lining Via Maggio, Via de' Serragli and Via Guicciardini. Luca Pitti was only a successful entrepreneur of raw French cloth, but he grew fat on Cosimo de' Medici's largesse, was ambitious, greedy and ungrateful. He accepted presents from rich citizens seeking favours from him in the Signoria. Cosimo even gave him 20,000 gold florins. But soon after Cosimo's death. Pitti plotted against Cosimo's son, Piero the Gouty, and was lucky enough to be forgiven by him. Pitti's mania for *grandezza* (which the early Medici were so careful to avoid) was poured into his palace, begun in 1458. Never before, remarked Machiavelli, had a private citizen of Florence built himself a palace calculated to be in royal isolation from his neighbours on top of a hill. Its construction caused strong public reaction – because there was a shortage of living-space at the time which was aggravated by the construction of the great palaces. In order to build his, Pitti used his authority in the Signoria to demolish many houses to make way for the site and made no effort to find his evicted neighbours new quarters.

The Palazzo Pitti was built of stone quarried from what later became the Boboli Gardens. The palace itself rests on an ancient quarrying yard. Although the Pitti family built the palace only to a width of seven windows, they set the scale for its future development. The roughness and the size of the enormous stone blocks were deliberate evocations of super-human forces and proportions bound to provoke awe. As Taine says, these are not stones 'but fragments of rock and almost sections of mountains'. There are bigger palaces in Europe but none more grandiose. The Pitti remains a symbol of immovable power and crushing strength.

In 1549, Buonaccorso Pitti sold the palace for 9,000 florins to Eleonora of Toledo, the wife of Cosimo I. She never liked the shut-in life of the Palazzo Vecchio and she saw in the Pitti and the land behind it a chance for the family and the court to enjoy the freedom of gardens and splendid views, removed from the noise and commotion of the centre of Florence.

For the rest of the century, the new Grand Ducal Palace and the Boboli Gardens grew together. Ammannati saw to the building of the great cortile and the enlargement of the palace, and Tribolo, followed by Buontalenti, to that of the gardens. Later, Ammannati's nephew, Giulio Parigi, saw to both. Through all of them came the spirit of imperial Rome. In fact, many of the artists who contributed to the Pitti-Boboli complex came fresh from Rome. Ammannati had seen Michelangelo and Vignola at work on the grandiose new villas and gardens for the Pope and his court. Valerio Cioli, an expert in restoring antique statuary, was put to work carving figures for the Boboli Gardens. They all remembered the great scale of ancient and modern Rome, the recently discovered grottoes, the imperial villa on the Palatine, the splendour of white marble statuary casually placed in courtyards and dark green shrubbery. In Florence, all this took a new turn. Florence had no visible antique remains to inhibit the super-abundant fantasies of her artists. What Florentines always had was an enthusiasm for erudition, archaeology and masquerades. In the hands of Ammannati and Buontalenti, the result was a bizarre decorative style. Stairs took the form of gryphon wings; there were surprises in the grottoes and in the hedges; there were even jokes made in stone. Morgante, Cosimo's favourite dwarf, was transformed by Valerio Cioli into a Bacchic travesty of Neptune calming the waters of the sea. Every Florentine recognized the rhetorical gesture from Ammannati's and Giambologna's monumental versions, which became ridiculous with Morgante astride the turtle.

THEATRE AND THE MEDICI COURT. The spirit of allegory and the theatre animated the style of the court and its surroundings. Like the rooms, the courtyard and the Boboli Gardens were conceived as a frame for *grandezza*. Operas, jousts and mock naval battles were staged in Ammannati's cortile and in the garden amphitheatre above it. The grottoes of Buontalenti and Bandinelli were *tableaux vivants* frozen in stone, stucco and paint. A stone Perseus charges through the still water of the pool to rescue Andromeda from the sea-monster in Alfonso Parigi's Isolotto.

Versatility and virtuoso performances were expected as a matter of course. Tribolo knew as much about hydraulics as about sculpture. Buontalenti was as famous for his fireworks as for his villas and fortresses. For the baptism of a Medici prince he decorated the Baptistery, for the older children he made a Christmas crêche with mechanical figures, and for a Medici wedding he conceived a stage device for the Gods of Olympus to descend from a cloud offering their congratulations. Giulio Parigi had a school in his home on the Via Maggio where Euclid was read and instruction given on perspective, mechanics, civil and military architecture. Local and foreign aristocrats were among the pupils. These artists handled many diverse projects at the same time and they worked fast. Giovanni da San Giovanni was so quick that Baldinucci tells the tale that he frescoed an entire scene while the Grand Duke was at his supper. The culmination of all this talent and versatility were the court theatricals. The fêtes of Louis XIV at Versailles and some of Diaghilev's productions for the *Ballets Russes* are derived from them. For the wedding of Ferdinando I and Christine of Lorraine, a musical entertainment was staged at the Pitti with props and costumes by Buontalenti. In it Apollo descended to earth with Bacchus and the personifications of Rhythm, Harmony, and the Three Graces, and then shot a fire-breathing monster. In 1661, for the marriage of Cosimo III and Marguerite of Orleans, 'the World in Festivity' was produced in the amphitheatre of the Boboli. A huge mechanical figure of Atlas carrying the world on its back staggered around the amphitheatre. Suddenly the globe he carried burst open with four pretty girls representing Europe, America, Asia and Africa.

Even in daily life, the Medici household teemed with allegories – in the tableware, in the grottoes, in the fountains, on the ceilings. It was all a perpetual masquerade to impress upon Tuscany (and those others who might care in the rest of Europe) the glories of the Medici dynasty at a time when it was actually in decline. Cosimo I appeared in the guise of Neptune and Perseus (the Oceanus Fountain in the Isolotto and the fountain in the hemicycle beyond it). A Medici princess was transformed into a colossus of Plenty and set at the top of the garden, and in the Grand Duke's reception hall, Giovanni da San Giovanni and Cecco Bravo frescoed *The Muses' Flight from Parnassus to Florence*.

THE GALLERIA PALATINA. It was in this spirit of recalling past glories that towards the end of the sixteenth century the Medici princes and Grand Dukes began to assemble the picture galleries which now make up the Pitti and the Uffizi. Some of the pictures came down from the papal bequests of Leo X and Clement VII. More were accumulated through purchase, marriage and commission. The Pitti picture collection dates almost entirely from the High Renaissance and Baroque periods. It includes 16 Andrea del Sartos, 13 Raphaels, 12 Titians and 8 Tintorettos. When Ferdinando II (1610–70) married Vittoria della Rovere of the ruling family of Urbino, the collection expanded. This was when Titian's *Magdalen, La Bella,* and the superb *Portrait of the grey-eyed nobleman* (No. 92) came to Florence. To accommodate all these pictures Ferdinando had the Pitti widened. Between 1641 and 1606 the five principal rooms of the gallery were painted with murals designed by Pietro da Cortona but largely carried out by Cirro Ferri. The themes refer to the Virtues which should guide a prince from youth through old age. The Hall of Venus (Room I) alludes to a loving and kindly nature, the Hall of Apollo (Room II) to the patronage of the fine arts, the Hall of Mars (Room III) to strength, the Hall of Jupiter (Room IV) to the virtues of peace, and the Hall of Saturn (Room V) to prudence and knowledge.

The most beautiful murals in the palace, however, were painted in the Sala della Stufa (Room (XXIX) between 1637 and 1640 by Pietro da Cortona. He brought to Florence the warm, grandiose manner of the Roman Baroque. The subjects (the Ages of Gold, Silver, Copper and Iron) were taken from Ovid's *Metamorphoses.* The Golden Age alluded to the age of Ferdinando's rule; in it are the boughs of laurel (a Medici symbol) and oak (the sign of the della Rovere). But the real Golden Age of the arts was not in Florence then, but in Rome. Pietro da Cortona's style did not take root among the Florentine painters, who were still living off the cool mannered style of the late sixteenth century. Even the work of the best of the Florentine decorators, such as Giovanni da San Giovanni's allegory of *The Muses' Flight from Parnassus to Florence* on the ground floor of the Pitti did not meet with Pietro da Cortona's approval. He conceded that the work had vigour and dash, but noted that the treatment of ancient legend was inexact and therefore, he thought, unworthy for a prince. After Pietro da Cortona's final departure from Florence in 1647, the warm breeze of the Roman Baroque ceased. Baldinucci tells us of the Florentine reaction in a story of two painters who came to look at Pietro's handiwork. Matteo Rosselli's comment to Francesco Curradi was: 'Oh Curradi, Oh Curradi, how small we are! Admit it. How very tiny we are.' (*O Curradi, O Curradi, quanto noi siam piccini! Che dite, siam ben piccini.*)

It was Cardinal Leopoldo (1617–75), Ferdinando II's brother, who originally proposed the formation of the Pitti and Uffizi galleries, the purchase of drawings in bulk, and the start of the great collection of artists' self-portraits. He added his pictures to the Grand Duke's collection. From him come Veronese's *Portrait of a Man* (No. 108) and the *Daniele Barbaro* (No. 216).

PRINCE FERDINANDO DE' MEDICI. The most interesting of the later Medici art patrons was Prince Ferdinando (1663–1713), the son of priggish Cosimo III and the flighty Marguerite of Orléans. At the age of fifteen he learned the complicated art of ivory-turning from Filippo Sengher and an example of his fine workmanship is still to be seen in the Museo degli Argenti. Ferdinando had a taste for Venetian painting, and besides collecting the old masters, became the patron of Sebastiano Ricci and Giuseppe Maria Crespi when they were still unknown. He bought up altarpieces in Florentine churches (Raphael's *Madonna del Baldacchino* from S Spirito and Fra Bartolommeo's *St Mark* from S Marco) and had copies set in their places. He also introduced the public art exhibition as we know it. Hitherto, pictures were shown on holidays such as Corpus Christi as part of a festive display of goods of all kinds. In 1701, Ferdinando organized a formal exhibition of about 250 pictures in the cloister of the Annunziata on St Luke's Day (the patron saint of painters) and prepared a catalogue for it. He lent more than twenty pictures from his own collection, including seven Venetians but not a single Florentine. At his villa at Pratolino there was a theatre famous throughout Italy. Ferdinando directed the productions, procured the best designers (e.g. the Bibbiena from Bologna) and the best composers (Alessandro and Domenico Scarlatti, and Handel). The Prince wrote music himself and when Scarlatti's pieces seemed too melancholy he insisted that the composer revise them to something more cheerful. Ferdinando was Cosimo III's eldest son; unfortunately, he died before his father. He was deeply mourned and it was said that the last signs of *brio* and joy in Tuscany died with him. The Pitti acquired 300 pictures from him.

POPULAR THEATRE: MYSTERY PLAYS. It was not only the Medici court who loved the theatre. The entire neighbourhood between the Pitti and the Carmine was involved in theatrical productions. Each church had its special play performed on the appropriate feast day or for the entertainment of visiting dignitaries. The Sforza in 1471 were treated to the spectacle of the *Pentecost* in S Spirito. S Felice's speciality, the *Annunciation* play, was put on (even though it was out of season) for the arrival of King Charles VIII of France in 1494. Some of the best artists in Florence made the props for the plays. While Masolino was at work on the murals in the Brancacci Chapel in 1425, he painted a cloud and a pair of angel's wings for the Carmine's production of the *Ascension of Christ and the Consignment of the Keys to St Peter*. Vasari says that Brunelleschi was the designer of the marvellous mechanical Paradise used in S Felice's *Annunciation* play, which had hundreds of little lamps which could be lit and extinguished at will. To finance these productions the whole city was involved. The Commune made a contribution, as did the parishioners. For the Carmine play, there are records of donations from the Brancacci and Capponi families, as well as from the still obscure young monk, Fra Filippo Lippi.

The Carmine's play was staged by the lay confraternity called the *Compagnia di S Maria delle Laudi e di S Agnese*. Their meeting hall or oratory, founded in 1264, still nestles beside the east flank of the church. Its members met about thirty times a year. Those who missed a meeting had to stand holding a candle before the statue of Our Lady while lauds were sung. The members included patricians and artisans. The company also ran a hospice for destitute widows, helped the poor, and provided dowries. For many years the inventory of the play's elaborate props and costumes was kept by the painter, Neri di Bicci, who had a large and flourishing atelier nearby. There was a mask for God the Father, red hose and wings with glitter for the angels, and all kinds of pulleys and beams, lamps and wooden clouds. On the occasion when the Oecumenical Council was assembled in Florence in 1439, new wings for the angels were made of ostrich plumes.

The theme of the production was always the Ascension to commemorate the day of the Carmine's consecration. Days before the play, heralds went about Florence announcing the programme. The interior of the church was filled with banners, pennants and flowers. The stage was in the middle of the nave, raised above the heads of the crowd. An aggregate of moveable clouds which enclosed God the Father and Christ was hung from the beams of the crossing and the Mount of Olives was built inside the arcaded enclosure of the monks' choir. Suspended among the clouds were little boys dressed as angels and great stars of gilt metal, wood and parchment on which more angels and seraphim were painted. After an introductory song, one of the suspended clouds was let down and Christ descended upon the stage. The dialogues owned by the company show that the words were sung to music, the Parte Guelfa paying the pipers. As Christ ascended the cloud again, he was pulled upwards amid showers of rose-petals, *ginestra* and lilies.

Sometimes these productions were staged at great risk to life and limb. When the *Pentecost* play, produced in S Spirito by Buontalenti, was given to celebrate the marriage of Virginia de' Medici and Cesare d'Este, the singers in the clouds were so frightened that they remained mute at the moment when the clouds burst open to the words of '*O benedetto giorno*'. One courageous singer finally saved the day, the chorus took heart, and the play went on. But this was one of the last times an elaborate mystery play was given in the neighbourhood. The annual play at the Carmine had ceased some fifty years before when the strain on the crossing beams threatened to pull down the roof. Furthermore, the musical drama by then had become secularized and the great theatrical efforts were concentrated on pageants for the Grand Ducal court.

The taste for the theatre remains in the neighbourhood even though both Court and miracle plays have long since gone. Every other year, the Maggio Musicale stages operas in the Boboli in front of the Meridiana or in the amphitheatre. For several years, the *Concorso Ippico Nazionale* (the national horse trials) have been held in the hemicycle beyond the Isolotto with its frame of magnificent sycamores and the long view up the Viottolone. Here a tall gaunt princess of Savoy usually competes with the best riders in Italy, including a small blonde young lady bearing the name of Paolucci di Càlboli, whose ancestor figures in the *Divine Comedy*. Just beyond the Boboli, beyond the ilex hedges and the potting-sheds, and over a few blocks, in the Via de' Serragli, the neighbourhood crowds the Teatro degli Artigianelli on Wednesday evenings during the winter. Here Wanda Pasquini, who used to run a nearby mercer's shop, leads her wonderful troupe of actors in comedies in S Frediano dialect. The tickets cost only 250 lire, but the seats have to be reserved in advance because the place is always packed with an audience egging the players on to side-splitting improvization.

The Boboli Gardens have become a free public park. They, the Cascine and the Fortezza di Belvedere are the only public parks in the city. The other large gardens – those of the Torrigiani and Annalena – are all private. The Boboli is the perfect place for solitary rambles, picnics, and children. There are shady paths, long views and occasional benches. One can parade by the grandiose monuments or play hide-and-seek in the bushes among statues of a friendlier character – bird catchers, gamesters, peasants and dogs. Two coral-coloured stone mastiffs glumly watch a fountain by the Cioli consisting of a farmer emptying his cask into a tub with a bare-bottomed stone child gleefully clutching the rim. This is the favourite fountain of Oltrarno children. Here their dirty hands are washed and thirsty infants are held up for a drink.

THE WAY TO SAN MINIATO. The way from the Oltrarno to S Miniato goes along the Via de' Bardi, past S Niccolò, through the S Miniato gate and the old city wall up a steep, winding road which brings one immediately into the country among orchards, olives and vines. The Via de' Bardi was once a popular quarter too. Before the Bardi came, it was called Borgo Pidiglioso, or 'full of fleas', because it was inhabited by the very poorest Florentines. At No. 30 there was in the thirteenth century a hospital of which a few faceted columns remain in the courtyard. Petrarch's mother, Eletta Canigiani, was born here. The hospital was transformed into a palace during the next century and by a curious coincidence it became in 1465 the property of a branch of the Bardi family also called Canigiani. At the bottom of the staircase, inside, a laughing, half-clad girl of stone greets each visitor to the courtyard, which despite its ruinous state is one of the loveliest examples of early Renaissance palace architecture. All the windows, cornices and colonettes are of the greatest delicacy. No one knows who the architect was except that he must have been a student of Brunelleschi and Michelozzo – and a good one.

The Palazzo Capponi at No. 36, built around 1420 for Niccolò d'Uzzano, has a splendid rusticated façade and an imposing bossed wooden door. Inside (ring for the porter) is a staircase with a splendid porphyry lion at its base which was once part of an ancient Roman sarcophagus. A few doors further on is the old church of S Lucia dei Magnoli, built originally in the eleventh century. The church, rebuilt many times, was popularly known as St Lucy Among the Ruins (*S Lucia fra le Rovinate*) because of the devastating landslides which swept down from the slope owned by the Magnoli family. A marble tablet commemorating the landslide of 1547 is set into the retaining wall opposite the church. A story has it that to this particular catastrophe Bernado Buontalenti owed his fortune. As a small boy he was trapped in the ruins of one of the houses on the street. Informed of the pitiful situation, Cosimo I did everything he could to rescue the child. When Bernado was saved he was taken to the palace, where he was eventually trained to be the court architect designer of fêtes, and jack-of-all-trades. As a man of many talents, Buontalenti lived up to his name.

In front of the Palazzo Mozzi the Via de' Bardi becomes the Via S Niccolò, the name of the church a bit further eastwards. S Niccolò is one of the city's oldest parishes, although the church we see today dates almost entirely from a late-sixteenth-century rebuilding campaign. The church, originally founded around 1050, was entirely rebuilt in a Brunelleschian style early in the fifteenth century. At the behest of the Quaratesi family, Gentile da Fabriano and Masaccio painted altarpieces which have since been either lost or dispersed. But a lyric view of the Arno Valley is still visible in the Castagnesque mural in the sacristy.

One of the final acts of the Republic took place in the little piazza in front of S Niccolò. There, in 1529, the captains of the Florentine troops swore to defend the city to the last man against the joint forces of the Medici Pope (Clement VII) and Charles V. Michelangelo served as overseer of the fortifications and lent the city a thousand *scudi* for its defences. But a year later, after a long siege, Florence capitulated. Michelangelo hid in the belfry of S Niccolò from Baccio Valori's men. The Pope intervened with an offer of immunity if he would take up his work for the Medici tombs in S Lorenzo. With heavy heart Michelangelo complied.

Michelangelo's patriotism was much like Dante's. He was devoted to the republican spirit of the city but was forced to spend most of his life away from it. He had reason to share Dante's opinion of his mean countrymen: 'Never have I associated with more ungrateful and arrogant people than the Florentines.' Michelangelo was frequently the victim of malicious gossip. He was taunted by letters with rumours of his own death. He was accused of cowardice during the siege, and until recent evidence appeared to the contrary, the accusation stuck. As hatchers of gossip and plots, the Florentines to this day are without peers.

SAN MINIATO. S Miniato lords over Florence from the south-east. Its steep hillside was transformed into a kind of pedestal of balustraded ramps and staircases by Giuseppe Poggi in the last century. S Miniato and the Baptistery are the most beautiful Romanesque churches of the city and among the few ever to have had their façades completed. Bishop Hildebrand, who led a successful clerical reform movement, decided to rebuild the old church of S Miniato soon after 1018. Miniato was the earliest Florentine saint. He was martyred on the spot by the Emperor Decius around A.D. 250. The construction and decoration of the church took two centuries to complete. Like the Baptistery's exterior, an arcade of black and white marble was drawn across the façade. So balanced and harmonious is its design, so classic in feeling, that many Renaissance architects mistook it for a model of ancient Roman workmanship. Inside, some of the dark columns have Corinthian capitals which really are antique, others are Byzantine (such as the one on top of the next to last column on the right side of the choir). Entirely unclassical in design and intention is much of the decoration. The splendid inlaid pavement in the nave and the walls of the monks' choir and the pulpit, all completed by 1207, are like oriental embroideries. Indeed, the patterns (the beasts and the Signs of the Zodiac) are of eastern origin. They reached Florence from Byzantium via trade and the Crusades.

Nothing further in the way of broad comprehensive schemes was added during the rest of the thirteenth and fourteenth centuries. The murals in the aisles are a patchwork quilt – all bits and pieces. The next occasion for a harmonious addition occurred in 1459 when the Cardinal of Portugal happened to die in Florence as he was passing through the city. The young cardinal was a prince: the King of Portugal's cousin and the brother of the Austrian Empress. The best talents then available in Florence were mobilized to make a memorial chapel for him at S Miniato.

The chapel is unique in Florentine architecture of the Quattrocento because in it architecture, sculpture and painting were given an equal role. It is a combination of Brunelleschian architecture and rich pictorial décor, blending the antique, the late medieval and the Renaissance. The architecture was based on a model prepared by Antonio Manetti, who died before the chapel's construction can have progressed very far. It was carried out by Giovanni Rossellino, the elder brother of Antonio and Bernardo, who were responsible for the cardinal's tomb and throne. The painters, Baldovinetti and the Pollaiuolo brothers, took pains to harmonize their compositions with the architecture and sculpture, which were finished first. All the walls and even the floor and ceiling echo one another's forms and colours. The carved marble curtain (which was originally painted and gilt) framing the cardinal's tomb is repeated in the dark-red curtain which Pollaiuolo's angels hold aside for the altar. Antonio Rossellino's tondo of the *Madonna and Child* echoes the round windows on the adjacent walls and Baldovinetti's *Annunciation* takes up the tones and motif of the porphyry and serpentine inlays on either side of the throne below. Even the roundels of Luca della

Robbia's glazed terracotta ceiling are the reciprocals of the whorls in the pseudo-Cosmatesque mosaic pavement.

Despite the harmonious result of combining so many different media, the scheme had no successor in Florence as far as we know. Versions of it reappeared in S Gimignano (Collegiata) and Naples (S Anna dei Lombardi) – cities where ornament was traditionally more extravagant than the comparatively austere canons of Florence usually allowed. Behind the legs of the cardinal's patron saints in the altarpiece (which is a copy of the original by the Pollaiuoli now in the Uffizi) is a tantalizing glimpse of the winding Arno seen from a bird's-eye view. One has only to go outside for a similar view, with the same river and all Florence at one's feet.

Chapter 10

The Florentine Countryside: 'Il terreno amico'[1]

❧

SUMMARY OF EXCURSIONS TO BE MADE IN THE ENVIRONS

1. Santa Margherita a Montici via Arcetri and Pian dei Giullari.
A 45-minute walk from the Via de' Bardi or Piazza S Felicita. Starting up the Costa S Giorgio from Piazza de' Rossi (behind S Felicita) one comes to *S Giorgio sulla Costa* (occupied by Vallombrosans since 1520, was rebuilt by G. B. Foggini, 1705) on the right side of the street at the point where it joins the Costa Scarpuccia. It contains an early 14th c. *Madonna and Child* by a follower of the S Cecilia Master. At No. 11 – Galileo's house before his exile to Pian dei Giullari. The *Porta S Giorgio* built *ca* 1280 with a mural of the *Madonna and Child with SS Leonard and George* by Bicci di Lorenzo (1430). On the other side of the gate, copy of the late 13th c. relief of *St George and the Dragon* (original now in the Palazzo Vecchio). To the right of the gate, entrance to the *Fortezza di S Giorgio** (or di Belvedere). The grounds surrounding the fortress are a public park from which the most magnificent views are to be had of Florence and its surroundings. The fortress itself was built (1590–5) at the order of Grand Duke Ferdinando I. The architect was Buontalenti, who probably used a plan prepared by Don Giovanni de' Medici (who also planned the Cappella dei Principi of S Lorenzo). The fortress used to be a repository for many of the murals detached from structures in and around Florence. To see them go to the Superintendency of Galleries (Via della Ninna 5) for further information.

Returning to the Porta S Giorgio, continue along the Via S Leonardo. On the left is *S Leonardo in Arcetri* – a much restored 11th c. church famed for its early 13th c. marble inlay pulpit (brought here from S Pier Scheraggio in 1782). On the altar, a

[1]Earth, the friend – Piero Vettori, 1569.

SUMMARY OF SOME EXCURSIONS

triptych by Lorenzo di Niccolò; at the left – *Madonna of the Holy Girdle* by Neri di Bicci (1467); at the right – an *Annunciation* by the same master. The Via S Leonardo crosses the Viale dei Colli (for S Miniato and Piazzale Michelangelo turn left) and continues until it bends to the left into the Via del Pian dei Giullari. As the road steepens, the *Villa Capponi,* renowned for its garden, is on the left (No. 3). At the cross-roads at the top of the hill: on the left, the *Torre del Gallo* – a 19th c. reconstruction of a medieval nucleus. It contains fragments of cloisters and palaces collected and installed here during the last century by Bardini, the antiquary. Beside the tower is the neglected 15th c. *Villa 'La Gallina'* which once belonged to the Lanfredini family who served Lorenzo the Magnificent as ambassadors. In one of the rooms, remains of a mural of nude dancers by Antonio del Pollaiuolo (*ca* 1464–71). Difficult to visit due to frequent change of owners. Inquire at Soprintendenza ai Monumenti, Palazzo Pitti.

Further on, at Via del Pian dei Giullari (Nos. 40–2) is the *Villa Gioiello* where Galileo spent the last years of his life.

At the fork in the road, take the left turn. At Via di S Margherita a Montici No. 75 is the *Villa Ravà,* where Francesco Guicciardini wrote his *Histories* between 1537 and 1540. The church of *S Margherita a Montici,* built early in the 14th c., contains two contemporary pictures by the St Cecilia Master. From here one can walk further: either down to Florence again or on to Ponte a Ema and Antella.

2. To Antella and Strada in Chianti.

This is a splendid trip to do on a bicycle (or take the bus from Piazza Ferrucci). From the Ponte S Niccolò and Piazza Ferrucci proceed eastwards along the Lungarno, turning right on Viale Giannotti . . . Follow the signs to *Badia a Ripoli.* The Badia is the old abbey on the left founded by Benedictine monks in 790. To the right of the highroad is *S Pietro a Ripoli.* which contains a muralled *Pietà* and *Annunciation* by a follower of Gerini (late 14th c.) and a painted cross of the late Trecento. Take the cross-road to the south and continue to *Ponte a Ema* and, passing through the village, continue on the Strada Chiantigiana along the bank of the Ema for about 500 metres. Take a road on the left and continue for about 1 km. At a fork in the road is a farm-house beside a grey stone *oratory dedicated to St Catherine* built by the Alberti family and painted with murals by Spinello Aretino (*ca* 1387). Taking the road to the right, proceed over the hill and down to Antella. Another alternative is to take the road back to the Via Chiantigiana and

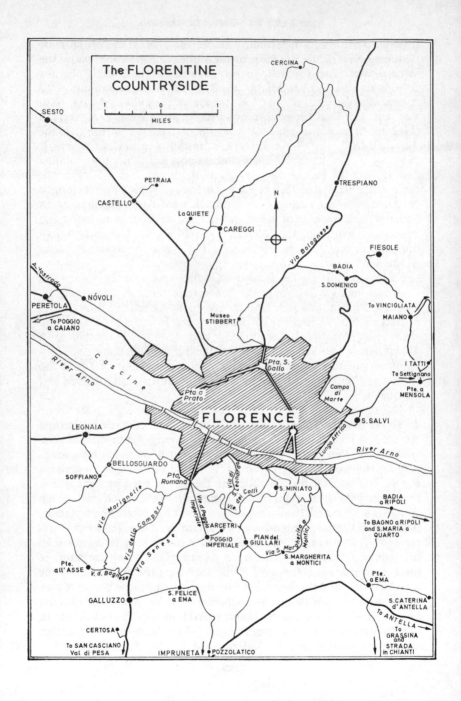

The FLORENTINE
COUNTRYSIDE

MILES

SESTO

CERCINA

PETRAIA

CASTELLO

La QUIETE

CAREGGI

TRESPIANO

N

Via Bolognese

FIESOLE

BADIA

S.DOMENICO

A-Autostrada

PERETOLA

NÓVOLI

To POGGIO
a CAIANO

Museo
STIBBERT

To VINCIGLIATA

MAIANO

River Arno

Cascine

Pta S.
Gallo

I TATTI

To Settignano

Pte. a
MENSOLA

Pta a
Prato

FLORENCE

Campo
di
Marte

S. SALVI

LEGNAIA

Lungo Affrico

River Arno

BELLOSGUARDO

Pta
Romana

SOFFIANO

Via Marignolle

Via della Campora

Via di S.Leonardo

Via dei Colli

Via.

S. MINIATO

Via di Pog
Imperiale

ARCETRI

BADIA
a RIPOLI

To BAGNO a RIPOLI
and S.MARIA a
QUARTO

POGGIO
IMPERIALE

PIAN del
GIULLARI

Via S. Margherita
a Montici

Via Senese

Pte.
all'ASSE

V. d. Bagnese

S. MARGHERITA
a MONTICI

Pte.
a EMA

GALLUZZO

S. FELICE
a EMA

S.CATERINA
d'ANTELLA

To ANTELLA

CERTOSA

To SAN CASCIANO
Val di PESA

IMPRUNETA

POZZOLATICO

To
GRASSINA
and
STRADA
in CHIANTI

continue on through *Grassina,* past the Ugolino (the golf club of Florence) and on to the Impruneta turn-off. The whole way is a succession of superb views.

3. To Bagno a Ripoli, Quarto, and Ruballa. Take the same route as in Excursion 2 as far as Badia a Ripoli (or take bus No. 32). Continue straight on to Bagno a Ripoli. Take the road on the left to *S Maria a Quarto,* a charming porticoed church on the hillside with a fine view of Florence and the Arno valley. There are also some late 14th and early 15th c. paintings inside. Return to Bagno a Ripoli, taking either of the two roads going uphill (the steeper dirt road is the quieter, more beautiful one); on the highway go on from Fonte del Pidocchio to La Corte, where one can see the towered church of S Quirico a Ruballa just below on the right. Continue on the main highway for a few hundred metres to Osteria Nuova and on the right is *S Giorgio a Ruballa,* which contains an altarpiece of the *Madonna with SS George, Matthias and a Donor* (1336) by Bernado Daddi. The painted cross is attributed to Taddeo Gaddi.

4. To Villamagna and Incontro. Proceed as in Excursion No. 2 to Piazza Ferrucci, then follow road on south bank of Arno and signs indicating Nave di Rovezzano and Candeli, taking turn-off for Villamagna and Incontro. At Villamagna, church of *S Donnino* has many fine paintings of the 14th and 15th centuries including works by Mariotto di Nardo and Francesco Granacci. The road with many beautiful views ends at Incontro where there is a Franciscan convent.

5. To Impruneta via Poggio Imperiale. A good 1½ hours' walk from Poggio Imperiale (take bus No. 37 or Black 11A to Via Gelsomino, or direct C.A.P. bus from Piazza Stazione near the corner of Via Nazionale. The former imperial villa of *Poggio Imperiale* was until 1487 the country house of the Baroncelli. In 1548 Cosimo I acquired it from the Salviati. But the villa was named by the Grand Duchess Maria Maddalena of Austria who bought it in 1622. It was rebuilt by G. M. Paoletti, G. Cacialli and P. Poccianti and later became the residence of Napoleon's sister, Elisa Baciocchi. Now it is the seat of the new regional government of Tuscany as well as a fashionable girls' school. Following the road to the right, one descends to *S Felice a Ema* which contains a *Madonna and Child* by Giovanni del Biondo (1387). If one proceeds down the road to the right one comes to Galluzzo, which is very close to the *Certosa di Val d'Ema* (*see* Excursion 6). Taking the road to the left, one continues eastwards and then south to another fork in the road. The uphill road to the right leads to Pozzolatico and goes on to Impruneta.

The church of *S Maria dell' Impruneta* ('Santa Maria in Pineta') originally built on property belonging to the Buondelmonti family in the 11th c. Legend has it that the site of the church was fixed by sending a cart loaded with building stones drawn by two guideless bullocks who by themselves found the spot. The present church was built under the patronage of Antonio degli Agli, who was the *pievano* here from 1439 to 1477. The church honours a miraculous image of the Madonna which was carried down to Florence in times of extreme distress. The church was shattered during the war and has been carefully restored. The large polyptych, painted in 1375 by Pietro Nelli and a Gerinesque master, was virtually destroyed. Nevertheless it has been installed in a much mended state behind the high altar. On either side of the chancel are two tabernacles designed by Michelozzo with glazed terracotta décor by Luca della Robbia (the one on the right is the Cappella della Croce; that on the left, the Cappella della Madonna). The marble predella of the Miraculous Madonna is by a follower of Donatello. In the sacristy, a *Trinity* by Mariotto di Nardo (1418).

6. The Certosa di Val d'Ema. Take bus No. 36 or 37 from the Porta Romana or Piazza S Maria Novella. Walk up path and ring bell at gate for a monk who will open the doors and show the way (offering expected). The church and cloister founded in 1338 with funds provided by Nicola Acciaioli, the Florentine banker who served the Angevin Kings of Naples as Grand Seneschal. Nicola and his descendants are buried beneath magnificently carved panels in a subterranean chapel beneath the monastery church of S Lorenzo. The church itself was heavily restored in the last century. In the choir, murals by Poccetti. The former *Palazzo degli Studi* now contains a museum. Here are the detached murals by Pontormo of *Scenes from the Passion* which he painted between 1523 and 1525. They are among the most dramatic and bizarre inventions of Florentine painting. Other pictures here by Mariotto di Nardo, Albertinelli, Bronzino and Lucas Cranach. In the pharmacy, liqueur, honey and lavender may be bought from the monks.

A road opposite the Certosa leads to Impruneta (*see* Excursion 5) and is about a 45-minute walk.

7. To Bellosguardo and Legnaia. A steep walk or a drive (no bus connection). Bellosguardo is a 20-minute walk from Piazza Tasso. Up the Via Villani to Piazza S Francesco di Paola: at No. 3, the *Villa S Francesco,* the house of Adolf Hildebrand, the sculptor and critic who made his home a gathering-place for German artists and men of letters towards the end of the last century. Many of the villas of Bellosguardo were – still are – occupied by foreigners. The *Villa della Torre di Bellosguardo,* which has the most splendid view of Florence, houses the American School of Florence. It is much restored. On the façade is a marble group attributed to Francavilla (late 16th c.). From the Piazza there are two roads: the one on the left goes towards the Via di Marignolle, which, if followed to the end, brings one close to the Certosa di Val d'Ema; the right-hand road proceeds in the direction of Soffiano, the slopes of which are full of anemones and wild tulips in spring. Taking the latter road, one passes the *Torre di Montauto* (original crenellated structure) where Nathaniel Hawthorne was a guest. After some 20 minutes' walk one descends to the cemetery of Soffiano. Proceed westwards for about five minutes to the former *Villa Carducci-Pandolfini* on the outskirts of Legnaia. The villa is on the right side of the road, now part of a farm; the custodian will show one the remains of Castagno's murals including a *Madonna and Child* and the figures of *Adam and Eve.* The rest of the cycle (the celebrated *Uomini Famosi*) is now temporarily installed in the Uffizi.

8. San Casciano, Val di Pesa. Take SITA bus from Via S Caterina di Siena No. 15. Some of the most beautiful walks are to be made from here. In the town itself, the church of the Misericordia (built in 1335) has a fine cross painted by Simone Martini and a *Madonna and Child* by Ugolino da Siena. Walk to *Sant' Andrea in Percussina* (3.1 km.): take the road on the right just before entering S Casciano. After passing the 18th c. Villa Antinori on the right, one comes to the church of S Maria a Casavecchia – just off the road about 200 m. with a 16th c. della Robbia altarpiece. Continuing on the main road one comes to Spedaletto with Machiavelli's old house on the left.

Another fine walk from S Casciano is that to *Cerbabia* (1 to 1½ hours). On the way, stop at the little church at Argiano (S Maria e Angiolo). Just before the descent to Cerbaia is the Romanesque church of S Giovanni in Sugana which has a *Coronation of the Virgin* by Neri di Bicci (1478–81), a 13th c. baptismal font, and a Gaddesque Cross.

9. To Settignano (Bus No. 10 from Piazza S Marco). On the way, see the Stadio Comunale at Campo di Marte designed by Pier Luigi Nervi (1932) with its beautiful flying concrete ramps. From the Via Lungo Affrico turn right at Piazza L. B. Alberti and proceed along the Via Aretina, turning left on the Via di S Salvi. At No. 16 is the former refectory of the *Convent of S Salvi* (now an insane asylum) which is open to the public (ring custodian's bell). Inside is Andrea del Sarto's *Last Supper*, commissioned by the Vallombrosan monks in 1519. Persist northwards until the Via Settignanese. At Ponte a Mensola: the church of *S Martino* on the slope to the left, rebuilt *ca* 1460, contains pictures by Taddeo Gaddi (*Madonna with SS Lucy and Margaret*), Zanobi Machiavelli (*Annunciation*) and Neri di Bicci (*Madonna and Child with Saints*). Taking the road on the left at Ponte a Mensola there is a turn-off at the right for Corbignano. Keeping to the main road, one passes the *Villa I Tatti* – the site of the Berenson Library, now belonging to Harvard University; visits on Wednesday afternoons by appointment – Tel. 60.32.51. The picture collection here includes masterpieces by Domenico Veneziano and Sassetta. Continuing uphill, one comes to the castle of Vincigliata, a piece of mock-medievalry created around a medieval tower in 1855 for John Temple-Leader. If one continues on this road for about an hour one reaches Fiesole. Returning to the Via Settignanese, proceed to **Settignano.**

In the piazza of Settignano, church of the Assunta containing a della Robbia altarpiece and a pulpit by Bernardo Buontalenti and Gherardo Silvani (1602). Taking the Via di S Romano from the piazza, turn right on the Via Rossellino. After about 1 km. is the *Villa Gamberaia* (No. 74), famous for its garden. To visit it, try ringing the bell; or telephone for permission to the Società Immobiliare 'La Gamberaia' (Tel. 697-205).

10. Fiesole (Bus No. 7 from Piazza S Marco). By car there are two main routes: (1) Via degli Artisti-Via Pacinotti-Viale Alessandro Volta-Via della Piazzola-S Domenico; (2) from Piazza della Libertà (also known as Piazza Cavour or Piazza S Gallo) take the north-eastern street, Viale Don Minzoni, to Piazza delle Cure, then follow Via Boccaccio (at Nos. 115/123 – *Villa Schifanoia* which boasts a garden based on a Renaissance plan; at No. 126, *Villa Palmieri,* said to be the site of an episode in Boccaccio's *Decameron*) to Piazza S Domenico.

Church and Convent of San Domenico, originally built between 1406 and 1435 for the monks of the Dominican Observance. The interior is a late 15th and 16th c. remodelling based upon the Badia Fiesolana. The porch added in 1635 by Matteo Nigetti, who was also responsible for the campanile.

Interior: first altar on left – altarpiece by Fra Angelico (*ca* 1428) with background repainted by Lorenzo di Credi so as to be in harmony with a new frame (*ca* 1501). In the frame, Saints and Angels by Rossello di Jacopo Franchi and at the bottom on either side two late 14th c. panels. The predella is a copy of the original by Angelico now in London at the National Gallery. Second altar – *Adoration of the Magi* begun by Sarto and Sogliani and finished by Santi di Tito; third altar – *Annunciation* by Jacopo da Empoli (1615) and a fine wooden Crucifix attributed to Andrea Ferrucci (*ca* 1510). Vestibule on left leads to the **Oratory of S Donato** (1792); behind the altar, a late 13th or early 14th c. wooden crucifix. Choir rebuilt (1603–6) by G. Caccini. On right side of nave: first altar – *Christ Crucified with Mary and St Jerome* (*ca* 1500); second altar – *Baptism* by Lorenzo di Credi and a copy of Perugino's altarpiece now in the Uffizi.

Convent: ring bell at entrance to right of church portico. Entrance vestibule has a lovely staircase, probably by a late 17th c. follower of Buontalenti. In the chapter-room (last room on left at end of corridor): mural of the *Crucifixion* by Fra Angelico (*ca* 1430). Other murals by Angelico from this series detached during last century, now in the Louvre and the Hermitage. Also here are Angelico's detached mural and sinopia of the *Madonna and Child*, originally a lunette in the cloister. In 1449, Fra Angelica was elected prior of S Domenico for a three-year term and he returned from Rome to assume his duties here.

Taking the road just to the north and west of S Domenico one comes to the **Badia Fiesolana*** which was the cathedral of Fiesole until 1118. **Facade:** *ca* 1150. The church was taken over by Augustinian canons in 1439, and largely rebuilt between 1456 and 1469 with funds provided by Cosimo and Piero de' Medici. To visit the inside of the church and convent, ring the custodian's bell. The **interior of the church** is one of the finest examples of Florentine architecture of the 15th c. The architect's name is unknown. Its style shows the strong influence of both Brunelleschi and Alberti. Brunelleschi was dead by then, Alberti occupied elsewhere, and other reasons exclude Michelozzo from being responsible for the building. Nevertheless, the names of Alberti and Manetti have been suggested. In the first chapel on the left: a *Pietà* by Botticini and a *Madonna and Child* by a follower of Jacopo della Quercia. The high altar was designed by Pietro Tacca (1612). In the vestibule between the church and library: a lavabo by Francesco di Simone Ferrucci (1461–6), splendid pietra-serena door-frames with some of the most beautifully inscribed letters of the Renaissance. The double-storeyed garden loggia to the south is one of the earliest completed parts of the convent. In the refectory, mural by Giovanni da S Giovanni (1629).

315

In 1752, the Tuscan agricultural academy (Accademia dei Georgofili) was founded here by the abbot, Ubaldo Montelatici.

Returning to Piazza S Domenico, proceed up the main road. At Regresso is the turn-off on the right for *Maiano*. Keeping to the main road to Fiesole, one passes the Villa Medici on the left, probably built by Michelozzo for one of Cosimo il Vecchio's sons between 1455–61. Between 1774 and 1776 it was remodelled for Lady Orford, the widow of Robert Walpole.

At last one reaches *Fiesole* at the top of the hill. The town occupies the site of a Roman settlement. There is insufficient evidence that the Etruscans were ever settled here or at the Campo di Marte below Fiesole. The *Roman amphitheatre* (open summer: 10.00–12.00, 15.00–19.00; winter 09.30–12.30, 14.00–17.00; admission fee 200 lire) Built in the 1st c. B.C. Additions were made under Claudius and Septimius Severus. A small museum contains urns and vases. In 1125 the Florentines destroyed Fiesole except for the *Cathedral*, begun in 1028. Campanile added in 1213. Building enlarged in 1256 and 1348, restored between 1878 and 1883. *Interior:* the glazed terracotta figure of *S Romolo*, the titular saint, over the central door was originally made by Giovanni della Robbia (1521) for another church at Castello in Val di Sieve. At the right of the raised choir is the *Salutati Chapel* with sculpture by Mino da Fiesole (the tomb and fine portrait of Bishop Leonardo Salutati, *ca* 1464) and murals by Cosimo Rosselli. On the high altar, triptych by Bicci di Lorenzo (*ca* 1450). In the sacristy is kept Bishop Salutati's beautiful velvet mitre adorned with silver-gilt and enamel ornaments. In the crypt: a Sienese iron gate (1349).

Museo Bandini (winter: 10.00–12.30, 14.00–17.00; summer 10.00–12.30; 14.00–18.00; admission fee 50 lire) contains fine furniture, maiolica and pictures by Bernardo Daddi, Taddeo Gaddi, Lorenzo Monaco, Jacopo del Sellaio, and others. A printed guide in every room.

On the east side of the Piazza is the 14th c. town hall (or *Palazzo Pretorio*) with its double loggiaed façade added in 1463. Next door, on the right, is *S Maria Primerana,* a small oratory rebuilt during the Renaissance. Façade: 1585. Inside: self-portrait of Francesco da Sangallo (1542), late 14th c. mural by a follower of Gerini, and a painted cross of the same time.

Taking the steep road at the western end of the piazza, one reaches *S Francesco.* The Franciscans moved in early in the 15th c. The convent was rebuilt in 1905–7. Inside the church: an early 15th c. *Mystic Marriage of St Catherine* and a *Crucifixion* by Neri di Bicci.

The *Annunciation* on the high altar attributed to Raffaellino dei Carli and the frame to Benedetto da Maiano. On the left wall: an *Immaculate Conception* by Piero di Cosimo and an *Adoration of the Magi* (mid-15th c.).

Behind Fiesole to the north-east, at **Caldine,** is the church and convent of **S Maria Maddalena** in Pian di Mugnone, which since the 15th c. has been used by the *frati* of S Marco in Florence as a hospice. There are murals of the *Annunciation* (1515) and *Noli me Tangere* (1517) by Fra Bartolommeo. The *Madonna* on the high altar is by the Master of the Horne Triptych (early 14th c.).

11. Museo Stibbert, Via Bolognese, Cercina (Bus No. 25 from Piazza S Marco). For the *Museo Stibbert:* from Piazza della Libertà take the road to the north-west leading to the Barriera di Ponte Rosso, then take the road again to the north-west: Via Vittorio Emanuele II; a few steps to the right is Via Federico Stibbert. At No. 26 is the Museum (09.00–14.00 weekdays; 09.00–12.00 Sundays; admission fee 300 lire) which was left with its contents to the city. Stibbert fought with Garibaldi, collected armour, tapestries, maiolica and pictures spread through some 70 rooms. There are paintings by Jacopo Bassano, G. B. Moroni, Hobbema, Mariotto di Nardo, Neri di Bicci, Crivelli and Cosimo Tura. There are also Napoleon's robes worn when he was crowned King of Italy.

Returning to the Via Bolognese: No. 120, *Villa 'La Pietra'* – once belonged to Francesco Sassetti, the general manager of the Medici bank. His descendants sold it to the Capponi family. Around 1697 the house was rebuilt, based on a design by Carlo Fontana. Subsequently, the garden was turned into a semi-wild *'giardino inglese'* and it is ironical that Arthur Acton, the English father of the present owner, laboured for years to turn it back again into a terraced Italian garden full of statues and urns. Housed in the villa is one of the most beautiful collections of Italian painting and sculpture still in private hands in Florence.

At the first stop after Trespiano (the Communal Cemetery), get off. A road on the left leads after half an hour's walk to the *Pieve of S Andrea a Cercina* which already existed in the 11th c. Inside are murals attributed to the young Domenico Ghirlandaio. There is also a charming cloister. Proceeding onwards down the Valley of the Terzolle, the road eventually reaches Careggi.

12. Careggi, Petraia, Castello and La Quiete. For Careggi take bus No. 14C from Piazza del Duomo; for Castello and Petraia take bus No. 28 from Piazza della Stazione; by car, follow the road to Sesto

Fiorentino from Via del Ponte del Romito (behind the Fortezza da Basso which is north-east of the station). Petraia and Castello closed Monday – hours 09.30–16.30 in winter, 09.30–18.30 summer.

The former *Medici Villa of Careggi* overlooks the many pavilions of the Medical Centre of Florence. It is now a nurses' dormitory. To visit the villa, go to Soprintendenza alle Gallerie at Via della Ninna 5 for a letter to the custodian. The villa was bought in 1417 by Lorenzo di Giovanni di Bicci de' Medici. Several decades later Cosimo had Michelozzo enlarge and remodel it. The courtyard is one of the best examples of how rich in line and refined in proportion the apparent simplicity of early Medicean architecture can be. Under Lorenzo, Giuliano da Sangallo added the loggiaed wings on the south. Just above Careggi is the villa known as *Le Fontanelle* which belonged to Marsilio Ficino.

The villas of *Petraia* and *Castello* were also Medici properties. In the 14th c. Petraia belonged to the Brunelleschi; in 1427 it was bought by Palla di Noferi Strozzi. In 1468 the Salutati acquired it, and in 1575, the family sold it to Cardinal Ferdinando de' Medici. Buontalenti transformed the medieval castle into a princely villa with a garden full of ilex and pines. In the garden is a fountain of *Venus wringing out her Hair* by Giambologna, based on an idea of Tribolo's. Originally the fountain was at Castello. Inside: the cortile has a fresco cycle of events from Medici history by Volterrano (1636–48) which was painted for Don Lorenzo de' Medici (Ferdinando I's fourth son). Otherwise the rooms of both Petraia and Castello were entirely redecorated in the last century by the House of Savoy.

The *Villa of Castello* was acquired by the nephews of Cosimo il Vecchio. Duke Cosimo I had Tribolo lay out the garden on a highly elaborate plan conceived by Benedetto Varchi. It was so ambitious that even Tribolo's successor, Buontalenti, was unable to realize all the fountains, statues, grottoes, secret gardens and labyrinths. One of the remants of this scheme was the Venus fountain, now at Petraia, which originally was known as the Fountain of the Labyrinth. Still at Castello is a grotto with stone and bronze animals, some of which may be by Giambologna. The figure of *Apennine* shivering with cold in the middle of a pond is by Ammannati. The *Fountain of Hercules crushing Antaeus* is at its original site. The upper part by Tribolo was left unfinished at his death in 1550. Ammannati finished it in 1559 according to Tribolo's model. The bronze *putti* around the rim of the basin are probably by Pierino da Vinci.

Returning along the main road back towards Florence, take the left turn-off at Le Panche into Via delle Montalve, which at the junction with Via di Boldrone brings one to the *Villa La Quiete,* the conservatory of the Montalve nuns. The property once belonged to the *condottiere,* Niccolò da Tolentino, whom Castagno painted in the Duomo. In 1650 a member of the Medici court, Eleonora Ramirez di Montalvo, turned it over to the nuns. To see the gallery of pictures, ring the bell. There is a fine *Coronation of the Virgin* by a close follower of Botticelli, an altarpiece by Ridolfo Ghirlandaio, and other works of the 14th and 15th c. On the floor above is a mural by Giovanni da S Giovanni of *La Quiete dominating the Winds* (*ca* 1620).

Not far away at Sesto Fiorentino, the Ginori porcelain factory has opened a fine new museum of Florentine chinaware; this is the *Museo di Doccia* at Viale Pratese No. 13. Hours: weekdays and holidays: 09.30–13.00, 15.30–18.30; closed Mondays and Sundays. Tel. 44.89.150. Bus No. 28 from Piazza Stazione.

13. To Peretola, Quaracchi and S Andrea a Brozzi. This is a good trip to do on a bicycle, the whole way is flat. Going through the Cascine, turn right after 1½ km. at the Piazzale delle Cascine into the Via delle Cascine, continuing until Piazza Puccini. Turn left and continue straight on, passing the turn-off for the Autostrada. At the next fork in the road, take the right-hand road towards Campi and Prato and after two or three minutes one reaches the village of *Peretola.* This was the home of the Vespucci family. In Piazza Garibaldi is the 14th c. church of S Maria. In the porch are 14th and 15th c. murals. Inside on the right is a baptismal font by Mino da Fiesole (1467). Nearby a mural with the story of *St Leonard and Four Saints* by Giusto d'Andrea. In the apse is the fine ciborium by Luca della Robbia (1441–3).

Just to the south-west of Peretola is *Quaracchi* (from '*ad claras aquas*'). At the Villa Lo Specchio is the Franciscan College, library and publishing house. This was once the magnificent 15th c. villa of the Rucellai, famous for its garden. Continuing along the highway, one reaches Brozzi. The church of *S Andrea a Brozzi* is an 11th c. structure rebuilt in the 15th c. The portico was added in the 17th c. If closed, ring the curate's bell at Via della Villa No. 2. Inside is an *Annunciation with Saints* attributed to Giovanni dal Ponte (*ca* 1420); above, lunette with *SS Albert and Sigismund* attributed to Raffaellino dei Carli (1520); *Madonna and Four Saints* by Francesco Botticini (late 15th c.). On the left wall is one of Domenico Ghirlandaio's early works: the *Madonna Enthroned between SS Sebastian and*

Julian with the *Baptism* above.

One can continue along this road for another 9½ km. to Poggio a Caiano.

14. Poggio a Caiano*, Artimino*, and Carmignano*. Take Lazzi bus from Piazza della Stazione; or SACA bus from Piazza S Maria Novella. The Villa at *Poggio a Caiano* is at present closed but sometimes admission is obtainable from the Soprintendenza dei Monumenti at Palazzo Pitti. This was once the country seat of the Cancellieri family of Pistoia. Later, it became the property of the Strozzi and the Rucellai families. In 1479 Lorenzo the Magnificent bought it from Giovanni Rucellai. In 1480 Giuliano da San Gallo was charged with remodelling it. Under Leo X (Lorenzo's second son), the loggia, the pediment and the pseudo-classical frieze of glazed terracotta (attributed to Andrea Sansovino) were probably added. Inside the loggia, Filippino Lippi painted a mural of the *Demise of Laocoön,* of which only faint traces remain. The present curving staircases leading up to the loggia were a later addition. Inside the villa, only one room remains with its original Medicean décor – this is the great *Salone* which was once the courtyard of the early 15th c. building. Its walls are covered with allegorical scenes deliberately chosen by Paolo Giovio as parallels to events in Medici history. The *Return of Cicero from Exile* (begun by Franciabigio in 1521 and finished by Allori *ca* 1580) refers to Cosimo il Vecchio's return from Venice. The *Consul Flaminius in Council with the Achæns* alludes to Lorenzo the Magnificent at the Diet of Cremona, when he upset the plots of the Venetians (by Allori, 1579–82). *Julius Ceasar receiving Tribute* refers to the gifts sent by the Sultan of Egypt in 1487 to Lorenzo, which included the famous giraffe installed in the Via della Scala (by Andrea del Sarto, 1521, completed by Allori in 1582). The *Moorish King receives the Victorious Scipio in Spain* alludes to Lorenzo's embassy to Naples (by Allori 1579–82). In the lunette of the eastern wall is Pontormo's *Vertumnus and Pomona* (1521) – an allegory in which the protagonists are called upon to help the ailing laurel (symbolic of the Medici).

Three km. to the south of Poggio a Caiano is *Carmignano.* Inside the church of S Michele is Pontormo's beautiful *Visitation* (*ca* 1528). From here one can proceed by car or on foot to **Vinci** – the birthplace of Leonardo.

To the south-west of Poggio a Caiano, about 6 km., is the town and villa of *Artimino.* The Villa Ferdinanda, as it was called, was built as a hunting-lodge for Grand Duke Ferdinando I by Buontalenti in

Detail from Pontormo's *Visitation* (*ca* 1528) in San Michele, Carmignano

Farmhouse on the Via Chiantigiana between Florence and Greve

1594. Here are some of the most splendid views of Tuscany: the long ones towards Florence, Prato, Pistoia and Empoli; and the more intimate ones of the walled medieval village and the olive-clad slopes and beautifully proportioned farm-houses.

'IL TERRENO AMICO'

The Florentines, be they ever so intellectual, have always had their roots in the soil. Florentine art and the Florentine countryside have fortified each other's character. The quarries of Settignano, Maiano, Carmignano and Boboli provided the stones – the cool blue-grey *pietra serena* and the tough golden-brown *macigno*. The fruits, the flowers and tender shoots have been caught in the bronze and marble framing Ghiberti's doors and gracing Desiderio's tabernacles. They crop up in the capitals of columns and in the delicate friezes, adding lightness and freshness to the classical austerity of Brunelleschi and Alberti. The land itself is the work of generations of farmers who are really born architects. The slopes, the plains, the rises and declivities are shaped, not deformed, by the human hand. The stone walls, the rows of olives and vines, the pitch of roof, the set of cypress here, umbrella pine there – all seem calculated to complement each other.

The art of Rome, Naples, Bologna and Genoa has always been thoroughly urban. One feels their joy in noise and chaos, in the weight of monuments and history. For them perspective, for instance, was only a useful device for making bigger views, superhuman illusions. The Florentines, on the other hand, have never lost sight of the human measure of things; for them, perspective was a means of defining, measuring, articulating the actual world about them; a way of seeing all objects in their proper proportion. The visual scrutiny of the Florentine is merciless. Like good farmers, they prune away the weak line, the superfluous detail. Remarkably, this has never blunted an appreciation of the unique or the bizarre – so long as it is well made. The Florentines of the fourteenth, fifteenth and early sixteenth centuries weeded out what was mediocre and confused. But with all this rigorous selection, there was also poetry and affection. The rustic stood side by side with elegance in the masonry and furniture of Florentine villas and palaces, in the planting of their fields and in the neatness and frankness of their speech.

How many great Florentines have come from the country! The Strozzi, Portinari and Covoni came from Fiesole, the Vespucci from Peretola, and the Guicciardini from the Val di Pesa. Desiderio, the

Rossellini and Benedetto, famous as sculptors and stonemasons, came from Settignano and Maiano. Michelangelo was born in Caprese and spent his early boyhood in Settignano too. Leonardo came from the village of Vinci. Brunelleschi's family stemmed from the slopes of Sesto. (There is still a Brunelleschi active in Florence, a stone-mason, who hails from Antella.) Giotto and Castagno were from Mugello farms, Masaccio and Masolino from S Giovanni Valdarno – not far from the birthplace of Poggio Bracciolini at Terranova.

The thrift, economy and restraint of the good farmer are also characteristics of the colour and expression of Florentine art. It is by the choice of the crucial moment or gesture, or by the arrangement of the forms that the Florentine reveals the full significance of a story or an event. The characteristic colours of the Florentine palette of the fourteenth and fifteenth centuries are earthy colours: cool olive-greens and greys, suffused browns and ochres, burnt orange, pale pinks ,deep wine-reds and purples.

The mentality of the prudent farmer gave the Florentines their reputation as misers. They rather confess poverty than wealth, for to admit abundance is to risk lowering prices and raising taxes. If you ask a Florentine how he is or how his work is going it is never *benissimo* or *splendido*. Extravagance, vagueness and sentimentality are looked on with suspicion. Riches are for the Milanese, extravagance for the Roman, and to wear one's heart on one's sleeve is for Neapolitan sailors.

Much of this is changing now. Since the war, tourism has taken the place of agriculture as the backbone of the Florentine economy. The farmers are leaving the land in droves for higher pay and easier hours in town. Few Florentine families can rely any longer on getting their oil, wine, fowls and fruit from their tenant farmers or country relations. Where the farm and villa were once a necessity, they are now the greatest luxuries. The city's youth, when formal education is finished, yearns to move northwards – to Milan and Turin. In and around Florence there is no future on the land and there are too few opportunities in business and the professions.

The look of the land is gradually changing too. The profits in agriculture are low because the land does not lend itself to mechanized farming. Rather than change the centuries-old crops of the vine and olive, land-owners and farmers prefer giving up altogether. The old Medici villas of Careggi, Petraia and Castello are almost surrounded by the industrial suburbs of Rifredi and Sesto. The slopes of S Casciano and Impruneta, famous for their vineyards, have been marred by thousands of concrete posts which have replaced the improvised wooden stakes formerly used to support the vines. Almost gone are the teams of white oxen and their cursing drivers. The Autostrada del Sole has slashed a great arc through the peaceful plain from Peretola to Antella. The arthritic olives around Poggio Imperiale and Pozzolatico stand untended. At the present pace, there are about twenty-five years left to enjoy the beauty of the classical Florentine countryside. The marvel is that it is still so close to the centre of the city: ten minutes' walk from the Via de' Bardi or Piazza Tasso, fifteen minutes by bicycle from the Porta Romana down the Via Senese.

THE LAND. The main crops of the Florentine countryside are oil and wine. Their cultivation is in itself an art requiring talent, insight, patience and great experience. Piero Vettori, in a treatise written in 1569, reminded his readers that among the Greeks Minerva was the patroness of 'everything made with great skill and every work of the mind'. The cultivation of the olive, he said, was one of the arts enjoying Minerva's protection, and he might just as well have added that of the vine. Each neighbourhood has its own variety. The quality has shifted from district to district with the centuries. In the sixteenth century the best red Trebbiano came from the slopes of Fiesole and from the plain around S Giovanni Valdarno. The red wine of Carmignano has been prized since the Trecento; Francesco di Marco Datini and his friend, Ser Lapo Mazzei, delighted in it, and Grand Duke Cosimo III sent frequent gifts of it to Queen Anne of England. The wine from Artimino, just above Carmignano, is still fine, but few are left to tend the vanishing vineyards there. An old man and his twelve-year-old grandson see to the curing of the great casks and bottle and label the flasks by hand. On early summer days, one can if one likes go up to Artimino and sit with them in the cool wine-cellar built next to the medieval wall surrounding the town. As one helps them glue labels, the old man will talk lovingly by the hour of the secrets of pruning the vines and the olives, punctuating his discourse now and again with glasses of the rich, woody wine.

The best white wines were from plants originally brought from the Aegean Islands. San Gimignano's famous *Vernaccia* came from Cretan cuttings imported late in the thirteenth century. In 1383, we are told that Messer Vieri de' Bardi had *Vernaccia di Corniglia* brought to the Val d'Arno from Portovenere. Ser Alamanno Salviati had cuttings from Greece for the *moscadello grosso* or *zibibbo bianco*, which we know as the Salamanca grape. Some of the names of Florentine wines are a delight. Franco Sacchetti, the late-fourteenth-century novella-writer, mentions *angiola, verdolina, san colombano* and *cimiciattola* (Novella No. 177). As far as I know, no Florentine names for grapes ever had the sour smack of the Lucchese *Strozzapreti* (choke priests). *Malvasia* was a grape imported from Crete and it was already famous in Lorenzo de' Medici's time. Today one of the best white wines is called *Machiavelli* (there is also a good *Machiavelli* red), not because of the sharp bite of its namesake but because it is grown on the old Machiavelli property just outside S Casciano. Another is *Perseto*, from the nearby slopes of Mercatale. The adjectives for good wines in Florence, red or white, have always been the same: *franco, schietto* and *gagliardo* (sincere, downright or unadorned, and vigorous). The same adjectives describe Florentine architecture, Florentine speech and pronunciation.

The trouble with most Tuscan wines has always been that they travel badly and that they have to be drunk fairly quickly. In the eighteenth century there were eighty-seven varieties of wine, of which only three-fifths could last five to eight months, one-fifth barely a year, and the remaining fifth – if it lasted three years – caused universal amazement. The exceptions were the wines of Montepulciano, the Chianti, and Artimino. We are told in a farmers' almanac of the time that one should begin to sell and drink the new wine of Antella, Careggi, Castello, Settignano and Carmignano between January and the end of Lent, for they were sure to suffer from the heat. This weakness in the native product provoked the Medici Grand Dukes to experiment with plants imported from Corsica, Sicily, Naples and Candia. Of the 211 different types of grape cultivated in Tuscany then, 150 had been imported by Cosimo III. It was Cosimo who first made a market in England for Chianti wines. Since the end of the last century, when phylloxera attacked all the vines of Europe, the old plants have been grafted on the phylloxera-immune American grape. To make these wines last for export, the commercial houses are forced to add chemicals or heavier south Italian wines to their blends to increase the alcohol content. This is to the shame and disgust of the private Florentine vineyard-owners, who defend their product with the seals of the *putto* and the *gallo nero* (black cock).

A variety of fig and the now common artichoke were introduced around 1466 by Filippo Strozzi who brought them from Naples. The different varieties of fig rival those of the grape. Save for the *pisani*, however, their names derive not from places but from human types. There are *badaloni, cavalieri, lazzari, lardaioli* and *picciolluti* (large fat ones, cavaliers, beggars, pork butchers and dwarfs). Among the names of pears and plums, there are *Pere del Signore, Bugiarde pistoiesi* and *Cosce di monaca* (pears of the Lord, Pistoiese liars and nuns' thighs).

Like Filippo Strozzi, Lorenzo the Magnificent was also a zealous farmer. As soon as he purchased Poggio a Caiano from Giovanni Rucellai in 1479, he became a farmer-entrepreneur. He introduced a kind of cheese manufacture, formerly the speciality of Lombardy, planted mulberry trees to increase silk manufacture, imported rabbits from Spain, pigs from Calabria, pheasants and peacocks from Sicily. Perhaps it was for these enterprises that the theme of Vertumnus and Pomona was selected as the subject for Pontormo's mural in Poggio a Caiano's great hall, which was devoted to praising Medici achievements.

As for the humble potato, it seems only fitting that it was introduced to Tuscany from Spain and Portugal by the barefoot Carmelite monks (the Scalzi) early in the seventeenth century.

The relationship between land-owner and farmer still follows the medieval system known as *mezzadria*. In theory, the owner provides the *mezzadro* or *contadino* with living quarters and the necessary equipment. In exchange, half the produce is supposed to go to the owner. In practice, he now receives much less and the entire *mezzadria* system is being legislated out of existence. The only trouble is that nothing really practical in Tuscany is being put in its place. Co-operatives, as they exist in Scandinavia and America, are unknown here and the individualism of centuries makes their acceptance in Tuscany unlikely. But the separate land-owners, the *padrone* or ex-*contadino*, can no longer afford to pay for the running expenses.

VITA IN VILLA. A villa, as defined by the dictionary of the Accademia della Crusca, is a piece of land with a house. In the literature of the twelfth and thirteenth centuries little is said of villa life. Most people sought refuge within the walls of the towns. There they were safe from the bands of freebooters and the troops of the warring communes, who burnt, blackmailed and stole everything they could find on the land. The oldest villas around Florence were all miniature fortresses. The medieval nuclei of Careggi and Castello are like this, and the Torre del Gallo at Arcetri and the castle of Vincigliata near Settignano were rebuilt in this style during the last century. Once the Florentine countryside was safe from attack, the tradition of life in the villa began.

Besides the peace and produce it offered, the villa was also a retreat from the contagious diseases which swept the city. When such dangers struck, the entire family of Lorenzo the Magnificent, for instance, were packed off to Careggi or to the more remote Cafaggiolo. Already in the thirteenth century, the Alighieri had a country house at the foot of Fiesole near what is now the youth hostel of Villa Camerata. Boccaccio's family had a house above the Mensola on the slope of Corbignano. The setting for Boccaccio's *Decameron* was a Fiesolan villa, sometimes identified as the Villa Palmieri.

Towards the end of the Trecento the villa became the fashionable setting for learned conversation. Coluccio Salutati, the Florentine chancellor, made a habit of collecting learned guests at his house in the country. A novella of Giovanni da Prato tells us of such gatherings in Antonio degli Alberti's villa above Antella called *Il Paradiso*. For example, at one party in May 1389 the guests were learned gentlemen, prelates and ladies, many of whom were well-known Florentines. They took refreshment beside a fountain in the garden. The table was set with silver vases. There were precious wines, exotic fruits, cherries, melons, and dewy figs (one wonders where figs were obtained in May!). One of the guests, Francesco degli Organi, had his portable organ with him. As he played a nightingale flew about brushing his head with its wings. Little birds in the nearby cypresses took up the notes and boys and girls danced to the music. Then the group retired indoors for the midday meal and discussion. To the wonder and admiration of everyone, the ladies took part in the talk. In the afternoon they all returned to the garden and the learned Fra Luigi de' Marsili (the Augustinian scholar of S Spirito) told amusing stories and led more serious talk (including a debate about why the nightingale had flown around Francesco degli Organi's head). Next morning, while the ladies were at Mass, talk continued in the garden with Fra Luigi ceding his place as leader to another. Among the themes discussed were why Rome fell, the definition of good and bad government, the archaeology of Florence, the best use of money, and the reasons for prohibiting usury. Such was the ancestor of Ficino's Platonic academy.

For Leon Battista Alberti, the villa had a much more private function. 'Buy the villa to pasture your family, and not for the amusement of others' (*compera la villa per pascere la famiglia tua, non per darne diletto ad altri*). He believed that the country house, not the palace, was the proper background for the education of children. He remarked that boys raised in villa were accustomed to work in the strong sun and were therefore stronger and solider than those grown to laziness in the shade. For him the villa was 'a true paradise . . . in the villa you can escape the clamour, the tumult, the worldly storms of the piazza and the palace. In the villa you can hide yourself to avoid seeing . . . the great quantity of wicked mankind . . . Only the villa, above all else, is grateful, pretty, loyal and trustworthy. If you govern it with diligence and love, it will never cease to satisfy you; always heaping reward upon rewards . . . and when you are old and weary [in town], the villa [gives you] the greatest profit, making you refreshed, seasoned, complete and sound.'

In his treatise on architecture Alberti gives a description of how a villa should be built – down to the minute details of where the windows in the wine-cellar should be (they should face north so that the winds of the *tramontana* can ventilate the room and keep it dry). Sometimes it is thought that Alberti designed Giovanni Rucellai's famous villa at Quaracchi as he did his town house and chapel in Florence. From the diaries, it appears that Rucellai took greater pride in this villa than in his splendid palace, of which he says comparatively little. A wall surrounded the villa (known as Lo Specchio), but passers-by could admire something of the marvellous garden with its shrubs cut into the shapes of galleons, heraldic lions, dragons, camels, giants and centaurs. Rucellai's neighbours, the citizens of Quaracchi, believed that the town owed its fame to this garden and they offered to pay for its maintenance themselves. Like Petrarch and Buonaccorso Pitti, Rucellai loved to count the trees in his orchards. There was a pond full of fishes surrounded by evergreens, and near by, on the bank of the Arno, he kept a little boat equipped with nets and rods so that he could go off by himself to fish.

Cosimo de' Medici had his library in his villa at Careggi. He saw to the pruning of his vines and olives, but as far as we know, he was not interested in exotic gardens or bizarre shrubbery. His wife, the thrifty Contessina, did not share her husband's philosophical and literary interests but she too was much occupied with the practical affairs of the villa. Once she asked Cosimo why he spent so many hours in his library in silent meditation. His reply was, 'When we are going to our country house you are busy for a fortnight preparing for the move, but since I have to go from this life to another, does it not seem to you that I ought to have something to think about?' All the procurement, large and small, for Medici palaces and villas was left to Contessina. She even saw to the maintenance of the cheese moulds and decided which of the old ones should be sold. In her old age, when her daughters-in-law assumed her former duties at Careggi, she still kept a critical eye on the oil-making.

Near Careggi was Marsilio Ficino's villa – the gift of his affectionate patron, Cosimo. Ficino is among the first to give us the idyllic picture of life at the villa. He advised those who, like himself, suffered from melancholy, to divert themselves out of doors, beside limpid streams, in sight of green trees, strolling in woods, gardens and meadows. The arts of the fields and the study of letters were, he maintained, the happiest of combinations. Often he would go off for a picnic on the hills of Fiesole with Pico, or visit the Canigiani at Campoli, the Valori at Maiano, and the Cavalcanti at Rignano. His own villa at Careggi, besides being a private refuge, also served as a studio and school. In one of the rooms was a pulpit from which Ficino delivered his lessons in philosophy, and against the opposite wall a bust of Plato. In another room was a mural of a terrestrial globe with Democritus laughing on one side and Heraclitus weeping on the other.

Ficino spent most of his time at Careggi during the spring and autumn. These are still the traditional seasons to spend 'in villa'. The climate then is gentle and one can see to the planting and to the harvest. The summer was too hot for the country. Many Florentines, in the days when beach resorts were still undreamt of, preferred to spend these months in the cool dark rooms of their palaces, surrounded by books and papers. But there were some exceptions. Here is a letter of one of Poliziano's pupils, Michele Vieri, who towards the end of the fifteenth century wrote from his villa of Lecore to Pietro Ridolfi in Florence:

Here I am to satisfy your curiosity about how I pass the summer days in this villa of mine of Lecore, and what my literary fancies here are. I get up early, walk about the little garden in my long dressing-gown where I refresh myself with the cool morning breeze, [then] I withdraw to my little study where I scan the pages of some poet or other, study Quintilian's precepts, and not without stupor I read Cicero's orations. I enjoy Pliny's letters, these are my real delight, and I compose epigrams. But I like [to compose] elegiac verses better. After lunch I sleep a little [while] my father, who is here with me, dedicated as he is to the pleasures of literature, corrects, adds, adorns and re-orders my compositions . . . and after a nap I divert myself with chess or backgammon. Near the villa is a vineyard, good and large, with much fruit. In the middle flows a fresh brook with a great quantity of little fish. There are very dense shrubs and nightingales which day and night complain of their ancient injuries in song. In this place I read something and then go with my lute singing verses, sometimes improvised and sometimes studied. Then when the sun is lower I play ball. In this way the whole summer passes by until the influence of the sicknesses in town cease. I don't cultivate my fields, since I am occupied with literary studies. I don't have here a library like that of the Sassetti or the Medici; but I do have a little shelf full of corrected texts that I treasure more than any rich ornament.

One Florentine who hated life in the country was Machiavelli. His residence on his farm near S Casciano was forced upon him as an exile from public service. He called his house L'Albergaccio – 'the wretched hotel'. Here he wrote *The Prince* and the *Discourses*. He too wrote a letter of how he spent his day which, save for the game of backgammon, gives a very different picture of life in the country from Vieri's at Lecore. After seeing to his woodsmen and to chores about the farm,

I move on to the road, to the inn: I talk to those who pass by, asking them news of their towns, hearing various things and noting the different tastes and fancies of men. Meanwhile, comes the hour of the midday meal when I with my band go to eat those victuals which this poor place and my meagre means have to offer. Having eaten, I return to the inn where there is usually the inn-keeper, a butcher, a miller and two bakers. With these I reduce myself to stupidity (*m'ingaglioffo*) for the rest of the day, playing cards and backgammon from which arise a thousand arguments and infinite contemptuous angry words . . . Thus sunk among such vermin I blow away the cobwebs from my brain by giving vent to this malice which is my fate – being pleased to let it trample me underfoot in this way to see if even it would be ashamed of such treatment.

It was only at night that Machiavelli left all these trivialities behind and entered his study to write and commune with his ancient heroes of politics and literature.

The furniture of the Florentine villa of the fourteenth and fifteenth centuries was not specially sumptuous. The house of a well-to-do Tuscan farmer today resembles the accounts of the old *ville signorili*. The rooms were spacious – sometimes six to seven metres high with walls a metre thick. There were red brick floors, whitewashed walls, occasionally a mural, a stone tabernacle with wooden doors, a few wall cupboards and a large fireplace. There was little more furniture – a table with a few stools on the ground floor, truckle-beds and *cassoni* upstairs.

The murals which have come down to us from the Quattrocento villas of rich Florentines usually have a pedagogical, moralistic theme. For the Carducci villa at Legnaia, Castagno covered the walls of the *salone* with heroes from Biblical, ancient Roman, and Florentine history. Most of this decoration is now in the Uffizi, but sections of it are still in the villa. Each figure represents a specific virtue or a memorable deed. For a villa belonging to the Tornabuoni, Botticelli painted Minerva introducing Lorenzo Tornabuoni to a tribune of the Liberal Arts, while Venus and the Graces offered gifts to a girl of the family. These are the murals now in the Louvre. The only outspokenly pagan decoration which has survived is Antonio Pollaiuolo's frieze of nude dancers in the now dilapidated villa at Arcetri originally owned by the Lanfredini.

THE MEDICI AND FIESOLE. The slopes of Fiesole are full of associations with the earlier Medici and their companions. One of Cosimo's sons built a villa there. Ficino came over from Careggi to savour a glass of fine Trebbiano with Pico and Poliziano, who both had houses on the hillside. Poliziano's villa, the Villa Diana, still stands on the Via delle Palazzine (No. 11). Sometimes Lorenzo came to be with them all at the villa built by his uncle. Even Fiesole's oldest church, the Badia, owed its transformation to the Medici.

About 1455 Cosimo's younger son, Giovanni, began to build himself a villa on the site of a house called Belcanto which he bought from the Bardi family. It is one of the first villas we know of that was built only for pleasure. The land was no good for farming. It was stony and steep, making the building costs high because the house had to be built into the hillside with many retaining walls and terraces. But the view was superb. Cosimo disapproved of the project, saying that he preferred a view consisting entirely of his own property. In this we see the lingering feudalism in Cosimo's taste. His son belonged entirely to the Renaissance; what he wanted was the magnificent view of Florence and the surrounding countryside. Belcanto, probably the work of Michelozzo, may well have been based on Pliny's well-known description of his own Tuscan villa with its terraced gardens. Certainly, it was one of the first real villas in the modern sense of the word, because it was conceived primarily for leisure rather than as a venture in practical farming.

While it was under construction, Giovanni's father and older brother Piero began to have the ancient Badia rebuilt. In all Cosimo's buildings the character of villa and monastery seem to merge. There is a monastic simplicity about the palace in Florence and the villas at Careggi and Cafaggiolo which he had Michelozzo rebuild for him. As for the churches he commissioned (S Marco, S Lorenzo, and finally the Badia Fiesolana), they have the lightness and freshness of the villa in the cloisters and loggias, the radiant white walls, and in the burgeoning stone ornaments of every capital and frieze.

The Badia was Cosimo's last project. Perhaps more than any of the others it bears the clearest imprint of his taste and character. It is interesting to compare his intentions for the Badia with those of Nicola Acciaioli, the patron of the Certosa di Val d'Ema built just a century before on the opposite side of Florence. Like the Badia, the Certosa was the foundation of a famous old Florentine of immense wealth built to perpetuate his name and to settle his account with his Maker. In 1356, Acciaioli wrote to his brother, saying: 'I want it to be the most noble place in all Italy . . . this monastery and its decorations alone belong to me for all time to come, and will preserve my name in my country. And if the soul is immortal, as Monsignor the Chancellor says, then my soul, wherever it is ordered to go, will delight in this building.'

Acciaioli had himself buried in a beautifully carved marble tomb, but such outspoken bombast was foreign to Cosimo's character and it seems that he viewed the hereafter with considerably more piety and less *sang-froid*. He left strict orders that he was to be buried without pomp in a wooden coffin. Nevertheless, the Medici *palle* are to be found everywhere in the Badia: on the capitals, over the doors, on the wooden beams of the loggias, on the library windows, and on the vaults of the church. Sometimes the *palle* are framed by a shield, elsewhere slender ribbons flutter about them, and inside the church they are painted red and set upon a gold field encircled by green laurel. There was at least one contemporary who charged Cosimo with vainglory for all this, and the Abbot of the Badia, the learned Timofeo Maffei of Verona, wrote many letters in defence of his benefactor. Like Nicola Acciaioli, Cosimo had a room set aside for himself in the convent and provided a library for the monks. He spent 80,000 *scudi* for construction work, 2,000 for furnishing the convent, 4,000 for books and furniture for the church, and 8,000 for books and manuscripts for the library. For these last items, he turned to Vespasiano da Bisticci, who immediately put forty-five scribes to work. After twenty-two months, two hundred volumes were ready.

Cosimo followed the construction of the Badia very closely. According to Vespasiano, he came every day to see how the work was coming along. One of his accountants thought he would shock his master by telling him that in one year more was being spent on the Badia than on S Lorenzo. To which Cosimo replied that this only showed that more was being accomplished in Fiesole than in Florence.

The name of the Badia's architect is never mentioned in the many surviving documents. One wonders if a model or a plan was left earlier by a great designer who could not be present to supervise its execution. The church interior and the garden loggia are of noble restraint, structure as well as every frieze and cornice in exquisite proportion. The only later additions made inside the church are the tabernacles at either end of the transept and the inlaid altar, which were installed by a Medici Grand Duke in the seventeenth century. Otherwise the church is as it was when it was consecrated in 1466. The style is simpler, more classical than Michelozzo's, closer to Alberti's. More than any other Florentine building, the Badia Fiesolana approaches the Platonic character of Alberti's ideal temple, the beauty of which lay entirely in the lines and proportions of an architecture which abjured painting and sculpture.

Whoever the Badia's architect was, it is interesting that the old Romanesque façade was retained. Indeed, the width of the inlaid façade determined the width of the nave, and many of its ornamental motifs served as a point of departure for the Quattrocento interior. There are the fluted archivolts surrounding the blind arches which reappear inside as frames for the chapels. The delicate string course, the black and white colour scheme, even the three small windows, were all taken over in the new church.

A few years after the Badia was consecrated and Cosimo and Piero de' Medici were dead, the façade was no longer pleasing to the abbot. He wrote to Lorenzo the Magnificent, begging him to complete the work begun by his father and grandfather, complaining that the new church was still with a medieval façade. But Lorenzo did nothing about it. Poliziano and Pico sometimes stayed at the Badia as the abbot's guests to use the splendid library which has since been dispersed. In March 1492, as Lorenzo lay mortally ill at Careggi, his son Giovanni was formally invested as a cardinal at the Badia. Pico was one of the witnesses. In 1516 Lorenzo's third son, Giuliano, died there when only thirty-seven years of age.

LATER MEDICI VILLAS. Towards the end of the fifteenth century the tone of noble restraint characteristic of the Florentine villa began to change under the influence of the re-discovery of the ancient villas of Rome. Already in the 1450's Giovanni de' Medici's villa at

Fiesole was probably sited with a Plinian model in mind. Thirty years later, his nephew Lorenzo the Magnificent began to have the façade of the villa at Poggio a Caiano remodelled and redecorated with neoclassical motifs contrived by Giuliano da Sangallo and Filippino Lippi. At Careggi, Lorenzo ordered sculpture and exotic plants for the garden. He had Verrocchio make the *Putto with a Spouting Dolphin* (now in the Palazzo Vecchio) for a fountain there.

Careggi was the favourite villa of the early Medici. Cosimo il Vecchio, Piero the Gouty and Lorenzo all died there. Lorenzo continued the tradition begun by his grandfather of gathering the Platonists of Florence either at the Medici villa or at Ficino's nearby. When he died, Poliziano and Pico were at his side. Lorenzo did not wish to receive the Last Sacrament in bed: 'It shall never be said that my Lord, who created and saved me, shall come to me in my room.' So with the help of his friends he rose to meet the priest. But soon he had to be carried back to his bed. One of his last thoughts uttered to Pico was 'I wish that death had spared me until your library had been complete.' Two years later, when Piero de' Medici fled from Florence, Careggi was looted and burned. Although Duke Alessandro and Cosimo I had Pontormo and Bronzino repair some of the damage, the villa was never again the intimate family retreat it had been in the fifteenth century. Compared to the later Medici villas, Careggi is relatively small and bucolic.

During the sixteenth century Castello, Pratolino, Poggio a Caiano and Petraia became the favourite country houses of the Medici. It was their sumptuous, courtly style which has come to be associated with the modern idea of the villa. Under Leo X, Lorenzo's second son, Poggio a Caiano acquired its gabled loggia and its frieze of pseudo-antique reliefs. The old open courtyard was transformed into a great reception hall with murals by Andrea del Sarto, Franciabigio and Pontormo glorifying the Medici in the guise of ancient Roman histories. The villa was used more for receptions than as a private retreat. Emperor Charles V was entertained here in 1536 and generations of Medici brides stopped there to prepare themselves for their ceremonial entries into Florence. In 1581 Montaigne was received by Francesco I and Bianca Cappello. To Montaigne, Poggio a Caiano seemed a modest place compared to the chateaux of France: 'It is marvellous that such a small pile can hold one hundred beautiful rooms. Among other things, I saw on the beds a great many beautiful materials, but of no value: they are nothing but poor speckled stuffs woven of very fine wool and sparse strands of silk of the same colour. We saw the Duke's distillery, and his lathe workshop, and other instruments – for the Duke is a great mechanic.'

Montaigne was much more impressed by Pratolino. Francesco I had had the villa built for his beloved Bianca long before he was able to marry her in 1579. Although Montaigne was patronizing about the quality of the villa's furniture, he thought the garden miraculous. Little of the original garden remains, but from all accounts it was less formal and much more bizarre than the Boboli. There were grottoes by Buontalenti and fountains by Ammannati and Giambologna. Great obelisks flanked the villa, the lawns concealed trick fountains, and there is still a pond with the colossal figure of Apennine. The grottoes had movable scenery. In one corner of the garden a bronze satyr by Giambologna sat astride a cask and spouted water. There were hydraulic organs played by stone muses, a mechanical shepherdess walked to a well, filled her pail, and returned to her niche and a satyr played a bagpipe. Scattered through the shrubbery were antiquities and pseudo-antiquities, many of which have since been transferred to the Boboli Gardens. Pratolino was the Grand Ducal amusement park and it was here that Prince Ferdinando later staged his operas with the help of the Scarlatti, the Bibbiena, and Handel.

Castello, by comparison, must have been very sedate. The place was already in Medici hands in the fifteenth century. When Cosimo I inherited it, he had a scholar think up a scheme for the garden. It was conceived as a grandiose allegorical treatise made of water, plants, marble, bronze and stone. The plan called for over fifty statues, a series of elaborate hydraulic systems, fountains, grottoes, labyrinths and secret gardens. Tribolo, Ammannati, Buontalenti and Giambologna all worked hard on it, but the garden was never completed. Nevertheless, Vasari could boast that it was the 'richest, the most magnificent, most ornate garden of Europe'. In 1571 Cosimo I retired to Castello with his new wife, Camilla Martelli, after he had turned over the political administration of the Grand Duchy to his son. He had ruled Tuscany for thirty-seven years and for the remaining three years of his life he dedicated himself to the cultivation of jasmine at Castello.

In the garden of Petraia, just below Castello, the Lorrainers in the eighteenth century continued with exotic jasmines. But they also bred dozens of new varieties of lemons. Many of these are still there in their original terracotta *orci*, fired at the kilns of Impruneta which stamped the year and the Grand Ducal emblem in the clay.

COUNTRY PAINTERS. It is an odd coincidence that one runs into the same painters again and again when one goes about the country roads of Florence. There is the S Cecilia Master, for instance, one of the first in the fourteenth century to take up Giotto's new style. Apart from his chief work in the Uffizi, his panels keep one company all the way from S Giorgio sulla Costa to S Margherita a Montici. Then there is the prolific Neri di Bicci who probably had the largest painter's atelier in Florence during the Quattrocento. He was the third generation of a family of painters and this may account for his popularity; people were simply used to ordering pictures from the Bicci. Though a mediocre painter, he was quick to adopt the inventions and novelties of others. He was in great demand in Florence as well as among the country parishes. Neri's works crop up at Arcetri in S Leonardo, near Settignano at S Martino a Mensola, above Cerbaia at S Giovanni in Sugana, and at Morrocco in the Val di Pesa. He must have been an excellent businessman, supervising his large shop, keeping up production, and looking after the inventories of the Carmine's *Compagnia di S Agnese*. There was more room in Florence in the 1460s and 1470s for him, Benozzo Gozzoli, Cosimo Rosselli and Baldovinetti than for Piero della Francesca, whose spirit was much more akin to that of Brunelleschi, Alberti and the Humanists. Instead, after a visit to Florence in the late 1430s and early 1440s when he collaborated with Castagno and Domenico Veneziano at S Egidio, Piero found steady work only with the burghers of Borgo S Sepolcro and Arezzo and at the courts of Rimini and Urbino. The Florentines preferred pictures of sweeter sentiment, rich in ornament and anecdotal detail – all qualities which Piero della Francesca disdained. The fact was that the really popular style of the fifteenth century was not set by Masaccio and Donatello, but by Fra Angelico and Ghiberti.

Castagno was an exception in mid-fifteenth-century Florence. He was the only painter who maintained the sternness and simplicity of Masaccio. The apocryphal story Vasari repeats about Castagno's murder of Domenico Veneziano may be an indication that Castagno's manner in painting as well as in private life made many ill at ease. There is the memory of his frightening effigies of punished criminals and there remains the rustic, unadorned severity of his religious murals and of the heroes and heroines from the Carducci villa near Legnaia.

There is nothing rustic or particularly bucolic about Pontormo – either in his style or in the patrons who commissioned him. Yet his most important murals are all to be found in the country. Secluded surroundings were congenial to his retiring nature and to his artistic vision. He came to Florence from the village of Pontormo, near Empoli (Pontormo's real name was Jacopo Carrucci). One of his most beautiful pictures, the *Visitation*, is in the church at Carmignano half-way between his own village and the villa at Poggio a Caiano where he painted for the Medici. In Florence, Pontormo painted portraits of courtiers and aristocrats and supplied the Pucci and Capponi with altarpieces and murals. Pontormo was the first to break with the canons of the classical High Renaissance style as these had been formulated by Fra Bartolommeo, Raphael and Andrea del Sarto. With him, the restraint and rationalism so characteristic of Florentine expression were cast aside. One has only to go to the villa at Poggio a Caiano and to the Certosa di Val d'Ema to see how fast this change occurred and how radical it was.

Pontormo painted the lunette of *Vertumnus and Pomona* in the Medici villa between 1520 and 1521. The composition is balanced, the colours warm and earthy, and the figures are lyrically disposed in the relaxed postures of those who sit out the heat of a stifling summer day. The very next year, after an outbreak of plague in Florence, Pontormo fled to the Certosa. There, during the next five years, he was involved with five scenes from the Passion. In these symmetry, weight, mass, classical proportions, natural colours were thrown to the winds. Instead, inspired by the late Gothic elements in Dürer's prints, Pontormo painted distorted figures moving with pain and difficulty in unexplained spaces. The colours are of a shrieking violence; it is almost as if colours rather than human figures assume the roles of actors in the drama. These murals of Christ's Passion were, in a way, a personal *Via Crucis* for Pontormo. All the conventions were ignored in order to render his own hallucinated vision of the theme. With the years he became more and more neurotic. He had a morbid interest in his own bad health and he lived as a recluse. Although Vasari deplored the influence of German art on his hitherto graceful style, Pontormo was greatly admired by his contemporaries and he never seems to have lacked work. In Florence then a man could be as eccentric as he liked so long as his work was beautifully made and truly felt.

IMPRUNETA. From the Certosa and Pontormo's haunting pictures, it is but a short hour's walk to the hill town of Impruneta. The walk is more beautiful, perhaps, than the goal – unless one happens to go there during the great fair towards the end of September. The fair at Impruneta has been held for more than three centuries.

A country road near Pian de' Giullari

Head of a man from Fra Angelico's *Deposition*, originally painted *ca* 1440
for the church of Santa Trinita, now in the San Marco Museum

Jacques Callot made an engraving of it in 1620 which he dedicated to Grand Duke Cosimo II. Originally, the *festa* celebrated the miraculous figure of the Virgin which was believed to have been painted by St Luke himself. But the real object of the fair was the autumn harvest. It is the last opportunity before winter for a great binge. The wines of the Elsa and Pesa valleys are rolled out by the demi-john. Chickens, pigeons and sucking-pig turn on dozens of spits. A cattle-market is held on one side of the great piazza. Then there are stalls upon stalls hung with garlands of hazel nuts. There is an endless supply of paper-thin anise biscuits called *brigidini*, bars of white *torrone*, and almond toffee boiling in iron cauldrons. Balloons, plastic toys and candles are all sold together. Vats of pickled olives and artichokes stand on the cobblestones and tables are heaped with home-cured hams and great loaves of saltless country-style bread. It all lasts two or three days, and for weeks beforehand the walls of Florence are plastered with broadsides announcing the days of the fair. Everyone who can think up a good excuse leaves his job and goes with family and friends to gorge himself at Impruneta.

There are similar fairs all over Tuscany in September and October. But the one at Impruneta is the largest and noisiest of all. Once it is over, the Florentine *contadini* settle down for the winter. The country roads and villas have their last burst of colour too as the *Vite del Canadà* covers the walls with its brilliant crimson mantle. Then come the grey mists. The twinkling lights and chrysanthemum garlands of *Ognissanti* and the Day of the Dead are the last flicker of country festivity before the first almonds burst into bloom in the spring. The old folk muffled in shawls, black stockings and felt slippers scurry silently through the streets. The tourists have gone, and the Florentines return from their villas and once more take possession of their city.

Practical Information

❧

Florence has a double street-numbering system for private and for commercial addresses. The latter are always numbered in red. Where the red number applies, this is indicated in brackets at the end of the address.

1. HOTELS AND PENSIONS

(*** expensive, ** not cheap, * moderate)
Near the Station
*** HOTEL BAGLIONI E PALACE, Piazza dell' Unità Italiana 6. Tel. 23.846
*** HOTEL MINERVA, Piazza S Maria Novella 16 (swimming-pool), Tel. 28.45.55
** HOTEL BONCIANI, Via de' Panzani 17, Tel. 27.00.39
*** HOTEL KRAFT, Via Solferino 2 (swimming-pool), Tel. 28.42.73
** HOTEL ROMA, Piazza S Maria Novella 8, Tel. 27.03.66
*** HOTEL VILLA MEDICI, Via del Prato 42 (swimming-pool), not far from the Cascine, Tel. 26.13.31
*** HOTEL CARLTON, Piazza Vittorio Veneto 4a (view over the Cascine), Tel. 27.70

Near the Centre (Piazza della Repubblica)
* HOTEL HELVETIA E BRISTOL, Via dei Pescioni 2, Tel. 28.78.14
*** HOTEL SAVOY, Piazza della Repubblica 7, Tel. 28.33.13
* HOTEL PORTA ROSSA-CENTRALE, Via Porta Rossa 19, Tel. 28.75.51
** PENSIONE PENDINI, Via Strozzi 2, Tel. 27.01.56
*** PENSIONE BEACCI-TORNABUONI, Via Tornabuoni 3, Tel. 27.26.45
** ALBERGO SIGNORIA, Via delle Terme 1.
* PENSIONE MONA LISA, Borgo Pinti 27 (garage), Tel. 24.041
* ALBERGO FIRENZE, Piazza de' Donati 4, Tel. 24.203
* LOCANDA ELISA, 11 Via dell' Oche, Tel. 29.64.51

Near or along the North Bank of the Arno
* HOTEL BERCHIELLI (near Ponte S. Trinita), Lungarno Acciaioli 14, Tel. 29.49.06
*** HOTEL AUGUSTUS, 5 Vicolo dell' Oro, Tel. 28.30.54
** PENSIONE CONSIGLI, Lungarno Vespucci 50, Tel. 24.172
** PENSIONE HERMITAGE (near Ponte Vecchio), Vicolo Marzio 1, Tel. 29.69.70
**PENSIONE QUISISANA E PONTE VECCHIO, Lungarno Archibusieri 4, Tel. 27.66.92
* PENSIONE RIGATTI (near Ponte alle Grazie), Lungarno Diaz 2, Tel. 23.022
* HOTEL JENNINGS-RICCIOLI, Corso dei Tintori 7, Tel. 28.27.65
*** HOTEL MEDITERRANEO (near Ponte S Niccolò), Lungarno del Tempio 44, Tel. 67.22.41
*** HOTEL EXCELSIOR-ITALIA, Piazza Ognissanti 3, Tel. 29.43.01
*** HOTEL LUCCHESI, Lungarno della Zecca Vecchia 38 (near Biblioteca Nazionale), Tel. 29.88.56

Oltrarno
* PENSIONE BANDINI, Piazza S Spirito 9 (splendid loggia, lift), Tel. 27.53.08
** PENSIONE PITTI PALACE, Via Barbadori 2, Tel. 28.22.57
* PENSIONE ANNALENA (near the Boboli Gardens), Via Romana 34, Tel. 22.24.02
** ALBERGO LUNGARNO, Borgo S Jacopo 12 (book well in advance), Tel. 26.03.97
* PENSIONE LA SCALETTA, Via Guicciardini 13, Tel. 28.30.28

On the near-by hillsides
*** HOTEL VILLA BELVEDERE, Via B. Castelli 3 (garden view, swimming-pool). Closed in winter. Tel. 22.25.01
*** PARK PALACE, Piazzale Galileo 5 (swimming-pool, terraces), Tel. 22.24.31
*** VILLA S MICHELE A DOCCIA, Fiesole, Tel. 59.451
** PENSIONE BENCISTÀ, Via Benedetto da Maiano 2, Fiesole, excellent, Tel. 59.163
*** VILLA LA MASSA, Via La Massa 8, Candeli (Bagno a Ripoli) (two swimming-pools, good restaurant, night club, open from March 1st to October 31st), Tel. 69.50.51
** PENSIONE VILLA LE RONDINI, Via Bolognese 224 (swimming pool, tennis, own bus service to centre), Tel. 40.02.71
** HOTEL-VILLA PARK SAN DOMENICO, Via Piazzola 55, Tel. 57.66.97

2. PLACES TO EAT

(*** very expensive, ** expensive, * moderate price)
All restaurants are subject to change and they are recommended as giving their respective standards when going to press. The best bargains in food are to be had at the *tavole calde* which serve hot meals at the counter. The following restaurants, *trattorie* and *tavole calde* are listed according to their neighbourhood. Autumn is perhaps the most interesting culinary season in Florence, when game and mushrooms abound. Good to eat then are *fagiano, porchetta, fegatelli di maiale, pappardelle alla lepre* (pheasant, sucking-pig, pigs' livers, pasta with hare sauce). To help understand the menu, here is a list of common dishes with their English equivalent:

Gnocchi – dumpling of semolina, potato flour, or corn meal
Penne – long macaroni
Taglierini – usually home-made egg noodles
Tortellini – pockets of pasta with meat inside folded into crescents
Brodo – broth
Arrosto di vitello – roast veal
Cotoletta alla milanese – breaded veal cutlet
Bistecca – beefsteak
Lombatina – a large cutlet or chop
Pollo – chicken
Manzo bollito – boiled beef
Abbacchio – roast lamb
Arista – roast pork
Osso-buco – veal steak with marrow-bone from shank
Stufatino – stew
Fagioli – kidney beans
Fagiolini – green string beans
Melanzane – egg-plant (aubergine)
Peperonata – stewed peppers
Piselli – peas
Cavour – sweet cake of meringue, whipped cream and chocolate
Zucotto – Florentine version of trifle with chocolate and ice-cream used instead of jam
Macedonia – fruit salad
Pesca sciroppata – canned peaches
Uva – grapes
Fichi – figs
Mela o pera cotta – baked apple or pear
Wine is usually ordered not by the closed bottle or flask, but open:

by the glass (*un bicchiere*), quarter-litre (*un-quarto*), half-litre (*mezzo*). Water is ordered *naturale* (tap-water) or *minerale* (bottled mineral water).

Near Piazza della Signoria
** CAVALLINO corner of Via de' Cerchi and Piazza della Signoria, closed Wednesdays
** DA PENNELLO, Via D. Alighieri 4, Tel. 294.848
** PAOLI, Via dei Tavolini, 12 (red), Tel. 21.62.15
** ANTICO BARILE, Via dei Cerchi 40 (red)
* FRIZZI, Borgo degli Albizzi 76 (red). Very cheap, a favourite of office workers.
* NELLA, Via delle Terme, 19 (red). Simple family cooking
* LA BUSSOLA, Via Porta Rossa 58 (red); open all night. Counter service is reasonable, table service expensive, closed Mondays
* GASTONE, Via del Proconsolo 55 (red)
** BUCCA DEL ORAFO, Via dei Girolami 28 (near Ponte Vecchio), Tel. 23.619 excellent artichoke omelettes
*** DONEY, Via Tornabuoni 10
*** GEORGE & DRAGON, Borgo SS Apostoli 33 (red), expensive and smart, Tel. 28.73.08
*** OLIVIERO, Via delle Terme 51 (red), evenings only, international cuisine, elegant, Tel. 28.76.48
** BEPPINO ALLA POSTA, Via Pellicceria 10, closed Wednesdays
** PASQUINI, Via Val di Lamona 2 (red)
* IL FAGIANO, Via dei Neri 57, Tel. 28.78.76

Near Piazza del Duomo
* LA CAMPANA, Borgo S Lorenzo 24 (red); specially good for *pizza* and a quick snack; open until 2 a.m. Occupies the site of an old inn, 'L'Angiolo', where Montaigne stayed
* TAVOLA CALDA E RISTORANTE PIETRO, Piazza di S Giovanni 5, north side of the Baptistery, quick service
** FIOR DI LOTO, Via dei Servi 35 (red), excellent Chinese cuisine
** DA CAFAGGI, Via Guelfa 33 (red), closed Mondays

Near Santa Croce
** RISTORANTE ANTELLESI, Piazza S Croce 21, good food in beautiful rooms of an old palace, Tel. 29.51.05
** TRATTORIA NATALINO, Borgo degli Albizzi 17 (red), on Mercatino di S Piero, rustic ambience, speciality fish, Tel. 26.34.04

** AL CAMPIDOGLIO, Via del Campidoglio 8. Much in demand for civic banquets

** GIOVACCHINO, Via Tosinghi 2, restaurant and snack bar, Tel. 23.276

* SELF-SERVICE, Via de' Pecori 5

Near Santa Maria Novella

** BUCA DI MARIO, Piazza Ottaviani; 16 (red)

** OTELLO, Via Orti Oricellari 28 (red). Has a garden

** AL GIRARROSTO, Piazza S Maria Novella 9–10 Especially good for game

*** SABATINI, Via de' Panzani 41 (red) – Tel. 211.559

** SOSTANZA, Via del Porcellana 25 (red); speciality – steaks

** FIASCHETTERIA 'IL LATINI', Via dei Palchetti 6 (red) (west side of Palazzo Rucellai)

** CANTINETTA ANTINORI, Piazza Antinori 3. Comfortable, quiet for a sandwich, soup, hot dish or glass of Antinori wine (Tuscan specialities)

*** BUCA LAPI, Via del Trebbio 1 (red). Excellent steaks, a rich tourist's favourite, Tel. 23.768

*** HARRY'S BAR, Lungarno Vespucci 22 (red). Excellent, fashionable for aperitif or a meal, Tel. 29.67.00

Oltrarno

** CELESTINO, Piazza S Felicita 4 (red), Tel. 29.65.74

*** CAMMILLO, Borgo S Jacopo 57 (red). Very good but always crowded. Closed Thursdays

* ANGIOLINO, Borgo S Spirito 36 (red). Closed Mondays

* TRATTORIA DEL CARMINE, corner of Piazza del Carmine and Borgo S Fediano. Closed Sundays

** LA BEPPA, just outside the Porta S Miniato, turn right: it is at the end of the street. In summer one eats under the trees, Tel. 29.63.90

* SELF-SERVICE OLD BRIDGE, Via de' Bardi 64–66 (red). Quick cafeteria serice, splendid views. Closed Mondays

** ALFREDO SULL' ARNO, Via de' Bardi, 56 (red). Terrace with fine view. Closed Wednesdays

* TRATTORIA DA NELLA, Via Romana 123 (red)

* LE SORELLE, Via S Niccolò 30 (red). Closed Tuesdays, Tel. 28.44.22

** LA GREPPIA, Lungarno Ferruci 8, Tel. 68.12.341

** TRATTORIA VITTORIA, Via della Fonderia 52 (red), Tel. 22.56.57 Seafood.

On Outskirts or Near Florence

** ANTICO CRESPINO, near Poggio Imperiale, Largo Enrico Fermi 15. Garden at rear, Tel. 221.155

** OMERO, Via del Pian dei Giullari 11 (red), behind the provisions store. Terrace with splendid view (reserve beforehand, Tel. 220.053)

* BIBE, Via delle Bagnese, near Galluzzo (turn right after the Esso Station on the Via Senese after passing through Due Strade)

** RASPANTI, Fiesole, on the road going east from the piazza. Large terrace, fine view, indifferent food.

** CAVE DI MAIANO, three minutes' walk north of the church. Rustic garden with a splendid view towards Vincigliata, closed Thursdays, Tel. 59.133

** LA TERRAZZA, Calenzano, behind the provisions store. Splendid view

** TRATTORIA DALLA 'EDY', Piazza Savonarola 9 (red). Garden, excellent quality at reasonable price, closed Saturdays

* TRATTORIA DA TITO, Lungarno Bellariva. Open terrace on river, good family cooking. Open April through October

** RISTORANTE 'DA DELFINA' ($\frac{1}{2}$ hour's drive to one of the most beautiful spots in Tuscany). Above Poggio a Caiano near the Medici villa of Artimino, advisable to reserve. Closed Tuesdays. Tel. 871.8074

** ZOCCHI, Via Bolognese (near Pratolino). Always crowded; view towards Fiesole, Tel. 88.90.00

* GIRARROSTO, Pontassieve ($\frac{1}{2}$ hour's drive), Tel. 83.02.048

** CENTANNI, just above Bagno a Ripoli on the road to S Donato in Collina. Surrounded by olive groves and farms. Via Centanni 7. Closed Fridays. Tel. 63.01.22

** AI DUE GIOGHI (TRESPIANO), Via Bolognese 9–11, Tel. 40.10.01

** DA OSVALDO, Via G. D'Annunzio 51 (red). Garden (at Ponte a Mensola, below Settignano). Closed Wednesdays. Tel. 60.21.68

** CASTELLO MEDICEO DI GRASSINA, Via delle Fonti 4 Grassina, Tel. 64.06.51

For those who like to take picnic lunches: got to a *forno* or *panificio* for bread; then, to a *pizzicagnolo* or *pizzicheria* for cheese, ham, etc. Here are some words to help you there:

prosciutto cotto – cooked ham

prosciutto crudo – smoked, uncooked ham, an Italian speciality usually eaten with melon or figs

burro – butter

formaggio – cheese (*Bel Paese, Parmigiano, Stracchino* and *Mascarpone* – cream cheeses; *Gruviera, Olandese* – Edam; *Pecorino* – sheep's milk cheese)

olive – olives

uova – eggs

succo di pomodoro – tomato juice

succo di pompelmo – grapefruit juice

finocchiona – good local salame

Wine can be bought here, but more cheaply and better at a vitner's. Fruit is sold not only in shops but in piazzas (S Spirito and S Lorenzo in the mornings and behind S Felicita all day in good weather).

3. SPECIALITY FOOD AND WINE STORES

(From September through May food and grocery stores are closed Wednesday afternoons)

GRANA MARKET, Piazza S Pier Maggiore; cheese galore!

CALDERAI, Via dell' Ariento 31 (red) and Via Calimala 19 (red); all the Tuscan country specialities and a fine selection of French cheeses and excellent liverwurst from Meran.

PRIMIZIE, Via Tosinghi. Specialists in out-of-season fruits and vegetables

PROCACCI, Via Tornabuoni 64 (red). Famed for truffle sandwiches – *panini tartufati*

OLD ENGLAND STORES, Via Vecchietti 28 (red). Teas, jams, wines

FRUSCONI, Via Guicciardini 3–5 (red)

PEGNA, Via dello Studio 8, excellent for spices

4. BAKERS AND CONFECTIONERS

FORNO INGLESE (BALBONI E MULLER), Via della Vigna Nuova 35 (red)

FORNO on the Via de' Cerchi near the Via del Corso and

FORNO in the Via dei Tavolini

ROBIGLIO, Via Tosinghi 11 (red); and Via dei Servi 102 (red)

RUGGINI, Via de' Neri 76 (red)

SIENI, Via dell' Ariento 29 (red)

PASTICCERIA E BAR OTELLO, Via S Agostino 11 (red) – excellent *mille foglie*

5. TEA-ROOMS AND BARS

CENNINI, Borgo S. Jacopo 51 (red) – excellent pastry
DONEY, Via Tornabuoni 10
GIACOSA, Via Tornabuoni 83 (red)
GILLI, Piazza della Repubblica
RIVOIRE, Piazza della Signoria
BAR-TEA ROOM S FRANCESCO, Via S Francesco 18, Fiesole
MAIOLI, Via Guicciardini 43 (red)

6. FOR A QUICK SNACK

'PERCHÈ NO?' Via dei Tavolini, ice cream supreme
DONNINI, Piazza della Repubblica – especially for hot sandwiches
MOTTA, corner of Piazza del Duomo and Via Martelli
ROSTICCERIA 'DA MORENO', Via Val di Lamona (near the main post-office between the Mercato Nouvo and Pellicceria)
PICCADILLY, Via Por S Maria 43R, pizza bar; tables out of doors with a view of Palazzo di Parte Guelfa
MODERN SNACK BAR, Borgo S Jacopo 19 (red)
CAVINI, Piazza delle Cure 23 (red) – excellent ice-creams
CANTINETTA ANTINORI, Piazza Antinori 3
BAR-GELATERIA VIVOLI, Via Isolo delle Stinche 7 (red), near Teatro Verdi – excellent ice creams
BAR-CALAMAI, Via del Agnolo near Via Verdi; hot brioches!

7. FOR THEATRE AND CONCERT TICKETS, VILLA VISITS, ETC.

Tickets to be obtained either from travel bureaux or from the theatres directly. For further information consult information officer in the Loggia de' Rucellai in Via della Vigna Nuova. The cheaper tickets at the Teatro Communale (*Seconda gradinata*) are highly recommended: acoustics and visibility are good and there are chairs. At the Teatro della Pergola the seats in the *Loggione* (the cheapest tickets) consist of stone steps!
ARNO-AGENZIA VIAGGI, Piazza degli Ottaviani 7 (red) top of Via de' Fossi; also has tickets for the Teatro Metastasio, Prato.

8. BANKS AND EXCHANGES

BANCA D'AMERICA E D'ITALIA, Via Strozzi 4

CREDITO ITALIANO, Via Vecchietti 11

UNIVERSALTURISMO, Via Speziali 7 (red). Foreign currency exchanged at the best rates behind the travel agency.

9. POSTAGE STAMPS, POST-OFFICE, TELEPHONES AND TELEGRAMS

Postage stamps, salt, cigarettes and candles are all sold at bars which are also licensed tobacconists. Their sign is *tabacchi* or simply T.

The Central Post-Offices near the Piazza della Repubblica (and in Via Pietrapiana at the corner of Via Verdi). To send a letter or a package with special handling ask for postage *Raccomandata*; with special delivery: *Espresso*. Packages weighing more than 2 kilos must be sent parcel post (*pacco postale*). Money orders are taken on the first floor of the main post office.

Telegrams are sent on the ground floor of the post office. Undelivered telegrams may be picked up at Via Anselmi 1 (the north side of the post-office building).

Public telephones in Italy do not function with coins, but with *gettoni* costing 50 lire, purchasable at bars or inside the post-office.

10. SHIPING AGENT

UNIVERSAL EXPRESS COMPANY, Piazza Goldoni 1

11. LEATHER GOODS, UMBRELLAS LUGGAGE

Apart from the outdoor markets in S Lorenzo, the Mercato Nuovo, the Loggia of the Uffizi, and the leather school of S Croce:

BRUSCOLI, Via Montebello 56 (red)

GUCCI, Via Tornabuoni 73–75 (red)

DUGINI, Via della Vigna Nuova 69 (red)

GHERARDINI, Via della Vigna Nuova 57 (red)

SILVIA, Umbrellas, excellent repair service, Via dei Conti 45 (red)

SIGNORINI, Via S Gallo 27 (red), Tel. 28.75.00

ROBERTA, Borgo S Jacopo 36

12. SHOES

Florence is full of shoe-stores, where all varieties and prices are to be found. In addition:

FERRAGAMO, Via Tornabuoni 16 (red)
GILARDINI, Via de' Cerretani 8 and 20 (red)
MANTELLASSI, Piazza della Repubblica 25 (red)
VARESE, Via de' Cerretani 45 and 55 (red)
RASPINI, Via de' Martelli 5–7 (red) and Via Por S Maria 70–74 (red)
STILE, Via Cavour (close to Piazza S Marco)
For problem feet: ALFREDO LOTTI, Via dell' Agnolo 87; NISTRI, Via della Vigna Nuova 87 (red)

13. STRAW

Mercato Nuovo
PAOLI, Via della Vigna Nuova 26 (red), specializes in raffia work, mats, novelties, etc.
Chiasso Cornino and Via delle Terme – items of a more rustic nature
Mercato di S Lorenzo

15. FABRICS

Silks for Garments: FERMO VALLI, Via Strozzi 4 (red)
S.A.T.A.S., Via Strozzi 24 (red)
Silks for Furnishings: LISIO, Via de' Fossi 45 (red). Woven in the style of the 15th, 16th and 17th c.
RUBELLI, Via Tornabuoni 3 (red)
Cotton, linen, etc.: CASTAGNOLI, Via Orsanmichele 12 (red). Especially good for linen towels and hand-dyed *canapa*
GHEZZI, Via Calzaiuoli 110 (red)
MAZZONI, Via Orsanmichele 14 (go upstairs)
Woollens (see also same shops as under Silks):
OLD ENGLAND STORES, Via Vecchietti 28 (red)
CASA DEI TESSUTI, Via de' Pecori 20–4 (red)
Passementerie: SILVI, Via dei Tavolini 5 (red) – infinite choice of designs and made to order
PASSAMANERIA S LORENZO, Borgo S Lorenzo 22 (red)
Mercers: ZUFFANELLI, Via Lamberti 1 – excellent for ribbons
QUERCIOLI E LUCHERINI, Via Calimala 13 (red) – excellent for threads and ornamental tapes in cotton

16. CLOTHING

Ready-to-wear clothing is still rather uncommon for women's wear and the prices are usually as much or higher than what it costs for a dressmaker's job. For those who have not the time to order clothing here is a short list:

FATA, Via Tornabuoni 26 (red)

EMILIO PUCCI, Via de' Pucci 6

MORADEI, Borgo S Lorenzo 15–17 (red). Excellent for very reasonably priced sportswear, lingerie, stockings

H. NEUBER, Via Strozzi 32 (red). English, French and American sportswear

FERRAGAMO, GIOVANNA, Via Tornabuoni 2, first floor

PRINCIPE, Via Strozzi 21–27 (red) – chiefly for young people

FRANCESCHINI, Vicolo dell' Oro 2, hat-maker for ladies

GALLERIA DELLA MODA, Via Calimala 23 (red), moderate prices

OLD ENGLAND STORES, Via Vecchietti 28 (red). A Florentine favourite. The shop has an excellent tailor in Signor Dino and dressmaker in Signore Vittoria and Anna Maria

VALDITEVERE, Lungarno Soderini 1 (first floor). Sportswear and made-to-order department. Materials usually hand-woven in Tuscany and Umbria. Reasonable prices

ZANOBETTI, Via Calimala 3 (red). Elegant sportswear for men and women

INNOCENTI, Via Tosinghi 18 (red)

ANICHINI (children's and infants' wear), Via del Parione 59

FICOZZI, Piazza Frescobaldi 10 (red). Will knit sweaters in cotton or wool to suit any style or measure at a reasonable price and fairly quickly

Sometimes UPIM (corner Via dei Speziali and Piazza della Repubblica, also at Via Gioberti 78 with parking lot) and STANDA (Via de' Panzani 31 (red) turn up items of surprising elegance at very low cost – roughly comparable to Marks & Spencer in England

17. GLASSWARE AND CROCKERY, HOUSEHOLD GOODS AND SILVER

DUILIO '48', Via Calzaiuoli 56 (red). In the basement is a selection of Empoli glassware

CANTAGALLI, Via Tornabuoni. Opposite Palazzo Strozzi

VIA PORTA ROSSA 21 (red). Glazed terracotta ware from Tuscany, Emilia and the Veneto

RICHARD-GINORI, Via Rondinelli 7. Elegant porcelain
TEGHINI, Via Strozzi 7–9, probably the widest and best selection of classical silverware patterns
BRANDIMARTE, 18 Via Bartolini (near Porta S Frediano) silverware of original and often beautiful design, wholesale prices
IL POLIZIANO, Via Rondinelli 22 (red)
MANETTI E MAZINI, Via Bronzino 125 – excellent for copying old ceramics
CERAMICHE DE SIMONE, Via Parione 52
IL TEGAME, Piazza G. Salvemini 7 – glassware and pottery from the Italian provinces
BARTOLINI, Via dei Servi 30 and Piazza S Giovanni 22 (red)
M.I.T.A.L., Via Cappello 25, Impruneta. Terracotta pots etc. There are several other kilns near here as well as near Antella

18. PHOTOGRAPHS, REPRODUCTIONS, ETC.

ALINARI, Via Nazionale 6; branches in the Via Strozzi and on the Lungarno Corsini
GABINETTO FOTOGRAFICO DELLA SOPRINTENDENZA ALLE GALLERIE, Piazzale degli Uffizi 2 (Hours: 11.00–13.00 Mon., Wed., Fri.). This is where much of the best black and white photography can be obtained of works of art in Tuscany
PINEIDER, Piazza della Signoria and Via Tornabuoni 76 (red)

19. PAPERS, BOXES, STATIONERS, ETC.

GIANNINI, Piazza Pitti 19. Florentine papers
ORLANDINI, Borgo SS Apostoli 27 (red). Papers and all sizes of boxes
ROMEO and PISTOLI, both in Via Condotta
PINEIDER, Piazza della Signoria and Via Tornabuoni 76 (red)
S. DAVITE, Via Nazionale 81 (red), Printers of fine stationery
RIGACCI, Via de' Servi 71 (red). Artists' supplies
SCATOLINI, Via dell' Anguillara 66 (red). Excellent for coloured papers of all kinds

20. PICTURE-FRAMES

Several shops on the Via Proconsolo end of Via Pandolfini.
MOSCARDI, Via Tornabuoni 25 (red). Expensive
LAZZERI, Via Ricasoli 26 (red). Excellent work at reasonable price
BARTOLOZZI E MAIOLI, Via Mattio 13 (red). Excellent copyists of

antique examples

21. BOOKSHOPS

CALDINI, Via Tornabuoni 91 (red)
FELTRINELLI, Via Cavour. The city's best selection of paperbacks
SEEBER, Via Tornabuoni 70 (red)
PORCELLINO, corner of Mercato Nuovo and Via Calimaruzza
SALIMBENI, Via Matteo Palmieri 6 (red); also antiquarian books
CENTRO DI, Piazza de'Mozzi 1 (red); superb for art books and catalogues

22. BOOKBINDERS

ATHOS, Borgo SS Apostoli at the Via Por S Maria end
BRUSCOLI, Via Montebello 56 (red)
VANGELISTI, Via Gignoro 105, Tel. 60.79.37

23. ANTIQUE SHOPS

Via de'Fossi, Via della Spada, Via de' Pepi, Borgo SS Apostoli, Borgo Ognissanti, and around Piazza S Spirito

24. LIBRARIES

BIBLIOTECA NAZIONALE, Piazza Cavaleggeri. Groundfloor rooms free for consultation. For access to the historical collections upstairs a letter of introduction is required from some learned institution or from the consulate. This also applies to the BIBLIOTECA RICCARDIANA, the BIBLIOTECA LAURENZIANA and the ARCHIVIO DI STATO
BIBLIOTECA MARUCELLIANA, Via Cavour 43
BRITISH CONSULATE, Lungarno Corsini 2. A public reading-room with a good selection of English periodicals
BRITISH INSTITUTE, Lungarno Guicciardini 9. Open to members
FRENCH INSTITUTE, Piazza Ognissanti 2. Reading-room is free to the public. Lending library service.
GABINETTO VIEUSSEUX, ground floor of Palazzo Strozzi. Begun early in the last century. Books and periodicals in the main European languages. Open to members. Rates available for 3 months
KUNSTHISTORISCHES INSTITUT Via Giusti 44; open to qualified students of history of art
HARVARD UNIVERSITY CENTER FOR RENAISSANCE STUDIES (Villa

'I Tatti'), 26 Via di Vincigliata, Ponte a Mensola
ISTITUTO NAZIONALE DI STUDI SUL RINASCIMENTO, Palazzo Strozzi
ISTITUTO OLANDESE DI STORIA DELL'ARTE (Dutch Art Historical Institute), Viale Torricelli 5, occasionally there are very fine exhibitions here open to the public.

25. PHARMACIES

COMUNALE, Via de'Serragli 2 (red). Open nights
FARMACIA DI S MARIA NUOVA, Via Bufalini 2 (red). Open nights
FARMACIA INGLESE, Via Tornabuoni 97 (red)
FARMACIA DI S MARIA NOVELLA, Via della Scala 16. Has existed since the 17th c. They make a very good verbena soap.

26. EMERGENCY TELEPHONE NUMBERS

AMBULANCE and FIRST AID: 21.22.22
FIRE: 222.222
POLICE: 113 21.21.21
HIGHWAY POLICE: 57.77.77
PUBLIC ASSISTANCE IN AN EMERGENCY: 113
FOR DISABLED AUTOMOBILES: 116

27. CHILD CARE SERVICE

BABY'S CLUB (nursery and kindergarten) will accommodate children of transient visitors too; Via del Salviatino 6 – Tel. 602.751

28. BICYCLE AND CAR HIRE

To hire a bicycle, ask the custodian of any bicycle or motorscooter *Posteggio* (garage for such vehicles). There is one very helpful on in Via delle Terme. Should one place be out of supply, ask for advice for the next likely garage.
For car hire: EUROPA GARAGE, Borgo Ognissanti 96, also for
        repairs – Tel. 29.22.22
        FIAT-SADEM, Viale Belfiore 51–61, Tel. 48.07.01
        HERTZ, Via Maso Finiguerra 33 (red) – Tel. 282-260

29. SPORTS

CLUB ALPINO ITALIANO, Palazzo Pazzi, Via Proconsolo 10. 18:00–20.00 weekdays

Swimming: BELLARIVA, Lungarno Diaz; there are also public slides and swings for children which are open in the spring and summer; CASCINE, guest membership available for visitors at the tennis club – Via degli Olmi – Tel. 36.75.06

Golf: UGOLINO GOLF CLUB, Via Chiantigiana (guest rates)

Tennis: Cascine

Ski-ing: many sports shops rent boots and skis. CIRRI on Via S Gallo 19–25 (red) is very good. Buses leave for Piazza S Maria Novella (SACA bus line) and Piazza della Stazione (LAZZI bus line) between 6 and 7.30 a.m. for Abetone in the mountains above Pistoia. Seats must be reserved a day or so in advance.

Seaside: during the summer a fast train (the Freccia del Tirreno) makes the trip from Florence to Viareggio in an hour. LAZZI and SITA buses go there too and on to Forte de' Marmi, Marina di Pietrasanta, and Ronchi in two hours.

30. YOUTH HOSTELS

VILLA CAMERATA, Viale Augusto Righi 2–4 – Tel. 610.300
OSTELLO S. MONACA, Via S. Monaca 6 – Tel. 29.67.04
CASA DELLO STUDENTE, Piazza Indipendenza, 15 – Tel. 47.15.81
Camping, Viale Michelangelo 80 – Tel. 663.938
TAVERNELLE, Val di Pesa – Tel. 827.009 (In the Chianti country) Via Roma 137

31. CONSULATES

GREAT BRITAIN, Lungarno Corsini 2 – Tel. 284.133
U.S.A., Lungarno Vespucci 38 – Tel. 298.276-7
FRANCE, Piazza S Trinita 1 – Tel. 23.509
GERMANY (WEST), Borgo SS Apostoli 22 – Tel. 29.47.22
SWITZERLAND, Via Tornabuoni 1 – Tel. 27.61.42

32. FESTIVALS, FAIRS, MARKETS, MUSICAL SERIES, ETC.

Scoppio del Carro, Piazza del Duomo, *Easter Sunday morning*

Mostra-Mercato dell' Artigianato (International Handicrafts Fair), Parterre, Piazza S Gallo late *April–May*

Festa del Grillo, Cascine, *Ascension Day*

Maggio Musicale (opera, theatre, concerts), *May–June*

Calcio in Costume (soccer game in costume), Piazza della Signoria, around *St John's Day (June 24th)*

Fireworks on St John's Day. Piazzale Michelangelo (best seen from the Fortezza di Belvedere or along the Arno), *June 24th* at 21.30

Festa delle Rificolone (children parade through the city with lighted lanterns to the SS Annunziata on the evening before the Virgin's Birthday), *September 8th*

Fiera degli Uccelli (Bird Fair), Porta Romana, *late September or early October*

Fair at Impruneta, usually late *September*

Saturday afternoon concerts (Amici della Musica), Teatro della Pergola, *October* through *April*

Winter Symphonic Series, Teatro Communale, *November* through *March*

Summer opera season in the Teatro Communale

Summer concert series in the cortile of the Palazzo Pitti

Bibliography

Chapter 1

ACTON, HAROLD, *The Last Medici*,
London, 1932
ARTOM-TREVES, GIULIANA, *The
Golden Ring*, London, 1955
*Atti del . . . convegno internazionale
per la pace e la civiltà cristiana*,
Florence 1952, 1953, 1954, 1955,
1956
BARON, HANS, *The Crisis of the Early
Italian Renaissance*, Princeton, 1955,
vol. 1, pp. 5–6, 49, 85–7, 117,
168–76, 338–409; vol. II, p. 493,
note 47
CHASTEL, ANDRÉ, *Art et Humanisme
au Temps de Laurent le Magnifique*,
Paris, 1959, p. 182
CONTINI, GIANFRANCO, *Poeti del
duecento*, Milan-Naples, 1960,
p. 414
FIUMI, ENRICO, 'La demografia
fiorentina nelle pagine di Giovanni
Villani', *Archivio Storico Italiano*,
CVIII (1950), pp. 78–158
GOETHE, J. W. VON, *Italienische Reise*,
ed. H. von Einem, Hamburg, 1954,
p. 113
GOMBRICH, ERNST, 'The Early Medici
as Patrons of Art', *Italian
Renaissance Studies*, London, 1960,
pp. 279–311
Illuminated Books of the Middle Ages,
Walters Art Gallery, Baltimore,
1949, no. 193
MACHIAVELLI, NICCOLÒ, *Istorie
fiorentine*, book VII, *Opere complete*,

Florence, 1843, pp. xii, 284–5,
1106–8
MOMMSEN, T. E., *Medieval and
Renaissance Studies*, Ithaca, 1959,
pp. 75, 83–4, 106f, 129
PAATZ, WALTER and ELIZABETH,
Die Kirchen von Florenz, Frankfurt
am Main, 1940–1954, vol. v, p. 50
RUSKIN, JOHN, 'The Vaulted Book',
Mornings in Florence, 1876,
(reprinted in Florence in 1945), p. 95
SCHEVILL, FERDINAND, *History of
Florence*, New York, 1936, pp.
220–2, 227–9, 282, 446
STENDAHL (Henri Beyle), *Rome,
Naples, et Florence*, Paris, 1826,
pp. 205–17
TAINE, HIPPOLYTE, *Voyage en Italie*,
Paris, 1874, vol. II, pp. 34, 93–4
VASARI, GIORGIO, *Le vite dei più
eccellent pittori, scultori e architettori*,
Florence, 1878–85, vol. II,
pp. 419–21
VESPASIANO DA BISTICCI, *Vite di
uomini illustri*, ed. P. D'Ancona and
E. Aeschlimann, Milan, 1951,
pp. 405–30
VILLANI, GIOVANNI, *Cronica*, book
VIII, chapter xxxvi; book XI,
chapter xciv
VILLARI, P., *La storia di Girolamo
Savonarola*, Florence, 1898, vol. I,
pp. 194, 200–3
WACKERNAGEL, MARTIN, *Der
Lebensraum des Künstlers in der
florentinischen Renaissance*, Leipzig,
1938, pp. 257–83

YOUNG, G. F., *The Medici*, London 1911, vol. II, p. 463

Chapter 2

ALBERTI, LEON BATTISTA, *Ten Books on Architecture*, facsimile edition of James Leoni with additional notes by J. Rykwert, London, 1955, book VIII, chapter vi

BALDINUCCI, FILIPPO, *Delle notizie de' professori del disegno da Cimabue in qua*, ed. Florence, 1770, vol. VI, p. 27; vol. VII, p. 94*f*

BEARZI, BRUNO, 'Considerazioni di tecnica sul S Ludovico e la Giuditta di Donatello', *Bollettino d'Arte*, XXXVI (1951), pp. 119–23

BERTI, LUCIANO, *Il principe dello Studiolo*, Florence, 1967

BOOTH, CECILY, *Cosimo I, Duke of Florence*, Cambridge, 1921, p. 247

BORGHINI, V., *Il Riposo*, Florence, 1584, pp. 164, 592–4, 639

BRAUNFELS, W., *Mittelalterliche Stadtbaukunst in der Toskana*, Berlin, 1953, pp. 96, 104, 166, 199, 204

CAVALCANTI, GIOVANNI, *Istorie fiorentine*, Florence, ed. 1839, book III, p. 77

CELLINI, BENVENUTO, *Ricordi, prose e poesie di B.C.*, Tassi ed., Florence, 1829, vol. II, pp. 474–5

CHASTEL, op. cit., p. 276

DAVIDSOHN, ROBERTO, *Firenze ai tempi di Dante*, Florence, 1929, pp. 476–7

DAVIDSOHN, ROBERT, *Forschungen zur Geschichte von Florenz*, Berlin, 1908, vol. IV, pp. 194, 499*ff*

Firenze, Touring Club Italiano, Milan, 1964, p. 118

FREY, KARL, *Die Loggia dei Lanzi*, Berlin, 1885, pp. 15–16, 31–5

GROTE, ANDREAS, *Das Dombauamt in Florenz 1285–1370*, Munich, 1961, *passim*, p. 30

Idem, 'Cellini in gara', *Il Ponte*, XIX (January 1963)

GUARNIERI, GINO, *I cavalieri di Santo Stefano*, Pisa, 1960, pp. 41–2

HEIKAMP, DETLEF, 'L'antica sistemazione degli strumenti scientifici nelle collezioni fiorentine', *Antichità Viva* (1970 – no. 6)

HEISS, A., *Les Médailleurs de la Renaissance*, Paris, 1881–7, vol. II, p. 32

HETZER, THEODOR, *Erinnerungen an italienische Architektur*, Godesburg, 1951, p. 94

JANSON, H. W., *The Sculpture of Donatello*, Princeton, 1957, vol. II, pp. 3, 41, 78, 198–201

KEUTNER, HERBERT, 'Der Giardino Pensile der Loggia dei Lanzi und seine Fontäne', *Kunstgeschichtliche Studien für Hans Kauffmann*, Berlin, 1956, pp. 241–4; 'Zu einigen Bildnissen des frühen Florentiner Manierismus', *Mitteilungen des Kunsthistorischen Institutes in Florenz*, vol. VIII, no. 3, (1959), pp. 149–50

LENSI, A., *Palazzo Vecchio*, Milan-Rome, 1929, pp. 8, 25–6, 35–40, 49, 60–1, 119, 202, 255–6, 264–9, 275–93

LIMBURGER, W., *Die Gebäude von Florenz*, Leipzig, 1910, pp. 12, 112, 173

MISSIRINI, M., *La Plazza del Granduca di Firenze*, Florence, 1830, p. 15

MOISÈ, FILIPPO, *Del Palazzo de' Priori: oggi Palazzo Vecchio*, Florence, 1843, pp. 52–4, 66, 81–2, note 1, 168

Mostra documentaria e iconografica di Palazzo Vecchio, Florence, 1957, fig. 21, p. 5

Notizi e Guida di Firenze, Piatti, 1841,

pp. 447–8 note 2

PAATZ, op. cit., vol. I, pp. 442–8; vol. V, p. 230

PAMPALONI, G., *Mostra documentaria e iconografica di Firenze al tempo di Dante*, Florence, 1959, p. 15

PANOFSKY, ERWIN, *Renaissance and Renascences in Western Art*, Stockholm, 1960, p. 170

PASSERINI, LUIGI, 'Del Monogramma di Cristo', *Curiosità storico-artistiche fiorentine*, Florence, 1866

PATRIZI, P.. *Il Giambologna*, Milan, 1905, pp. 39, 124, 139, 142

PAUL, JÜRGEN, *Der Palazzo Vecchio*, Florence, 1969, pp. 55 and passim

RODOLICO, FRANCESCO,*Le pietre delle città d'Italia*, Florence, 1953, pp. 10, 24–5, 236

SALVINI, ROBERTO, 'Una possible fonte medioevale di Leonardo e il suo autore,' *Studien zur toskanischen Kunst: Festschrift für Ludwig Heinrich Heydenreich*, Munich, 1964, pp. 266–74

SIEBENHÜNER, HERBERT, *Das Kapitol in Rome, Idee und Gestalt*, Munich, 1954, pp. 18, 28–9

SINIBALDI, GIULIA, *Il Palazzo Vecchio di Firenze*, Rome, 1950

TAINE, op. cit., p. 101

TOLNAY, CHARLES DE, *The Youth of Michelangelo*, Princeton, 1947, vol. 1, pp. 29–30, 93–7, 151–5; vol. III, pp. 98–103

VASARI, op, cit., vol. I, p. 603- note 1; vol. VII, p. 622; vol. VIII, pp. 530, 565

VILLANI, op. cit., book VIII, chap. 26

VILLANI, MATTEO, *Cronaca*, bk. III, chap. 58

WILDE, JOHANNES, 'The Hall of the Great Council of Florence', *Journal of the Warburg and Courtauld Institutes*, VIII (1944–5), pp. 65–81; 'Michelangelo and Leonardo', *Burlington Magazine*, XCV (1953), pp. 65–77; *Michelangelo's 'Victory'* (The Charlton Lecture), London, 1954

WILES, B. H., *The Fountains of Florentine Sculptors*, Cambridge (Mass.), 1933, pp. 13, 19, 50–4

WIND, EDGAR, 'Donatello's Judith: a Symbol of "Sanctimonia" ', *Journal of the Warburg and Courtauld Institutes*, I (1937–8), pp. 62–3

YOUNG, op. cit., vol. II, pp. 246, 252–3, 266–7, 278, 291–2, 299, 302,

Chapter 3

ARCINIEGAS, GERMÀN, *Amerigo and the New World*, New York, 1955, *passim*

ARGAN, GIULIO CARLO, 'The Architecture of Brunelleschi and the Origins of Perspective Theory in the Fifteenth Century', *Journal of the Warburg and Courtauld Institutes*, IX (1946), pp. 96–121

BECHERUCCI, L. and G. BRUNETTI, *Il Museo dell' Opera del Duomo*, 2 vols. Milan 1969–70

BALDINI, UMBERTO, 'L'orologio di Paolo Uccello nel Duomo di Firenze', *Commentari*, XXI (1970), pp. 44–50

BORSOOK, E., *The Mural Painters of Tuscany*, London, 1960, pp. 10, 149–50

BRAUNFELS, op. cit., pp. 22–3, 116–18, 129, 137, 143–7, 148–51, 154–6, 172–3, 216–30

CANTINI, LORENZO, *Saggi storici d'antichità toscane*, vol. III, Florence, 1796, pp. 118–20

CAVALLUCCI, C. J., *S Maria del Fiore*, Florence, 1881, pp. 26–30, 43, 49,

158–9, 181–2

CHASTEL, op. cit., pp. 121–2, 181–2

CRISPOLTI, V., *Santa Maria del Fiore alla luce dei documenti*, Florence, 1937, pp. 60–1, 348, 377–9, 449

DAVIDSOHN, *Firenze ai tempi di Dante*, op. cit., 20, 82, 92, 474, 477–8, 523

DAVIDSOHN, *Forschungen*, op. cit., vol. IV, pp. 194, 213, 396, 462, 509, 521; vol. V, pp. 322–3

DAVIDSOHN, *Geschichte von Florenz*, vol. I, Berlin, 1896, p. 18

FABRICZY, CORNEL VON,, *Filippo Brunelleschi*, Stuttgart, 1892, pp. 6, 79, 122–3

FREY, *op. cit.*, p. 464; Idem, *Scritte da M. Giorgio Vasari*, Munich, 1911, pp. 349–53

GAYE, GIOVANNI, *Carteggio inedito d'artisti dei secoli* XIV, XV, XVI, Florence, 1839, vol. I, p. 125; vol. II, pp. V–VII

GROTE ,op. cit., pp. 20, 28–9

GUAITA, MARIA LUIGIA (editor), *Firenze*, Florence, 1962, p. 24

HAFTMANN, W., 'Ein Mosaik der Ghirlandaio-Werkstatt aus dem Besitz des Lorenzo Magnifico', *Mitteilungen des Kunsthistorischen Institutes in Florenz*, VI (1940–1), pp. 98–108

HETZER, op. cit., p. 88

HOLMES, G., 'How the Medici became the Pope's Bankers,' *Renaissance Studies*, London, 1968, pp. 362*ff* and 373.

JANSON,, op. cit., vol. II, pp. 119–29, 225–8

KENNEDY, RUTH WEDGWOOD, *Alesso, Baldovinetti*, New Haven, 1938, pp. 113, 133–4

KIESOW, GOTTFRIED, 'Zur Baugeschichte des Florentiner Domes', *Mitteilungen des Kunsthistorischen Institutes in Florenz*, X (1961), pp. 1–22

KRAUTHEIMER, RICHARD, and TRUDE KRAUTHEIMER-HESS, *Lorenzo Ghiberti*, Princeton, 1956, pp. 4, 6, 31–46, 133–4, 197–8, 214, 234–44, 254–6, 315, 323

LAPINI, AGOSTINO, *Diario fiorentino*, Florence, ed. 1900, pp. 201, 203

LISNER, MARGRIT, *Luca della Robbia: Die Sängerkanzel*, Stuttgart, 1960, pp. 5–7, 14–19

LOPES PEGNA, MARIO, *Firenze dalle origini al medioevo*, Florence, 1962, pp. 165, 292, 299–307, 331

MAGUIRE, YVONNE, *The Women of the Medici*, London, 1927, pp. 55–6

MAMMI, D. M., *Ragionamento Istorico sovra i carri che si conducono al Tempio di S Gio. Battista di Firenze*, Florence, 1766, pp. 7–8

MARQUAND, ALLAN, *Luca della Robbia*, Princeton, 1914, pp. 3–7, 34–40, 183

MCCARTHY, MARY, *The Stones of Florence*, New York, 1959, p. 47

MEISS, MILLARD,*Painting in Florence and Siena after the Black Death*, Princeton, 1951, p. 49

MIDDELDORF, U., 'Ein Jugendwerk des Amadeo', *Kunstgeschichtliche Studien für Hans Kauffmann*, Berlin, 1956, pp. 136–42

MÜNTZ, EUGÈNE, *Les Précurseurs de la Renaissance*, Paris & London, 1882, p. 44

OFFNER, RICHARD, *A Critical and Historical Corpus of Florentine Painting*, section III, vol. V, New York, 1947, p. 94

PAATZ,, *Kirchen*, op. cit., vol. II, pp. 173–4, 196–202, 243; vol. III, pp. 25, 35–6, 329, 334–6, 369–85, 406, 431, 503; vol. IV, pp. 31, 194, 198, 302–5; vol. V, p. 35

PASSERINI, LUIGI, *Storia degli stabilmenti di beneficenza e d'istruzione elementare gratuita della città di Firenze*, Florence, 1853, pp. 8–9, 13

POGGI, GIOVANNI and I. B. SUPINO, 'La compagnia del Bigallo', *Rivista d'Arte*, II (1904), pp. 189–214

POGGI, GIOVANNI, *Catalogo del Museo dell' Opera del Duomo*, Florence, 1904, pp. 8–10

POPE-HENNESSY, JOHN, *Italian Gothic Sculpture*, London, 1955, pp. 14–16, 25, 53–5, 182, 185–7, 198, 218–19; *Italian Renaissance Sculpture*, London 1958, pp. 18–19, 43, 62–3, 267, 292, 294; *Paolo Uccello*, London, 1950, pp. 14, 144

PRAGER, FRANK D., 'Brunelleschi's Inventions and the Renewal of Roman Masonry Work', *Osiris*, IX (1950), pp. 457–554; 'Brunelleschi's Patent', *Journal of the Patent Office Society*, XXVIII (1946), pp. 109–35

SAXL, F., 'The Classical Inscription in Renaissance Art and Politics', *Journal of the Warburg and Courtaulds Institutes*, vol. IV (1940–1), p. 25

SCHEVILL, op. cit., p. 73

SINIBALDI, GIULIA, and GIULIA BRUNETTI, *Pittura del Duecento e Trecento: catalogo della mostra Giottesca di Firenze del* 1937, Florence, 1943, p. 365

TOLNAY, *Michelangelo*, op. cit., vol. V, Princeton, 1960, pp. 86–8, 149–50, 168–70

VASARI, op. cit., vol. II, pp. 378–9; vol. IV, pp. 305–9; vol. VII, pp. 243–4

VILLANI, GIOVANNI, op. cit., book VI, ch. 33; book VIII, chs. 3, 9

WACKERNAGEL, op. cit., pp. 24–43

Chapter 4

ACTON, op. cit., p. 194

AMMIRATO, SCIPIONE, *Istorie fiorentine*, ed. Florence, 1647, bk. VII, p. 358; bk. IX, p. 464; bk. XI, p. 606; bk. XIV, p. 765

ANTAL, F., *Florentine Painting and its Social Background*, London, 1948, pp. 67–70, 78, 92–3, 97–8, 126, 131-note 13, 149, 151

BALDINI, U. and L. BERTI, *Il mostra di affreschi staccati*, Florence, 1958, pp. 6–7, 63–4

BERNARDINO DA SIENA, *Le prediche volgari*, ed. Bianchi, 3 vols., Siena, 1888

Idem., Bib. Naz., Florence, *MSS. Conventi Soppressi*, F. VI., 1329, fol. 37.

BIGAZZI, F., *Iscrizion e memorie della città di Firenze*, Florence, 1886, pp. 89–90, 180, 201, 350–1, 354, 369, 374

BORSOOK, op. cit., pp. 64, 131–2

BRAUNFELS, op. cit., pp. 22, 33, 148–50, 187, 190

BRUCKER, G. A., *Florentine Politics and Society* 1342–1378, Princeton, 1962, pp. 46–8, 74, 110–11, 132–3, 145, 313–14

BURGER, F., *Geschichte des florentinischen Grabmals*, Strassburg, 1904, pp. 42, 44, 84–7, 137

CANTINI, L., *Legislazione toscana*, Florence, 1802, vol. IV, pp. 46, 304–5

CAROCCI, G., *Firenze scomparsa*, Florence, 1878, pp. 77*f*; 'I Tabernacoli di Firenze', *Arte e Storia*, XXIV (1905), pp. 7–8, 27–8

CAVALCANTI, op. cit., vol. I, pp. ix-note 16, xxi; vol. II, p. 498

CHIARINI, MARCO, 'Il Maestro del Chiostro degli Aranci' etc., *Proporzioni*, IV (1963), pp. 1–24

COCCHI, A., *Notizie storiche intorno antiche imagini di Nostra Donna che hanno culto in Firenze*, Florence,

1894, pp. 123–4

CORAZZINI, G. O., 'Diario fiorentino di Bartolommeo di Michele del Corazza (1405–38)', *Archivio Storico Italiano*, serie V, vol. XIV (1894), p. 241

D A V I D S O H N, *Firenze ai tempi di Dante*, op. cit., pp. 11, 45–6, 51–3, 60, 112, 150–1, 163–9, 222–3, 267–8; *Geschichte*, op. cit., vol. II, part I, pp. 112, 122–3, 129–35, 150–1, 163, 168–9; vol. IV, part II pp. 52–9 64–6; *Storia di Firenze*, vol. V, ed. Sansoni, Florence, 1962, pp. 322–3

DURANTI, FRANCESCO, Appendix in Donato Velluti's *Cronaca di Firenze*, Florence, 1731, p. 148

Firenze, Touring Club Italiano, op. cit., p. 133

FORTUNA, A.M., *Andrea del Castagno*, Florence, 1958, p. 109

FRANCIONI, DOMENICO, *Storia Del SS Miracolo seguito in Firenze nel 1230 nella ven. Chiesa di S Ambrogio*, Florence, 1875, pp. 34–5, 133

FREY, *Loggia dei Lanzi*, op. cit., p. 71

GAMBA, C., *Il Museo Horne a Firenze*, Florence, 1961

GARNERI, A., *Firenze e dintorni*, San Casciano, 1924, pp. 142, 147, 148, 166, 249–54, 258–9, 261–2

GEMELLI, A., *Il Francescanesimo*, 7th ed., Milan, 1956, pp. 5–30, 36, 46, 101, 104

GRIFI, E., *Saunterings in Florence*, 8th ed., Florence, 1930–1, p. 369

HALL, M. B., 'The "Tramezzo" in S Croce, Florence and Domenico Veneziano's Fresco,' *Burlington Magazine*, CXII (1970), pp. 797–9

HETZER, op. cit., p. 42

JANSON, op. cit., vol. II, pp. 7–12, 44–8

KENNEDY, op. cit., pp. 166, 192–3

KAUFFMANN, G., *Florenz*, Stuttgart, 1962, pp. 194–8, 210, 320–1, 345

LASCHI, G., P. ROSELLI and P. A.

ROSSI, 'Indagini sulla Cappella dei Pazzi', *Commentari*, XIII (1962), pp. 24–41

LIMBURGER, op. cit., pp. 3, 28, 37, 45, 55, 82, 96, 123, 143, 152, 159–60

MARCHINI, G., *I palazzi del popolo nei comuni toscani del medio evo*, Milan, 1962, pp. 155–6

MARTINI, G., *Mostra documentaria e iconografica del Palazzo del Podestà (Bargello)*, Florence, 1963, pp. 3-16, 19, 21, 29, 33

MASI, G., 'La pittura infamante nella legislazione e nella vita del comune Fiorentino, Sec. XIII–XVI', *Studi di diritto commerciale in onore di Cesare Vivante*, Rome, 1931, pp. 23–5

MOISÈ, F., *Santa Croce di Firenze*, Florence, 1845, pp. 73, 114–17, 125, 152–3, 165, 319, 437

OFFNER, *Corpus*, op. cit., sec. IV, vol. II, p.97

ORIGO, IRIS, *The Merchant of Prato*, London, 1957, pp. 68–9, 75; *The World of San Bernardino*, London, 1963, pp. 35, 41, 127, 183

ORZALESI,, O., *Della chiesa di S Ambrogio in Firenze e dei suoi restauri*, Florence, 1900

L'osservatore fiorentino, vol. V, Florence, 1821, pp. 5–6, 10–11, 48, 53–5, 123–5

PAATZ, *Kirchen*, op. cit., vol. I, pp. 284, 291, 502, 507–8, 523, 536, 542, 544; vol. II, pp. 103, 131, 359*ff*; vol. III, pp. 304, 311, 591; vol. IV, pp. 359*ff*, 690–2; V, pp. 5–6; 'Zur Baugeschichte des Palazzo Podestà (Bargello) in Florenz', *Mitteilungen des Kunsthistorischen Institutes in Florenz*, III (1919–32), 287–321

PAGNINI DEL VENTURA, G., *Della decima e delle altre gravezze*, etc., Lisbon and Lucca, 1766 vol. IV., pp. 170–1

POPE-HENNESSY, *Italian Gothic Sculpture*, op. cit., p. 196; *Italian Renaissance Sculpture*, op. cit., pp. 35, 41–4, 267, 276, 294, 297–9, 305; *Italian High Renaissance and Baroque Sculpture*, London, 1863, vol. I, pp. 61–2

PROCACCI, UGO, *La Casa Buonarroti*, Milan, 1965, p. 5.

RIDOLFI, ROBERTO, *La stampa in Firenze nel secolo XV*, Florence, 1958, pp. 14–20

RONDONI, GIUSEPPE, 'I giustiziati a Firenze del secolo XV al secolo XVIII', *Archivio Storico Italiano*, XVIII (1901), pp. 222–35

ROSS, JANET, *Florentine Palaces and their Stories*, London, 1905, pp. 116–19, 146–9, 208–33

ROSSI, FILIPPO, *Il Museo Horne*, Milan, 1966

SAALMAN, H., 'Filippo Brunelleschi: Capital Studies', *Art Bulletin* XV-2 (June 1958), pp. 127–9, 135; 'The Authorship of the Pazzi Palace', *Art Bulletin*, XLVI (1964), pp. 388–94

SALMI, M., *Andrea del Castagno*, Novara, 1961, pp. 56–7

SALVINI, R., *Botticelli*, Milan, 1958, vol. II, p. 69

SANPAOLESI, PIERO, 'Costruzioni del primo quattrocento nella Badia fiorentina', *Rivista d'arte*, XXIV (1942)), pp. 143–79

SCAIFE, WALTER, *Florentine Life During the Renaissance*, Baltimore, 1893, p. 140

SCHEVILL, op. cit., pp. 40, 99–102, 158*ff*

SHORR, DOROTHY C., *The Christ Child in Devotional Images in Italy during the XIV Century*, New York, 1954

TAMASSIA, NINO, *La famiglia italiana nei secoli decimoquinto e decimosesto*, Milan, 1910, pp. 146–8

TINTORI, L. and E. BORSOOK, *Giotto: the Peruzzi Chapel*, New York, 1965

TOLNAY,, *Michelangelo*, op. cit., vol. I, pp. 8, 11, 41, 126, 129

TORRICELLI, CESARE, *Da Firenze a Firenze*, Florence, 1929, pp. 364–6

VILLANI, MATTEO, op. cit., bk. III, chap. 43

bk. III, chap. 43

WILES, op. cit., p. 88

WITTKOWER, RUDOLF, *Architectural Principles in the Age of Humanism*, 3rd ed., London, 1962, p. 39; *Art and Architecture in Italy, 1600 to 1750*, Harmondsworth, 1958, p. 258

Chapter 5

AMMIRATO, op. cit., bk. XIX, p. 1022

ANTAL, op. cit., pp. 73–4, 79–80, 84–9, 87

ARCINIEGAS, op. cit., pp. 4–11, 25–6, 80

BALDINI and BERTI, op. cit., p. 5

BARGELLINI, P., *Aspetti minori di Firenze*, Florence, 1958, p. 29

BECKER M., 'Church and State in Florence on the Eve of the Renaissance (1343–82)', *Speculum*, XXXVIII (1962), pp. 509–27

BORSOOK, op. cit., pp. 140–1, 143–4, 147–8, 158–9, 160–2

Idem., 'Documents for Filippo Strozzi's Chapel in S Maria Novella and other Related Papers,' *Burlington Magazine*, Nov.–Dec., 1970, pp. 737–45, 800–4.

BRAUNFELS, op. cit., p. 92

BROCKHAUS, E.. *Ricerche sopra alcuni capolavori d'arte fiorentina*, Milan, 1902, pp. 83–100

BRUCKER, op. cit., pp. 9-note 26, 32–3

BURGER, op. cit., *passim*

CAROCCI, op. cit., pp. 56–9

BIBLIOGRAPHY

DAVIDSOHN, *Firenze ai tempi di Dante,* op. cit., pp. 134, 214–19; *Geschichte,* op. cit., vol. IV, pt. 2, pp. 54–9

DOREN, A., *Die Florentiner Wollentuchindustrie,* Stuttgart, 1901, vol. I, pp. 28–9, 34, 87, 109

EDLER, F., *Glossary of Medieval Terms of Business,* Cambridge (Mass.), 1934, pp. 409, 419

FRIEDMAN, DAVID, 'The Burial Chapel of Filippo Strozzi in S Maria Novella in Florence,' *L'Arte,* IX (March 1970), pp. 108–31

JANSON, H. W., 'Ground Plan and Elevation in Masaccio's Trinity', *Essays in the History of Art presented to Rudolf Wittkower,* London, 1967, pp. 83–8.

KAUFFMANN, op. cit., pp. 223, 272–3

LAMI, G., *Lezioni di antichità toscane e specialmente della città di Firenze,* Florence, 1766, vol. II, pp. 614–17

LAUTS, JAN, *Domenico Ghirlandaio,* Vienna, 1943, pp. 48–9

LIMBURGER, op. cit., p. 130

MARCUCCI, LUISA, 'Del polittico di Ognissanti di Giovanni da Milano', *Antichità Viva,* no. 4, vol. 1 (1962), pp. 11–19

MARIOTTI, F., *Storia del lanificio toscano,* Turin, 1864, pp. 26–7, 41–4

MARRI, G. C., *Mostra documentaria e iconografica degli antichi ponti di Firenze,* Florence, 1961, pp. 3–6

MEISS, op. cit., pp. 9–14, 57–79, 83, 99–104, 160–3

MONTI, G. M., *Le confraternite medievali dell' alta e media Italia,* 2 vols., Venice, 1927

OFFNER, *Corpus,* op. cit., sec. III, vol. V, pp. 88–92; sec. IV, vol. II, pp. 47–9

ORIGO, *The Merchant of Prato,* op. cit., pp. 59–75; *The World of San Bernardino,* op. cit., p. 201

ORLANDI, S., *S Maria Novella e i suoi chiostri monumentali,* Florence, 1956, pp. 3–19, 24, 28–31, 43–8, 57, 60–2; 'La cappella e la Compagnia della Purità in Santa Maria Novella di Firenze', *Memorie domenicane,* II–III (1958), pp. 3–11

ORZALESI, op. cit., p. 7

PAATZ, *Kirchen,* op. cit., vol. II, p. 131; vol. IV, pp. 406–44

PAGNINI DEL VENTURA, op. cit., vol. III, 1766, pp. 261–3

PANELLA, A., 'Politica ecclesiastica del comune fiorentino dopo la cacciata del Duca d'Atene', *Archivio Storico Italiano,* LXXI (1913), p. 318

PANOFSKY, E., 'A Letter to St Jerome', etc., *Studies in Art and Literature for Belle Da Costa Greene,* Princeton, 1954, pp. 102–3

PICCHI, G., 'Tabernacoli fiorentini', *Illustrazione Toscana e dell' Etruria,* Serie II – Anno X (September 1932), pp. 8–15

POPE-HENNESSY, *Italian Renaissance Sculpture,* op. cit., pp. 35, 267, 298–9

SCHEVILL, op. cit., pp. 97–8

SCHLEGEL, URSULA, 'Observations on Masaccio's Trinity Fresco in S Maria Novella', *Art Bulletin,* XLV (1963), pp. 19–33

VASARI-MILANESI, op. cit., vol. III, p. 261

VON SIMSON, OTTO, Lecture on the Trinity, Kunsthistorisches Institute, September 7th, 1965

WITTKOWER, *Architectural Principles,* op. cit., pp. 41–7

WOOD-BROWN, J., *The Dominican Church of Santa Maria Novella,* Edinburgh, 1902, pp. 3–18, 55–71, 82–3, 90–1, 145

Chapter 6

ABBONDANZA, R., *Mostra documentaria e iconografica della fabbrica degli Uffizi*, Florence, 1958, 1958, pp. 3–5

ACKERMAN, J. S., *The Architecture of Michelangelo*, London, 1961 (catalogue volume), p. 144

ALINARI, V. and A. BELTRAMELLI, *L'Arno*, Florence, 1909, pp. 115–19

ALMAGIÀ, R., 'Il primato di Firenze negli studi geografici durante i secoli XV e XVI', *Atti della Società Italiana per il Progresso delle Scienze*, XVIII (1929), 6–9, 14–19

BALDACCINI, R., *Il Ponte Vecchio*, Florence, 1947, pp. 10–11, 28

BANDINI, ANGELO MARIA, *Vita di Amerigo Vespucci*, Florence, 1898, p. 19

BARATTA, M., *Leonardo da Vinci negli studi per la navigazione dell' Arno*, Rome, 1905, pp. 4–6

BAROCCHI, PAOLA, 'Il Vasari architetto', *Atti dell' Accademia Pontaniana*, VI (1956), pp. 113–36

BARTOLI, L. and E. A. MASER, *Il museo dell' opificio delle pietre dure di Firenze*, Prato, 1953

BEAZLEY, C. R., *The Dawn of Modern Geography*, vol. III Oxford, 1906, pp. 288f, 324–6

CANTINI, op. cit., vol. VI, p. 305

CAROCCI, op. cit., pp. 54–61, 69–73, 77, 82–3

CELLINI, op. cit., vol. III, p. 272

CHURCHILL, S. J. A. and G. C. E. BUNT, *The Goldsmiths of Italy*, London, 1926, pp. 31, 67.

CINI, F., *L'Argonautica*, etc., Florence, 1608

CLARK, K., *A Catalogue of the Drawings of Leonardo da Vinci . . . at Windsor Castle*, Cambridge, 1935, pp. 142–3; *Leonardo da Vinci*,

Cambridge, 1952, pp. 58–9, 86, 131–2

CODAZZI, ANGELA, *Storia delle carte geografiche*, Milan, 1958, pp. 86–7, 96–7

DAMI, L. and B. BARBADORO, *Firenze di Dante*, Florence, 1921, pp. 7–8

DAVIDSOHN, *Firenze ai tempi di Dante*, op. cit., pp. 11, 442–3, 457, 492–5; *Forschungen*, op. cit., vol. IV, p. 290; *Geschichte*, op. cit., vol. IV, part 2, pp. 31, 271–2

DE BROSSES, CHARLES, *Selections from the Letters of de Brosses*, ed. Lord Gower, London, 1897, vol. I, p. 261

DEL BADIA, IODOCO, *Miscellanea fiorentina*, vol.. II, Florence, 1902, pp. 3–7, 191

DORINI, U., 'Come sorse la fabbrica degli Uffizi', *Rivista Storica degli Archivi Toscani*, V (1933), pp. 1–9, 20

EDLER, op. cit., p. 419

ETTLINGER, L. D., 'A Fifteenth-Century View of Florence', *Burlington Magazine*, XCIV (1952), pp. 160–7

FAVARO, ANTONIO, *Galileo Galilei*, Milan, 1939, pp. 10–11, 19

Firenze, Touring Club Italiano, op. cit., pp. 246–8, 255

'Firenze: sviluppo e problemi urbanistici', *Urbanistica*, XXIII (No. 12–1953), p. 14

FOLLI, I., *I ponti e le porte di Firenze*, Florence, 1904, p. 2

FOLLINI, V. and MODESTO RASTRELLI, *Firenze Antica, e Moderna*, vol. I, Florence, 1802, p. 400

FRANCESCHINI, P., *Relazione delle Feste fatte in Firenz sopra il ghiaccio del fiume Arno il 31 Dicembre*, 1604, Florence, 1885

FRANCHI, A., *Ponte a Santa Trinita*, Florence, 1957, pp. 14, 42, 51–2

FREY, *Loggia dei Lanzi*, op. cit., p. 5

GRIFI, op. cit., pp. 343–4, 368–9, 399

GUAITA, op. cit., *passim*

GUCCERELLI, D., *Stradario storico biografico della città di Firenze*, Florence, 1929, pp 48–9

HEIKAMP, DETLEF, 'La Tribuna degli Uffizi come era nel Cinquecento,' *Antichità Viva*, III–3 (May 1964), pp. 11–30

HONOUR, HUGH, 'The Palazzo Corsini, Florence', *Connoisseur*, CXXXVIII (1956), pp. 160–5

IMBERT, G., *La vita fiorentina nel seicento*, Florence, 1906, chapter IX

KRAUTHEIMER, op. cit., p. 13

KRIEGBAUM, F., 'Michelangelo e il ponte a S Trinita', *Rivista d'Arte*, XXIII (1941), p. 139

KRIS, ERNST, *Meister und Meisterwerke der Steinschneidekunst in der italienischen Renaissance*, Vienna, 1929

LABARTE, JULES, *Historire des Arts Industriels*, Paris, vol. II, 1864, pp. 277, 391–2, 403, 408, 416, 421, 423, 456–7, 508–11

LAPINI, op. cit., pp. 104, 145, 152–3

LEONARDO DA VINCI, *Trattato della Pittura*, ed. A. Borzelli, Lanciano, 1913, vol. I, p. 30

LIMBURGER, op. cit., pp. 30–2, 119, 124–5

LOPES PEGNA, op. cit., p. 13–14

MANNI, D. M., *Della Vecchiezza Sovraggrande del Ponte Vecchio di Firenze*, Florence, 1763, p. 18

MARCUCCI, LUISA, *Gallerie Nazionali di Firenze: I Dipinti Toscani del secolo XIV*, Rome, 1965, pp. 11–13 and *passim*

MARRI, op. cit., pp. 3–7, 25–7

ORR, M. A., *Dante and the Early Astronomers*, London, 1956, p. 102

PAATZ, *Kirchen*, op. cit., vol. II, pp. 381–94

PAGNINI DEL VENTURA, op. cit.,

vol. II, p. 36

PAPINI, R., 'Il nostro ponte tale e quale', *La Nazione*, August 3, 1957, p. 5

PASSERINI, LUIGI, *Gli Alberti di Firenze*, Florence, 1869, vol. I, pp. 11–13

PELLEGRINI, CARLO, *La Contessa d'Albany e il salotto del Lungarno*, Naples, 1951

PRAGER, 'Brunelleschi's Patent', op. cit., 120–1

PREZZINER, G., *Storia del pubblico studio e delle società scientifiche e letterarie di Firenze*, vol. II, Florence, 1810, pp. 29*f*, 38

RICHTER, J. P., *The Literary Works of Leonardo da Vinci*, London, 1939, vol. II, pp. 181–3

RILLI, JACOPO, *Notizie . . . intorno agli uomini illustri dell' Accademia Fiorentina*, Florence, 1700, pp. xvii–xix

RODOLICO, op. cit., p. 245

ROSS, op. cit., pp. 31–7, 42, 151–4, 307–8, 314–15

SALMI, MARIO, *Masaccio*, Milan, 1948, pp. 138–9

SALVINI, ROBERTO, *La galleria degli Uffizi: catalogo dei dipinti*, Florence, 1952

SANDBERG-VAVALÀ, EVELYN, *Uffizi Studies*, Florence, 1948

SCHEVILL, op. cit., pp. 105*ff*, 133–44, 265–83, 347–8, 490*f*

Stradario storico e amministrativo della città e del comune di Firenze, Florence, 1929, pp. 27, 32

TINGHI, CESARE, 'Diario e cerimoniale della corte medicea, etc.', Bib. Naz. Firenze, *MSS. Fondo Gino Capponi*, 261, vol. I, c. 221

UZIELLI, GUSTAVO, *La vita e i tempi di Paolo dal Pozzo Toscanelli*, Rome, 1894, pp. 7, 11, 376, 391–3, 527, 569–75, 580–6

BIBLIOGRAPHY

VASARI-MILANESI, *Vite*, op. cit., vol.
II, p. 593; vol. VI, p. 62–3
VASARI, G. and A. CONDIVI, *Le vite di
Michelangelo Buonarroti*, ed. K.
Frey, Berlin, 1887, pp. 56–61, 136–7
VILLANI, op. cit., book VIII, ch. 70
VODOZ, EDUARD, 'Studien zum
architektonischen Werk des
Bartolomeo Ammannati',
*Mitteilungen des Kunsthistorischen
Institutes in Florenz*, VI (1941), pp.
3–4
YOUNG, op. cit., vol. II, pp. 347*f*, 378,
405*f*, 441–3

Chapter 7

ANTAL, op. cit., pp. 36, 74, 224
ALBERTI, *Ten Books on Architecture*,
op. cit., bk. V, chs. III, XIV
AVERARDO DEGLI ALBERTI to
GIOVANNI DI COSIMO DE MEDICI,
letter of 23rd March, 1443,
Archivio di Stato, Florence, M.A.P.,
Filza IX, n. 558
BALDACCINI, RENZO, 'S Trinita nel
periodo gotico', *Rivista d'Arte*,
XXVII (1951–2), p. 73
BERNARDINO DA SIENA, op. cit., vol.
I, p. xxii; vol. III, pp. 206–9, 232,
240, 250
BERTI, LUCIANO, *Palazzo Davanzati*,
Florence, 1958, p. 8
BIAGI, GUIDO, *The Private Life of the
Renaissance Florentines*, Florence,
1896, 0p. 32
BINI, G. and P. BIGAZZI (editors), *Vita
di Filippo Strozzi il vecchio scritta da
Lorenzo suo figlio con documenti*,
etc., Florence, 1851
BOMBE, WALTER, 'Die Novelle der
Kastellanis von Vergi in einer
Freskofolge des Palazzo Davizzi-
Davanzati zu Florenz' *Mitteilungen
des Kunsthistorischen Institutes in*

Florenz, voll II (1912–17), p. 2; 'Una
Casa Medioevale Fiorentina', *Vita
d'Arte* (1911), pp. 2–4
BORSOOK, 1960, op. cit., pp. 32, 141–2,
159–62
BRAUNFELS, op. cit., pp. 5, 101, 207,
211–14, 215
BRUCKER, op. cit., pp. 16, 23, 99–101,
134, 368–70, 382; 'The Medici in the
Fourteenth Century', *Speculum*,
XXXII (1957), pp. 1–26
BRUNETTI, GIULIA, 'Una testa di
Donatello, *L'arte*, 1969, pp. 81–94
CANESTRINI, GIUSEPPE, *La scienza e
l'arte di stato . . . della repubblica
fiorentina e dei Medici*, Florence,
1862, p. 149
CAROCCI, G., *Palazzo Davanzati*,
Florence, 1910, p. 9
CHASTEL, op. cit., p. 163
CLAYTON, SIR RICHARD, *Memoirs of
the House of Medici, etc.*, from the
French of M. Tenhove, Bath, 1797,
vol. I, pp. 401–2-note
COHN, WERNER,'Franco Sacchetti und
das ikonographische Programm der
Gewölbemalereien von Orsan-
michele', *Mitteilungen des
Kunsthistorischen Institutes in
Florenz*, VIII (1958), pp. 65–7, 74;
'Zur Ikonographie der Glasfenster
von Orsanmichele', *Mitteilungen des
Kunsthistorischen Institutes in
Florenz*, IX (1959), pp. 1–12
DAMI and BARBADORI, op. cit., pp.
53–5, 118, 126–7, 141
DAVIDSOHN, *Firenze ai tempi di Dante*,
op. cit., pp. 172–5, 465–7
DEL LUNGO, ISIDORO, *La donna
fiorentina del buon tempo antico*,
Florence, 1906, pp. 52–3
DOMINICI (BEATO), GIOVANNI,
Regolo del governo di cura familiare,
ed. D. Salvi, Florence, 1860, part IV,
pp. 130–3, 154–8, 164, 185
DOREN, A., *Le arti fiorentine*, Florence,

364

1940, vol. I, pp. 5, 183ff, 242; vol. II, p. 237

DORINI, U., 'Il Palagio dell' Arte della Lana', *Rassegna Nazionale* (May 16th, 1905), p. 5; *Notizie storiche sull' università di Parte Guelfa in Firenze*, Florence, 1902, pp. 3–9, 34–41

EVANS, ALLAN, *Francesco Balducci Pegolotti: La pratica della mercatura*, Cambridge (Mass.), 1936, pp. 360–1, 374, 378

FRANCESCHINI, P., *L'oratorio di San Michele in Orto*, Florence, 1892, pp. 17–18, 87–92

FREY, *Loggia dei Lanzi*, op. cit., p. 1

GARNERI, op. cit., pp. 82–3, 121

GIACCHI, PIRRO, *Dizionario del vernacolo fiorentino*, Florence-Rome, 1878, p. 76

GIOVANNOZZI, VERA, 'La vita di Bernardo Buontalenti scritta da Gherardo Silvani', *Rivista d'Arte*, XIV (1932), pp. 505, 524; 'Ricerche su Bernardo Buontalenti', *Rivista d'Arte*, XV (1933), pp. 299–327

GLASSER, HANNELORE, 'The Litigation concerning Luca della Robbia's Federighi Tomb,' *Mitteilungen des Kunsthistorischen Institutes in Florenz*, XIV (1969), pp. 1–32

GOMBRICH, op. cit., pp. 307–8

Idem., 'From the Revival of Letters to the Reform of the Arts.' *Essays in the History of Art Presented to R. Wittkower*, London, 1967, pp. 71–82

GUAITA, op. cit., p. 211

GUCCERELLI, op. cit., pp. 89, 124, 251, 301, 384

GUTKIND, CURT, *Cosimo de' Medici*, Florence, 1940, pp. 8, 11–12, 70-note 1, 50, 56-note 1

GUZZONI DEGLI ANCARANI, CARLA, *La cronica domestica toscana dei secoli xiv e xv*, Lucca, 1920, pp. 89, 130, 141–2, 159–62, 165, 169–70

HAFTMANN, W., *Das italienische Säulenmonument*, Leipzig and Berlin, 1939, pp. 138–41

HEYDENREICH, L. H,. 'Die Cappella Rucellai von San Pancrazio in Florenz', *Essays in Honor of Erwin Panofsky*, vol. I, New York, 1961, pp. 219–29

JANSON, 1957, op. cit., pp. 18–19, 49–50

KAUFFMANN, op. cit., pp. 301–2, 311–13, 378–80

KRAUTHEIMER, op. cit., pp. 71–100

LANDUCCI, LUCA, *Diario fiorentino dal 1450 al 1516*, ed. I. del Badia, Florence, 1883, pp. 57–9

LAPINI, op. cit., p. 27

LENKEITH, NANCY, *Dante and the Legend of Rome*, London, 1952, pp. 19, 92

LENSI, op. cit., pp. 40–4

LIMBURGER, op. cit., pp. 18, 85, 112–13, 131–2, 164–5

LISNER, MARGRIT, 'Zur frühen Bildhauer-Architektur Donatellos', *Münchener Jahrbuch der Bildenden Kunst*, IX–X (1958–9), pp. 72–127

LITTA,, F., *Famiglie celebri italiane*, series I, vol. V, plates I, IX, XVIII

LOPES PEGNA, op. cit., pp. 18, 83, 132–8, 332–4

LOPEZ, ROBERT S. and IRVING, W. RAYMOND, *Medieval Trade in the Mediterranean World*, New York, 1955, pp. 423–4

MAGUIRE, op. cit., pp. 6, 13, 34, 38, 51–2, 61, 72–3, 103, 157

MARCHINI, GIUSEPPE, 'Aggiunte a Michelozzo', *La Rinascita*, VII (1944), pp. 24–51; *Le vetrate italiane*, Milan, 1956, p. 228

MARCOTTI, FILIPPO, 'Dell' arte e del commercio della paglia da cappelli, etc.', *Atti dei Georgofili*, N.S., I (1853), pp. 5–9

MARCOTTI, G., *Un mercante fiorentino*

e la sua famiglia, Florence, 1881, pp. 10–16, 81–7

MARKS, L. F., 'The Financial Oligarchy in Florence under Lorenzo', *Italian Renaissance Studies*, London, 1960, pp. 125, 128*f*

MARQUAND, ALLAN, *Giovanni della Robbia*, Princeton, 1920, pp. 15–17

MASI, BARTOLOMEO, *Ricordanze . . . dal 1478 al 1526*, ed. G. O. Corazzini, Florence, 1906, p. 14

MEISS, op. cit., p. 78*ff* and *passim*

MORPURGO, S., 'Bruto, "il Buon Giudice", nell' udienza dell' Arte Arte della Lana in Firenze', *Miscellanea di Storia dell' Arte in Onore di I. B. Supino*, Florence 1933, pp. 141–63

OFFNER, R., 'A Ray of Light on Giovanni del Biondo and Niccolò di Tommaso', *Mitteilungen des Kunsthistorischen Institutes in Florenz*, VII (1956), pp. 182–7; *Corpus*, op. cit., sec. III, vol. II, part I, p. 104; sec. III, vol. VI, p. 106; sec. IV, vol. II, p. 39

ORIGO, *The Merchant of Prato*, op. cit., pp. 59, 87, 149*f*, 154–5, 178–9, 200, 225, 254–9, 265, 270, 274–6, 280–2, 288

Idem., 'The Domestic Enemy: the Eastern Slaves in Tuscany in the Fourteenth and Fifteenth Centuries,' *Speculum*, XXX (1955), pp. 321–66

PAATZ, *Kirchen*, op. cit., vol. I, pp. 228–57, 411–12,; vol. III, pp. 615–27, 632, 645; vol. IV, pp. 168–9, 482–6, 508; vol. V, pp. 213–16, 219, 278*f*, 289, 310, 313, 355

PAGNINI DEL VENTURA, op. cit., vol. II, pp. 116, 124

PAOLO DA CERTALDO, *Libro di buoni costumi*, ed. A. Schiaffini, Florence, 1945, ch. 155, pp. 126–8

PATZAK, BERNHARD, *Die Renaissance- und Barockvilla in Italien*, vol. II, Leipzig, 1913, pp. 29, 49, 150

POGGI, GIOVANNI, *La cappella e la tomba di Onofrio Strozzi nella chiesa di Santa Trinita* (1419–23), Florence, 1903, pp. 8–13

POLIDORI CALAMANDREI, E., *Le vesti delle donne fiorentine nel Quattrocento*, Florence, 1924, pp. 64–7, 94, 113–4

POPE-HENNESSY, *Italian Gothic Sculpture*, op. cit., pp. 53, 219; *Italian Renaissance Sculpture*, op. cit., pp. 7, 28–9, 47, 295

ROSS, op. cit., pp. 1–9, 43, 47

RUCELLAI, GIOVANNI *Giovanni Rucellai ed il suo zibaldone*, ed. A. Perosa, London, 1960, vol. I, pp. 23–4, 60, 117

SAALMAN, HOWARD, 'Florence Santa Trinita I and II, etc.', *Journal of the Society of Architectural Historians*, XXI, no. 4 (Dec. 1962), pp. 179–87

SANDBERG-VAVALÀ, EVELYN, *Studies in the Florentine Churches*, Florence, 1959, pp. 6–13

SAPORI, ARMANDO, *Studi di storia economica medievale*, Florence, 2nd ed., 1946, p. 642

SCHEVILL, op. cit., pp. 30–43, 46, 143, 153, 208, 268–82, 307, 400*ff*

SCHIAPARELLI, ATTILIO, *La casa fiorentina e i suoi arredi*, Florence, 1908

STEGMAN, CARL VON and HEINRICH VON GEYMÜLLER, *Die Architektur der Renaissance in Toscana*, Munich, 1885–1908, vol. IV, pp. 6–7, 15; vol. VII, pp. 14–16

STROZZI, ALESSANDRA
 MACINGHI NEGLI, *Lettere di una gentildonna fiorentina*, ed. C. Guasti, Florence, 1887, pp. 5, 14–22, 110–11, 116–18, 154–5, 180–1, 475, 493

STROZZI, LORENZO, *Vita di Filippo di Matteo Strozzi*, ed. by G. Bini and P. Bigazzi, Florence, 1851, pp. 25–8, 31–2, 42, 45–6, 65–6, 71

UGURGIERI DELLA BERARDENGA, CURZIO, *Gli Acciaioli di Firenze nella luce dei loro tempi*, 2 vols., Florence, 1962

VASARI-MILANESI, *Vite*, op. cit., vol. II, pp. 371–2; vol. IV, pp. 443–8; vol. V, pp. 350–2

VENTURI, A., *Storia dell' arte italiana*, Milan, 1923, vol. IV, pp. 443–8; vol. VIII, part I, pp. 416–20; vol. XI, part 2, pp. 455–6, 493*ff*

VESPASIANO DA BISTICCI, op. cit., pp. 387–98

VILLANI, op. cit., bk. XI, ch. xcii

VOLPI, GUGLIELMO, 'Affeti di famiglia nel Quattrocento', *Vita Nuova*, II (1891), p. 9

WARBURG, ABY, *Gesammelte Schriften*, Leipzig-Berlin, 1932, vol. I, pp. 146–51, 161–2

WILES, op. cit., p. 100

WITTKOWER, *Art and Architecture in Italy*, 1600 *to* 1750, op. cit., p. 361

WOODWARD, W. H., *Studies in Education during the Age of the Renaissance*, 1400–1600, Cambridge, 1906, pp. 59–61

YOUNG, op. cit., vol. II, p. 238

ZOBI, ANTONIO, *Notizie storiche sull' origine e progressi dei lavori di commesso in pietre dure, etc.*, Florence, 1853, pp. 105–7

Chapter 8

ACKERMAN, op. cit., vol. I, pp. XXX, 15, 22, 41–3; vol. II, pp. 20, 33–43

ADY, CECILIA M., *Lorenzo dei Medici and Renaissance Italy*, London, 1955

ALBERTI, *Ten Books on Architecture*, op. cit., bk. VII, chs. x, xi

ANGELO POLIZIANO'S TAGEBUCH, ed. A. Wesselski, Jena, 1929, pp. 3, 79

ANTAL, op. cit., pp. 109, 115

ARCINIEGAS, op. cit., pp. 32–7

ARGAN, 'The Architecture of Brunelleschi, etc.', op. cit., p. 113; *Brunelleschi*, Milan, 1955, pp. 75–7

BARON, op. cit., vol. I, pp. 165, 172–3

BIAGI, LUIGI, *L'Accademia di Belle Arti di Firenze*, Florence, 1941, p. 19

BIBLIOTECA NAZIONALE, Florence, *MS. II, IV*, 324, folio 108 recto and verso (the account of the wedding of Lorenzo the Magnificent)

BORSOOK, 1960, op. cit., pp. 24–34, 151–2, 162–3

BROWN, ALISON M., 'The Humanist Portrait of Cosimo de' Medici Pater Patriae', *Journal of the Warburg and Courtauld Institutes*, XXIV (1961), pp. 186–94

BRUCKER, *Florentine Politics and Society*, op. cit., p. 80

CANTIMORI, DELIO, 'Rhetoric and Politics in Italian Humanism', *Journal of the Warburg and Courtauld Institutes*, I (1937–8), pp. 83–100

CASTIGLIONE, BALDASSARE, *Il Cortegiano*, bk. I; bk. II, ch. xxiii

CHABOD, FEDERICO, *Machiavelli and the Renaissance*, London, 1958, pp. 25, 72, 77, 99, 183–4

CHASTEL, op. cit., pp. 45*ff*, 136

CHIAPELLI, A., *Arte del Rinascimento*, Rome, 1925, pp. 192*f*

CIANFOGNI, PIER NOLASCO, *Memorie istoriche dell' ambrosiana R. basilica di S Lorenzo*, Florence, 1804, pp. 166, 188–9

CONDIVI, ASCANIO, *Vita di Michelangelo* (written 1553), Florence, 1944, pp. 13–14, 95, 122

CRUTTWELL, MAUD, *Antonio Pollaiuolo*, London & New York,

1907, pp. 66–8, 133–4

DAVIS, CHARLES, review of 'Bartolomeo Ammannati Architetto', by M. Fossi in *Journal of Architectural Historians*, 1969, p. 304

DELLA TORRE, ARNALDO, *Storia dell' accademia platonica di Firenze*, Florence, 1902, pp. 639–43, 739–41

DEL LUNGO, ISIDORO, *Florentia: uomini e cose del Quattrocento*, Florence, 1897, pp. 119, 407*ff*

DEL PIAZZO, MARCELLO, 'Architettura e storia', *Il santuario di Firenze*, Florence & Milan, 1957

DE ROOVER, RAYMOND, 'Lorenzo il Magnifico e il tramonto del banco dei Medici', *Archivio Storico Italiano*, CVII (1949), pp. 172–81; *The Medici Bank*, Oxford, 1948, pp. 1, 45, 60–6

FASOLA, GIUSTA NICCO, 'La nuova spazialità', *Leonardo: saggi e ricerche*, Rome, 1954, pp. 293–311

FELICE, BERTA, *Donne medicee avanti il principato*, Florence, 1904, pp. 40, 43

FILARETE, ANTONIO, *Trattato dell' architettura*, ed. W. von Oettingen, Vienna, 1896, bk. XXV, p. 667

FIORILLI, CARLO, 'I dipintori a Firenze nell' arte dei Medici e Speziali e Merciai', *Archivio Storico Italiano*, LXXVIII (1920), p. 42

FORTUNA, op. cit., *passim*

FRASER JENKINS, A. D., *Journal of the Warburg and Courtauld Institutes*, XXXIII (1970), p. 165

GARNERI, op. cit., pp. 204–5, 214

GAYE, G., *Carteggio inedito d'artisti*, vol. I, Florence, 1839, p. 191

GINORI-CONTI, PIERO, *La basilica di S Lorenzo di Firenze*, Florence, 1940, pp. 30, 46–94, 114

GOMBRICH, E. H., 'Botticelli's Mythologies', *Journal of the*

Warburg and Courtauld Institutes, VIII (1945), pp. 14–19, 21, 55; 'The Early Medici as Patrons of Art', op. cit., *passim*; 'Renaissance and Golden Age', *Journal of the Warburg and Courtauld Institutes*, XXIV (1961), pp. 306–9

GRIFI, op. cit., ed. 1896, pp. 134, 187, 287–9

GUTKIND, op. cit., pp. 162, 322–3

GUZZONI DEGLI ANCARANI, op. cit., p. 131

HAMILTON, PAUL C., 'Andrea del Minga's Assunta in S Felicita', *Mitteilungen des Kunsthistorischen Institutes in Florenz*, XIV (1970), pp. 466–8

HATFIELD, RAB, 'The Compagnia de' Magi', *Journal of the Warburg and Courtauld Institutes*, XXXIII, (1970), pp. 107–61

HEYDENREICH, L. H., 'Die Tribuna der SS Annunziata in Florenz', *Mitteilungen des Kunsthistorischen Institutes in Florenz*, III (1931), pp. 268–85; 'Spätwerke Brunnelleschis', *Jahrbuch der preussischen Kunstsammlungen*, LII (1931), pp. 5–7, 20

HYMAN, ISABELLE, 'New Light on Old Problems: Palazzo Medici and the Church of San Lorenzo', *Journal of the Society of Architectural Historians*, XXVIII (1969), p. 216

JANSON, 1957, op. cit., pp. 126, 132–40, 214–18

KAUFFMANN, op. cit., pp. 75–82, 85, 103, 112–38, 226, 353

LANKHEIT, KLAUS, *Florentinische Barockplastik 1670–1773*, Munich, 1962, pp. 43, 86*f*

LAVIN, IRVING, 'The Sources of Donatello's Pulpits in San Lorenzo', *Art Bulletin*, XLI (1959), pp. 20–38

LIPARI, ANGELO, *The Dolce Stil Novo*

according to Lorenzo de' Medici, New Haven, 1936, pp. 17, 73, 120–1, 126, 129, 139, 140–3, 332

LISNER, MARGRIT, 'Die Büste des Heiligen Laurentius in der Alten Sakristei von San Lorenzo', *Zeitschrift für Kunstwissenschaft*, XII (1948), pp. 51–70

LORENZO DE' MEDICI IL MAGNIFICO, *Opere*, ed. by A. Simoni, 2nd edition, Bari, 1939, vol.I, pp. 16,18

LOWINSKY, E. E., 'The Medici Codex', *Annales Musicologiques*, V (1957), p. 67

MACHIAVELLI, NICCOLÒ, *Il Principe*, Chapter X, XVII, XXV

MAGUIRE, op. cit., pp. 47, 96, 136–7, 184

MANETTI, ANTONIO, *Vita di Filippo di Ser Brunellesco*, ed. E. Toesca, Florence, 1927, pp. 19–22, 66–7

MARTINES, LAURO, *The Social World of Florentine Humanism*, Princeton, 1963, pp. 161–2

MARZI, DEMETRIO, *La cancelleria della repubblica fiorentina*, San Casciano, 1910, pp. 366, 405–7f

MILANESI, GAETANO, *Le lettere di Michelangelo*, Florence, 1875, pp. 448–59

MOOREHEAD, ALAN, *The Villa Diana*, London, 1951, pp. 3, 107–21, 141–50, 174

MORINO, UGO, *La. R. accademia degli immobili ed il suo teatro 'La Pergola'* Pisa, 1926

MÜNTZ, op. cit., p. 108

PAATZ, op .cit., vol. I, pp. 62, 65–8, 121, 212–15; vol. II, pp. 197, 498–500, 502–7, 514, 566-note 207; vol. III, pp. 9–19, 34–40, 178–9

PATZAK, op. cit., vol. II, pp. 22–5, 107f, 150

PICCOLOMINI, ENEA SILVIO, 'The Commentaries of Pius II', *Smith College Studies in History*, ed. F. A.

Gregg and L. C. Gabel, XXII (1936–7), pp. 161–3, 165

PIERACCINI, GAETANO, *La stirpe de' Medici di Cafaggiolo*, Florence, 1924, vol. II, 1925, pp. 289–90

POLIZIANO, AGNOLO, *Operum*, London, 1546, p. 100

Idem., *Prose volgari inedite e poesie latine e greche edite e inedite*, ed. by I. Del Lungo, Florence, 1867, p. 47

POPE-HENNESSY, JOHN, *Fra Angelico*, London, 1952, pp. 7, 12, 20–1, 176; *Italian High Renaissance and Baroque Sculpture*, op. cit., Text Volume, pp. 18, 20–3, 25, 27, 33f, 61–3; Catalogue Volume, pp. 24–5, 36; *Italian Renaissance Sculpture*, op. cit., pp. 19, 270, 280, 285–9, 303; *Paolo Uccello*, op. cit., pp. 150–1

PREVITALI, GIOVANNI, 'Una data per il problema dei pulpiti di San Lorenzo', *Paragone*, CXXXIII (January 1961), p. 51

PREZZINER, op. cit., vol. I, pp. 130–2, 138, 149–50

ROBB, NESCA A., *Neoplatonism of the Italian Renaissance*, London, 1935, pp. 31–2, 57–61

ROGERS, ERNESTO, Introduction to *Italy Builds* by G. E. Kidder Smith, London, 1956, p. 10

RONDONI, GIUSEPPE, 'Ordinamenti e vicende principali dell' antico studio fiorentino', *Archivo Storico Italiano*, series IV, XIV (1884), pp. 41–64, 194–220

ROSCOE, WILLIAM, *The Life of Lorenzo de' Medici*, London, 1797, vol. I, pp. 20, 45–9, 159–60; vol. II, pp. 71, 85–6, 131–2, 143–4, 149–50, 284–6; Documents, LXIV, LXVI

SAALMAN, 'Capital Studies', op. cit., pp. 113–37

SALMI, *Andrea del Castagno*, op. cit. pp. 54, 56

SANPAOLESI, P., 'La casa fiorentina di Bartolommeo Scala', *Studien zur toskanischen Kunst; Festschrift für L. H. Heydenreich*, op. cit., pp. 275–88

SAXL, op. cit., p. 23

SCHEVILL, op. cit., pp. 359–61, 378, 388–9, 483

SCHIAPARELLI, op. cit., p. 136

SHEARMAN, JOHN, *Andrea del Sarto*, 2 vols., Oxford, 1965; 'The Chiostro dello Scalzo', *Mitteilungen des Kunsthistorischen Institutes in Florenz*, IX (1960), pp. 207–20

SUMMERS, DAVID, 'The sculptural Program of the Cappella di S Luca in the Santissima Annunziata, *Mitteilungen des Kunsthistorischen Institutes in Florenz*, XIV (1969), pp. 67–90

TAINE, op. cit., p. 113

TIGRI, G., *Canti popolari toscani*, Florence, 1860, p. iv

TOLNAY, *Michelangelo*, op. cit., vol. III, pp. 61–3, 70–5

UZIELLI, *Toscanelli*, op. cit., pp. 14–16

VASARI, GIORGIO, *La Vita di Michelangelo nelle redazioni del 1550 e del 1568*, ed. by Paola Barocchi, Milan-Naples, 1962, vol. I, pp. xxii, 121, 210–1

VESPASIANO DA BISTICCI, op. cit., pp. 257, 261, 405–30, 435–6

VILLARI, op. cit., vol. I, pp. xix-note 1, 197–9, 529

VITRUVIUS, *Ten Books on Architecture*, Loeb Library Edition, 1955, bk. III, ch. I

WACKERNAGEL, op. cit., pp. 156, 162, 235–46, 257–71

WALSER, ERNST, *Poggius Florentinus*, Leipzig-Berlin, 1914, pp. 18–19

WHITE, JOHN, 'Developments in Renaissance Perspective', *Journal of the Warburg and Courtauld Institutes*, XIV (1951), pp. 49–52

WITTKOWER, R., *Architectural Principles*, op. cit., pp. 3–5, 6, 9–10, 14–15, 17–19, 28

WÖLFFLIN, HEINRICH, *Classic Art*, trans. by P. and L. Murray, London, 1952, pp. 214–15, 231, 241

WOOD BROWN, J., *The Builders of Florence*, London, 1907, pp. 408–11

YOUNG, op. cit., vol. I, pp. 79, 132–3, 156–7, 160

ZOBI, op. cit., pp. 195–6

Chapter 9

ACTON, op. cit., pp. 78–9, 284–5

BACCHI, GIUSEPPE, 'La compagnia di S Maria delle Laudi e di S Agnese del Carmine di Firenze', *Rivista Storica Carmelitana*, II (1931), pp. 137–151; III (1931), pp. 12–39, 97 122

BALDINUCCI, op. cit., ed. 1842, vol. II, pp. 493, 499, 516, 521–2, 539; vol. III, pp. 136, 147; vol. IV, p. 141

BAROCCHI, PAOLA, *Il Rosso Fiorentino* Rome, 1950, p. 41

Idem and R. RISTORI, *Il carteggio di Michelangelo*, Florence, 1965, vol. I, p. 140

BELLANDI, P. S., O.S.A., *La chiesa di Santo Spirito di Firenze*, Florence, 1921, pp. 12–16

BELLANDI, P. GINO, *Le vicende dell' antico capitolo di Santo Spirito*, Florence, 1950

BERENSON, BERNARD, *Italian Pictures of the Renaissance: Florentine School*, London, 1963, vol. I, pp. 24, 29, 149–50, 185–6, 197, 207

BIADI, L., *Notizie sulle antiche fabbriche di Firenze non terminate*, Florence, 1824

BIGAZZI, *Iscrizioni*, op. cit., pp. 109, 323–4

BORSOOK, 1960, op. cit., pp. 25, 144–6,

156-7

BRAUNFELS, op. cit., p. 207

BRIGANTI, GIULIANO, *Pietro da Cortona*, Florence, 1962, pp. 92-9, 126, 215-17, 221

BURCKHARDT, JAKOB, *Cicerone*, Basel 1860, vol. I, p. 177

CAIOLI, P. PAOLO, 'Masaccio e i Carmelitani', *Rivista Storica Carmelitana* (1929), pp. 69-87

CAMBIAGI, GAETANO, *Descrizione dell' Imperiale Giardino di Boboli*, Florence, 1757

COX, JANET, 'Pontormo's Drawings for the Destroyed Vault of the Capponi Chapel', *Burlington Magazine*, XCVIII (1956), pp. 17-18

FISCHEL, OSKAR, *Raphael*, Berlin, 1962, pp. 84-5

FREEDBERG, SIDNEY, *Painting of the High Renaissance in Rome and Florence*, Cambridge (Mass.), 1961, vol. I, pp. 70, 179, 440, 478

GARNERI, op. cit., pp. 264-6, 306

GIOVANNOZZI, 'Ricerche su Bernardo Buontalenti', op. cit., p. 306

GUCCERELLI, op. cit., pp. 283, 451-3

GUTKIND, op. cit., pp. 48, 183-4

HARTT, F., G. CORTI, and C. KENNEDY, *The Chapel of the Cardinal of Portugal, 1434-1459*, Philadelphia, 1964

HASKELL, FRANCIS, *Patrons and Painters*, London, 1963, pp. 229-30, 233-5, 239-41

HEIKAMP, DETLEF, 'La grotta grande del Giardino di Boboli,' *Antichità Viva*, 1965 (n. 4)

HOLDERBAUM, JAMES, 'A Bronze by Giovanni Bologna and a Painting by Bronzino', *Burlington Magazine*, XCVIII (1956), pp. 439-45

JAHN-RUSCONI, A., *Il museo degli Argenti in Firenze*, Rome, 1935; *La R. Galleria Pitti in Firenze*, Rome, 1937

KAUFFMANN, op cit., pp. 204-9, 259, 286-301 345, 356-75

LIMBURGER, op. cit., pp. 55-6, 60, 80, 93, 146, 157

MASSON, GEORGINA, *Italian Gardens* London, 1961, p. 80

MORANDINI, FRANCESCA, *Mostra documentaria e iconografica di Palazzo Pitti e Giardino di Boboli*, Florence, 1960, pp. 3-4, 7-8

MORASSI, ANTONIO, *Il Tesoro dei Medici*, Milan, 1963

OFFNER, *Corpus*, op. cit., sec. IV, vol. I, 1962, pp. 66-9

PAATZ, *Kirchen*, op. cit., vol. I, p. 456; vol. II, pp. 30*ff*, 42, 46-9, 58, 64-7, 89; vol. III, pp. 188-90; vol. IV pp. 621-4; vol. V, pp. 118-22, 169-note 39

PIACENTI, KIRSTEN ASCHENGREEN, *Il Museo, degli Argenti a Firenze*, Milan, 1968; Idem, 'The Summer Apartment of the Grand Duke Ferdinand I', *Apollo*, (September 1977)

PROCACCI, UGO, 'Sulla cronologia delle opere di Masaccio e di e di Masolino tra il 1425 el il 1428', *Rivista d'Arte*, XXVIII (1953), pp. 31-4

PREZZINER, op. cit., vol. I, pp. 88-9

RODOLICO, op cit., p. 243

ROSS, op. cit., pp. 123, 182-7, 190, 195-6

SAALMAN, 'Capital Studies', op. cit., pp. 129-30

Idem. 'Paolo Uccello at San Miniato,' *Burlington Magazine*, CVI (1964), pp. 558-63

SALMI, MARIO, 'Nota sulla chiesa di Santo Spirito a Firenze', *Atti del I congresso nazionale di storia dell' architettura*, October 1936, pp. 1-16

SHEARMAN, JOHN, *Andrea del Sarto*, Oxford 1965, vol. II, p. 230*ff*

SOLDINI, F. M., *Il reale giardino di*

Boboli, Florence, 1789
VASARI-MILANESI, op. cit., vol. II, pp. 375–7, 381
VITALI, LAMBERTO, 'Three Italian Friends of Degas', *Burlington Magazine*, CV (1963), pp. 266–73
WARBURG, ABY, 'I costumi teatrali per gli intermezzi del 1589', *Gesammelte Schriften*, Leipzig, 1932, vol. I, pp. 264–66
WILES, *passim*
YOUNG, op. cit., vol. II, p. 410

Chapter 10
ACTON, op cit., pp. 83–4
Idem, 'An Anglo-Florentine Collection,' *Apollo*, LXXXVII (1965), pp. 272–83
Idem, *Merian/Florenz*, XXII (April 1969), pp. 51–2
ADEMOLLO, A., *Marietta de' Ricci ovvero Firenze dell' assedio*, ed. L. Passerini, Florence, 1845, vol. IV, pp. 1198, 1214
ALBERTI, LEON BATTISTA, *Opere volgari:* I libri della famiglia, ed. by Cecil Grayson, Bari, 1960, bk. I, p. 49; bk. III, pp. 199–201, 359
ANTAL, op. cit., p. 132
BACCHI, GIUSEPPE, *La Certosa di Firenze*, Florence, 1930, pp. 40–3
BIAGI, op. cit., p. 81
BIANCHINI, R., *L'Impruneta: paese e santuario*, Florence, 1932
CLARK, KENNETH, *Piero della Francesca*, London, 1951, pp. 30–1
DAVIDSOHN, *Firenze ai Tempi di Dante*, op. cit., pp. 589*ff*
DELLA TORRE, op. cit., pp. 174, 179–81, 639–41
FABRICZY, op. cit., pp. 584–5
Firenze, T. C. I., op. cit., pp. 239, 291–302, 310, 330–1, 337–8, 348, 385
FORTUNA, op. cit., pp. 7–8, 58–60
FRAENCKEL, INGEBORG, *Andrea del*

Sarto, Strassburg, 1935, pp. 148–9
FRIEDLAENDER, WALTER, *Mannerism and Anti-Mannerism in Italian Painting*, New York, 1958, pp. 3–28
FROMMEL, C. L., *Die Farnesina und Peruzzis architektonisches Frühwerk*, Berlin, 1961, pp. 85–7, 89
GAYE, op cit., vol. I, pp. 61–3, 191
GIGLIOLI, EDOARDO H., *Fiesole* Rome, 1933, pp. 50–68, 114, 144–6, 265–7
GOMBRICH, 'The Early Medici as Patrons of the Arts', op. cit., pp. 285*ff*, 295–7, 305
HERLIHY, DAVID, 'Santa Maria Impruneta,' in *Florentine Studies* ed. by N. Rubinstein, London, 1968, pp. 242*ff*
HEYDENREICH, 'Die Cappella Rucellai, etc', op. cit., pp. 219–29
HUTTON, EDWARD, *Country Walks about Florence*, London, 1908, pp. 147–8, 160–3, 212, 217, 225–7
IMBERCIADORI, EDOARDO, *Campagna toscana nel '700*, Florence, 1953, pp. 8–11, 205
KAUFFMANN, op. cit., pp. 334, 383–9
KLIEMANN, JULIAN, 'Vertumnus und Pomona zum Programm von Pontformos Fresko in Poggio a Caiano,' *Mitteilungen des Kunsthistorischen Institutes in Florenz*, XVI (1972), 293–328.
LENSI, ALFREDO, *Il museo Stibbert*, Florence, 1918
LENSI ORLANDI CARDINI, GIULIO CESARE, *Le ville di Firenze*, vol I, Florence, 1953, pp. 9–15, 26, 39–41, 54, 58, 77–8, 80, 82, 151; vol. II, 1954, pp. 8, 224, 258–9
LIMBURGER, op. cit., pp. 2, 69
LOPES PEGNA, op. cit., p. 31
MACHIAVELLI, *Opere complete*, op. cit. pp. 1107–8
MAGUIRE, op. cit., pp. 47, 51–2, 55–6,

BIBLIOGRAPHY

89

MARCHINI, *I palazzi del popolo*, etc.,
op. cit., pp. 59, 155

MARESCALCHI, A. and G. DALMASSO,
Storia della vite e del vino in Italia,
vol. III, Milan, 1937, pp. 488, 522,
711–12

MASSON, GEORGINA, *Italian Villas and
Palaces*, London, 1959, pp. 133–5,
159

MONTAIGNE, MICHEL DE, *Journal du
Voyage en Italie par la Suisse et
l'Allemagne en 1580 et 1581*, ed.
M. Rat, Paris, 1955, pp. 83–4, 87–8,
155–6

MOROZZI, GUIDO, 'The Certosa of
Galluzzo', *Florence*, XI (1960), p. 29

PAATZ, *Kirchen*, op cit., vol. IV,
p. 211; vol. V, pp. 50–1

PATZAK, op. cit., vol. II, pp. 117,
183-note 234

POLIZIANO, *Operum*, op. cit.,
pp. 100*ff*

POPE-HENNESSY, *Fra Angelico*, op.
cit., pp. 5, 24; *Italian High
Renaissance and Baroque Sculpture*,
op. cit., vol. I, pp. 72–8: catalogue
vol., pp. 24–5, 88

REARICK, JANET COX, *The Drawings
of Pontormo*, Cambridge (Mass.),
1965, vol. I, pp. 149–50, 172–4, 213*ff*,
257–8, 263, 310–11

RIDOLFI, ROBERTO, *Vita di
Niccolo Machiavelli*, Rome, 1954,
pp. 228–9

ROSCOE, op. cit., vol. II, p. 141

RUCELLAI, *Zibaldone*, op. cit.,
pp. 20–3, 27

SCAIFE, op. cit., pp. 91–2

SCHEVILL, op. cit., pp. 78–9

SHEARMAN, *Andrea del Sarto*, op.
cit., vol. I, pp. 19, 78–9

STEINWEG, KLARA, 'Zur
Ausstellung restaurierter Gemalde
in S Marco, Florenz', *Kunstchronik*,
XIII-2 (1960), pp. 39–42

TARGIONI-TOZZETTI, ANTONIO,
*Cenni storici sulla introduzione di
varie piante nell'agricoltura ed
orticoltura toscana*, Forence, 1853,
pp. 48–9, 52, 145–6, 185

TARGIONI-TOZZETTI, GIOVANNI,
*Relazioni d'alcuni viaggi fatti in
diverse parti della Toscana*, vol. V,
Florence, 1773, pp. 62–3

VASARI-MILANESI, op. cit., vol. VI,
p. 266

VETTORI, PIERO, *Trattato della
coltivazione degl' ulivi*, Florence,
1569, p. 32

VITALE-MAGAZZINI, D.,
Coltivazione toscana (original ed.
1634), Milan, 1842, pp. 8–11, 13,
21, 33–4, 64–5, 92, 119–21

VITI, VINCENZO, *La Badia
Fiesolana*, Florence, 1956, pp. 26,
46–7, 89–90, 92

WILES, op. cit., pp. 76–7

WINNER, MATTHIAS, 'Volterranos
Fresken in der Villa della Petraia',
*Mitteilungen des Kunsthistorischen
Institutes in Florenz*, X (1963),
pp. 220, 228

WOODWARD, op. cit., pp. 59–60

YOUNG, op. cit., vol. II, p. 299

Index